WINNIPEG JETS
The WHA Years Day By Day

Curtis Walker

PCMP Press
Tucson, Arizona

PCMP PRESS
P.O. Box 121
Tucson, Arizona
85702 USA

www.purple-cactus.tv

Copyright ©2010, 2013 Curtis Walker & PCMP LLC

The logo of the WHA Hall of Fame is a registered trademark, used with permission.

www.WHAhof.com
www.whaRACERS.com

All rights reserved. No part of this publication may be reproduced, stored in a retrieval system, or transmitted in any form or by any means electronic, mechanical, photocopy, recording, or otherwise without the prior written permission of the Publisher. Some graphic materials are believed to be in the public domain. Opinions expressed are solely those of the Author. Trademarks remain the property of their owners, and are shown for historical purposes.
This publication is not associated with the National Hockey League.

ISBN 978-0-9797337-2-7

Manufactured in the United States of America

First Electronic Printing April 2010
First Paper Printing June 2013

Editorial assistance by Timothy Gassen and Sarah Gassen
Additional layout and photo restoration by Timothy Gassen

Front Cover: 1976 WHA Jets program cover celebrating the team's first WHA championship.
Back Cover: (clockwise) 1978 program cover; Anders Hedberg scores versus the Houston Aeros; Bobby Hull on the cover of the 1975-1976 WHA league media guide.

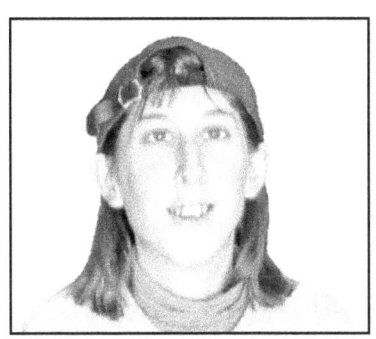

**Dedicated to the memory of Carli Anne Ward
18 March 1982 – 15 December 2007**

Your spirit will endure forever

Table of Contents

Introduction 6

Acknowledgements 6

Part I - The Games 7

Season I: 1972-1973 – The Maiden Voyage 7
    Scores and Stats 30
    Photos 33

Season II: 1973-1974 – A Blum Ending 38
    Scores and Stats 54
    Photos 56

Season III: 1974-1975 – This Team is Our Team 60
    Scores and Stats 80
    Photos 82

Season IV: 1975-1976 – The Payoff 88
    Scores and Stats 110
    Photos 112

Season V: 1976-1977 – A Trying Defense 118
    Scores and Stats 138
    Photos 140

Season VI: 1977-1978 – Another Crisis, Another Parade 144
    Scores and Stats 165
    Photos 167

Season VII: 1978-1979 – New Owners, New Team, Same Result 169
    Scores and Stats 192
    Photos 194

Epilogue 196

Part II - Records and Miscellany 198

The Players 198

Team Records 201
    Blowouts 201
    We Want Ten 202
    Friday The 13th 202
    The Terrible Trifecta 203
    Sunday's The Day 203
    By The Month 204
    Monsters of Maroons Road 204
    Best Periods 206
    Take A Shot 207
    Venues Jets Visited 209

Individual Records 209
Pulling The Goaltender 209
The Hot Line 210
The Heave-Ho 210
Best Individual Performances 211
The Top Opponents 212
In The Nets 213
Shutouts 213
Playmakers From The Crease 214
Bad Boys 215
For Openers 216
Ben Hatskin's Investment Paid Off 218
Hull's Victims 223
No Ordinary Joe 224
Overtime 229
Top 10 Dramatic Goals 231

In Memoriam 233

Bibliography 234

Introduction

The Winnipeg Jets competed in the World Hockey Association (WHA), a league founded by Dennis Murphy and Gary Davidson that began play in October 1972. The league survived for seven seasons until four of its remaining six teams, including the Jets, joined the rival National Hockey League (NHL) as expansion teams to start the 1979-1980 season.

This work provides a detailed day-by-day, game-by-game, season-by-season account of the Jets' seven seasons in the WHA, complemented by a listing of statistical records and assorted miscellany. The material comes from extensive research that includes newspaper articles, game programs, team publications, game summaries and first-hand interviews with former players.

From the team's inception and the groundbreaking signing of superstar Bobby Hull that got both the Jets and the new league off and running, through the influx of European players, two ownership changes, three AVCO World Trophy championships, training camps in Europe, international exhibitions in Moscow and Tokyo — all culminating in the Jets' entry into the NHL and the disbanding of the WHA — the reader will be able to follow the Jets through their memorable journey on a long road that had its share of detours and rough stretches.

In spite of many challenges, the Jets iced one of the best teams in hockey history during this time and they were the standard bearers of the WHA. This work attempts to preserve the memory of the Jets' outstanding accomplishments as well as honor those who made them possible, both on and off the ice.

Acknowledgements

There are a number of people I wish to thank. Above all else, I would be remiss not to single out Jets' founders Ben Hatskin and Dave Simkin along with all the other founding partners of the WHA, without whom the Jets or the WHA would never have existed. The Jets would have been sold and moved in 1974 without the tireless efforts and foresight of the Honourable Jack McKeag, Bob Graham and others who led the community ownership drive in which thousands of ordinary citizens of Winnipeg and Manitoba bought founders loans and memberships that raised the necessary capital to purchase the team. When the public corporation ran out of money, the group headed by Michael Gobuty stepped forward to buy the team and lead the Jets into the NHL.

Until I began gathering research material, I never realized how much effort members of the Jets Booster Club, led by Gary Bigwood, Walt Tyler, Rose Glesby, Ron Bunio, and others, put into the care and feeding of their favorite team. The passion and unconditional devotion of such dedicated fans is what made Ben Hatskin believe that Winnipeg could support major league hockey.

As I poured over so many of Reyn Davis' articles in the pages of the *Winnipeg Free Press*, I couldn't help but be reminded of the voice of Ken "Friar" Nicolson. My earliest memories of the Jets are beside a radio listening to the Friar on CJOB radio. The Friar's voice became synonymous with the Jets and I was a member of a generation he helped to grow into Jets fans. I didn't appreciate Davis' work at the time, but as I dug through the archives, I didn't need to read his obituary to discover that he loved his work and had a natural talent for sports writing.

The staff at the Millennium Library in the Micromedia Services remained patient as I made trip after trip to collect the pages of the past to put together this detailed diary of a beloved hockey team. Finally, I would like to thank Timothy Gassen for his dedication to preserving the memory of the WHA and for his efforts in bringing this work to fruition.

Curtis Walker
September 2009
Winnipeg, Manitoba

Part I - The Games

Season I: 1972-1973 - The Maiden Voyage

The incubation of the Winnipeg Jets began when Louis Hatskin and the former Annie Cohen immigrated to Canada from Proprask, Russia in 1911. They settled in Winnipeg and Annie gave birth to the couple's first child on 30 September 1917. The proud parents named him Benjamin.

On September 13, 1971, Ben Hatskin satisfied his desire to bring major league hockey to Winnipeg when he partnered with longtime friend Dave Simkin and together they paid a total of $25,000 to become a charter member of the fledgling World Hockey Association (WHA), a venture founded by Dennis Murphy and Gary Davidson just five months earlier. The paper entity that was officially born on December 27, 1971 would eventually take on a life of its own and attach itself to the hearts of many of Winnipeg's citizens. Hatskin took the name "Jets" for his new team, the same name as the junior team that he had owned for the past six seasons. Hatskin was an admirer of the National Football League's New York Jets, and he used the same moniker for his hockey teams.

Hatskin had originally inquired with National Hockey League (NHL) President Clarence Campbell about obtaining an expansion franchise for Winnipeg, but he was told that he would need an arena with 16,000 seats and a $7.2 million entry fee. Unfortunately, the seating capacity of the Winnipeg Arena was just over 10,000 and without a major upgrade the NHL was not an option. However, the WHA made no such restrictions and Hatskin bought into the new league.

Campbell also mockingly welcomed the new league, saying that it would be a good source of employment for "seniors and semi-pro players." Ben Hatskin had bigger plans. He believed the people of Winnipeg could support major league hockey and set about the task of giving it to them. He was a determined and proud man who strove to be the best in every endeavor he undertook. Hatskin's new hockey team, the city of its residence and the league it was part of would reap the benefits of that determination and vision for generations to come.

Hatskin became involved in both the sports and business world at an early age. He played six seasons for the Winnipeg Blue Bombers of the Canadian Football League (CFL) and participated in two Grey Cup championship games. With the Bombers, "Fats," as his teammates called him, once made an annual salary as high as $260. After his playing days, he stayed with football and coached at a local high school.

Off the gridiron, he was said to have once told his father, "The music I love to hear is played on a cash register." It didn't take long before his ears started ringing. He partnered with Les Lear in the horse racing business and he eventually went out on his own in 1957 with Hatskin's Farms. One of his horses won the 1959 Louisiana Derby, which netted him a prize of $50,000. Once the family sold its wooden box and corrugated paper box plants, Ben and his younger brother Ruben became involved in James Realty, Hatskin Containers, Lodge Investments, Triangle Acceptance, Universal Music and six other businesses over the years. Ben's latest speculative venture, however, would eventually make him a household name in the Manitoba capital.

Hatskin first needed to build an organization. With secretary Rosemary Delaronde at his side, he set about the task of giving life to a piece of paper.

During the winter of 1971, he hired Terry Hind as the Jets' Business Manager. Hind was the man Hatskin needed to spread the word and carry his passion into the community. Hind had an extensive track record of selling pro sports in Winnipeg, having worked for the Blue Bombers and two baseball teams, the Winnipeg Goldeyes and later, the Winnipeg Whips. Though his first love was baseball, he also had some hockey experience under his belt as manager of the Winnipeg Maroons. Hind also served as a Winnipeg city alderman from 1961-1965.

Hatskin then hired fellow CFL veteran Annis Stukus as his first General Manager. In addition to his 12-year playing career with the Toronto Argonauts, "Stuke", or the "Loquacious Lithuanian," was best known for building CFL teams in Edmonton and Vancouver but was also coming off a successful run as the general manager of the Western Hockey League's Vancouver Canucks.

Ron Lyon was added in January 1972 as the Director of Public Relations. Lyon was successful at the junior level in stops across Western Canada and he was arguably more enthusiastic about his work than Hatskin was. He started his sales career in the oil business and was operating hotels before moving on to the hockey world.

Hatskin then added Bill Robinson as the Director of Player Personnel. The meticulously well-dressed former host at Assiniboia Downs race track would be responsible for the Jets' scouting system. He started his new job by making his way across the North American continent, cataloging information on players the Jets hoped to sign. Robinson had an extensive hockey background as both a player and a coach. He once turned down a contract offer from the NHL's Chicago Blackhawks and went on to coach the University of Manitoba Bisons for 13 years.

On 12 February 1972, Hatskin and his small entourage traveled to Anaheim, California, site of the WHA's first General Player Draft, where the teams would divvy up the rights to NHL players, minor leaguers, juniors, Europeans, or anyone else a team wished to select. Hatskin identified goaltending as a priority and insisted that the Jets select seven or eight goaltenders in the hopes of signing two of them. He had already made a preliminary selection of Ernie Wakely of the NHL's St. Louis Blues, but he also needed a drawing card, so he also selected superstar winger Bobby Hull. The game's premiere player was in his 15th NHL season, all spent with the Chicago Blackhawks, where he won the NHL scoring championship three times and was twice named the NHL's most valuable player.

Over the span of the next two days, the league's 12 teams, including the Jets, made more than 1,000 selections. The Jets not only made sure to select a number of goaltenders, but also to select many players with Manitoba heritage. One notable exception was their last selection, Alexsei Kosygin, the sitting Premier of the Soviet Union. Though the pick was made in jest, most people in the hockey world thought the Jets had a better chance of getting Kosygin's signature on a contract than convincing Hull to sign with the Jets. Undeterred, Hatskin told Hull, "I'm gonna get you." Many questioned how serious he was. Those who doubted him would soon be eating their words.

Armed with the WHA rights to over 70 players, the Jets now had a team to build both on and off the ice. In March, Robinson began making contact with the players on the Jets' protected list, and the number of season tickets sold reached four figures. The job of selling a team with no players under contract was difficult and discouraging at times, but both Hind and Lyon worked tirelessly to get the team off the ground as best they could.

The last bureaucratic hurdle was cleared when the Jets posted a $100,000 performance bond on 16 April 1972, and the race was on to sign players. The next day, the Jets held informal talks with Art Stratton, Jim Hargreaves, Brian Cadle and the agents for Hull, Ted Harris and Joe Daley, each of whom were on the Jets' protected list.

Later that month, the Jets made 30-year-old winger Norm Beaudin their first signee. However, the club didn't announce the signing since they were afraid of a public backlash for signing a minor leaguer as their first player. Beaudin was a veteran of 10 pro seasons spent mostly in the minor leagues with only 25 NHL games to his credit split between the St. Louis Blues and Minnesota North Stars. The native of Montmarte, Saskatchewan spent the last three seasons with the Cleveland Barons of the American Hockey League (AHL), where he scored a total 97 goals and picked up the nickname of "Prairie Dog Frog" from the fans in Cleveland.

Over the course of the month of May, the lack of any announced signings prompted critics to begin calling the team the "Phantom Jets," but they were silenced when the Jets held a press conference at 10 a.m. on 24 May to announce that they signed 31-year-old goaltender Ernie Wakely, one of their preliminary selections in the General Player Draft. The pipe-smoking Flin Flon, Manitoba native and resident of Albuquerque, New Mexico signed a reported $160,000, three-year, no-trade, no-cut contract that was four pages in length. Wakely spent the previous three seasons with the Blues following many seasons in the Montreal Canadiens' farm system.

Two days later at the International Inn, the Jets held a 3:30 p.m. press conference to announce their second official signing. Joe Daley, a 29-year-old goaltender who had played last season with NHL's Detroit Red Wings, signed a $125,000, three-year contract, though he had reached a verbal agreement with the Jets three months earlier. The native of the Winnipeg suburb of East Kildonan played parts of five previous seasons with the Pittsburgh Penguins and Buffalo Sabres in addition to the Red Wings.

Veteran NHL goaltender Jacques Plante termed the new Jets' goaltending duo, "the best one-two combination in hockey," but Wakely and Daley still needed a team in front of them.

On 30 May, the Jets finally announced that they had signed Beaudin to a three-year contract. The Jets also announced that radio station CJOB had won the rights to air their games and that Ken "Friar" Nicolson and Stew McPherson would handle the on-air duties. Nicolson had been CJOB's Sports Director since July 1969 and he had circled the globe covering a wide variety of sports including football, baseball and curling, but hockey was his first love. As a youngster, Nicolson played both hockey and football, but a diagnosis of diabetes at age 18 forced him to turn to broadcasting sports instead of playing them.

Hatskin kept doggedly pursuing Hull, hockey's best player, and finally got him to agree to a meeting. Hatskin, Hull and his representative, Harvey Weinberg, along with Gary Davidson, all met in a roadside motel on the outskirts of Denver on 1 June. After 15 hours of meetings, Hull came away with an offer of $1 million in cash and a contract that would pay him an additional $1 million over five years, a significant raise over the $100,000 he made with the Blackhawks last season. The next day, Hull told Hatskin that he would decide within 10 days whether or not to accept the offer. Hatskin flew back to Winnipeg and was so confident that Hull would respond positively that he ordered 5,000 pictures of Hull.

Meanwhile, on 8 June, the Jets announced the signing of rugged 27-year-old winger Dunc Rousseau to a three-year deal. Though Rousseau was brought in to fill an enforcer's role, he had also showed a bit of a scoring touch in the minor leagues. He scored a career-high 35 goals with the Dayton Gems of the International Hockey League (IHL) four seasons earlier.

Negotiations continued with Hull, and on 16 June, Hatskin proclaimed that he was "99.99% sure" that Hull would sign with the Jets and that all that remained were to iron out the details in the 75-page contract that the Golden Jet would sign.

The team continued to grow. Three days later, Daniel Douglas Johnson, better known to his friends as Danny, put his signature on a Jets contract. The Jets had obtained the hard-working 27-year-old centerman's rights from the New York Raiders in exchange for the rights to Marc Dufour. Johnson represented himself in contract negotiations, but he did consult with Daley during the process. The two had been teammates in Detroit last season and were teammates once again with the Jets.

Defenseman Larry Hornung signed a three-year, no-cut, no-trade contract to bring the total number of players under contract to six. Like Johnson, Hornung acted as his own agent during the negotiations and became the second former member of the St. Louis Blues to sign with the Jets. Two weeks earlier, the 26-year-old native of Gravelbourg, Saskatchewan had been left unprotected by the Blues and the New York Islanders selected his NHL rights in the Expansion Draft, but he opted to sign with the Jets instead.

Much-travelled 30-year-old defenseman and Winnipeg native Bob Woytowich followed suit and left the Los Angeles Kings to become the seventh player to sign a contract with the Jets. The veteran nicknamed "Augie" was signed to provide a steadying influence on the blue line.

The Jets' next signing would be far more dramatic.

In the wee hours of the morning of 27 June, Robert Marvin Hull flew from Edmonton to Winnipeg under the cover of darkness. After catching a couple of hours sleep at the nearby International Inn, he returned to the airport at 6:30 a.m., where a throng of media had gathered. Hull boarded a plane bound for the Twin Cities, where his wife Joanne and three of his five children were waiting after flying in from Chicago. They rode in a 1938 Rolls-Royce to the Minnesota Club in downtown Saint Paul, where Hull put his signature on the league's portion of a contract that would pay him $2.75 million over 10 years to become the next member of the Jets. Hull would receive an annual salary of $250,000 for five seasons as a player and coach, $100,000 per year for another five years as a club executive and a signing bonus of $1 million from WHA Properties that was funded by all 12 teams in the league. Hull signed the contract with 11 different pens, each representing one of the other teams in the WHA.

Hull and his family then flew back to Winnipeg, where they were taken in a Rolls-Royce to a public signing ceremony to sign the Jets' portion of the contract at the corner of Portage Avenue and Main Street in the heart of downtown, where more than 5,000 onlookers gathered for the event. Rush-hour traffic came to a standstill, but the congestion mattered little to ecstatic Winnipeg hockey fans. The Jets now had themselves a bona fide superstar and the WHA gained instant credibility. They were the "Phantom Jets" no more.

Despite the whirlwind surrounding the blockbuster signing, the Jets still needed to fill spots on their roster and continued to sign players. On 5 July, they signed veteran centerman Wally "Mags" Boyer and minor-league defenseman Joe Zanussi.

Boyer was preparing to retire from hockey after a 14-year pro career to become a full-time motel owner, but the Jets convinced him to put off those plans for at least one season. The 34-year-old 5'8" slick speedster had spent time with four different NHL teams and was with the AHL's Hershey Bears for most of last season. Zanussi was also known as a fast skater, but he was 10 years younger than Boyer, and he earned the nickname "Tasmanian Devil" for his wild rushes up the ice. He had been in Detroit's camp as a winger last season until he was sidelined by a knee injury and subsequently returned for this third season with Fort Worth of the Central Hockey League (CHL).

Winger Cal Swenson, versatile centerman Garth "Scooter" Rizzuto, together with defensemen Steve Cuddie and Bob "Beaver" Ash rounded out the signings for the month of July. All four were veteran minor leaguers, though the 22-year-old Cuddie was both the youngest and the heaviest of the group. At 203 pounds, Cuddie was not afraid to use his weight to his advantage against opposing forwards. In order to be able to sign Cuddie, the Jets acquired his rights from the New England Whalers in exchange for the rights to veteran NHL defenseman Ted Green. Rizzuto came with a reputation of being quick on his skates and quick with his temper, while both Swenson and Ash weren't noted as being particularly fast in either of those categories. The Jets traded the rights to Ted Hampson to the Minnesota Fighting Saints so they could sign the 28-year-old Ash, the co-owner of a busy Esso service station outside Brandon, Manitoba, to a three-year contract. What the quietly intense Ash lacked in size he made up for with an abundance of savvy.

In August, the Jets signed Alvin Brian McDonald, better known as Ab, along with Christian Bordeleau, Jean-Guy Gratton and Milt Black. The 36-year-old McDonald, a veteran of four Stanley Cup championship teams, became the third member of the 1971-1972 Detroit Red Wings to sign with the Jets. Upon his signing, Hull expressed surprise that McDonald wasn't also named as an assistant coach. McDonald was a Winnipeg native who got his start in hockey playing at the Weston Community Club before advancing to the junior ranks and on to the NHL, where he spent 14 seasons. The 24-year-old Bordeleau, a centerman, had been one of Hull's teammates in Chicago and was known as a good two-way player. The 23-year-old Gratton came from the AHL's Hershey Bears and had a reputation as a good stickhandler, accurate passer and a finesse player. Black became the first graduate of the junior Jets to sign a contract with the pro Jets despite missing most of last season with a broken arm. The 23-year-old would soon be reunited with his former coach as the Jets named Nick Mickoski, coach of the junior Jets, as the bench coach to assist Hull with the pro Jets. Mickoski played 12 seasons in the NHL before turning to coaching, and he was Hull's teammate during the Golden Jet's first season with the Blackhawks. At the end of his playing career, he led the San Francisco Seals to two Western Hockey League (WHL) championships as a playing coach.

Rounding out the roster was forward William Fraser Sutherland, known to his friends as Bill, "Sudsie" or the "Old Goat," who signed a contract on the morning of 2 September. The 37-year-old noted practical joker was a veteran of 14 pro seasons and yet another member of the 1971-1972 Red Wings to join the Jets' inaugural lineup.

The Jets added trainer Diarmid McVicar and equipment manager Steve Adamski to the fold. McVicar was a native of Scotland who was a graduate of the Royal Infirmary School of Therapy in Glasgow. Adamski spent several years as a certified psychiatric nurse's aide in his native Brandon before joining the Jets.

Unfortunately, the signing of high-profile names like Bobby Hull and other NHL players to WHA contracts didn't escape the attention of the more established league, and they weren't about to take these signings lying down. The NHL launched legal action that prevented its former players from being available to the WHA's new teams, claiming that the controversial reserve clause bound players to their respective teams for life. Most notably, this prevented Hull from immediately joining the Jets.

Nonetheless, the Jets' inaugural training camp got underway on 14 September in Kenora, Ontario at the Kenora Recreation Center amid tight security and locked doors, though there was less than a full complement of players on hand. In any event, led by Mickoski and accompanied by both McVicar and

Adamski, the Jets still had 17 players on the ice: forwards Brian Cadle, Garth Rizzuto, Jean-Guy Gratton, Milt Hohol, Milt Black, Dunc Rousseau, Cal Swenson, Nels Jacobson, Freeman "Duke" Asmundson, Bill Sutherland, and Ab McDonald; defensemen Ron Hopkinson, Jim Pritchard, Joe Zanussi, and Steve Cuddie; goaltenders Gord Tumilson and Wayne Doll. Danny Johnson, Christian Bordeleau, Bobby Hull, Norm Beaudin, Wally Boyer, Bob Woytowich, Larry Hornung, Ernie Wakely, and Joe Daley all stayed away and worked out on their own instead. Ash had planned to go to Kenora, but a letter from the lawyers convinced him to join the latter group.

In defiance of the legal proceedings and the skeptics, most of the Jets took to the ice for their first exhibition game on the night of 1 October, when they dropped a 7-5 decision to the Minnesota Fighting Saints in Duluth, Minnesota. Asmundson, who was in camp on a tryout contract, had the honor of scoring the first Jets' goal.

Two nights later, the Jets made their debut at the Winnipeg Arena, where the Fighting Saints defeated the Jets again, this time by a score of 5-2. McDonald scored the first goal for the Jets in front of only 1,721 onlookers. The next night, they lost their third straight, a 6-3 decision at the hands of the Alberta Oilers in Edmonton. One night later, they finally picked up their first victory of the exhibition season, defeating the Los Angeles Sharks by a score of 2-1 before 3,000 onlookers in Regina, Saskatchewan. Three nights later, they beat the Sharks again by a score of 6-5 in front of a crowd of 1,851 in Winnipeg.

At the conclusion of the exhibition season, the Jets signed Asmundson, Cadle and Tumilson to contracts. All three were in camp on tryout contracts and earned spots on the final roster. The 29-year-old Asmundson, a big winger but a gentle man, earned his job playing the point on the power play and also filling on defense when needed. Cadle, who had just turned 24 and was arguably the most popular player the junior Jets ever had, was a skinny, tough hitter who made the team primarily on desire, while Tumilson was signed as insurance in case of injury to either Daley or Wakely. Two days before the games were to begin for real, the Jets appointed McDonald as their captain and Woytowich and Sutherland were each elected as assistant captains.

The Jets would start their first season in the Western Division along with the Fighting Saints, Oilers and Sharks, as well as the Houston Aeros and Chicago Cougars. The other six teams — the Cleveland Crusaders, New England Whalers, New York Raiders, Philadelphia Blazers, Ottawa Nationals and Quebec Nordiques — would comprise the Eastern Division. The Aeros were originally to be based in Dayton, Ohio, but were transferred to Houston in April, 1972, while the Nordiques franchise was once slated for San Francisco before settling in Quebec under new ownership.

On the evening of Thursday, 12 October 1972, the Jets took to the ice for its first regular season game. In front of 6,273 curious spectators inside New York City's Madison Square Garden, the Jets, without Hull or Woytowich, faced off against the Raiders. With Winnipeggers listening back at home to the voice of Stew MacPherson, referee Bob Sloan dropped the puck at center ice to begin the first Winnipeg Jets WHA game. It was a wide-open, entertaining affair that saw the Jets come out on top by a score of 6-4 on the strength of four goals from Bordeleau. The line of Bordeleau, Beaudin and Sutherland tallied nine points on the night in which the Jets never trailed. McDonald had the honor of scoring the first regular season Jets goal, taking a feed from Gratton during a scramble and poking the puck past Raiders goaltender Gary Kurt at the 8:14 mark of the first period. Hull was pleased with his team's performance, but he could do little other than act as a cheerleader between periods, as Mickoski handled the duties behind the bench.

The Inaugural Lineup

Goaltenders:	1	Joe Daley	Played last season with the Detroit Red Wings, previously had NHL time with the Buffalo Sabres and Pittsburgh Penguins. Had 140 NHL games over parts of five seasons.
	30	Ernie Wakely	Played the last three seasons with the St. Louis Blues after a lengthy pro career, mostly in the minor leagues.
Defensemen:	3	Bob Ash	Most recently had been with the Omaha Knights (CHL) and Providence Reds (AHL). Played the past prior eight seasons in the minor leagues.
	6	Steve Cuddie	Played last season with the Cincinnati Swords (AHL) and made his pro debut in 1970-1971 with the Salt Lake Golden Eagles (WHL).
	5	Larry Hornung	Split last season between the St. Louis Blues and Kansas City Blues (CHL). Had 48 NHL games, all with the Blues, and had six seasons of pro hockey under his belt mostly in the minor leagues.
	4	Joe Zanussi	Played the last three seasons with the Fort Worth Wings (CHL) and started his pro career with the Johnstown Jets before going to Fort Worth.
Forwards:	21	Freeman "Duke" Asmundson	Played the last three seasons with the Des Moines Oak Leafs (IHL). Had spent the past eight seasons in the minor leagues.
	11	Norm Beaudin	Split last season between the Minnesota North Stars and Cleveland Barons (AHL). Had a total of 25 NHL games split between the North Stars and St. Louis Blues over a lengthy pro career spent mostly in the minor leagues.
	19	Milt Black	Played the last two seasons with the Dallas Black Hawks (CHL), his first two years of pro hockey.
	7	Christian Bordeleau	Split last season between the St. Louis Blues and Chicago Blackhawks. Had a total of 205 NHL games split between St. Louis, Chicago, and Montreal.
	8	Wally Boyer	Played last season with the Hershey Bears (AHL) with the exception of one game with the Pittsburgh Penguins. Had a total of 365 NHL games split between the Penguins, Oakland Seals and Chicago Blackhawks in a career of 14 pro seasons.
	20	Brian Cadle	Split last season between the Des Moines Oak Leafs (IHL) and Columbus Golden Seals (IHL) after making his pro debut in 1970-1971.
	16	Jean-Guy Gratton	Played the last three seasons for the Hershey Bears (AHL), his only pro team since leaving junior hockey.

	17	Danny Johnson	Split last season between the Vancouver Canucks and Detroit Red Wings. Had 121 NHL games split between the Canucks and Red Wings, in addition to one game with the Toronto Maple Leafs.
	14	Ab McDonald	Split last season between the Detroit Red Wings and Tidewater Wings (AHL). Had 762 NHL games split between the Red Wings, St. Louis Blues, Pittsburgh Penguins, Boston Bruins, Chicago Blackhawks and Montreal in a 16-season pro career.
	15	Garth Rizzuto	Split last season between the Seattle Totems (WHL) and Rochester Americans (AHL). Had 37 NHL games with the Vancouver Canucks in 1970-1971.
	12	Dunc Rousseau	Played season with the Baltimore Clippers (AHL). Spent seven seasons in the minor leagues.
	10	Bill Sutherland	Split last season between the Tidewater Wings (AHL), St. Louis Blues, and Detroit Red Wings. Had 250 NHL games split between the Blues, Red Wings, Philadelphia Flyers, Toronto Maple Leafs, in addition to two playoff games with Montreal in a 17-season pro career.
	18	Cal Swenson	Spent the past four seasons with the Tulsa Oilers (CHL), where he made his pro debut in 1968-1969.

Did You Know?

Joe Daley and Joe Zanussi had both once played with the Johnstown Jets, the team that the Charlestown Chiefs were derived from in Slap Shot, a classic movie featuring a disbanding minor league hockey team based in a Pennsylvania mining town.

One night later, the Jets were back on the ice, this time at the Saint Paul Auditorium, the temporary home of the Fighting Saints until construction of their new arena was completed. The Jets were given an additional half hour of rest as they waited through the lengthy opening ceremonies that included an appearance from Minnesota Governor Wendell Richard Anderson, one of the Fighting Saints' choices in the General Player Draft. Before an enthusiastic sellout crowd, the home team took period leads of 2-1 and 3-2, but the Jets came up with two goals in the third period for a 4-3 victory. The game-winner came off the stick of Asmundson, who scored from his knees with only 1:29 left in the third period. Asmundson had been substituted in place of Sutherland alongside Bordeleau and Beaudin after Sutherland was forced out of the game in the third period with an injured knee. Daley was the star of the game for the Jets, as he kept his travel-weary teammates in the game in the early going, setting the stage for the late-game heroics.

Did You Know?

Goaltender Joe Daley played the entire 1972-1973 season without a mask.

Two nights later, it was time for the Jets to make their own home debut on Sunday night against the Oilers. Given how low the attendance had been at the two exhibition games, Hatskin was more nervous than any of the players. The Jets had 3,300 season ticket holders, but they needed more to at least attain an estimated 6,000 per game to break even. The Jets' single biggest customer was the Province of Manitoba, purchasers of 550 of season tickets for distribution to disadvantaged people throughout the province.

Did You Know?

The first ten rows of seats in the Winnipeg Arena were painted red and those seats were padded, while the remainder were painted blue and were cushioned only by plywood. Season tickets for 1972-1973 cost $257.40 in the red seats and $214.50 in the blue seats, and the price eventually rose to $380 for red seats and $220 in the blue seats for the 1978-1979 season. A lower-cost "gray" option was added that cost $140 per season in 1978-1979, which consisted of the upper rows of the blue sections.

Despite the absence of their star attraction, the Jets did draw 8,123 spectators to their first regular season home game, allowing Hatskin to breathe a little easier for the time being. Naturally, the Jets had plenty of opening ceremonies before the drop of the puck. Don Wittman, Master of Ceremonies, introduced Manitoba Lieutenant-Governor William John "Jack" McKeag, Winnipeg Mayor Stephen Juba, Manitoba Attorney General Al Mackling, WHA President Gary Davidson, Winnipeg Enterprises Chairman Sam Fabro, along with Hatskin and Hull. As expected, the latter two got standing ovations from the crowd. Wittman then introduced each player and Doug Crossley's rendition of *O Canada* brought the festivities to a close. With Jim Franks at the organ and Doug "Maxie" McIlraith manning the public address system, it was time to drop the puck.

After the action got underway, the Jets proceeded to lay an egg in front of the home crowd. They looked nothing like the team that gutted out a pair of road victories to open the season as they trailed by scores of 2-0 and 3-1 at each intermission. Johnson scored the historic first goal on home ice at the 7:11 mark of the second period, but the Jets never were closer than one goal down after the Oilers opened the scoring in the first period and cruised to a 5-2 win. The Oilers had had a 4 a.m. wake-up call in Cleveland on Sunday morning to get to Winnipeg in time for the game, but the nervous and jittery Jets could not take advantage of their weary opponents.

Two nights later, the Jets returned the favor for the Oilers, serving as the opponent for their home opener at the Edmonton Gardens. Unfortunately, it was the Oilers who again emerged victorious, this time by a 3-2 score in overtime as the Jets experienced their first taste of the WHA's extra 10-minute period to decide games tied after regulation time. Though the Jets played better than they had two nights earlier, it wasn't good enough and they wasted another fine performance from Daley in the process.

On Friday, 20 October, the Jets began a five-game home stand with a visit from the Fighting Saints. The Jets thoroughly outplayed their guests, but they could do no better than a 1-1 tie, thanks to Fighting Saints' goaltender Mike Curran, who stopped all but one of the 38 shots the Jets sent his way. Zanussi scored the Jets' only goal before a disappointing turnout of only 4,171 paying customers.

Next up on the schedule was a pair of games against the high-priced Philadelphia Blazers. The Blazers' roster featured former NHL stars Johnny McKenzie, Derek Sanderson and Bernie Parent, but they still were without a win as their plane touched down in Winnipeg. A crowd of 6,152 showed up to see this contingent of former NHLers adorned in gaudy orange and yellow uniforms and they were instead treated to a 6-3 Jets victory that broke their three-game winless streak. The Jets had the game well in hand early in the second period and got contributions from all four lines.

Two nights later, the Jets were hoping to have Hull and Woytowich available for the rematch, but the promised ruling from Judge A. Leon Higginbotham in U.S. Federal Court in Philadelphia didn't come. A lot of fans didn't come either, as only 4,736 paid to see the Jets rebound from an early 2-0 deficit to post a 5-3 win and sweep the back-to-back series. The underachieving Blazers showed a lot more heart than they had on Sunday evening, but it wasn't enough to earn them their first victory of the season. The Jets, with the win, pulled into a first-place tie with the Oilers in the Western Division.

Derek Sanderson put on a show, of sorts, for the spectators with his continuous abuse of referee Brent Casselman. For his efforts, he was assessed three minor penalties, two misconducts, and finally, a game misconduct. Bordeleau scored his ninth goal of the young season while Sanderson was serving one of his many stints in the penalty box.

Did You Know?

On 24 October 1972, Derek Sanderson was assessed 36 minutes in penalties, the highest individual total by an opponent in any game against the Jets during their seven seasons in the WHA.

The fourth of the five-game home stand was scheduled for Friday, 27 October against the Cougars. The Jets had again been promised a decision from the Philadelphia court, but the lengthy report had to be typed up before it could be made available. Hatskin tried to keep Hull's unavailability a secret in order to sell more tickets, but Nicolson spilled the beans on Friday morning.

The Cougars, dressed in no less off-the-wall uniforms than the team that just left Winnipeg, played it close to the vest, but the Jets scored three times in a five-minute span during the second period to break a scoreless tie. The Cougars rallied to narrow the gap to 3-2, but Beaudin's second goal of the game into an empty net sealed the victory. Wakely played perhaps his finest game of the season in backstopping the Jets to their third straight victory that moved them into sole possession of first place.

The game was played in front of only 4,135 paying customers, a number that was held down on account of both Hull's absence and the four and a half inches of snow that fell on Winnipeg. Since Hull wasn't in the Jets' lineup, there may have been more people watching in the stands than watching the live television broadcast in Chicago.

Sunday night, the Jets played host to the Aeros to complete the five-game home stand, but only 4,311 spectators were on hand to see it. The Jets were soundly outplayed in the first two periods, and only Daley's stellar goaltending kept the deficit down to 3-1 at the second intermission. The third period was a different story, as the Jets rallied for four goals to post a 5-3 win. They outshot their guests by a 25-4 margin and kept themselves in sole possession of first place before hitting the road for a pair of games in Chicago and Saint Paul.

The 6-2-1 Jets touched down in Chicago on Halloween night expecting a treat, but instead got another trick when they learned that Judge Higginbotham in Philadelphia still hadn't finished his report. Hull flew to Chicago with his teammates, but as a result of the delay in Philadelphia, he was still unable to play. The Cougars presented Hull with an award for his on-ice accomplishments in Chicago and the crowd of 6,727 fans gave him a standing ovation, but it was the Cougars who stole the show on that Tuesday night. Reggie Fleming led the way, as he and his teammates nearly ran the Jets out of the International Amphitheater. Despite the physical punishment they took, the Jets held a 1-0 lead going into the third period, but the Cougars scored three times in the final 20 minutes to post a 3-1 win, putting an abrupt halt to the Jets' four-game winning streak.

One night later, the Jets opened the month of November with their second visit of the season to the Saint Paul Auditorium to play the Fighting Saints. Despite the absence of a decision from the Philadelphia court, Hatskin made the decision to have Woytowich suit up. Woytowich was one of the former NHL players who were still not legally free to play, but his presence on the Jets' blue line in defiance of the courts did nothing for the Jets' fortunes on this night. Just as he had done in Winnipeg less than two weeks ago, goaltender Mike Curran was the difference once again, turning aside all 42 shots he faced, seven of which came off of Bordeleau's stick. The Jets controlled the play, but it was the Fighting Saints who controlled the scoreboard, scoring twice in the second period and once more in the third en route to a 3-0 win.

The Jets returned home for a pair of weekend games against the 6-5-0 Raiders. Just as they had done in the season opener, the two teams played another wide-open affair, but, this time, the Jets came out on the short end of the stick. Of the 15 goals scored in the game, the Jets only scored six of them. Defensively, the Jets left Wakely to fend for himself most of the night. The small gathering of 4,112 who were in attendance saw the Jets' losing streak grow to three games.

Short-Lived Terror

Bobby Sheehan scored twice in each of his first two games against the Jets, but he would only score three more against the Jets in his WHA career. Sheehan would go on to play a total 241 regular season games and five playoff games in the WHA for New York Raiders, New York Golden Blades, Jersey Knights, Edmonton Oilers and Indianapolis Racers.

The two teams were back on the ice on Sunday night to complete the weekend series. Another below-5,000 crowd saw a much different performance from the Jets this time around. The Jets learned their lesson and tightened up in their own end, not even allowing the Raiders a shot on goal until the second period. The Jets scored three times in the first period and never looked back in the 3-1 victory that put an end to their three-game losing streak.

There would be no time for celebration, as the 7-5-1 Jets boarded a plane early Monday morning bound for Boston to kick off a three-game Eastern road trip that evening against the Whalers. The Jets held off the Whalers for the first two periods, but fatigue caught up to them in the third. A 2-1 deficit quickly became a 6-2 defeat, and the Jets would carry on for a matchup against the Nordiques on Wednesday night.

While the Jets were in Quebec preparing to play the Nordiques, they finally got the news they were waiting to hear from Philadelphia. In a lengthy decision, Judge Higginbotham granted the WHA's request for a preliminary injunction that prevented the NHL from enforcing its reserve clause. In his decision, Higginbotham refused to make a finding as to whether or not the reserve clause was a violation of the Sherman Anti-Trust Act, but he did free the long list of former NHL players to play for their respective WHA teams until a final decision was made. The WHA would still have to post a $2.5 million bond by 20 November, and in the event that the final decision went in the NHL's favor, any financial damage the NHL suffered would be paid from the bond.

Though there was also a separate suit filed by the Blackhawks against Hull that Higginbotham had previously returned to a Chicago court, the bottom line was that Hull was free to play for the Jets. The ruling also officially allowed Woytowich, Daley, and Wakely to play, though all three had already long since been playing regardless of the NHL suit.

The mid-day news brought Quebecers out in droves, and a crowd of 10,126 packed Le Colisee to see Hull's historic WHA debut. Despite the addition of one of hockey's best players, however, the Jets still went into the game shorthanded, since Cadle and Rizzuto were out of the lineup and Daley was injured in the warmup. The Jets came out with a spirited effort, but all the hoopla surrounding Hull seemed to be more important than the game. The Jets found themselves more concerned with feeding their superstar and coach than with making the right play, and they wasted a 44-shot effort in a 3-2 defeat. Hull did record his first point as a Jet, but the assist didn't come until there were only five seconds left in the game. After the game, the Jets learned that Daley had fractured his thumb around the knuckle and would be lost to the team anywhere from three to six weeks. In addition, Sutherland flew back to Winnipeg after the game to get a second opinion on a troublesome arm problem.

The rest of the Jets moved on to Ottawa on Thursday night to meet the Nationals, who were winners of six of their past eight after dropping their first three games. Despite playing their fourth game in five nights, the Jets rebounded to hand the listless Nationals a 4-1 defeat in front of a season-high crowd of 5,034 at the Ottawa Civic Centre. Hull did record another assist, but it was the less celebrated foot soldiers who delivered the goods in this game.

The 8-7-1 Jets returned to Winnipeg for a game on the night of Friday, 10 November against the Fighting Saints, finishing off their third game in as many nights. Before the game, they got more bad news on the injury front when they learned that the bicep muscle on Sutherland's right arm was torn away from the bone and surgery might be required to reattach it. As a result, "Sudsie" would be out of action for at least four months.

An enthusiastic gathering of 7,487 turned out to see Hull's home ice debut and they came within a whisker of seeing Hull's first goal as a Jet, but his shot rang off the goal post on his first shift of the game. Unfortunately, the visitors took over the game from that point on and cruised to a 5-1 win. To make matters worse, Hull suffered some stretched knee ligaments when he was sent head over heels by Fighting Saints' defenseman Terry Ball.

After a day of some much-needed rest, the Jets were back on the ice on Sunday night to meet the Sharks. For starters, the crowd of 7,563 didn't have long to wait to see Hull's first goal as a Jet. Larry Hornung's shot deflected off a shin pad and back to Hull, who wasted no time putting the puck past goaltender George Gardner, bringing the crowd to its feet only three minutes into the contest. Gardner kept the game close, but the Jets used three unanswered third period goals to break a 2-2 tie and post a 5-2 victory. Hull scored again and Bordeleau netted his team-leading 11th goal of the season on a shorthanded breakaway.

The same two teams were back in action on Tuesday night at the Arena. An embarrassingly small crowd of only 5,105 saw the Jets score early and often in the 8-0 blowout. The Sharks tried to intimidate the Jets, but they were instead burned by four power-play goals. Ernie Wakely stopped all 24 shots he faced to earn the first shutout in Jets history. With the win, the 10-8-1 Jets climbed back into sole possession of first place in the Western Division, two points ahead of the Oilers and four ahead of the Sharks.

One night later, the Jets were back on the road with another first-place showdown in Edmonton. The sellout crowd of 5,200 saw the Jets control the first period, but the home team gradually took over as the game went on. In addition, Hull was slowed by the sore knee and was also feeling the effects of the flu. The Oilers scored once in the second period and twice more in the third to hand the Jets a 3-1 defeat.

Two nights later, the Jets were in Southern California to begin a two-game weekend series with the Sharks on Friday night at the Long Beach Arena. During the week, the Sharks had made various threats against the Jets, singling out Bordeleau in particular for his stickwork during the games the two teams played recently in Winnipeg. Once the game started, however, despite all the pre-game bluster, the Jets pulled away from their rough-and-tumble hosts with two goals in each of the first two periods en route to a comfortable 5-1 win.

Sunday night, 19 November, the two teams moved over to the Los Angeles Sports Arena for their fourth meeting in the span of one week. The Jets built up a 4-1 lead heading into the third period on the strength of two goals from Hull and they hung on for a 4-3 win. The Jets left Wakely to fend for himself in the final 20 minutes and only his spectacular work enabled the Jets to escape with two points. Their fourth win in as many meetings with the Sharks propelled the Jets back into sole possession of first place as they left California on a plane bound for Texas.

The Jets wrapped up their five-game road trip on Tuesday night with the first of two games against the Aeros at the Sam Houston Coliseum. Hull wasn't in the lineup, but that didn't stop the rest of the Jets from battling hard against the Aeros and coming through with a 4-2 win. Bordeleau led the way for the Jets with two goals, bringing his season total to 17.

On Thursday night, Hull returned to the ice, but Rizzuto was out on account of a cracked hand and Boyer had to miss the game with a cracked rib. The Jets rebounded from a 1-0 first period deficit with four goals in the second to take a 4-2 lead to the third despite the fact that they were being outplayed. The hard-nosed Aeros kept coming and broke through with three goals in the third, but Hull's goal late in the third sent the game to overtime. At the 3:50 mark of the extra period, Cuddie was sent off for tripping, and it only took 13 seconds of power play time for Keke Mortson to score the game-winner and send the Jets down to their second overtime defeat of the season.

The 13-10-1 Jets answered a 5 a.m. wake-up call on the morning of Friday, 24 November and they didn't reach Winnipeg for ten hours, where the well-rested Nordiques were waiting for them to begin a two-game weekend series. Despite playing in their fifth game in the space of eight days and second in as many nights, the Jets jumped out to a 3-0 lead in the first period, only to trail off and allow the Nordiques to tie the score with three goals of their own. However, the Jets summoned up some reserve energy and rallied with two goals in a span of 33 seconds midway through the third to propel them to a 5-3 victory. Taking himself off the line with Beaudin and Bordeleau, Hull placed himself alongside Swenson and Black and responded with two goals, including the game-winner.

During their 10-hour travel odyssey from Houston to Winnipeg, the WHA finally posted the $2.5 million bond that the U.S. Federal Court in Philadelphia had required as part of its decision that freed Hull and other former NHL players to play for their respective WHA teams. It was four days late, but it was the last hurdle that the league needed to clear to allow their star players to continue playing.

The Jets spent part of their off day on Saturday signing autographs after practice for 3,000 children, then they returned to the ice on Sunday night for a rematch with the Nordiques. For the second straight game, a crowd numbering over 7,000 was in attendance, and they saw the Jets erase an early 1-0 deficit with three first period goals on their way to a 4-1 win. Unlike Friday night's affair, the Jets didn't let the three-goal lead get away and they held the freewheeling Nordiques off the scoreboard the rest of the way.

On Tuesday night, the 15-10-1 Jets entertained the Oilers for the second time this season. The Oilers were missing their big gun, Jim Harrison, who was out of the lineup on account of a knee injury, and the Jets took full advantage, scoring once in each period to post a 3-0 victory. Wakely earned his second shutout of the season and the new line combinations continued to pay dividends on the scoreboard. The win was the Jets' first against the Oilers in four meetings and it allowed the Jets to widen their lead atop the division to eight points in front of a disappointing turnout of 4,421 patrons.

The two teams faced off against each other once again two nights later, this time in the Alberta capital. The Jets jumped out to an early 3-0 lead, but the Oilers rallied to tie the game at 3-3, sending the game to overtime. Hull had two good chances in the extra period, but he couldn't connect, and the game ended in a draw. Wakely, however, was the star of the night for the Jets as he stopped 40 of the 43 shots he faced to steal a point for his team.

The Jets were scheduled to begin a five-game home stand the next night to start the month of December, but getting back home was a bigger challenge than anything they had faced throughout the game. A blizzard was ripping through northern Alberta and the airport was brought to a virtual standstill. The Jets boarded a plane early the next day, but just before takeoff they got word that a planeload of cattle had gone down in a gravel pit a few miles away. Fortunately, the Jets' flight did not meet with the same fate, and they made it home safely and in time for the game.

Waiting for them were the Ottawa Nationals, who were making their first appearance in Winnipeg. With Ernie Wakely having started 15 games in a row, Hull decided to give his overworked goaltender a break and give Gord Tumilson his first start. The Nationals played a close-checking game to near perfection and broke open a 2-2 tie with two third period goals that gave them the lead for good. The Jets rallied to narrow the gap to a single goal, but they could get no closer and the game ended with the final score of 4-3 in the visitors' favor. In making his pro debut, Tumilson held his own and was given the sentimental choice as the game's first star. Sadly, the game was played in front of a crowd of only 5,106 despite the fact that Hatskin offered 500 $5.50 tickets at half price to kids 16 and younger.

The Jets continued to be plagued by the injury bug as Swenson sustained an ankle injury on Wednesday night against the Oilers and though he suited up against the Nationals, he wasn't able to play. Rizzuto's sore hand had been preventing him from gripping a stick and Hull's right elbow was so swollen that he couldn't extend it fully. He aggravated it further after a third period collision against the Nationals.

Battered, bruised and travel-weary, the Jets were back in action at the Arena on Sunday night to play the Fighting Saints for the fifth time. The Jets responded to the occasion and scored three times in the game's first five minutes, then cruised to a 5-1 victory. Larry Hornung scored twice and Woytowich added his first goal of the season as the Jets finally broke through against Mike Curran, who had yielded a total of two goals in his last three games against the Jets. The lone disappointment of the night was the poor turnout. Despite the presence of busloads of fans from Manitou and Morden who had made the trek to Winnipeg to see the game, only 4,790 saw the Jets extend their lead in the division to nine points over both the Fighting Saints and Sharks.

On Monday, 4 December, Dave Simkin, Hatskin's good friend, business partner and Jets' Vice-President for Finance, passed away suddenly at the age of 59.

Prior to the Jets' next game on Tuesday night against the Nordiques, the Jets held a moment of silence in Simkin's honor, then Beaudin opened the scoring two minutes into the game, but the Nordiques controlled the play for the rest of the night. The visitors scored four times in the second period and the Jets could only muster a meaningless goal from Hull with nine seconds left as the Nordiques handed the Jets a 4-2 defeat. The Jets lost their second of three games before a crowd of only 4,181 that was as listless as the team they had come to see.

The next afternoon, the Jets attended Simkin's funeral at 1 p.m. at Chesed Shel Emes Chapel, then they were back on the ice in the evening to do battle with the woeful 6-15-1 Cougars. The Jets took it to the

Cougars right off the opening faceoff and were full value for a 7-1 victory. Leading the Jets' attack was Jean-Guy Gratton, who was facing his former teammate with the Hershey Bears, Cougars' goaltender Andre Gill. Gratton told Gill before the game that he would score twice. Instead, Gratton scored three goals, which doubled his season goal total. The Jets' 18th win of the season was seen by a season-low turnout of 3,436, which was the only blemish on an otherwise satisfying win.

The Jets wrapped up their home stand on Friday night when the Aeros made their second appearance of the season in Winnipeg. The Jets broke open a 2-2 tie with four unanswered third period goals within a span of just over five minutes to rout the Aeros by a score of 6-2, giving those in the small, but appreciative gathering their money's worth. Hull scored two of the four goals in the final 20 minutes to pace the Jets, who packed their bags after the game for a seven-game, six-city road trip that would keep them away from home until after Christmas. However, they embarked on the rigorous road trip with the comfort of a well-earned 11-point lead atop the Western Division standings.

One night after disposing of the Aeros, the Jets made their first trip to the Cleveland Arena to meet the 17-10-1 Eastern Division-leading Crusaders. The Crusaders scored once in each of the first two periods and outshot the Jets by a 31-20 margin, but the Jets turned the tables in the third period. Hull and Johnson scored 63 seconds apart to tie the game at 2-2, and the score held until overtime. Hull set Black up for the game-winner three minutes into the extra period, sending the crowd of 8,204 home disappointed.

Two nights later, the Jets returned to the Boston Garden to battle the Whalers, but in the first two periods they were turned away time and again by goaltender Al Smith, who kept his team in the game. Mike Hyndman and Kevin Ahearn then scored late in the third period to break a 2-2 tie and give the hometown Whalers an eventual 4-3 victory. During the game, Hull added to his collection of bumps and bruises when he collided with Smith, and though he wasn't forced to leave the game, he did sustain a foot injury.

The Jets moved on to the City of Brotherly Love to meet the 8-19-0 Blazers for a pair of games starting on Wednesday, 13 December. The Jets controlled the play in the early going, but Blazers' goaltender Bernie Parent held them off the scoreboard until his teammates could respond. They did respond, and often, breaking open a 3-2 narrow lead at the second intermission with four goals in a span of just over two minutes early in the third period to make the score 7-2 and send the Blazers on to an easy victory. Christian Bordeleau and Duke Asmundson each scored late in the game, but the outcome had long since been decided in the Blazers' favor.

Friday night's rematch proved to be no different. The Jets were the better team in the early stages of the game, but they couldn't beat Parent. The Blazers scored three times in the second period and once more in the third before the Jets could break through with a pair of their own. Bordeleau and Hull scored twice each in the third and the Jets didn't go down without a fight, but the Blazers still prevailed by a score of 6-4 to sweep the pair of games. Not coincidentally, Derek Sanderson, who had spent the bulk of the time during the last meeting between the two teams back in Winnipeg throwing temper tantrums, missed both games against the Jets this time around with a back injury.

The Jets left Philadelphia bound for New York carrying a three-game losing streak with them as they prepared for a Sunday matinee against the Raiders. After a scoreless first period, the Raiders opened the scoring with two goals early in the second, but the Jets responded with one of their own and added three more in the third to take a 4-2 lead. The Raiders kept up the pressure on the Jets, but goaltender Ernie Wakely was excellent in a fine rebound performance after getting pummeled in Philadelphia and the Jets hung on for a 4-3 victory.

With a rare four-day break between games, the Jets were able to return home for a breather before they had to get back on a plane bound for Saint Paul to meet the Fighting Saints for the sixth time this season on Thursday night. It looked like the Jets caught a break when scheduled Fighting Saints starting goaltender Mike Curran couldn't make it through the warmup on account of tendonitis in his right leg, forcing 37-year-old backup Jack McCartan into action. McCartan, however, borrowed Curran's magic against the Jets and single-handedly kept them off the scoreboard for the first two periods. In the third, goals from Mel Pearson and Wayne Connelly gave the Fighting Saints all the cushion they needed, and with Wakely on the bench, Pearson scored his second of the period into the vacated net to seal the 3-0 victory. The win enabled the Fighting Saints to pull to within four points of the sliding Jets and the Fighting Saints also had the benefit of five games in hand over the Jets.

The 21-16-2 Jets, losers of four of their last five decisions, limped into Chicago to put a merciful end to their seven-game road trip. Waiting for them was a crowd of 8,856 spectators who came to see Hull play in Chicago for the first time as a Jet. In the first period, Hull scored his 19th goal of the season to the delight of the crowd, but the game was tied at 2-2 after one period. There was no more scoring until Butch Barber scored in the third period goal to break a 2-2 tie and put the Cougars back in front to stay. With time winding down, Hull sent Rick Morris hard into the boards, prompting Reggie Fleming to go after the Golden Jet. The ensuing melee put Hull off the ice for five minutes with a questionable fighting major and helped to quash any comeback hopes. The Jets went down to their fifth loss in six games, but despite the defeat, Joe Daley made a successful return after a six-week absence, enabling the Jets to return to their system of rotating their two main netminders.

The Jets were able to rest during the Christmas holidays and they were back on the ice at the Arena on Boxing Day for a rematch with the Cougars. Though Bill Sutherland made an unexpectedly quick recovery from his bicep injury, the Jets came into the game shorthanded once again. Joe Zanussi had to return home on account of an illness in the family, while the flu bug hampered both Bordeleau and Woytowich. Still, the gathering of 9,681, the Jets' largest of the season, saw their understaffed team completely dominate the game, but the Jets needed a third period goal from Gratton to break a 2-2 tie and escape with a 3-2 win. Cougars' goaltender Jimmy McLeod faced a 47-shot barrage and nearly stole the game for his team, but the Jets prevailed in the end. The Jets pulled six points ahead of the Fighting Saints and snapped the Cougars' brief winning streak at three games.

Aside from their attendance at the Rotary Club's Christmas party at the Hotel Fort Garry the next day, the Jets were able to enjoy some rest until their next game on New Year's Day in Edmonton against the Oilers. Despite being losers of eight of their last 11 games, the Oilers took it to the Jets, scoring three times in the second period to blow open what had been a 2-1 game after one period. The two teams split four goals in the third to close out the scoring in the 7-3 rout, much to the delight of the sellout crowd at the Edmonton Gardens, where the Jets again failed to record a win in their fourth try.

As they attempted to return to Winnipeg, the Jets were stranded in Edmonton on account of a blizzard, and they had to wait nearly a full day before they could take off and head for home. Once they finally got out of Edmonton, most of the team enjoyed a few days off for the All-Star break, but five members of the Jets were selected to play in the first WHA All-Star Game, which was held on the afternoon of Saturday, 6 January 1973 in Quebec City.

Hull, Bordeleau, Beaudin, Hornung and Wakely led the best of the Western Division against the best of the Eastern Division. Wakely started in goal and stopped all but one of the 18 shots he faced in the first period before being relieved by Jack Norris and later, Mike Curran. After Wakely departed, the Eastern Division All-Stars broke open a 1-1 game and cruised to a 6-2 blowout victory. Hull scored in the third period, while Beaudin and Bordeleau each registered one assist each in the game.

After the game, the five All-Star Jets hurried to catch a plane for Saint Paul to meet their teammates. The Fighting Saints hosted the Jets on Sunday afternoon in their second game at the brand-new $23-million Saint Paul Civic Center in front of a league-high crowd of 13,426 as well as a nationally televised audience on CBS. Jack McCartan stoned the Jets in the early going, just as he did the last time the Jets visited the Minnesota capital, but late in the second period, they broke through and opened the floodgates. Three late goals in the period broke a 1-1 tie, and the Jets added three more in the third to cruise to the 6-2 win. Reunited with Hull and Beaudin, Bordeleau tallied two of the three third period goals to pace the Jets' attack and give the Jets a five-point cushion atop the Western Division standings.

The Jets returned home to begin a six-game home stand on Wednesday against the Oilers, who made their third visit of the season to the Arena. The Oilers tried to slow the Jets down with stickwork and fisticuffs, but the Jets responded with goals. The Jets scored four times in the first period and added two more in the second to send the small, but enthusiastic gathering of 4,811 home happy. After the game, trainer Diarmid McVicar was kept busy tending to the players, but it was the visitors who were feeling the stinging pain of defeat.

The home stand continued with a pair of weekend games starting Friday night against the 24-14-1 Crusaders, co-leaders of the Eastern Division. The two teams put on quite a show for the 6,892 onlookers, but the Jets prevailed by a score of 5-3. Norm Beaudin scored the game's last goal into an empty net to seal the victory and he assisted on all of the other four goals the Jets scored. He was playing in front of his brothers Bob, Alain and Harvey, who had driven more than 300 miles from their hometown of Montmartre, Saskatchewan to see Norm in action.

On Saturday, the Arena hosted a track meet, leaving the staff scrambling to put the ice back in for Sunday's rematch between the Jets and Crusaders. As a result, the two teams spent most of the night fighting their way through the soft ice instead of each other. In spite of the conditions, however, Bob Ash and Steve Cuddie scored third period goals to break a 1-1 tie and send the Jets on to a 3-1 win that was largely made possible by Wakely's strong goaltending. In addition, several Crusaders had their jerseys stolen on Saturday and had to make do with junior Jets' uniforms on Sunday.

Winners of their last four games, the Jets began the second half of their six-game home stand against the Fighting Saints on the night of Tuesday, 16 January. The first two periods were a virtual carbon copy of Sunday night's sluggish affair, but after Wayne Connelly broke a scoreless tie five minutes into the third period, the Jets rose up and scored three times in just over three minutes to propel themselves to a 3-1 victory. The win increased the gap between the two teams to nine points in the race for first place.

The Jets closed out their home stand with another pair of weekend games, this time against the Whalers, the other Eastern Division first-place contender. Like the Crusaders before them, the Whalers were also making their inaugural appearance in Winnipeg and they were the last of the other 11 WHA teams to do so. The bigger and tougher Whalers took it to the Jets in the early going and only another strong outing from Wakely prevented the visitors from expanding their slim 1-0 lead. The Jets righted the ship and scored six unanswered goals en route to an impressive 6-2 victory before 9,208 paying customers, their second-largest crowd ever. Beaudin and Bordeleau scored twice each in the Jets' first win over the Whalers, a game that Hull called the Jets' finest performance of the season.

For the second time on the home stand, the visiting team became a victim of theft when three dozen sticks were stolen from the Whalers' dressing room on Friday morning. Come Sunday afternoon, however, the Whalers stuck it to the Jets, handing them a 7-2 defeat in front of a national television audience watching on CBC. It was the Jets' first loss on home ice since early December and Ab McDonald admitted after the game that the Jets might have been overconfident.

Despite the loss, however, the Jets still won five of the six games on the home stand and flew to Cleveland to play their first road game in 16 days, taking an eight-point lead in the Western Division with them to begin the four-game trip.

On Tuesday night, the Jets were much better against the Crusaders than they had been on Sunday afternoon, but they still lost, thanks to Ray Clearwater's second goal of the game 29 seconds into overtime. The next day, the Jets moved on to Boston to battle the Whalers for the third time in four games. They showed few ill effects of playing last night, but they couldn't get anything past goaltender Al Smith in the first period. Smith's teammates turned the game in the second and they proceeded to pummel the Jets. The result was a 6-1 defeat, the Jets' third consecutive loss.

Two nights later, the Jets limped into Quebec for a Friday night game against the Nordiques. With the hard-charging Aeros nipping at their heels in the standings, the Jets responded and took the play to the Nordiques, but they couldn't capitalize on the many chances they had and they were forced to settle for a 2-2 tie. They concluded their road trip two nights later against the struggling Nationals, losers of their last five games. The Nationals put on a show for their largest crowd of the season to date, but it was the Jets who persevered and escaped with a 5-4 victory. Referee Pierre Belanger was the center of controversy all night long, but the most notable incident occurred late in the third period when he waved off a potential game-tying goal by the Nationals. After the game, the crowd littered the ice with debris and Belanger, who earlier had his hair pulled by an enraged fan who had climbed over the boards, required no fewer than eight security guards to escort him out a side door for his own safety.

The Jets returned home with only three points to show for the four road games, but they still stood atop the Western Division standings with a 29-21-3 record, five points ahead of the Aeros.

While the Jets were celebrating their victory over Ottawa, the Jets announced changes in the ownership structure, necessitated by the death of former Vice President Dave Simkin. Ben Hatskin and his brother Ruben jointly retained their original 50 percent share of the team, with the remaining 50 percent being held by a group of Winnipeg investors, represented on the Board of Directors by D.E. McVittie as Vice President for Finance; A.J. Mercury as Secretary; and G.J. Simkin as Treasurer. Along with the Hatskin brothers, they formed the new board.

The Jets also announced that, in an attempt to bolster sagging ticket sales, they were offering eight-game packages in March that would assure buyers the right to purchase the same seats for upcoming playoff games. The package price was set at $52.80 for the red seats in the lower rows and $44.00 for seats in the blue seats of the upper reaches of the Arena.

After a break between games, the Jets returned to action against the Oilers on Friday night at the Arena to begin the February portion of their schedule. The Oilers took a 3-1 lead after two periods against their lethargic hosts, but the Jets stormed back in front of an intimate gathering of 6,346 and they tied the game at 3-3, thanks to goals by Hull and Gratton, but they couldn't get anything more past a beleaguered Jack Norris in the Oilers' net. Late in the third period, Jim Harrison again burned the Jets when he beat Wakely with only 3:19 left to play in regulation time, and, this time, the Oilers held the lead to capture their second win of the season in Winnipeg.

The 29-22-3 Jets packed their bags for another long road trip, and their first stop was a Sunday night rematch with the Oilers in Edmonton. The Jets rallied from a 2-0 deficit to take a 5-2 lead late into the third period, helped in part by Hull's three-goal outburst. After keeping the game within reach in the early going, Joe Daley was struck by a high stick late in the third period following an Oilers' goal. The enraged Daley pled his case to referee Bob Sloan to no avail and Wakely had to finish up the game while the barefaced Daley was being attended to at the bench. Wakely had to make only make one save the rest of the way, however, and the Jets held on for their first ever win in Edmonton.

The Jets moved on to Houston for a pair of critical meetings with the Aeros, the first of which came on Wednesday night. The Jets came out of the action-packed and hard-hitting first period with a 2-1 lead, but the tight-checking Aeros shut down the Jets and the threesome of Hull, Bordeleau, Beaudin — otherwise known as the Luxury Line — en route to a 5-2 comeback victory that shaved the Jets' lead atop the Western Division standings to a mere three points.

The two teams went at it again 24 hours later, but, this time, the Jets escaped with a narrow 3-1 victory, due mostly to a spectacular performance from Daley. For the second time in five games, the Jets had a potential game-tying goal against them disallowed, when referee Ray Thomas waved off Murray Hall's marker with 1:22 remaining in regulation time.

Still clinging to a five-point lead in the division, the 31-23-3 Jets left Houston and moved on to Los Angeles for a pair of games with the Sharks. On Saturday afternoon at the Los Angeles Sports Arena, Hull scored twice to lead the Jets to an early 3-0 lead, but the stubborn Sharks kept battling and they used two late second period goals to tie the game at 3-3. The teams traded goals in the third period, but Joe Szura's goal with only 3:24 left to play in regulation time looked like it might propel the Sharks to their first win over the Jets in five tries. With Wakely on the bench in favor of a sixth attacker, Dunc Rousseau pounced on a rebound in front of the Sharks' net and tied the game at 5-5 with only seven seconds left on the clock. The Jets controlled the overtime period and won in dramatic fashion when Beaudin pulled goaltender George Gardner out of position and put a backhand into the open net to secure the 6-5 victory.

The same two teams went at it again on Sunday night. The Sharks were determined to break their five-game losing streak against the Jets, but Daley, taking his turn in goal, held the Sharks at bay, while Danny Johnson added a pair of second period goals to stake the Jets to a 2-0 lead. Hull added another in the third, and Daley earned his first shutout as a Jet to complete the weekend sweep.

After a well-earned stop back in Winnipeg, the Jets flew into Chicago to resume their road trip on Thursday, 15 February against the Cougars. A crowd in excess of 9,000 packed the International Amphitheater to see Hull, the former Blackhawk star, and he didn't disappoint. Hull scored twice early and he added another in the second period as the Jets poured it on in a 7-2 rout of the Cougars, who lost for only the second time in their last eight games.

The Jets had little time to celebrate their victory, and instead, they answered a 6 a.m. wake-up call on Friday morning to catch a flight back to Winnipeg to begin a six-game home stand against the Aeros. The travel-weary Jets touched down in Winnipeg at noon, but their opponents would be no fresher, as they were also scurrying into the Manitoba capital after posting a 4-3 over the Oilers in Houston on Thursday night.

Once the game started, the Jets showed no ill effects of their hectic travel day and scored early and often en route to a convincing 7-0 win over their closest divisional pursuers. The biggest theatrics of the evening came near the end of the second period when Hull sent a shot from his own blue line that skidded through the pads of Aeros' goaltender Don "Smokey" McLeod and into the net. The Jets thought they had scored, but referee Bob Sloan disallowed the goal, claiming time had expired. In the aftermath of Sloan's call, Daley took a swing at the timekeeper with his stick, but, fortunately, he missed him. Inexplicably, Daley was not penalized on the play, but then a fan took up the cause and hit Sloan in the head, earning himself an early exit from the premises. Lost in the shuffle was the fact that Daley collected his second consecutive shutout, stopping all 31 shots he faced.

Riding a five-game winning streak, the Jets had a well-earned day off on Saturday, but they were back at it again on Sunday night for a rematch with the Aeros. This time around, the visitors clamped down defensively and kept the Jets at bay through most of the game, but the Jets rallied from a 2-1 deficit late in the third period to post a 4-2 victory. By sweeping the Aeros, the 36-23-3 Jets not only extended their winning streak to six games, but they pushed the Aeros into third place, one point behind the Fighting Saints.

After being run all over the continent, the Jets had a full week of rest before their next game against the new and improved Blazers. Since they last met the Jets in Winnipeg, the Blazers had bought out the contract of Derek Sanderson and replaced playing coach Johnny McKenzie with Phil Watson. After losing 16 of their first 20 games, the Blazers came into town only three games under the .500 mark and winners of seven of their last eight games.

The Blazers got on the board early and took advantage of the Jets' frustration over the bad Arena ice, but the Jets rallied and took it to the Blazers, turning a 3-2 deficit into a 5-3 win thanks to Beaudin's natural hat trick in the third period. A crowd of 8,047 saw the Jets win their seventh in a row, marking only the fourth time all season that the Jets broke the 8,000 barrier at the gate.

The Jets continued their home stand on Tuesday night against the Cougars, where they used two late second period goals from Milt Black to pull away from their guests and cruise to a 5-1 win before a crowd of only 4,242. Sporting a 38-23-3 record and a comfortable nine-point lead over the Aeros in the standings, the Jets opened the month of March with a pair of weekend games against the Sharks to close out their six-game home stand. On Friday night, the Sharks played it close to the vest, but the Jets built a 2-0 lead with single goals in each of the first two periods and held on for a 2-1 win. Joe Daley wasn't severely tested on the night, but his best save came in the final minute when he stopped Ted McCaskill to preserve the lead and the Jets' ninth win in a row. The Jets got on the board only 17 seconds into Sunday night's affair, but they again had to hold on to an identical 2-1 score for their tenth consecutive victory.

For the first time since mid-February, the Jets had to play a road game and on Tuesday night, they began a three-game eastern swing in Ottawa to meet the revitalized Nationals. A season-high crowd of 9,424 at the Ottawa Civic Centre saw the home team dominate from start to finish en route to a 5-2 victory, putting a decisive end to the Jets' winning streak in far less of a controversial affair than the last time the Jets had been in the nation's capital. In the defeat, the Jets wasted a strong performance from Daley, who admirably faced 42 shots including several breakaways.

The Streak

The Jets rattled off a team and league-high ten-game winning streak that lasted nearly a month, from 8 February 1973 to 4 March 1973, as they defeated four different opponents. During this time, the Jets extended a fragile three-point Western Division lead to 13 points, all but locking up the top spot with less than a month to go in the regular season.

1.	8 February	Houston Aeros	3-1
2.	10 February	Los Angeles Sharks	6-5 (OT)
3.	11 February	Los Angeles Sharks	3-0
4.	15 February	Chicago Cougars	7-2
5.	16 February	Houston Aeros	7-0
6.	18 February	Houston Aeros	4-2
7.	25 February	Philadelphia Blazers	5-3
8.	27 February	Chicago Cougars	5-1
9.	2 March	Los Angeles Sharks	2-1
10.	4 March	Los Angeles Sharks	2-1

Two nights later, the Jets took to the ice in Quebec in front of another large crowd at Le Colisee, where they pulled away from the stubborn Nordiques midway through the second period to post a 7-4 win. At least one member of the Luxury Line had a hand in all but one of the seven goals the Jets put past Nordiques' goaltender Richard Brodeur.

The Jets wrapped up their road trip on Saturday night in New York in front of 10,921 curiosity seekers, where Bordeleau collected his sixth goal on Madison Square Garden ice this season less than three minutes into the contest, but the Raiders rallied and played the Jets to a 2-2 draw through regulation time. In the extra period, Brian Bradley scored with only two minutes remaining to lift the Raiders to a 3-2 win, sending the Jets home with only one win to show for three games on the road.

Despite the disappointing defeat, the Jets still held a healthy 13-point lead atop the Western Division standings as they returned home via Saskatoon, Saskatchewan on account of foggy conditions in Winnipeg in time to open a six-game home stand against the Crusaders on Sunday night. The Crusaders took full advantage of the tired Jets and spanked them by the tune of 11-2 in front of 8,417 paying customers who were most displeased over the Jets' performance.

After a couple of days off, the Jets were back on the ice on Wednesday night against the Whalers. The Jets scored a pair of early goals, but the Whalers turned the tables and scored five unanswered goals to take a 5-2 lead. With the prospect of another blowout defeat staring them in the face, the Jets rallied and tied the game at 5-5 early in the third period, thanks to two goals from Hull and another from Joe Zanussi. Hull's third hat trick as a Jet wasn't enough, however, as the Whalers kept pressing and Ted Green swatted a rebound out of mid-air past Daley with 5:23 left in regulation time for what would prove to be the game-winner. The Whalers sealed the Jets' third straight loss with an empty-net goal in the final minute to send the crowd of 6,883 home disappointed. Despite the loss, however, the Aeros also lost and the Jets' magic number for clinching first place shrank to three points.

Hull's Hat Tricks

During the 1972-1973 season, Bobby Hull recorded three hat tricks, two on the road and one in Winnipeg. The Jets won both road games in which the Golden Jet scored three or more goals, while they lost the only time Hull scored three goals at home.

Game Date	Opponent	Goals	Opposing Goaltender
4 February 1973	Alberta Oilers	3	Jack Norris
15 February 1973	Chicago Cougars	4	Jim McLeod
14 March 1973	New England Whalers	3	Bruce Landon

Bordeleau had to leave Wednesday's game early after falling on his hip and Bob Ash remained hampered by a rib injury, so the Jets signed defenseman John Shmyr to a five-game tryout contract for some added depth. Shmyr, the younger brother of Crusaders' defenseman Paul Shmyr, had been playing amateur hockey in British Columbia when the Jets called.

Next up on the schedule was a pair of weekend games against the Nationals, winners of six of their last seven games. A Friday night crowd of numbering just under 5,000 saw the visitors break out in front with two early goals. The Jets could only muster a power-play goal from Johnson in response as the complacent Jets went down for the fourth straight game, this time by a score of 6-1. Sunday night's affair looked to be a repeat performance of Friday's lopsided defeat, but the Jets erased an early 2-0 deficit to tie the game in the second period. A controversial goal put the Nationals back in front before the intermission, but that didn't slow the Jets down. They were determined to bust out of their doldrums, but despite outshooting their guests by a margin of 14-3 in the final period, they couldn't get the equalizer, and the Jets went down by a score 3-2 at the half-empty Arena.

The Jets had four days to stew about their five-game losing streak before getting back on the ice on Thursday night to face the Oilers for the first time since early February. In spite of their recent woes, they held an 11-point lead atop the division standings and they needed only a single point to assure themselves of first place and the $2,500 bonus per player that it would bring.

The Oilers, however, would not be easy pickings for the Jets. Led behind the bench by General Manager Bill Hunter, who relieved Ray Kinasewich of his duties soon after they last saw the Jets, the Oilers came into the contest winners of their last five games and in hot pursuit of the last playoff position in the Western Division. Before the game, Hull, in his capacity as coach, shook up the second and third lines, hoping to spark the team by reuniting the trios of Ab McDonald, Danny Johnson, and Jean-Guy Gratton, along with Milt Black, Wally Boyer, and Dunc Rousseau.

The Jets took it to their guests, but despite numerous power plays and Hull's first penalty shot as a Jet, the Jets still trailed 1-0 entering the third period. The score held until the final minute of regulation time, when Beaudin took a feed from Rousseau in front and beat Oilers' goaltender Jack Norris to tie the game with only 16 seconds left on the clock and Wakely on the bench in favor of an extra attacker. Overtime settled nothing and the 41-29-4 Jets barely captured the necessary point to assure themselves of a first-place finish.

With their playoff position secured, the front office announced on Sunday that there would be no price increases for the first round of post-season action and they began selling playoff tickets to season ticket holders at 9:30 that morning. In the announcement, Hatskin added that a larger arena would be needed to keep the Jets in Winnipeg but that, as a temporary measure, more seats could be added in the $5.50 blue section, taking capacity up to 10,500, if demand for tickets warranted.

That night, the Jets closed out the home portion of their regular season schedule against the New York Raiders, who, like the Oilers before them, were locked in a tight battle for a playoff spot. In front of a crowd of 8,184, one of their best of the season, the Jets erased a 4-3 first period deficit and scored five unanswered goals to post an 8-4 victory, putting an end to a forgettable six-game winless streak. Both Beaudin and Hull collected their 10th point of the season, while Bordeleau saw his point total reach 99. The Jets opted to rest McDonald, Wakely, and Larry Hornung but their absence didn't prevent the Jets from collecting their 42nd win of the season.

Did You Know?

Though Ron Ward of the New York Raiders was held off the score sheet on the night of 25 March 1973 when the Raiders visited the Jets, his thirteen points against the Jets in the 1972-1973 regular season was the highest total of any opponent. Ironically, Ward would briefly play for the Jets late in the 1976-1977 season, his last as a player.

The Jets began their final road trip of the regular season on Wednesday in Chicago, where Hull dazzled another large crowd by scoring his 50th and 51st goals of the season. His second goal of the game came 55 seconds into overtime, giving the Jets to a 4-3 win over the Cougars.

Bobby Hull's 50-Goal Season

Despite being barred from playing in the first 14 games of the season, Bobby Hull still managed to score 50 goals in the 1972-1973 season, marking the sixth time in his pro career that he accomplished the feat. Of the 50 goals, Hull's favorite victim was the Chicago Cougars, against whom he scored nine times.

Two nights later, Hull and his teammates moved on to Cleveland, where, despite a strong showing, they went down to a 4-2 defeat. They had no fewer than four breakaways, but Crusaders' goaltender Gerry Cheevers stopped them all. The regular season finale came on Sunday, the first day of April, when the Jets went down by an identical 4-2 score at the hands of the Blazers. Gord Tumilson came off the bench to make only his second start of the season in goal, giving both Daley and Wakely a rest before the start of the playoffs.

The Jets were scheduled to open the playoffs on Friday night, but their opponent still remained undecided, as the Oilers and Fighting Saints finished the regular season tied for fourth place with identical 38-37-3 records. Amid some controversy, the league decided to hold a one-game playoff to decide who would be the last entrant into the playoffs. The Oilers were awarded home ice for that game on account of their superior record against divisional foes. The two teams split their eight regular season meetings evenly.

Unfortunately for the Oilers, their home rink, Edmonton Gardens, had already been booked for a rodeo, so the Oilers looked elsewhere for a place to play the game. After considering Vancouver, they decided on Calgary, so they took to the ice against the Fighting Saints at the Stampede Corral on Wednesday evening for the right to play the Jets in a best-of-seven series. The Fighting Saints made easy work of the Oilers, scoring once in each of the first two periods, then twice more early in the third to take a 4-0 lead. The Oilers did respond with a couple of their own, but it wasn't enough, and the Fighting Saints took the game and moved on to meet the Jets in Winnipeg.

With the matchup set, the Jets and Fighting Saints faced off on Friday night in front of a crowd of 7,354 at the Arena for Game 1 of the Western Division semi-final. Wearing their customary white jerseys, rather than the blue road uniforms they wore at home in the latter half of the regular season, the Jets got on the board first with a power-play goal from Hull, but the visitors played it close to the vest and held the Jets at bay. The 1-0 score held until the third period, when Fighting Saints' centerman Mike Antonovich picked up the puck after Zanussi had partially fanned on a shot. Antonovich sped down the ice and beat Ernie Wakely to tie the score, but less than three minutes later, all three members of the Luxury Line combined for Hull's second goal of the game to restore the Jets' lead. Bordeleau added an insurance marker with just under five minutes to play to give the Jets a 3-1 win and a 1-0 series lead. It was far from their best game of the year, but the Jets rose to the occasion when they had to and prevailed.

Two nights later, the same two teams went at it for Game 2 in front of an even larger crowd of 8,425. After the two teams traded goals less than a minute apart in the first period, Danny Johnson took a feed from Gratton on Jack McCartan's doorstep and put it home to give the Jets their second lead of the game early in the second. Later in the period, the Fighting Saints tied the score once again and pressed hard for their first lead of the series, but Daley was equal to the challenge. The Jets took the lead for good late in the period when the wily Wally Boyer scored his first of the playoffs. They extended their lead in the third when the Luxury Line combined for two more goals, giving the Jets a 5-2 win and a commanding 2-0 series lead.

During the game, the Jets took care of some awards. General Manager Annis Stukus presented Hull with a trophy for being the team's leading scorer, but Hull insisted that Beaudin also receive equal recognition, because the two had equal point totals during the season. Bordeleau, the other member of the Luxury Line, was not left out as he was not only called over to join in the festivities with Hull and Beaudin, but he was also presented with the most valuable player award. Hull, because he was also the coach, was excluded, and in over 1,000 mail-in ballots, Bordeleau edged out Beaudin by 20 votes and received a stereo system as the prize.

One person who wasn't on hand was Hatskin. He was in New York, meeting with representatives of at least six NHL teams to resume discussions that had started last week about a potential merger of the WHA and the NHL. Under the rumored plan that was to be discussed on Sunday and Tuesday were provisions to move two existing teams into Washington and Kansas City; dissolving the Raiders, who were a ward of the WHA; and having the remaining nine WHA teams play in one division. The plan also called for an entry fee of $4 million to be paid by each WHA team.

Meanwhile, back on the ice, after a Monday morning practice, the Jets flew to Saint Paul for Game 3 on Tuesday night. The crowd of 5,151 at the Saint Paul Civic Center, including a busload of fans from Winnipeg seated behind the Jets' bench, saw a wild first period in which the Jets netted only two of the six goals scored during the opening 20 minutes of action. To add injury to insult, late in the period, Hornung's shot caught Bordeleau on the ankle and though "Pepe" continued to play, he later had to leave the game and was taken to a local hospital. The game settled down and the Jets rallied to tie the score early in the third period, but the Fighting Saints broke the 4-4 tie with two goals just over three minutes apart and held on for the 6-4 victory, narrowing the Jets' lead in the series to 2-1.

After the game, the Jets got bad news regarding Bordeleau. The popular centerman would have to return to Winnipeg, where he would be fitted for a cast for his sprained ankle. He was ruled out for the remainder of the series, but was expected to be available if the Jets advanced to meet the winner of the series between the Aeros and the Sharks.

Without one third of the Luxury Line, the Jets returned to the ice on Wednesday night hoping to gain a split from the pair of games in Saint Paul. In Bordeleau's absence, Hull decided to insert the veteran Bill Sutherland between himself and Beaudin, but early returns didn't look positive as the Fighting Saints took an early lead. The Jets responded with a goal just over a minute later, and both goaltenders made the 1-1 score hold up until Terry Ball's second period goal restored the home team's lead at 2-1. The Jets applied plenty of pressure in the third period, but they were stopped time and again by goaltender Mike Curran, who was making his first appearance of the series after sitting out the first three games with a bad back. In the final minute of regulation time, the Jets pulled Joe Daley in favor of the extra attacker, and they finally got the equalizer when Sutherland put in a rebound to tie the game with only 45 seconds left on the clock. Three minutes into overtime, with Fighting Saints' defenseman John Arbour in the penalty box, Cal Swenson fed Beaudin out front, and he put the puck over a prone Curran to give the Jets a dramatic 3-2 come-from-behind victory. The Jets and their faithful were overcome with emotion and, fortunately, they had some time off to recover for Game 5 back in Winnipeg.

On Sunday night, another large crowd, numbering 8,852, turned out to see if their Jets could finish off the scrappy Fighting Saints in five games. Neither team held anything back and goals were being scored at a furious pace, but it was the Jets who used four quick second period goals to pull away from their determined guests and cruise to an 8-5 win. Beaudin led the way offensively with a seven-point performance as the Jets took both the game and the series.

Did You Know?

Norm Beaudin's three-goal, four-assist performance on 15 April 1973 would be the single highest point total a Jet would accumulate in a WHA regular season or playoff game.

In the other Western Division series, the Aeros defeated the Sharks by a score of 3-2 in Los Angeles on Tuesday night, taking the series four games to two and earning a date with the Jets in a best-of-seven series to decide the Western Division championship beginning on the night of Friday, 20 April. The Aeros had a couple of days off to rest after being pounded by the physical Sharks, while the Jets used the time to get Bordeleau healthy. Though he still had some pain in the ankle, he would be available for Game 1.

The series got underway before a disappointing crowd of 7,044 at the Arena and the Aeros tried to batter their hosts into submission, but it didn't take long before the Aeros began to show the effects of coming off a grueling six-game series against the Sharks. The Jets took full advantage and hit back on the scoreboard as they scored three times in the first period and coasted to a 5-1 victory. Wally Boyer led the way with two of the five goals in a performance that earned him first-star honors. As it turned out, the Jets hardly needed Bordeleau, who played only six shifts and wasn't very effective.

Game 2 got underway on Sunday night and the visitors showed a much stronger resolve than they had on Friday night, but all it got them was a parade to the penalty box. The Jets, however, were unable to take advantage of the five first period power play opportunities. The Aeros began to assert control in the second period, but Wakely held his team in the game. The game remained scoreless until late in the third period, when Dunc Rousseau put home a rebound past Don "Smokey" McLeod with only four and a half minutes to play, giving the Jets a 1-0 lead. The Aeros pressed hard for the tying goal, but Wakely made his best saves of the night as time was expiring and Beaudin's empty-net goal sealed the 2-0 victory that gave the Jets an identical edge in the series, much to the delight of the small, but vocal gathering of 5,029 paying customers.

The series shifted to Houston for Game 3 on Tuesday night and the Aeros defeated the visiting Jets in front of their enthusiastic supporters, but while Joe Daley was stopping the Aeros from denting the scoreboard, the Jets made the most of their few chances. After Zanussi opened the Jets' scoring, the trio of Sutherland, Hull and Beaudin combined for a goal with only one second left in the first period, which only served to further frustrate the home team. It was more of the same in the second period, and the Jets extended their lead to 3-0 before the Aeros came storming back, scoring a pair early in the third to get back in the game. Daley and the Jets held firm, however, and Bordeleau's late goal restored the two-goal margin and capped the 4-2 victory that gave the Jets a commanding 3-0 lead in the series. After the game, a couple of fans went after referee Bob Sloan and one of them hit Sloan with a punch, but local police intervened and prevented any further trouble.

The two teams returned to the ice two nights later with the Aeros looking to stave off elimination. The Jets had a slightly easier time of it as they used a late first period goal from Norm Beaudin to stake claim to a narrow 1-0 lead and Wakely made it hold up during a furious second period assault by the Aeros. The Jets hammered the final nail in the Aeros' coffin when Larry Horunug's backhand shot early in the third period made it through a maze of bodies and into the net. The Jets never looked back. Beaudin's ninth goal of the playoffs ended the scoring and the Jets took both the game and the series. The rough Aeros squad hammered the Jets physically every inch of the way, but it was the Jets, not the Aeros, who were advancing to the inaugural WHA final series.

While the Jets were taking care of their own series on Thursday night, the Whalers followed suit by defeating the Cleveland Crusaders by a 3-1 score in Boston, winning their best-of-seven Eastern Division final in five games. By virtue of finishing four points ahead of the Jets in the regular season standings, thanks to the Jets' late season slump, the Whalers earned home-ice advantage for the series that would open at the Boston Garden on Sunday, 29 April. The unavailability of the Arena from 4 May through 13 May on account of the Shrine Circus meant that Games 2 and 3 would be played in Winnipeg, with Games 4 and 5 played in Boston. If necessary, the Jets would have to play Game 6, a "home" game, at Maple Leaf Gardens in Toronto, and return for a decisive Game 7 in Boston.

The first WHA championship series opened on Sunday night at a busy Boston Garden that had hosted a National Basketball Association playoff game earlier in the day and a rock concert the night before. A crowd of only 6,526 saw the Jets face off against a Whalers team missing two of their key components during the regular season. During Game 4 of their series against Cleveland, the Whalers lost 100-point man Terry Caffery and top penalty killer John Danby and neither would be available for the championship series.

The Jets got on the board first as all three members of the Luxury Line combined on Beaudin's tenth post-season goal midway through the first period, but the Whalers took charge of the game with four goals of their own before the intermission. The Whalers added two more goals in the second period and the rout was on as the Whalers cruised to a 7-2 victory against a Jets team that showed little of the perseverance and determination they displayed in the first two rounds. Daley looked bad in yielding seven goals on only 25 shots in a matchup against his former teammate and roommate, Al Smith of the Whalers, but the blowout loss was a complete team effort.

After a couple of days between games, it was time for Game 2 on Wednesday night at the Arena, where the Jets were greeted with a standing ovation from the crowd of 8,655. The Jets rewarded their faithful with a goal in the first minute when Beaudin scored his 11th playoff goal to open the scoring and keep the fans on their feet. Christian Bordeleau put a shot off Whalers' defenseman Brad Selwood in the final minute of the first period to give the Jets a 2-0 lead, but the Whalers replied with one of their own a mere 26 seconds later, reducing the Jets' lead to a single goal before the intermission. The Whalers tied the game early in the second period, but the Jets responded with two of their own in short succession and Wakely's strong goaltending kept the two-goal lead intact into the third. The Whalers kept pressing and tied the game at 4-4 with two quick goals before the third period was four minutes old.

Soon afterward, Hornung sent a shot off both goal posts and the goal judge flipped the red light on to signify a goal. After referee Bob Sloan immediately and correctly ruled no goal, the fans littered the ice with all sorts of debris, including a 2x4, but fortunately, no one was hurt in the crowd's temper tantrum. With momentum on their side, the visitors kept the heat on the Jets and they soon took their first lead of the game. The Whalers doubled their lead just over a minute later when John Cunniff was sent in on a breakaway and scored his first playoff goal, putting the Jets down by two goals. The Jets had no heroic comeback in the offing this time and the Whalers capped the scoring with an empty-net goal and skated off with a 7-4 victory to take a 2-0 series lead against the discouraged Jets.

With the Shrine Circus ready to move in, the two teams were back on the ice less than 24 hours later as the Jets faced a must-win situation in Game 3, their last true home game of the series. A crowd of only 7,200 paying customers saw the Jets shake off the previous night's disappointment and stake themselves to a 2-0 lead with two late first period goals. Danny Johnson's third goal of the playoffs early in the second extended the lead to three goals, but the Whalers started another comeback. Rick Ley scored with five minutes left in the second and Winnipeg native Ted Green scored early in the third to narrow the Jets' lead to a single goal. Daley and the Jets kept the Whalers at bay, but with only 1:41 left, John French set Tim Sheehy up in front and though Sheehy's first shot was blocked, his second made it through to the back of the net, tying the game at 3-3. With their season hanging in the balance, the Luxury Line rose to the occasion as Hull put a rebound shot over a fallen Smith with only 64 seconds left in regulation time to give the Jets a 4-3 lead. The Whalers had no time to mount another comeback and the Jets hung on for the victory, trimming the Whalers' lead in the series to 2-1.

Two nights later, the series resumed in Boston for Game 4 in front of 13,697 enthusiastic Whalers supporters. Right from the start, the Jets opted to play a close-checking style, a strategy that had been employed so often against them, and it paid off in the early going. The Jets held the Whalers off the scoreboard in the first period and added one of their own when they capitalized on a giveaway in the Whalers' zone, resulting in Hull's ninth goal of the playoffs. Unfortunately, the Whalers broke through in the second period and put three goals past Wakely to take a commanding 3-1 lead to the second intermission. The Jets tried to get back in the game in the third period, but just when it looked like they might make a dent in the Whalers' lead, Mike Byers of the Whalers scored to make the score 4-1, snuffing out any comeback hopes on the part of the visitors. All the Jets could muster was a goal off a rush by Rousseau with six seconds left, but it was far too little and too late as the Whalers moved to within a game of capturing the inaugural WHA championship.

The two teams returned to the ice on Sunday afternoon for Game 5 in front of 11,186 spectators in the Boston Garden and a national television audience on CBS. The Whalers started the fireworks only 21 seconds into the contest and they didn't let up, putting five past Daley in the opening period, while the Jets could only respond with a pair of their own. An early second period goal from the Whalers made the score 6-2, but the Jets rallied with two quick goals and added another early in the third to trim the Whalers' lead to one goal. However, that was as close as the Jets could come and Larry Pleau scored a pair of goals in short succession to complete his hat trick and put the game out of reach. Duke Asmundson picked up his first goal of the playoffs to round out the scoring as the Whalers took the game by a score of 9-6 and the series four games to one, earning the title of the first WHA champions.

The Jets had a very successful season and gave it their all, but in the end, the Whalers' depth was the key to the series. The Luxury Line terrorized opposing goaltenders all season long and the strong tandem of Joe Daley and Ernie Wakely between the pipes was among the best in pro hockey, but the Jets needed more size and youth to get past the last hurdle of becoming champions of the infant league. As a consolation prize, each one of the Jets picked up $60,000 for being the loser of the championship series, money that was well earned despite the disappointing end to the season.

Beaudin's Bounty

Though the Jets failed to capture the WHA championship, Norm Beaudin's 28 points led all scorers in the 1973 WHA playoffs. Beaudin tallied 13 goals and 15 assists, and his total was two points better than Tom Webster and three better than his linemate and coach, Bobby Hull. He recorded at least one point in 13 of the 14 games the Jets played in the playoffs, and his single game high was a three-goal, four-assist performance on 15 April, when the Jets ousted the Fighting Saints in Game 5 of their first round series.

Game Date	Opponent	Period	Time	Result
6 April	Minnesota	1	6:37	Assist
6 April	Minnesota	3	10:03	Assist
6 April	Minnesota	3	15:04	Assist
8 April	Minnesota	1	5:25	Assist
8 April	Minnesota	3	0:57	Goal
8 April	Minnesota	3	19:15	Assist
10 April	Minnesota	2	8:56	Assist
11 April	Minnesota	4	3:12	Goal
15 April	Minnesota	1	2:31	Goal
15 April	Minnesota	1	14:22	Assist
15 April	Minnesota	2	3:15	Assist
15 April	Minnesota	2	4:15	Goal
15 April	Minnesota	2	5:29	Assist
15 April	Minnesota	2	17:06	Goal
15 April	Minnesota	3	7:13	Assist
20 April	Houston	2	1:42	Assist
22 April	Houston	3	19:22	Goal
24 April	Houston	1	19:59	Goal
26 April	Houston	1	14:20	Goal
26 April	Houston	3	14:22	Goal
29 April	New England	1	10:02	Goal
2 May	New England	1	0:33	Goal
2 May	New England	1	19:20	Assist
3 May	New England	1	15:23	Assist
3 May	New England	1	19:34	Assist
3 May	New England	3	18:56	Assist
6 May	New England	1	17:53	Goal
6 May	New England	2	3:15	Goal

1972-1973 Winnipeg Jets (43-31-4)

Regular Season

Date	Opponent		Date	Opponent	
12 Oct	@New York Raiders	6-4	22 Dec	@Chicago Cougars	2-3
13 Oct	@Minnesota Fighting Saints	4-3	26 Dec	Chicago Cougars	3-2
15 Oct	Alberta Oilers	2-5	1 Jan	@Alberta Oilers	3-7
17 Oct	@Alberta Oilers	2-3*	7 Jan	@Minnesota Fighting Saints	6-2
20 Oct	Minnesota Fighting Saints	1-1*	10 Jan	Alberta Oilers	6-1
22 Oct	Philadelphia Blazers	6-3	12 Jan	Cleveland Crusaders	5-3
24 Oct	Philadelphia Blazers	5-3	14 Jan	Cleveland Crusaders	3-1
27 Oct	Chicago Cougars	4-2	16 Jan	Minnesota Fighting Saints	3-1
29 Oct	Houston Aeros	5-3	19 Jan	New England Whalers	6-2
31 Oct	@Chicago Cougars	1-3	21 Jan	New England Whalers	2-7
1 Nov	@Minnesota Fighting Saints	0-3	23 Jan	@Cleveland Crusaders	4-5*
3 Nov	New York Raiders	6-9	24 Jan	@New England Whalers	1-6
5 Nov	New York Raiders	3-1	26 Jan	@Quebec Nordiques	2-2*
6 Nov	@New England Whalers	2-6	28 Jan	@Ottawa Nationals	5-4
8 Nov	@Quebec Nordiques	2-3	2 Feb	Alberta Oilers	3-4
9 Nov	@Ottawa Nationals	4-1	4 Feb	@Alberta Oilers	5-3
10 Nov	Minnesota Fighting Saints	1-5	7 Feb	@Houston Aeros	2-5
12 Nov	Los Angeles Sharks	5-2	8 Feb	@Houston Aeros	3-1
14 Nov	Los Angeles Sharks	8-0	10 Feb	@Los Angeles Sharks	6-5*
15 Nov	@Alberta Oilers	1-3	11 Feb	@Los Angeles Sharks	3-0
17 Nov	@Los Angeles Sharks	5-1	15 Feb	@Chicago Cougars	7-2
19 Nov	@Los Angeles Sharks	4-3	16 Feb	Houston Aeros	7-0
21 Nov	@Houston Aeros	4-2	18 Feb	Houston Aeros	4-2
23 Nov	@Houston Aeros	5-6*	25 Feb	Philadelphia Blazers	5-3
24 Nov	Quebec Nordiques	5-3	27 Feb	Chicago Cougars	5-1
26 Nov	Quebec Nordiques	4-1	2 Mar	Los Angeles Sharks	2-1
28 Nov	Alberta Oilers	3-0	4 Mar	Los Angeles Sharks	2-1
30 Nov	@Alberta Oilers	3-3*	6 Mar	@Ottawa Nationals	2-5
1 Dec	Ottawa Nationals	3-4	8 Mar	@Quebec Nordiques	7-4
3 Dec	Minnesota Fighting Saints	5-1	10 Mar	@New York Raiders	2-3*
5 Dec	Quebec Nordiques	2-4	11 Mar	Cleveland Crusaders	2-11
6 Dec	Chicago Cougars	7-1	14 Mar	New England Whalers	5-7
8 Dec	Houston Aeros	6-2	16 Mar	Ottawa Nationals	1-6
9 Dec	@Cleveland Crusaders	3-2*	18 Mar	Ottawa Nationals	2-4
11 Dec	@New England Whalers	3-4	22 Mar	Alberta Oilers	1-1*
13 Dec	@Philadelphia Blazers	4-7	25 Mar	New York Raiders	8-4
15 Dec	@Philadelphia Blazers	4-6	28 Mar	@Chicago Cougars	4-3*
17 Dec	@New York Raiders	4-3	30 Mar	@Cleveland Crusaders	2-4
21 Dec	@Minnesota Fighting Saints	0-3	1 Apr	@Philadelphia Blazers	2-4

Playoffs

Date	Opponent		Date	Opponent	
6 Apr	Minnesota Fighting Saints	3-1	24 Apr	@Houston Aeros	4-2
8 Apr	Minnesota Fighting Saints	5-2	26 Apr	@Houston Aeros	3-0
10 Apr	@Minnesota Fighting Saints	4-6	29 Apr	@New England Whalers	2-7
11 Apr	@Minnesota Fighting Saints	3-2*	2 May	New England Whalers	4-7
15 Apr	Minnesota Fighting Saints	8-5	3 May	New England Whalers	4-3
20 Apr	Houston Aeros	5-1	5 May	@New England Whalers	2-4
22 Apr	Houston Aeros	2-0	6 May	@New England Whalers	6-9

* - overtime

Scoring

Player	Regular Season									Playoffs								
	GP	G	A	Pts	PIM	+/-	PP	SH	Shots	GP	G	A	Pts	PIM	+/-	PP	SH	Shots
Bob Ash	76	3	14	17	39		0	0		13	1	3	4	4				
Duke Asmundson	76	2	14	16	54		1	0		12	1	2	3	8				
Norm Beaudin	78	38	65	103	15		5	0		14	13	15	28	2				
Milt Black	75	18	16	34	31		1	0		14	1	3	4	2				
Christian Bordeleau	78	47	54	101	12		6	3		12	5	8	13	4				
Wally Boyer	69	6	28	34	27		2	0		14	4	2	6	4				
Brian Cadle	56	4	4	8	39		1	0		3	0	0	0	0		0	0	
Steve Cuddie	77	7	13	20	121		0	0		12	0	1	1	10		0	0	
Joe Daley	29	0	1	1	10		0	0		7	0	0	0	0		0	0	
Jean-Guy Gratton	71	15	12	27	37		1	0		12	1	1	2	4				
Larry Hornung	77	13	45	58	28		5	2		14	2	9	11	0				
Bobby Hull	63	51	52	103	37		14	2		14	9	16	25	16				
Danny Johnson	76	19	23	42	17		4	0		14	4	1	5	0				
Ab McDonald	77	17	24	41	16		7	0		14	2	5	7	2				
Garth Rizzuto	61	10	10	20	32		4	0		14	0	1	1	14				
Dunc Rousseau	75	16	17	33	75		2	0		14	3	2	5	2				
John Shmyr	7	0	0	0	2		0	0		3	0	1	1	2		0	0	
Bill Sutherland	48	6	16	22	34		1	0		14	5	9	14	9				
Cal Swenson	77	7	21	28	19		2	0		14	1	5	6	7				
Gord Tumilson	3	0	0	0	0		0	0										
Ernie Wakely	49	0	0	0	0		0	0		7	0	0	0	0		0	0	
Bob Woytowich	62	2	4	6	47		0	0		14	1	1	2	4				
Joe Zanussi	73	4	21	25	53		1	0		14	2	5	7	6				

Goaltending

Goaltender	Regular Season										
	GP	Min	GA	GAA	Saves	Sv %	SO	EN	W	L	T
Joe Daley	29	1718	83	2.90	693	0.893	2	2	17	10	1
Gord Tumilson	3	138	10	4.34	55	0.846	0	0	0	2	0
Ernie Wakely	49	2889	152	3.14	1259	0.892	2	2	26	19	3
	Playoffs										
	GP	Min	GA	GAA	Saves	Sv %	SO	EN	W	L	
Joe Daley	7	422	25	3.55			0	2	5	2	
Ernie Wakely	7	420	22	3.14			2	0	4	3	

ABOVE LEFT: Bobby Hull gleefully accepts his $1,000,000 check from WHA President Gary Davidson.

ABOVE RIGHT: Norm Beaudin, the first player to sign a Jets contract.

LEFT: Ben Hatskin presenting Ernie Wakely with his jersey.

BOTTOM LEFT: Joe Daley, the second half of the original Jets goaltending tandem.

BELOW RIGHT: Ben Hatskin holds up a contract in the middle of the crowd that converged upon Portage Avenue and Main Street in downtown Winnipeg to see Hull sign with the Jets.

ABOVE LEFT: Jets founder Ben Hatskin.

ABOVE RIGHT: The first Jets off-ice team. **Top:** left to right, Business Manager Terry Hind, Director of Public Relations Ron Lyon, Director of Player Personnel Bill Robinson, and General Manager Annis Stukus. **Bottom**: Bench coach Nick Mickoski, trainer Diarmid McVicar, equipment manager Steve Adamski, and secretary Rosemary Delaronde.

LEFT: Stew MacPherson

RIGHT: Ken "Friar" Nicolson, the first voice of the Jets on radio station CJOB.

LEFT: Reyn Davis, the beat writer for the *Winnipeg Free Press*

RIGHT: Vic Grant, the beat writer for the *Winnipeg Tribune*.

LEFT: CBC's Don Wittman

RIGHT: Doug "Maxie" McIlraith. Wittman was the Master of Ceremonies at the Jets' first home game and McIlraith was the Jets' first public address announcer.

LEFT: Bobby Hull striking a pose.

LEFT: Manitoba Lieutenant-Governor William John (Jack) McKeag dropping the puck for the ceremonial faceoff at the Jets' first regular season home game. To his right is Jets captain Ab McDonald and to his left is Oilers captain Al Hamilton.

RIGHT: Nick Mickoski behind the bench during a home game against the Whalers.

ABOVE LEFT: All three members of the Luxury Line. Christian Bordeleau, Norm Beaudin, and Bobby Hull watch the action while Nick Mickoski looks on behind them.

ABOVE RIGHT: Norm Beaudin, Duke Asmundson, and Milt Black at the bench.

BELOW: The Jets and Cougars gaze upon a Booster Club sign in the north end.

ABOVE LEFT & CENTER: A maskless Joe Daley keeps his opponents at bay. **RIGHT:** Gord Tumilson

ABOVE LEFT: Danny Johnson in a pre-seaon game vs the Los Angeles Sharks.
RIGHT: Cal Swenson and Norm Beaudin buzz around the Whalers net.

BELOW: Wally Boyer tries to get around Andre Lacroix of the Philadelphia Blazers.
RIGHT: Bob Woytowich trudges off the ice.

Season II: 1973-1974 – A Blum Ending

The first off-season in Jets history saw Ben Hatskin showered with awards for all his work in getting the Jets and the WHA off the ground. In May, the Winnipeg Sales and Advertising Club named Hatskin the Winnipeg Man of the Year. In August, he was honored by *The Sporting News* as its choice for the top executive in hockey for the 1972-1973 season.

Losses on operations were larger than expected, but Hatskin still committed to operating the Jets in Winnipeg for the 1973-1974 season, eschewing interest from Vancouver, Detroit and Milwaukee. Ninety percent of last season's season ticket holders renewed their packages and there was considerable interest in the new "Jet Paks" available at a cost of $71.50 for 13 home games. The most popular Jet Paks were for games involving the Aeros, who now featured legendary former Detroit Red Wing Gordie Howe and his two sons, Marty and Mark. Unfortunately, the corporate community remained slow to jump aboard the Jets bandwagon, which kept attendance below the 7,500 mark that Hatskin estimated would be the financial break-even point. Borger Construction was the largest corporate season ticket holder with 28 tickets.

Around the WHA, there were a number of changes. The New York Raiders, the Jets' first regular season opponent, were sold and renamed the Golden Blades. The Philadelphia Blazers were sold to interests in Vancouver and made the cross-continent move to British Columbia. The Ottawa Nationals, who played their playoff games last season in Toronto, stayed there and became known as the Toronto Toros. The Alberta Oilers remained in Edmonton, but changed their name to reflect their home city. The Fighting Saints rejected an offer to purchase the club and move it to Detroit, so the Jets' closest geographic rival was staying put in Saint Paul. As a result of the Blazers' move west, Vancouver moved into the Western Division, forcing the Cougars into the Eastern Division to keep the 12-team league split down the middle.

Bobby Hull underwent successful elbow surgery in the off-season and, finally legally free to play, he looked forward to a healthy and full season with his new team. In June, the Jets traded Steve Cuddie to the Toros for rugged defenseman and Selkirk, Manitoba native Ken Stephanson. The cousin of Bill Masterton, the former Minnesota North Star who had died as a result of brain injuries sustained after falling during a game in January, 1968, Stephanson was best known for his size, strength and toughness, all attributes that the Jets needed.

The Jets signed 24-year-old Regina, Saskatchewan native Ron Snell on 13 June 1973. The diminutive winger was one of the Jets' selections in the 1972 General Player Draft and he signed a contract that also provided assistance for his education. Snell was coming off a 33-goal season with the Hershey Bears of the AHL and he was a former second-round draft choice of the Pittsburgh Penguins. On 24 July 1973, the Jets inked talented 21-year-old forward Dan Spring, who was a former first-round draft choice of the Chicago Blackhawks.

The Jets took part in both an Amateur Draft and Professional Draft and they were able to sign their third-round selection, 20-year-old right-winger Kelly Pratt, formerly of the Western Canada Hockey League's (WCHL) Swift Current Broncos. Pratt received an invitation to the Pittsburgh Penguins' training camp, but he opted to become the youngest member of the Jets after being bypassed in the NHL draft. The 5'8" Pratt, who was in the middle of his pipe-fitting apprenticeship, netted 81 goals over the past two seasons in Swift Current to go along with more than 200 penalty minutes and a reputation as a player who played the game hard and tough. Pratt had 14 major penalties last season, proving that he wasn't afraid to mix it up when necessary.

As training camp approached, the Jets rounded out their roster with more invitees to camp. Centerman Ted "Tuffy" Hargreaves, who had spent the past two seasons playing for and coaching the Nelson Maple Leafs of the Western International Hockey League (WIHL), sent the Jets a letter asking for a contract and he received an invitation to camp. Defenseman Jim Hargreaves, no relation to Ted, who had spurned the Jets' offers last year, signed with the Jets to give them some added muscle on the blue line. The former junior Jet who had shared the team's rookie of the year award with Neil Komadoski in 1968-1969 spent last season split between the Canucks and their farm team in Seattle. The Jets also added Terry Manukus and Aurel Beaudin to their training camp roster. Mankus, who had starred at the University of Illinois last season, was Hull's personal find, and Aurel Beaudin, six years younger than his more celebrated brother Norm, was with the WIHL's Kimberley Dynamiters.

During the off-season, Brian Cadle was released, and both Bill Sutherland and Wally Boyer retired. Sutherland moved on to sell beer for Molson Breweries, while Boyer, in making his retirement announcement a week before the start of camp, retreated to the relative comfort of running his motel in Midland, Ontario.

While a season ticket blitz was taking place at the Marlborough Hotel, where a makeshift ticket office was set up, the Jets' second training camp began at the Arena on 14 September 1973 under considerably less secretive circumstances than existed one year earlier. Aside from Christian Bordeleau, who was given a 10-day excused absence, the Jets had a full complement and the focus was on the ice, not in the courtroom. The workouts drew large crowds, some in excess of 1,000, to see the Jets prepare for their second season.

1973 Training Camp Roster

Goaltenders:	Joe Daley, Gord Tumilson, Ernie Wakely
Defensemen:	Bob Ash, Jim Hargreaves, Larry Hornung, John Shmyr, Ken Stephanson, Bob Woytowich, Joe Zanussi
Left Wingers:	Ted Hargreaves, Bobby Hull, Ab McDonald, Garth Rizzuto, Dunc Rousseau
Centermen:	Christian Bordeleau, Danny Johnson, Dan Spring, Cal Swenson
Right Wingers:	Duke Asmundson, Aurel Beaudin, Norm Beaudin, Milt Black, Jean-Guy Gratton, Terry Mankus, Kelly Pratt, Ron Snell

The exhibition season saw the Jets criss-cross the continent, playing a pair of games in Winnipeg, two in Milwaukee, one each in London, Ontario, Montreal and Edmonton. On 25 September, the Jets also participated in a "Hockey Spectacular" at Madison Square Garden that also involved the Whalers, Golden Blades and Aeros. More than 7,000 onlookers witnessed six 15-minute periods with equal participation from each team. On 30 September, the Arena was sold out for the first time for a Jets game as 10,077 paid to see Gordie Howe and the Aeros hand the Jets a 4-1 defeat.

Mankus and Aurel Beaudin failed to crack the lineup, as did holdovers Shmyr and Tumilson, but Ted Hargreaves earned a one-year contract on 4 October, impressing management with his ability as a checker and showing a penchant for scoring on the power play during the exhibition season. Pratt expected to be sent to the minors, but he was pleasantly surprised when the Jets decided to keep him.

Hornung was named as an assistant captain to replace the retired Sutherland, and the 1973-1974 edition of the Winnipeg Jets was ready to take to the ice. Three days after wrapping up their exhibition season in Edmonton, the Jets' first game of the season took place on the night of Wednesday, 10 October at the Pacific Coliseum in Vancouver, the new home of the relocated Blazers. The crowd numbered 12,452, the largest gathering to see the Jets since they visited the new Saint Paul Civic Center on a Sunday afternoon back in January. The Blazers moved without Andre Lacroix, the WHA's leading scorer last season, and goaltender Bernie Parent, the first NHL player to sign a WHA contract. The Blazers had to trade Lacroix because he had a clause in his contract preventing him from being traded to a Canadian team, while Parent had left the Blazers during the playoffs last season and returned to the NHL during the off-season.

The Jets opened the scoring four minutes into the contest thanks to a shot from Gratton that Blazers' goaltender Yves Archambault misjudged, but the Blazers countered with two of their own before the intermission. The Jets tied the game early in the second period and missed a golden opportunity to retake the lead when McDonald missed an open net, but then they had to hang on as only Wakely's brilliance preserved the tie going into the third. The two teams traded goals early in the third and the remainder of regulation time settled nothing, prolonging the game into overtime. In the extra period, it was the Blazers who were determined to break the tie, and after Wakely came up with two big stops, Jim Adair scored his second of the game to give the Blazers a dramatic 4-3 win over the disappointed Jets.

Picking On The Jets

Yves Archambault posted his only win of the 1973-1974 season against the Jets on 10 October 1973 and he would never win another game in major pro hockey. Jim Adair would score only 12 goals in 1973-1974, his only season in major pro hockey, but four of them came against the Jets.

The next day, the Jets boarded a plane for Edmonton to meet the Oilers on Friday night. For the first time with Hull in the lineup, the 5,200-seat Edmonton Gardens wasn't sold out to see the Jets, but a crowd of 4,809 saw the Jets face off against an Oilers' lineup that featured no fewer than eight new faces. The Oilers jumped out to a 3-0 first period lead and though the Jets kept battling back, they weren't able to get any closer than one goal down and the Oilers, paced by Jim Harrison's hat trick, skated off with a 6-4 win.

With nothing to show for their first two games, the Jets returned to Winnipeg for their own home opener on Sunday night to meet the Blazers for the second time in three games. In the hopes of sparking the Jets' attack, Hull decided to take himself off the Luxury Line and place himself alongside Spring and Snell while putting Rousseau alongside Bordeleau and Norm Beaudin. Off the ice, in the hopes of sparking ticket sales, Hull offered a steer from his ranch to a randomly-drawn paying customer, but even that value-added prospect only drew 6,661 fans to see the Jets open the home portion of their second season.

The Jets jumped out to a 3-0 lead in the first period and though the Blazers fought back with two quick goals in the second, the Jets replied with more of their own and cruised to a 6-3 win. Hull's decision to take himself off the Luxury Line paid off handsomely. All of the Jets' lines contributed, and the cause was aided by some shaky goaltending from Peter Donnelly in the early going. Season ticket holder Steve Zaplachinski was the winner in the drawing for the steer, but the biggest prize of the night was two points for the Jets.

On Wednesday night, the Jets were back on the road for the first of a two-game swing in Boston, where their season had ended in May. Joining them was Anthony Francis Huck, better known as Fran, who put his signature on a Jets' contract. The cigar-smoking Huck, a centerman who had played 58 games for the St. Louis Blues last season, was also a lawyer and acted as his own representative. To make room for Huck, the Jets assigned Milt Black to the Jacksonville Barons of the AHL.

Huck and his new teammates took to the ice against the Whalers, who were enjoying a much better start to their season than the Jets. Led by new coach Ron Ryan, the Whalers were unbeaten in their last four games and the paltry gathering of 4,537 saw them get the early jump on the Jets when Tom Webster scored only 22 seconds into the contest. The Jets, however, kept their composure and played it close to the vest, then they used three late third period goals to turn the tables on their hosts and skate off with a 3-1 win.

One night later, the Jets met the Golden Blades in New York. The crowd of fewer than 3,000 at Madison Square Garden saw the Jets jump out to an early lead and they cruised to a 6-1 win. Huck scored his first two goals as a Jet in his new team's third consecutive victory before the team returned home for a Sunday night matchup with the Fighting Saints.

Come Sunday night, the Jets and Fighting Saints were ready for the game, but the Arena ice wasn't ready for them. Okotoberfest, an annual beer festival, was held on the Arena floor on Saturday night, and as a result, the ice wasn't ready. Large chunks of ice kept breaking away, but the game still went ahead as scheduled. The jovial crowd numbering just over 7,000 enjoyed an entertaining game in which both goaltenders, Joe Daley and Mike Curran, staged a duel that wasn't settled until Bordeleau's slap shot rang off the goal post and into the net late into overtime, giving the Jets a thrilling 2-1 victory.

Winners of their last four games, the Jets had some time off before meeting the 2-6-2 Toros on Friday night. Led by the new line of Hull, Huck and Pratt, the Jets coasted to a 3-0 lead against the former Ottawa Nationals, but they eased up on their downtrodden guests and the Toros stormed back to tie the game with three third period goals, the third of which came with only 31 seconds to play in regulation time. Overtime settled nothing and the Jets were forced to settle for a 3-3 tie.

One night later, the Jets and a handful of their loyal supporters made their way to Saint Paul for a return engagement with the Fighting Saints to begin a three-game road trip. Despite the extra support in the stands, the Fighting Saints cruised to a 5-2 victory, handing the Jets their first defeat in 16 days that also allowed the Fighting Saints to pull into a second-place tie with the Jets, three points behind the 6-1-0 Oilers. The only bright spot on the evening came late in the second period when Ted Hargreaves scored his first goal as a professional, becoming the second Jet in as many days to accomplish the feat. Pratt had opened the scoring last night for his first professional marker.

The Jets moved on to Chicago for a Tuesday night date with the Cougars, whose lineup featured changes that included the additions of former Blackhawks Pat Stapleton and Ralph Backstrom. The Cougars got the early jump on the Jets and held them at bay as they won for only the second time in their first eight games. Snell became the third player in as many games to score his first goal as a Jet, but it was far from enough in the 4-1 defeat.

Did You Know?

John Shmyr, who played briefly with the Jets in the latter part of the 1972-1973 season and attended training camp in 1973, assisted on the Cougars' first goal at 3:36 of the first period on 30 October 1973. His assist marked the first point recorded against the Jets by a former Jets' player.

One night later, the Jets moved on to Cleveland, hoping to salvage something from their three-game road trip against the 5-1-2 Crusaders. In front of only 2,910 spectators at the Cleveland Arena, the game went back and forth before Jim Wiste broke a 4-4 tie with only six and a half minutes to play in regulation time, sending the Jets down to an eventual 6-4 defeat. Hull tried to spark the Jets by reuniting the Luxury Line, but the trio combined for only one of the Jets' four goals on the night.

The Jets returned home Thursday afternoon to prepare for a Friday night encounter with the 2-7-2 Golden Blades as they bid the month of October adieu. The game was no classic, but the Jets used two goals from Ron Snell and hung on for a 3-1 win to bust out of a four-game winless streak. Hull, however, was so disappointed in his own performance that he came back on the ice after the game to skate around the rink as a form of self-punishment.

The new and improved Nordiques were next on the schedule for a Sunday night contest as the Jets looked to sweep the weekend home stand before heading back out on the road. Led by new coach and general manager Jacques Plante, along with key additions Rejean Houle and Serge Bernier, the 8-5-0 Nordiques came into Winnipeg in first place in the Eastern Division. In front of a season-high crowd of 8,029, the two teams traded a pair of goals until the Jets broke out with six unanswered goals and turned a seesaw affair into a blowout. Hull scored four times for only the second time as a Jet and added an assist to lead the Jets in the 8-2 rout.

With their record back over the .500 mark, the 6-5-1 Jets boarded a plane to begin a road trip that would see them play three games in four nights, the first of which was on Tueday night against the same Nordiques. This time it was the Nordiques who had the upper hand during the play, but Ernie Wakely's 31 saves were just enough to earn a single point for the Jets in a 2-2 tie.

The point came at a high price, however, as the Jets lost no less than four players to injury during the game. First, Huck was lost on account of a charleyhorse he sustained in an inadvertent collision with referee Bill Friday. Two members of the defense corps, Woytowich and Ash, were also lost due to charleyhorses, and Beaudin suffered two hip pointers during the game.

One night later, the Jets moved on to Boston and, looking every bit like a battered and bruised team, they went down to a humiliating 9-2 defeat at the hands of the Whalers. To add further injury to insult, the Jets lost Joe Zanussi in the game's final minute thanks to a hard hit from Whalers' defensman Rick Ley.

Despite their ups and downs, the 6-6-2 Jets remained in second place behind only the red-hot 9-1-0 Oilers as they traveled west to Cleveland to meet the Crusaders again on Saturday night. The Jets battled back from an early 2-0 deficit to tie the score, but two goals in the final minute and a half of regulation time gave the Crusaders a 4-2 victory that sent the visitors limping home with only one point to show for their latest three-game road trip.

The Jets had no time to catch their breath, as they had to rush home for a Sunday night engagement against the 5-11-0 Sharks. Before a crowd of 6,253 at the Arena, the Jets jumped out to a quick 2-0 lead and then hung on as Joe Daley kept the Sharks at bay. A frustrated Daley let his temper boil over during the second intermission and his teammates responded by turning a paper-thin 3-2 lead into a 6-2 rout. It wasn't pretty, but the Jets still captured their two points and pulled their record back to the .500 mark at 7-7-2, which was good enough for third place, one point behind the Fighting Saints and eight behind the Oilers.

There was to be no rest for the travel-weary Jets, who were back on a plane on Monday afternoon bound for Vancouver to meet the 3-13-0 Blazers on Tuesday night. Since handing the Jets a 4-3 defeat to start their new life on the West Coast, the Blazers had won only two games since and came into the contest losers of their last ten games. The Blazers' lineup featured a couple of new additions, hard-hitting defenseman Ralph MacSweyn and goaltender George Gardner, who were both obtained from the Sharks in exchange for forward Ron Ward, who would be joining his third team in just over one season.

A surprisingly good crowd of 8,366 at the Pacific Coliseum saw their heroes, buoyed by solid contributions from the pair of new players, jump out to a 3-1 first period lead against the Jets. However, the frustrated Jets kept plugging away and they eventually tied the score at 3-3 early in the third period. The Blazers showed some rare resilience and Jim Adair, the overtime hero when the Jets were last in Vancouver, put the Blazers back in front to stay. The Jets were unable to mount another comeback and the Blazers skated off with a 6-4 victory, putting a merciful end to their long losing streak at the Jets' expense.

The embarrassed Jets returned home to face the 13-1-0 Oilers on the night of Friday, 16 November. A crowd numbering nearly 8,000, the second highest total of the season, saw the determined Jets dominate the visiting Oilers, but the Jets still held only a slender 1-0 lead entering the third period despite outshooting the Oilers by a margin of 38-18. Jim Harrison's goal early in the third period tied the score, but the Jets remained patient and Hull broke the deadlock with just over two minutes left in regulation time. The proud Oilers did all they could to get back in the game, but Daley rose to the occasion and Hull's second goal of the game into an empty net sealed a 3-1 win for the Jets, who put an end to the Oilers' 11-game winning streak.

Fresh off their bounceback performance against the Oilers, the Jets took off for Toronto to begin and end their second one-game road trip in less than a week, in the hopes of winning away from Winnipeg for only the third time in 12 tries. Before a packed house of 4,479 in the cozy Varsity Arena, the Jets jumped out to a quick 2-0 first period lead only to have the Toros rally for three goals in each of the next two periods to hand the Jets a 6-2 defeat.

To make matters worse, the Jets lost Hornung to a serious injury to his right knee that was later diagnosed as a stretched medial ligament, keeping him out of the lineup for an estimated four to six weeks. For the first time in his career, the defenseman jokingly called "Paul," in reference to the former Green Bay Packer of the same surname, would be sitting on the sidelines due to injury. He and his teammates returned home to entertain the Crusaders on Wednesday night to begin a brief two-game home stand.

Despite the nine inches of snow that had fallen over the past three days, nearly 5,000 fans made it to the Arena to see the Jets jump out to a 2-0 first period lead, just as they had done on Sunday. This time, they kept the pressure on and, led by Bordeleau's first hat trick since his four-goal performance in the Jets' regular season debut last year, they cruised to a 6-2 victory against a tired Crusaders team that showed the effects of playing two games in as many nights. The win kept the Jets unbeaten at home and evened their record at 9-9-2, which was still good enough for second place, one point ahead of both the Fighting Saints and the Aeros and eight behind the Oilers.

Two nights later, the Jets prepared to do battle with the Blazers for the fourth time this season. The Blazers came in led by their third coach of the season as Andy Bathgate assumed control of the bench duties. Bathgate had made his coaching debut the previous night and the Blazers responded with a shocking 7-1 upset of the Oilers at the Pacific Coliseum. The Blazers got the early jump in the lackluster affair, but the Jets woke up and rallied from a 2-0 deficit to eventually take a 3-2 lead early in the third period. However, the Blazers and goaltender Peter Donnelly held firm, setting the stage for the tying goal off the stick of Don Burgess with just under four minutes to play. The Blazers had a chance for victory in the final minute of regulation time, but Wakely stopped Danny Lawson, the WHA's top goal scorer last season, who was sent in alone on a breakaway. The game went to overtime, where the Blazers capitalized on an untimely fall by Bob Woytowich to score the winning goal halfway through the extra period, sending the crowd home disappointed after seeing their Jets suffer their first loss of the season on home ice.

Did You Know?

Though his team lost on the night of Friday, 23 November 1973, Christian Bordeleau became a father for the first time the next day as his wife Jocelyne gave birth to Christian Bordeleau, Jr.

The reeling fourth-place Jets left Winnipeg for a three-game road swing that began on Sunday night in Saint Paul against the Fighting Saints. The Jets came out strong, but the Fighting Saints matched their effort and took a 3-1 lead in the second period. The Jets rallied to tie the score at 3-3 early in the third period, but they couldn't get anything more past Mike Curran and Steve Cardwell's second goal of the game broke the deadlock at 8:20 of the third period as the Fighting Saints went on to a 5-3 victory.

Two nights later, the Jets continued their road trip against the well-rested Sharks in Southern California. The Sharks, led by new coach and former captain Ted McCaskill, took leads of 2-0 and 4-2, but the Jets mounted a comeback each time to tie the score, and the game went to overtime. It took less than two minutes into the extra period for Brian McDonald to find a loose puck in the crease and stuff it into the net, giving the Sharks their first victory over the Jets in 10 tries and sending the Jets down to their third consecutive defeat.

The floundering Jets had no time to rest and they were right back on a plane bound for Houston for a Wednesday night encounter with the Aeros and the Howe family to wrap up their three-game road trip. The shorthanded Jets, missing no fewer than three defensemen, gave up three goals in a minute and a half early in the second period and odds of the visitors busting out of their three-game losing streak appeared bleak. However, the Jets kept plugging along and gradually chipped away at the 3-0 deficit and Ron Snell's second goal of the game with less than five minutes remaining in regulation time gave the Jets a 4-3 lead. Unfortunately, the Aeros came back and tied the score in the final minute of the third period and, after a scoreless overtime period, the two teams settled on a 4-4 tie.

Though the Jets' road woes were troubling, they wouldn't have to worry about being away from home again until mid-December. They flew home to begin an eight-game home stand that started on Friday night against the Sharks to bring an end to the miserable month of November. In need of another healthy body in the lineup, the Jets also decided to summon Milt Black from Jacksonville, since both Bob Ash and Larry Hornung were still sidelined due to injuries.

In front of a season-low gathering of only 4,635 spectators, the listless Jets proved to be no match for the visiting Sharks, who broke open a 2-1 game in the third period with three goals en route to an easy 5-2 victory. With the win, the Sharks pulled themselves within three points of the fourth-place Jets. After the game, a furious Hull called his team "gutless" when speaking with the *Winnipeg Free Press*, and none of those few who witnessed the contest could disagree with that assessment.

Next up for the 9-13-3 Jets was a date with the Nordiques on Sunday, 2 December, but not before holding a team meeting to clear the air in the dressing room. The Jets also assigned Kelly Pratt to Jacksonville and Hull juggled the lines again to try and spark the team. The Jets responded and overcame a 2-0 first period deficit to post a 5-3 victory, peppering Nordiques' goaltender Serge Aubry with 45 shots on the night. Fran Huck scored three of his team's five goals as the Jets put an end to their five-game winless streak.

On Wednesday night, the Oilers made their second appearance of the season in Winnipeg and the Jets hoped to make it two wins in a row while the Oilers came into town winners of only three of their last 10 games. With their general manager behind the microphone as the fill-in public address announcer, the Jets took to the ice and battled the first-place Oilers in a spirited affair that was tied at 1-1 entering the third period. The Jets broke the deadlock when Hull put home a rebound for his 18th goal of the season. They never looked back as they won by a score of 3-1 for the second time in as many meetings with their Alberta rivals, moving into a third-place tie with the Fighting Saints in the process. During the third period, Ernie Wakely reluctantly became the first Jets' goaltender to fight an opponent as he went toe to toe with Jim Harrison of the Oilers.

The fourth game of the marathon home stand took place two nights later with the Toros providing the opposition. Before a disappointing Friday night crowd numbering just under 5,000, the Jets erased an early deficit and broke a 2-2 tie with five unanswered second period goals en route to a comfortable 7-4 win. Wakely stopped 22 shots over the last two periods to earn the victory after replacing Joe Daley, who had to leave the game on account of the flu. The two points kept the 12-13-3 Jets in the thick of the logjam in the Western Division standings as they remained in a three-way tie for second place along with the Fighting Saints and the Aeros, who each sat seven points behind the frontrunning Oilers.

On Sunday night, the Jets played host to the Jersey Knights, who started the season as the New York Golden Blades until their relocation to Cherry Hill, New Jersey in late November. Since moving south, the Knights had won four of their seven games under new playing coach Harry Howell, but they were still without road uniforms featuring their new logo, so the Jets were forced to wear their road blues at home while the Knights wore white.

The crowd of 4,589 made it through 2½ inches of snow and braved the 15°-below Fahrenheit temperature to see the Jets come out strong only to be stopped time and again by Knights' goaltender Joe Junkin. The Jets eventually broke through, however, and they took their first lead of the night early in the second. From there, it was Wakely's turn to shine at the other end of the ice and he made the slender lead hold up for the 3-1 victory, the Jets' fourth win in a row. The Jets evened their record at 13-13-3 and they remained in a three-way tie for second place. The game also marked the first time the Jets had won in their road blues that featured their new logo, since their first two victories on the road came in the blue uniforms that still bore last season's logo.

Game six of the eight-game home stand took place on Wednesday night when Gordie Howe, his sons and the rest of the Aeros came to Winnipeg to do battle with the Jets. The 16°-below temperature outside did nothing to freeze the demand for tickets as the Howes not only easily sold out the Arena for the second time in as many visits, but many fans had to be turned away at the box office, forcing some of those who missed out to sneak in.

The five-figure crowd saw the Aeros dominate the game's early stages and only Daley's strong goaltending kept the Jets within two goals. Though the Jets tried to mount a comeback, it was a case of too little, too late, and the Aeros held on for a 3-2 win that bumped the Jets down to fourth place.

The home stand continued two nights later with a game on Friday, 14 December against the Sharks. The season-low gathering of 4,049 saw a scoreless first period but plenty of action as Hull fought Ron Garwasiuk in response to a high stick from the Sharks' winger. After getting out of the penalty box, the Golden Jet opened the scoring midway through the second period with his trademark booming slap shot, but he still wasn't done playing the role of enforcer for the night. Early in the third period, Hull leveled Garwasiuk, leaving him doubled over in pain at center ice and knocking him out of action for the rest of the game. Meanwhile, in the Jets' end of the rink, Wakely made the one-goal lead hold up with a sparkling 32-save performance as the Jets again evened their record at 14-14-3.

The game was over, but the action continued off the ice when two fans doused Sharks' coach Ted McCaskill with beer. Under abuse from nearby spectators earlier in the game as well, the Sharks took matters into their own hands and headed into the stands to take revenge. McCaskill, Bart Crashley, Reg Thomas, Garwasiuk, and others climbed over the railing to pursue the battle. Hull came over and played the role of peacemaker, earning himself a bleeding nose, puffy lip and a red, swollen eye for his trouble.

The longest home stand in Jets history came to an end on Sunday night when the Fighting Saints flew into Winnipeg for their second visit of the season. Right from the start, it was the visitors who took the play to the Jets, who had only Daley to thank for keeping them in the game. He couldn't do it all himself, however, and the Fighting Saints used two goals from Wayne Connelly to erase a 2-1 Jets' lead and skate off with a 3-2 victory, much to the chagrin of the 6,259 hardy Winnipeggers who paid to see the contest.

A four-game road trip was next on the schedule for the fourth-place Jets and it began on Tuesday night in Chicago against the much-improved Cougars. A frustrated Hull tried shaking up the lines again, and his team responded. The Jets held a 3-0 lead at midway point of the third period, but then the roof caved in. The Cougars scored a pair of goals just over a minute apart to get back to within one goal, then in the final minute, Bob Liddington was left alone in front of a beleaguered Wakely and he scored to tie the game at 3-3 in dramatic fashion. Neither team could score in overtime, so they each had to settle for a single point.

The enraged Jets headed south for Houston for an important Wednesday night encounter with the Aeros, who took full advantage of their downtrodden guests, scoring early and often in a 10-0 rout. It was statistically the worst defeat the Jets had suffered in their brief history and was every bit as ugly as the score indicated.

The Jets had some time to catch their breath before their next game in Boston, where they met the Whalers on Saturday night. The Jets did an about-face and used a solid team effort, combined with a 22-save shutout performance from Wakely to defeat the Eastern Division leaders by a score of 2-0 for only their third road victory of the season.

Before the Christmas break, the Jets boarded a southbound bus bound for Cherry Hill to meet the Knights for the first time in their new home and wrap up their four-game road trip on Sunday afternoon. Sadly, the Jets were unable to duplicate their success on Saturday night and couldn't rally from a 4-1 deficit and went down to an eventual 6-3 defeat.

The Jets limped home for the holidays still in fourth place, three points behind the Fighting Saints and four behind both the Oilers and hard-charging Aeros. Their next action came on Boxing Day with the Cougars providing the opposition at the Arena, where an unusually large crowd of 8,356 was on hand to see the game. The Jets came out strong and took a 2-0 first period only to have the Cougars again come back and tie the score late in the second. The Jets pressed on and Hull broke the deadlock with his 20th goal of the season and they held on for a 4-2 victory.

It was back on the road for the Jets, who started a three-game swing on Saturday night in Quebec. After two first period goals from Alain "Boom Boom" Caron, the Jets stormed back and scored four times and used some tight checking combined with Daley's superb goaltending to hold off the Nordiques and claim a 4-3 victory. One night later, the Jets visited Toronto for the second time this season. The Jets fought back from a 2-0 deficit, only to have the Toros rebound with three of their own to post a 5-2 victory.

Did You Know?

Steve Cuddie became the first former Jets player to score against the Jets when he scored at 19:32 of the second period on 30 December 1973. Cuddie scored seven goals for the Jets in 1972-1973 and this goal was only his third of the season for the Toronto Toros.

The 17-18-4 Jets wrapped up their three-game road swing on New Year's Day with their first visit of the season to Edmonton. The game went back and forth and wound up tied at 3-3 through regulation time, but it was the Jets who captured the victory when Hull set up Huck for his 16th goal of the season in the first minute of overtime. The win, the Jets' third straight over the Oilers, vaulted them into a tie with the slumping Oilers for second place, each only two points back of the first-place Aeros.

On the heels of only their second winning road trip of the season, most of the Jets returned home to await the Whalers' first appearance of the season in Winnipeg on Friday night. Hull, Wakely and Huck flew to Saint Paul to represent the Western Division at the second annual WHA All-Star Game on Thursday night. Hornung was also selected to play in the game but was unable to go on account of the knee injury that had sidelined him for the past month and a half. Before a crowd of 13,196 at the Saint Paul Civic Center, the Western Division All-Stars, who were also coached by Hull for the second consecutive year, went down to an 8-4 defeat at the hands of their Eastern Division counterparts. Hull was the only Jet who recorded a point when he set up Mike Walton's second period goal.

One night later, the three All-Star Jets rejoined their teammates, including Huck, who was able to go despite suffering a hyperextended knee during the All-Star Game. Unfortunately, three other Jets couldn't answer the bell. In addition to Larry Hornung's knee injury, Ken Stephanson was out with an ankle injury and Christian Bordeleau had to miss the game on account of bronchitis. The Whalers came into town with problems of their own, as injuries to regular goaltenders Al Smith and Bruce Landon forced them to turn to 28-year-old untested second-year pro Bill Berglund, who had to suit up with a uniform that had his name written on tape stuck to the back.

Before a crowd numbering 8,601, the largest of the season for a game that didn't involve Gordie Howe, the Jets got on the board first, but the Whalers seized control of the game and took a 4-1 lead to the second intermission. The shorthanded Jets threw everything they had at the Whalers in the third period, but despite goals from Hull and Ted Hargreaves and the encouragement from a vocal crowd, it wasn't enough and the Whalers escaped with a 4-3 victory.

With the one-game home stand behind them, the Jets left town to start a three-game road trip in Houston on Sunday night. Improbably, the 18-19-4 Jets had a chance to pull into a first place tie with the Aeros with a win, but things didn't go any better for the Jets than they had in their last visit to the Lone Star State. With four players in the sick bay, the Jets were once again no match for the Aeros, who cruised to a 7-1 blowout victory. Daley again weathered the full force of the onslaught and faced no fewer than 46 shots on the night.

The Jets picked up the pieces and moved on to Southern California to meet the cellar-dwelling Sharks on Tuesday night. Jean-Guy Gratton opened the scoring with an early second period power-play goal, but the Sharks, losers of seven of their last nine games, responded with two goals in each of the second and third periods and handed the Jets a 4-1 defeat. The Sharks, who once had been an automatic win for the Jets, won for the third time in five meetings between the two teams this season.

With trade rumors swirling around the struggling Jets, on Tuesday, they called up both Kelly Pratt and Cal Swenson from Jacksonville to join the team back in Winnipeg. Pratt's physical presence had been sorely missed during his absence and the Jets hoped that Swenson, one of last season's regulars who was demoted in October, could add some offensive punch. Swenson left Jacksonville as the Barons' leading scorer.

Before returning home to meet the pair, the Jets moved north for their third game in four nights to wrap up the road trip in Vancouver against the Blazers. The two teams traded goals until the Jets broke open a 3-3 tie and pulled away for an eventual 6-4 win, marking their first victory in three tries at the Pacific Coliseum.

Two nights later, the 19-21-4 Jets and their reinforced lineup took to the ice against the Oilers to begin a four-game home stand. Before a crowd of 6,566 of the hardiest Winnipeggers who had braved a bitter mid-January cold snap, the Jets got the early jump on their guests with three first period goals en route to a 7-4 win. Hull scored a pair for the victorious Jets and Swenson added one in his first game back from Florida, but the Jets lost Norm Beaudin to a series of injuries that included a bruised shoulder, pulled groin muscle and a jammed thumb.

After hosting a gathering of children on Saturday morning for an intra-squad game and an autograph session, the Jets returned to the ice on the night of Sunday, 13 January to play host to the well-rested Cougars, who hadn't played since Tuesday. The Jets took a 2-0 lead early in the second period and with the help of Daley and the red posts behind him, the Jets held on for a 3-1 win. The Jets' third consecutive victory put them into sole possession of second place, two points ahead of the third-place Oilers and only two back from the first-place Aeros.

The Jets had a few days off to allow the members of the walking wounded to recover before welcoming the Crusaders to Winnipeg on Friday night. A crowd of just under 7,000 took time out from shoveling snow to see the Jets, buoyed by Hornung's return to the lineup, erase a 3-2 second period deficit with five unanswered goals in a 7-3 win. Hull scored twice for the Jets, giving him 29 for the season, but more importantly, the Jets remained in second place and pulled their record above the .500 mark for the first time since early November.

On Sunday night, the Jets wound up the home stand with a visit from the Knights, who had broken a four-game losing streak in Vancouver one night earlier. Despite playing their third game in as many nights, the Knights jumped out to a quick 2-0 lead, but the visitors' momentum was short-lived and the Jets dominated the rest of the way. When it was all said and done, the Jets celebrated a convincing 9-3 victory, their fifth in a row. Hull scored three times for his second hat trick of the season and fifth as a Jet, while Fran Huck added five assists despite leaving his skates at home and having to call to have them retrieved before the game.

For the second time in as many weeks, the Jets had some time between games, so they spent the week working out at St. John's Ravenscourt School before travelling to Edmonton to meet the Oilers on Friday night. The Oilers were without Jim Harrison, their leading scorer, who had been struck by an errant puck and broken his nose earlier in the day, but his absence didn't prevent the Oilers from taking a 3-2 lead early in the third period of a very chippy contest. However, the Jets responded with goals from the red-hot Hull and Danny Johnson, whose second goal of the game proved to be the winner in a 4-3 victory.

The second-place Jets moved on to Saint Paul for a Sunday night game, where they were joined by three busloads of their most loyal supporters who had made the trek from Winnipeg to see their heroes try and extend their winning streak to seven games. The boosters partied through the weekend, but the good times ended soon after the game started. The Fighting Saints dominated from the start and the final result was a 12-2 drubbing that pleased the vast majority of the season's largest crowd at the Saint Paul Civic Center.

The 24-22-4 Jets and more than 100 of their disappointed fans returned home for a pair of weekend games to open the month of February. Friday's opponent was the 20-31-0 Sharks, who were making their fourth and final visit of the season to Winnipeg. Missing Bob Woytowich, who was out on account of back spasms, and a lot of paying customers, the Jets still got off to a quick start thanks to a pair of goals by Beaudin, and then sat back and protected their lead. Wakely did the rest, stopping 19 shots in the third period and 38 shots overall to earn his second straight shutout over the Sharks as the Jets coasted to a 4-0 victory that kept them in second place.

The Jets wrapped up the weekend with a Sunday night date against the Cougars. After the visitors rallied from a 2-0 deficit, Kelly Pratt set up Dan Spring in front for the eventual game-winner as the Jets held off the Cougars to post a 4-2 victory and make the outside temperature of 35º-below a little less uncomfortable for the 6,032 fans who made their way home after witnessing the contest. Unfortunately, the Jets' injury list gained another member during the game when Ron Snell sustained a charleyhorse after being hit by Reggie Fleming.

On Monday, the Jets boarded a place bound for Chicago to complete a home-and-home series with the Cougars on Tuesday night. The Jets would have to try and extend their winning streak to three games not only without Snell, but also without Woytowich, Ash, and McDonald. The captain came down with a case of the flu to put him on the sidelines. The Cougars took full advantage of the depleted Jets' lineup and had the visitors down by a score of 3-0 midway through the second period and cruised to a 3-1 victory.

The Jets returned home for another weekend home stand starting on Friday night against the fourth-place Fighting Saints, who came into Winnipeg winners of five of their last six games and only three points behind the second-place Jets. Despite having both Ab McDonald and Woytowich back in the lineup, two goals by George Morrison put the Fighting Saints up by a 2-0 score before the game was five minutes old. The Jets showed some resilience by continuing to press on and they took the lead for the first time in the game when Hull completed his third hat trick of the season early in the third period. With everything going the Jets' way, the Fighting Saints scored a back-breaking shorthanded goal late in the third to tie the score, then Mike Walton's breakaway goal in overtime gave the visitors a 4-3 victory. By virtue of the Aeros' 6-2 win over the Oilers, the 26-24-4 Jets remained in second place, but by only one point ahead of the Fighting Saints and two ahead of the Oilers.

Sunday night brought a chance at redemption with the first-place Aeros' second regular season appearance of the season at the Arena. Before a sellout crowd that endured a hearty sampling of some Winnipeg's worst winter weather just for the privilege of seeing Gordie Howe, the Aeros controlled the first two periods and only a superb effort by Ernie Wakely kept the Jets within a pair of goals heading into the third period. With less than two minutes to play, the Jets rose from the ashes and scored twice to tie the game and nearly won it in the dying seconds. There was no scoring through the overtime period and the game ended in a 2-2 tie.

The Jets left Winnipeg to begin a three-game road trip in Los Angeles on the night of Tuesday, 12 February against a Sharks team that was coached once again by Terry Slater, who had replaced Ted McCaskill behind the bench. In addition to their second coaching change of the season, the Sharks entered the game with a litany of problems, both on and off the ice. Stuck in the basement of the Western Division, the Sharks were in the throws of a six-game losing streak and rumors were rampant about the potential relocation of the team to Detroit for next season. However, the Jets were in no position to show the Sharks any mercy. After a scoreless first period, the Jets jumped out to a quick 2-0 lead and held off the Sharks the rest of the way en route to a 4-2 victory that snapped the Jets' three-game winless skid and put the Jets back into sole possession of second place.

The next night, it was on to Houston to meet the Aeros for their fourth and final regular season appearance in Texas. Unfortunately, the Jets fared no better than they had in each of their last two visits to the Sam Houston Coliseum, which had ended in lopsided defeats. The Aeros jumped out to a 3-1 first period lead and never looked back in handing the Jets a 5-1 loss that widened the gap between the two teams in the standings to a dozen points.

On Friday night, the Jets closed out their road trip with their last regular season visit to the Saint Paul Civic Center in a showdown for second place. Buoyed by a season-high crowd numbering 12,044, thanks to an aggressive phone sales campaign, the Fighting Saints had little difficulty with the Jets and disposed of their guests by a score of 7-1. Only Daley's outstanding goaltending prevented a wider margin of defeat as the Fighting Saints bumped the Jets down to third place.

The Jets returned home for a Sunday night engagement against the Whalers, who were in the midst of a heated battle with the Toros and Nordiques for supremacy in the Eastern Division. The crowd of 7,217, who enjoyed their first taste of above-freezing temperatures since the new year, saw the Jets struggle out of the gate, but the two teams still ended up tied at 2-2 through regulation time as the Jets missed many opportunities to bury their guests. In overtime, the Whalers' John Cunniff, playing in only his second game since his recall from the minor leagues, fired a shot that went off Wakely and trickled into the net. His second goal of the game gave the Whalers a 3-2 victory and sent the Jets' record back to the .500 mark at 27-27-5.

The Jets didn't play on Tuesday, but it was one of the most important days in the brief history of the WHA and the future of pro hockey. An out-of-court settlement to the $50-million antitrust lawsuits brought by the WHA against the NHL was reached and signed by representatives of both leagues in front of Judge Leon A. Higginbotham. Though NHL President Clarence Campbell emphasized that this agreement was not a merger, its terms were far-reaching. They agreed to respect each other's contracts, compete in a limited number of exhibition games, as well as enter into negotiations for more exhibition games and possibly even interleague games, and drop all pending claims and counter claims. In addition, the NHL agreed to pay $1.75 million to cover the WHA's legal bills and not to oppose the WHA's use of NHL arenas. The latter point was a sticky issue during the negotiations, but the WHA won out. The NHL also agreed not to interfere with WHA teams who wished to do business with minor league teams that were controlled or affiliated with the NHL. For the WHA's part, they agreed not to sign NHL players after 1 August, and not to sign NHL players until they had completed the option year on their contracts.

Next up on the schedule for the sliding Jets was a date with the Oilers in Edmonton on Wednesday night. The Oilers were missing key contributors Jim Harrison, Tom Gilmore and Rusty Patenaude due to injury, as well as Doug Barrie due to suspension, but that didn't stop the home team from dominating the game from start to finish. Joe Daley single-handedly kept his team in the game, but the Oilers were able to get enough past the beleaguered goaltender to post a 4-1 victory. The win lifted the fourth-place Oilers to within a single point of the third-place Jets.

Hoping to put the brakes on their four-game losing streak, the Jets returned home to host the Toros on Friday night at a half-empty Arena. The Jets shortened their bench and Hull juggled the lines one more time and also reunited the Luxury Line in the hopes of getting the Jets back on track. The Toros drew first blood, but the Jets responded with three of their own, two of them coming from the newly formed trio of Ab McDonald, Danny Johnson, and Jean-Guy Gratton. The Toros rallied to tie the score at 3-3 late in the third period, but Hull finished off an end-to-end rush with a hard shot that restored the Jets' lead with only two minutes remaining. The Jets sweated out the remaining seconds and escaped with a 4-3 victory that put a couple more points between themselves and the fourth-place Oilers.

The 28-28-5 Jets wrapped up another weekend home stand with a Sunday night visit from the Cougars, who were desperately trying to crawl back into the playoff hunt in the Eastern Division. The Jets stuck with their shortened bench and new line combinations and in front of yet another half-empty Arena, the two teams went back and forth in a wide-open affair but the Jets had the only two goals by the midway point of the second period. The on-ice action temporarily gave way to some off-ice action when Larry Mavety of the Cougars was assessed a two-minute penalty by referee Bob Kolari and was subsequently ejected after throwing a temper tantrum. On his way off the ice, he threw his stick at some drunken fans behind the Cougars' bench and the fans responded by throwing beer at the enraged defenseman. Mavety and bench coach Jacques Demers headed for the stands, but playing coach Pat Stapleton pulled Demers back so hard that Demers hit his head on the ground. Police interceded and order was eventually restored. The focus turned back to the ice, where both teams picked up where they left off. The Cougars could only manage to get one of their 42 shots past Daley and Hull sealed the eventual 3-1 victory with an empty-net goal in the game's final minute.

It was back on the road for the Jets, who touched down in Quebec to battle the Nordiques on Tuesday night. Four Quebec goals late in the first period quickly put an end to any thoughts of the Jets extending their brief winning streak to three games and the Nordiques cruised to a 7-1 victory.

From there, the Jets moved on to meet the Toros at the Ottawa Civic Centre, last season's home rink for the franchise, where a surprisingly large crowd of 7,236 turned out to see the former Nationals do battle with the Jets. It took less than a minute for the Toros to take the lead and the early goal proved to be the game-winner as the Jets were foiled time and again by goaltender Gilles Gratton en route to a 3-0 defeat.

The 29-30-5 Jets bid adieu to the month of February with a quick turnaround flight back to Winnipeg to meet the Fighting Saints on Friday night and kick off a three-game home stand. Joining the team was Bill Sutherland, a key contributor from last season's roster, whom Hull cajoled into coming back. "Sudsie" was still not in game shape, but he was at least available for spot duty and on the power play. The Jets again fell behind early and despite firing 41 shots at Mike Curran in the Fighting Saints' net, they were blanked for the second time in as many nights as the visitors skated off with a 4-0 win. Not only did the Jets' third straight loss put them nine points behind the second-place Fighting Saints, but the Oilers' victory over the Aeros pulled them within a single point of the third-place Jets. In a dramatic reversal of fortune, the team that the Jets eliminated in five games in the first round of last season's playoffs won seven of the eight meetings between the two teams this season.

Did You Know?

Mike Walton, with his goal on 1 March, raised his season total against the Jets to nine, more than any other player would score against the Jets in the 1973-1974 season.

The Jets returned to the ice on Sunday night against the Nordiques, where they busted out of both their three-game losing streak and two-game goal-less drought in a big way during a wild 8-6 victory. Hull scored three of his team's eight goals to register his fourth hat trick of the season and his third goal gave him a total of 700 as a professional. The third period power-play goal was his 45th of the season and his teammates left the bench to congratulate him on the historic accomplishment, but more importantly, the win kept the Jets two points up on the fourth-place Oilers.

The Road To 700

On the night of 3 March 1974, Bobby Hull scored his 700th goal as a professional. 604 of his total came as a member of the Chicago Blackhawks, while the remaining 96 came in a Jets uniform. His total was accumulated over 15 NHL seasons and 2 WHA seasons.

Season	Goals	Season	Goals	Season	Goals
1957-1958	13	1963-1964	43	1969-1970	38
1958-1959	18	1964-1965	39	1970-1971	44
1959-1960	39	1965-1966	54	1971-1972	50
1960-1961	31	1966-1967	52	1972-1973	51
1961-1962	50	1967-1968	44	1973-1974	45
1962-1963	31	1968-1969	58		

After playing three games in four nights, the Jets had a breather before their next game, Friday night against the Crusaders. Before just over 6,000 onlookers at the Arena, the Jets threw everything they had at their guests, only to be stoned by Crusaders' goaltender Gerry Cheevers. Norm Beaudin's late first period goal was all they could get past the stubborn Cheevers, while the Crusaders pumped four past Wakely, sending the Jets down to a 4-1 defeat.

The 30-32-5 Jets left Winnipeg to begin a three-game road swing starting in Chicago on Saturday night. Tied for third place with the Oilers, the Jets were joined by 42 boosters who had spent more than 17 hours on a Grey Goose bus to see the game. The boosters, who arrived in Chicago at 12:30 p.m. on Friday, greeted the players at the Executive House hotel on Saturday afternoon and both groups headed for the International Amphitheater for the main event. The game was a seesaw affair that wound up tied at 4-4 through regulation time, but it was the Cougars who emerged victorious when Larry Mavety was the recipient of an inadvertent pass from Huck and went in alone on Daley to score the winning goal.

After suffering their second defeat in as many nights, the Jets boarded a plane to meet the Knights in Cherry Hill on Monday night, while their disappointed boosters boarded a bus on Sunday morning for another long trek on the highway for their return trip to Winnipeg. To add to their woes, the Jets learned that Hull wasn't going to be able to play against the Knights, nor against the Crusaders on Wednesday night due to a stomach ailment. At the half-empty, 4,000-seat Cherry Hill Arena, the Knights ran roughshod over the visiting Jets and won easily by a score of 10-2. In suffering their third consecutive defeat and sixth loss in seven games, the Jets missed an opportunity to pull into sole possession of third place and left Cherry Hill still tied with the Oilers.

The Jets moved on to Cleveland, where they again fell behind early. They rallied with three third period goals to tie the score at 3-3, only to have Jim Wiste score off a rebound with 7:32 to play in regulation time. The Jets pressed hard for the equalizer, but it was not to be as the Jets went down to a 4-3 defeat, their fourth in a row.

Did You Know?

While the Jets were being beaten in Cleveland on Wednesday, 13 March 1974, Jets President Ben Hatskin, along with Bobby Hull, announced the formation of the Bobby Hull 700-Goal Scholarship Fund. The fund, started with donations from Hatskin and the Jets Booster Club, was set up to assist students "to be enrolled in a university or college to pursue the attainment of excellence as a player or participant in any sport while maintaining educational endeavors." The Fund was subsequently kicked off in a pre-game ceremony on 29 March.

The 30-35-5 Jets returned to Winnipeg to begin a three-game home stand on Friday night against the Blazers in fourth place, two points behind the third-place Oilers with only eight games left on the regular season schedule. Hull was again available as a player, but he opted to leave Nick Mickoski in charge behind the bench rather than reassume the coaching duties himself. The crowd of just over 5,200 shivered through an unseasonably cold mid-March evening to see the Jets come out strong, only to fall behind by two goals in the second period. Eventually, the Jets broke through against Blazers' goaltender Peter Donnelly and they persevered in a 7-5 victory that wasn't assured until Ron Snell's empty-net goal with one second remaining, giving Mickoski his first win as the head coach.

Did You Know?

Nicholas Mickoski had a playing career in the NHL that encompassed 705 regular season and 18 playoff games. His last NHL season came in 1959-1960, when he played 18 games for the Boston Bruins. Mickoski was later inducted into the Manitoba Hockey Hall of Fame.

Two nights later, the Jets were back on the ice facing the Eastern Division leading Whalers on St. Patrick's Day. Nearly 7,000 onlookers saw the visitors get the early jump on the scoreboard, but the Jets quickly turned the tables on their guests and routed the Whalers by a score of 10-1 in what was undoubtedly the Jets' finest performance of the season to date. Nine different scorers did the damage as the Jets remained tied with the third-place Oilers and secured a playoff berth in the process.

The Jets had a break before their next game on Friday night against the Aeros, but on Monday night, they were in action off the ice at the Marlborough Hotel in downtown Winnipeg, where the Booster Club held its first annual Awards Night and Banquet. Spending around $4,000 of their own money to stage the event, the boosters presented Fran Huck with the most popular player award, Joe Zanussi was named the most exciting player, Jean-Guy Gratton was selected as the most improved Jet, and Hull was presented with a special award for "untiring efforts and dedication to hockey." Huck, Zanussi, and Gratton each received stereo component sets, while Hull was given an engraved Olympic coin set. The boosters also presented the voice of the Jets, Ken "Friar" Nicolson, with a portable television set for his "editorial contributions and tireless efforts."

Back on the ice, the first-place Aeros, who were 24 points ahead of the 32-35-5 Jets, flew in to town after a Thursday night game in Ottawa against the Toros and were greeted by another sellout crowd at the Arena to see Gordie Howe. Before the game, the Jets got a scare when Huck closed his car door on the middle finger on his left hand. The finger swelled up and though Huck was able to play, he had trouble holding his stick. In addition, Joe Daley made the start in goal, since Ernie Wakely was under the weather with flu-like symptoms. The Jets jumped out to a 2-1 lead, but the Aeros fought back with three unanswered goals and expertly kept the Jets at bay the rest of the way to a 4-2 victory.

Most of the Jets boarded a plane for a Sunday matinee at the Los Angeles Sports Arena to play the Sharks for the final time this season, but with a playoff berth already in hand, they opted to leave a large contingent behind, including Hull, Beaudin, Bordeleau, McDonald, Hornung, and Woytowich. Wakely made the trip to serve as Daley's backup, but the doctor advised that he not play if it could be avoided. Not surprisingly, the visitors were no match for the Sharks, who easily disposed of the Jets by a score of 6-3. Marc Tardif scored four goals to lead the Sharks' attack.

The fourth-place Jets returned home still two points back of the Oilers to open their final home stand of the regular season on Friday night against the Aeros once again. Unfortunately, Wakely remained behind in Los Angeles, confined to a hospital after being diagnosed with pneumonia, leaving the Jets to scramble during the week to find a backup for Daley. They first turned to Gord Tumilson, who had spent last season with the Jets as their third-string goaltender, but his WHA rights were held by the expansion Indianapolis Racers. The Jets then arranged for the loan of third-stringer Frank Blum from the Toros, but starter Gilles Gratton went down with an injury, so they made a last-minute substitution of York University graduate Bill Holden.

With Daley between the pipes and Holden on the bench as his backup, the two teams faced off on Friday night before the traditional Gordie Howe sellout crowd, which didn't get to see the proud veteran because he was out of the lineup on account of a foot injury. The Jets fell behind, but they kept pressing and were able to overcome a 4-3 third period deficit on their way to a 7-5 victory, their first in eight meetings with the Aeros this season. The game was briefly interrupted when Hull scored his 50th goal of the season in the third period to give the Jets their first lead of the night. Dave Meyers, perhaps the most fanatical of the Jets' faithful, came out onto the ice to congratulate the Golden Jet personally. The win kept the Jets within four points of the third-place Oilers, who had won earlier in the week and were winning in Saint Paul as the Jets were in the process of defeating the Aeros.

The Jets closed out the month of March with a Sunday night engagement against the Blazers at the Arena. With Daley making his fifth consecutive start while Wakely remained in a Los Angeles hospital, the Jets took a 2-0 lead only to have the visitors tie the score on goals 12 seconds apart. The game went to overtime tied at 3-3, and Huck scored the winner two minutes into the extra period to give the Jets their second consecutive victory.

Unfortunately, while the Jets were celebrating their 34th victory of the season, the Oilers were in the process of defeating the Cougars by a score of 4-1 in Edmonton, and in so doing, they clinched third place in the Western Division. As a result, the Jets' first-round playoff matchup against the first-place Aeros was set and tickets went on sale the next morning. Due to a scheduling conflict at the Sam Houston Coliseum, Games 1 and 2 of the series would take place in Winnipeg, starting on Monday, 8 April, before the series shifted to Houston.

With nothing left to play for, the Jets entertained the Oilers on Wednesday, 3 April in their regular season home finale. Prior to the game, Hull was given more trophies to add to his burgeoning collection. He earned one for being the Jets' leading scorer and another for being the most valuable player. Labatt Breweries, presenters of the latter award, also made a donation to the Bobby Hull 700-Goal Scholarship Fund. Hull also earned a watch from Independent Jewellers in honor of his 700th goal as a professional, but he instead asked them to make one for his 3-year-old daughter, Michelle. Once the game started, the lead kept changing hands, but regulation time settled nothing and the two teams went to overtime. After the Jets failed to connect on a power play opportunity, the Oilers came back down the ice and Ross Perkins fed Tom Gilmore for his fourth goal of the game that gave the visitors a 6-5 victory.

The Jets moved on to Vancouver to close out their regular season schedule on Thursday night. Daley got the night off and the Jets turned the goaltending chores over to Bill Holden, who made only his second pro appearance. The Blazers put two goals past Holden in the first five minutes of the game and didn't look back as the home team ended their season on a positive note with a 4-2 win. For their part, the Jets finished the season with a record of 34-39-5, a 17-point drop from their first-place finish one year ago.

The Captain's Ship Comes In

On 4 April 1974, Ab McDonald, the Jets' first captain, scored his last goal as a professional. He made his NHL debut in the 1958 playoffs and played in 762 regular season and 84 playoff games before racking up 147 regular season and 18 playoff games as a Jet. Following is a listing of all of 31 goals McDonald scored as a Jet.

	Opponent	Period	Time	Goaltender
12 Oct 1972	@New York Raiders	1	8:14	Gary Kurt
13 Oct 1972	@Minnesota Fighting Saints	3	7:31	Mike Curran
22 Oct 1972	Philadelphia Blazers	2	2:31	Bernie Parent
5 Nov 1972	New York Raiders	1	13:01	Gary Kurt
12 Nov 1972	Los Angeles Sharks	3	4:45	George Gardner
19 Nov 1972	@Los Angeles Sharks	2	18:41	George Gardner
21 Nov 1972	@Houston Aeros	1	15:26	Don McLeod
23 Nov 1972	@Houston Aeros	2	15:48	Don McLeod
24 Nov 1972	Quebec Nordiques	3	10:44	Jacques Lemelin
26 Dec 1972	Chicago Cougars	2	10:56	Jimmy McLeod
1 Jan 1973	@Alberta Oilers	3	13:44	Jack Norris
7 Jan 1973	@Minnesota Fighting Saints	2	8:16	Jack McCartan
19 Jan 1973	New England Whalers	3	3:08	Bruce Landon
28 Jan 1973	@Ottawa Nationals	2	13:34	Gilles Gratton
10 Feb 1973	@Los Angeles Sharks	3	9:10	George Gardner
16 Feb 1973	Houston Aeros	1	12:51	Don McLeod
16 Feb 1973	Houston Aeros	2	4:00	Don McLeod
15 Apr 1973	Minnesota Fighting Saints	2	5:29	Mike Curran
3 May 1973	New England Whalers	1	19:34	Al Smith
10 Oct 1973	@Vancouver Blazers	2	5:13	Yves Archambault
7 Nov 1973	@New England Whalers	2	2:38	Bruce Landon
28 Nov 1973	@Houston Aeros	3	8:58	Don McLeod
29 Dec 1973	@Quebec Nordiques	2	12:30	Serge Aubry
15 Feb 1974	@Minnesota Fighting Saints	1	12:01	Mike Curran
17 Feb 1974	New England Whalers	2	5:42	Al Smith
22 Feb 1974	Toronto Toros	2	14:42	Gilles Gratton
26 Feb 1974	@Quebec Nordiques	2	19:25	Richard Brodeur
3 Mar 1974	Quebec Nordiques	2	4:48	Richard Brodeur
15 Mar 1974	Vancouver Blazers	3	10:04	Peter Donnelly
15 Mar 1974	Vancouver Blazers	3	11:38	Peter Donnelly
4 Apr 1974	@Vancouver Blazers	1	15:31	Peter Donnelly

Ready or not, the Jets returned home for Game 1 of the Western Division semi-final on Monday night against an Aeros team that had finished 28 points ahead of them in the standings. To add to the Jets' woes, not only were the Jets still without Wakely, but Bordeleau couldn't answer the bell on account of a bout with the flu. For the first time ever, Gordie Howe stepped on to the Arena ice in front of some empty seats as only 8,446 were in attendance to see the game. Once the puck was dropped, Howe and his teammates took control of the game early on and kept it. The Aeros asserted themselves both physically and on the scoreboard and only Daley's brilliant goaltending kept the Jets within striking distance. The Jets scored twice in the third period, but the late rally was far from enough and the Aeros were full value for their 5-2 win that gave them a 1-0 lead in the best-of-seven series.

The two teams returned to the Arena ice on Wednesday night for Game 2, where the Jets at least had a weakened Christian Bordeleau available. This time around, the Jets opened the scoring and had plenty of chances on the power play to add to their lead, but their pitiful performance with the man advantage mirrored their regular season ranking of 11th in the 12-team league. A myriad of goal posts, missed empty nets and errant passes came home to roost as the Aeros first tied the score, then took a 3-1 lead midway through the third period. The Aeros again masterfully held the Jets at bay and skated off with a 3-2 win, taking a 2-0 series lead back to Houston with them.

Both teams got on a plane on Thursday morning headed for Texas in anticipation of Game 3 on Saturday night at the Sam Houston Coliseum. On Friday night, however, after taking in the Houston Astros' 5-3 National League victory over the Los Angeles Dodgers at the Astrodome, Daley had to be rushed to hospital, complaining of a sharp pain in his chest. The diagnosis was pneumonia and with Bill Holden unavailable due to a broken thumb he sustained in the regular season finale, the Jets again had to scramble to find a goaltender. On Saturday morning, they found one when the Toros graciously consented to loan Blum to the Jets under emergency conditions and the Sudbury, Ontario native boarded a plane in Cleveland and arrived in Houston in the afternoon in time for the game.

Blum thought that he was coming to Houston to be Wakely's backup, but instead, he was the starter as the Jets took to the ice to try and get back in the series. Wearing jersey number 27, Blum was greeted rudely by the Aeros, who scored early and often on their way to an easy 10-1 victory that put the Jets one game away from an early playoff exit. Blum faced a total of 44 shots on the forgettable evening and was only able to stop 34 of them.

One night later, the two teams went at it one more time as the Jets tried to keep their season alive in Game 4. Though they would not have to contend with Gordie Howe, who had stayed at home in bed with the flu, the rest of the Aeros were plenty formidable enough. Unlike the previous night, the Jets got through the opening minutes unscathed, but the Aeros broke through and built up a 4-0 lead late in the second period. With the Aeros and their rabid fans smelling blood, the Jets summoned up some pride and made a game of it without the help of Fran Huck, who let his frustration get the better of him and took off his uniform and walked out during the second intermission. The rest of the Jets scored three more times in the third period, but the Aeros held off the Jets and won by a score of 5-4. During the frantic third period, Blum became the second Jets' goaltender to be involved in a fight when he scrapped with Andre Hinse and showed some fighting spirit that had been in short supply at times during the season.

The second season of Jets hockey could only be described as a major disappointment. After the game, Hull bemoaned the lack of spirit and effort that had taken the Jets so far last season and vowed that changes would be made. Joe Daley would later characterize the season as a "disaster" and few could argue. Late in the season, *Winnipeg Free Press* reporter Don Binda wrote, "The Jets are probably the most unpredictable team in hockey. One night the team looks like a million dollars and the next night they might look quite ordinary."

In the aftermath of the Jets' premature exit from post-season play, Sutherland announced the first change of the off-season and said that he was retiring for the second and final time. There would be more changes to come, on and off the ice.

Scores and Stats

1973-1974 Winnipeg Jets (34-39-5)

Regular Season

Date	Opponent	Score	Date	Opponent	Score
10 Oct	@Vancouver Blazers	3-4*	1 Jan	@Edmonton Oilers	4-3*
12 Oct	@Edmonton Oilers	4-6	4 Jan	New England Whalers	3-4
14 Oct	Vancouver Blazers	6-3	6 Jan	@Houston Aeros	1-7
17 Oct	@New England Whalers	3-1	8 Jan	@Los Angeles Sharks	1-4
18 Oct	@New York Golden Blades	6-1	9 Jan	@Vancouver Blazers	6-4
21 Oct	Minnesota Fighting Saints	2-1*	11 Jan	Edmonton Oilers	7-4
26 Oct	Toronto Toros	3-3*	13 Jan	Chicago Cougars	3-1
27 Oct	@Minnesota Fighting Saints	2-5	18 Jan	Cleveland Crusaders	7-3
30 Oct	@Chicago Cougars	1-4	20 Jan	Jersey Knights	9-3
31 Oct	@Cleveland Crusaders	4-6	25 Jan	@Edmonton Oilers	4-3
2 Nov	New York Golden Blades	3-1	27 Jan	@Minnesota Fighting Saints	2-12
4 Nov	Quebec Nordiques	8-2	1 Feb	Los Angeles Sharks	4-0
6 Nov	@Quebec Nordiques	2-2*	3 Feb	Chicago Cougars	4-2
7 Nov	@New England Whalers	2-9	5 Feb	@Chicago Cougars	1-3
10 Nov	@Cleveland Crusaders	2-4	8 Feb	Minnesota Fighting Saints	3-4*
11 Nov	Los Angeles Sharks	6-2	10 Feb	Houston Aeros	2-2*
13 Nov	@Vancouver Blazers	3-5	12 Feb	@Los Angeles Sharks	4-2
16 Nov	Edmonton Oilers	3-1	13 Feb	@Houston Aeros	1-5
18 Nov	@Toronto Toros	2-6	15 Feb	@Minnesota Fighting Saints	1-7
21 Nov	Cleveland Crusaders	6-2	17 Feb	New England Whalers	2-3*
23 Nov	Vancouver Blazers	3-4*	20 Feb	@Edmonton Oilers	1-4
25 Nov	@Minnesota Fighting Saints	3-5	22 Feb	Toronto Toros	4-3
27 Nov	@Los Angeles Sharks	4-5*	24 Feb	Chicago Cougars	3-1
28 Nov	@Houston Aeros	4-4*	26 Feb	@Quebec Nordiques	1-7
30 Nov	Los Angeles Sharks	2-5	28 Feb	@Toronto Toros	0-3
2 Dec	Quebec Nordiques	5-3	1 Mar	Minnesota Fighting Saints	0-4
5 Dec	Edmonton Oilers	3-1	3 Mar	Quebec Nordiques	8-6
7 Dec	Toronto Toros	7-4	8 Mar	Cleveland Crusaders	1-4
9 Dec	Jersey Knights	3-1	9 Mar	@Chicago Cougars	4-5*
12 Dec	Houston Aeros	2-3	11 Mar	@Jersey Knights	2-10
14 Dec	Los Angeles Sharks	1-0	13 Mar	@Cleveland Crusaders	3-4
16 Dec	Minnesota Fighting Saints	2-3	15 Mar	Vancouver Blazers	7-5
18 Dec	@Chicago Cougars	3-3*	17 Mar	New England Whalers	10-1
19 Dec	@Houston Aeros	0-10	22 Mar	Houston Aeros	2-4
22 Dec	@New England Whalers	2-0	24 Mar	@Los Angeles Sharks	3-6
23 Dec	@Jersey Knights	3-6	29 Mar	Houston Aeros	7-5
26 Dec	Chicago Cougars	4-2	31 Mar	Vancouver Blazers	4-3*
29 Dec	@Quebec Nordiques	4-3	3 Apr	Edmonton Oilers	5-6*
30 Dec	@Toronto Toros	2-5	4 Apr	@Vancouver Blazers	2-4

Playoffs

Date	Opponent	Score	Date	Opponent	Score
8 Apr	Houston Aeros	2-5	13 Apr	@Houston Aeros	1-10
10 Apr	Houston Aeros	2-3	14 Apr	@Houston Aeros	4-5

* - overtime

	Scoring															
	Regular Season								Playoffs							
Player	GP	G	A	Pts	PIM	+/-	PP	SH	Shots	GP	G	A	Pts	PIM	+/-	PP	SH	Shots
Bob Ash	60	2	18	20	30		0	0		4	0	1	1	2			
Duke Asmundson	72	5	14	19	85		0	0		4	0	1	1	2			
Norm Beaudin	74	27	28	55	8		5	0		4	3	1	4	2			
Milt Black	47	6	9	15	14		0	0		4	1	1	2	0			
Frank Blum										2	0	0	0	5		0	0
Christian Bordeleau	75	26	49	75	22		5	1		3	3	2	5	0			
Joe Daley	41	0	1	1	4		0	0		2	0	0	0	0		0	0
Jean-Guy Gratton	68	12	21	33	13		4	0		2	0	0	0	0		0	0
Jim Hargreaves	53	1	4	5	50		0	0									
Ted Hargreaves	74	7	12	19	15		0	2		4	0	1	1	10		0	0
Bill Holden	1	0	0	0	0		0	0									
Larry Hornung	51	4	19	23	18		1	1		4	0	0	0	0		0	0
Fran Huck	74	26	48	74	68		2	2		4	0	0	0	2		0	0
Bobby Hull	75	53	42	95	38		9	1		4	1	1	2	4			
Danny Johnson	78	16	21	37	20		2	0		4	1	0	1	5			
Ab McDonald	70	12	17	29	8		2	0		4	0	1	1	2			
Kelly Pratt	46	4	6	10	50		1	0									
Garth Rizzuto	41	3	4	7	8		1	1									
Dunc Rousseau	60	10	8	18	39		0	0		4	0	0	0	0		0	0
Ron Snell	70	24	25	49	32		5	0		4	0	0	0	0		0	0
Dan Spring	66	8	16	24	8		1	0		4	0	1	1	0		0	0
Ken Stephanson	29	0	7	7	24		0	0		3	0	2	2	10		0	0
Bill Sutherland	12	4	5	9	6		0	0		4	0	0	0	4		0	0
Cal Swenson	25	5	4	9	2		0	0		1	0	0	0	0		0	0
Ernie Wakely	37	0	0	0	9		0	0									
Bob Woytowich	72	6	28	34	43		1	0		4	0	0	0	0		0	0
Joe Zanussi	76	3	22	25	53		0	0		4	0	0	0	0		0	0

	Goaltending										
	Regular Season										
Goaltender	GP	Min	GA	GAA	Saves	Sv %	SO	EN	W	L	T
Joe Daley	41	2454	163	3.99	1239	0.884	0	4	19	20	1
Bill Holden	1	60	4	4.00	24	0.857	0	0	0	1	0
Ernie Wakely	37	2254	123	3.27	1061	0.896	3	2	15	18	4
	Playoffs										
	GP	Min	GA	GAA	Saves	Sv %	SO	EN	W	L	
Frank Blum	2	120	15	7.50			0	0	0	2	
Joe Daley	2	119	8	4.03			0	0	0	2	

ABOVE: Bobby Hull shows off the new Jets road blues that debuted in the 1973-1974 season.

New faces for the 1973-1974 season:

TOP LEFT: Ted Hargreaves
TOP MIDDLE: Dan Spring
TOP RIGHT: Fran Huck

SECOND ROW LEFT: Kelly Pratt
SECOND ROW MIDDLE: Ken Stephanson
SECOND ROW RIGHT: Ron Snell

BOTTOM RIGHT: Jim Hargreaves

ABOVE: Christian Bordeleau prepares for a faceoff against the Aeros.

RIGHT: Bobby Hull fires a shot while Fran Huck looks for a rebound. The legendary Gordie Howe of the Aeros tries to offer some defensive support.

BELOW: Norm Beaudin fires a shot against the New York Golden Blades while linemates Bobby Hull and Christian Bordeleau look on.

ABOVE: Ernie Wakely covers up in front of the north end goal.

LEFT: Joe Daley keeps the Minnesota Fighting Saints off the scoreboard while wearing the mask he began using in the 1973-1974 season.

BELOW: Ernie Wakely contends with Don Herriman of the New York Golden Blades.

Season III: 1974-1975 – This Team is Our Team

It wasn't long after the dust settled on the bitterly disappointing 1973-1974 season that work began on the 1974-1975 season. For starters, amid losses exceeding $400,000 each of the previous two seasons, Hatskin and the Simkin family decided to put the team up for sale. As early as January, Hatskin made Jack McKeag aware of the dire situation regarding the future of the Jets. Operating costs had risen sharply and combined with declining attendance and the burden of a 10 percent provincial sales tax, the financial picture wasn't pretty. It was after that meeting with Hatskin that McKeag got a group together and first breached the idea of a community-owned team.

Hatskin and the Simkin family decided to put the team up for sale. As early as January, Hatskin made Jack McKeag aware of the dire situation regarding the future of the Jets. Operating costs had risen sharply and combined with declining attendance and the burden of a 10 percent provincial sales tax, the financial picture wasn't pretty. It was after that meeting with Hatskin that McKeag got a group together and first breached the idea of a community-owned team.

Once all parties realized that no local offers were forthcoming, the unprecedented concept in the world of professional sports took flight. Because Hatskin and the Simkin family genuinely wanted the team to stay in Winnipeg, they agreed to a discounted sale price of $2.3 million to a public group led by McKeag, Inter-City Gas President Bob Graham, chartered accountant William Shields, lawyer Nestor Swystun, and James Burns. They needed a down payment of $600,000 and an additional $300,000 in operating capital, with the rest payable over the next eight years at an interest rate of 9 percent.

After giving the group a five-week extension, Hatskin needed a commitment by 1 July or the team would be sold to private interests for $3.5 million. Detroit, Milwaukee, San Diego, Miami and New Orleans were all mentioned as possible destinations of the so-called "Bobby Hull franchise," but the campaign to keep Winnipeg as the only destination for the Jets was off and running.

Raising the money became the challenge. In the early stages of the process, Manitoba Premier Ed Schreyer implied that the group would get some financial assistance from the Province of Manitoba, so they came up with a plan whereby the Province and the City of Winnipeg would be asked for a $300,000 interest-free loan with the remaining amount coming from contributions from members of the general public. After meeting with Schreyer, the group was informed that the Province could not provide direct assistance, but the Premier indicated that the group would be given rights to a lottery as a means of generating additional revenue. However, the City of Winnipeg did agree to a $300,000 loan, but now the group had to raise $600,000 from the public.

While the efforts to keep the team in Winnipeg were happening, the on-ice product needed just as much attention and the Jets turned their eye across the Atlantic to sign a pair of Swedish stars. In early May, centerman Ulf Nilsson and winger Anders Hedberg were introduced at a press conference at the Viscount Gort Hotel near the Arena after the pair of 23-year-olds each signed two-year, no-cut, no-trade contracts with the Jets.

Dr. Gerry Wilson, who was studying at a Stockholm university on an exchange program, discovered the pair and urged the Jets to sign both of them. Hedberg was completing his education at the same university where he met Dr. Wilson and the two eventually became good friends and colleagues. Hedberg had turned down an offer from the Vancouver Canucks years before in order to finish his education and had also turned down a more lucrative offer this year from the Toronto Maple Leafs in favor of the Jets. Though Hedberg admitted to being largely unaware of the circumstances regarding the Jets' immediate future, he was lured by the appeal of playing with both Nilsson and Hull. After playing left wing for the previous two seasons in Sweden, however, Hedberg would have to make the switch to the right side to play with them.

Nilsson, an intelligent playmaker who dabbled in woodworking when off the ice, also had an offer from the Buffalo Sabres, but chose to sign with the Jets instead. The pair of Swedes had played with each other on their national team and though they didn't play on the same club team, they practiced at the same rink and had developed a friendship.

Winger Willy Lindstrom was another Swede on the Jets' radar, but he opted to stay in Sweden. However, they bagged another Swedish star when 30-year-old defenseman Lars-Erik Sjoberg chose the Jets over the California Golden Seals and was introduced as the newest Jet in late May. At the press conference announcing the signing, the former captain of the Swedish national team cited Bill Robinson as the greatest influence in his decision to join the Jets. The wily veteran was a quick skater who possessed considerable strength despite his small 5'8" stature and was described as the "Bobby Orr of international hockey." Sjoberg was also a student of the game and was well on his way to his doctorate in the science of physical education.

The signings from overseas didn't stop there. Over the course of the tumultuous off-season, the Jets added a pair of Finns, 26-year-old centerman Veli-Pekka Ketola and 25-year-old defenseman Hexi Riihiranta. Ketola had starred with his hometown team in Pori, Finland and led them to three national titles. He turned down an offer from the Detroit Red Wings so he could sign a three-year deal with the Jets. Riihiranta played for his hometown team in Helsinki and spurned an offer from the Boston Bruins in favor of joining the Jets. The Jets rounded out their European contingent when they outbid the Seals for a second time, this time to sign 29-year-old Swedish goaltender Curt Larsson. The noted practical joker had spent the past 10 seasons with Sodertalje SK in Sweden and was an All-Star in the Swedish First Division and at the World Championships this past season.

Domestic signings included a pair of 22-year-old defensemen, Mike Ford and Perry Miller. Ford was an eighth-round draft choice of the Detroit Red Wings in 1972 and had toiled in their farm system for the past two seasons. Miller, a Winnipeg native who spent his childhood on the rinks of the Weston area, had played the past two seasons with the Charlotte Checkers of the Southern Hockey League. The Jets would ultimately convert Miller, a hard skater, good shooter, mean hipchecker and renowned fighter, into a winger.

The Jets made 16 selections in the 1974 WHA Amateur Draft and signed two of them. Twenty-year-old centerman Randy Andreachuk, the Jets' first-round selection and seventh overall pick, signed a two-year deal as did Ron "Bam Bam" Ashton, another 20-year-old whom the Jets selected in the fourth round. Andreachuk had racked up 46 goals and 97 points with the Kamloops Chiefs of the WCHL last season and Ashton, also a fifth-round selection of the Minnesota North Stars, came with a tough reputation after piling up 232 penalty minutes with the Saskatoon Blades last season.

Off the ice, the Jets, heeding Hull's suggestion, hired 59-year-old Winnipeg native Rudy Pilous as their new coach and signed him to a two-year deal. After a brief pro playing career, Pilous had held a variety of off-ice positions at all levels of hockey that included coaching, managing, promotion, and ownership over the past 32 years. Most notably, Pilous coached the Chicago Blackhawks to a Stanley Cup championship in 1961. Pilous had spent the past three seasons behind the bench of the WCHL's Brandon Wheat Kings, where he held the dual role of Head Coach and General Manager. Out were both Annis Stukus and Nick Mickoski, though the latter was offered a scouting job in the organization.

The WHA held an Expansion Draft to stock the rosters of two new expansion teams, the Indianapolis Racers and Phoenix Roadrunners, and the Racers selected Bob Ash, Jim Hargreaves, and Cal Swenson off the Jets' roster. In addition to Bill Sutherland's second retirement, the popular Ab McDonald also retired and teamed up with Sutherland at Molson Breweries, while the Jets released Joe Zanussi. Fran Huck, who was named last season's most popular player, signed with the Fighting Saints for a reported salary of $75,000. At odds with both Hull and Christian Bordeleau, his unexcused absence from the third period of Game 4 of last season's playoff series against the Aeros was the last straw as far as the Jets were concerned. Kelly Pratt, a part-time contributor last season, was the next to go when he signed with the Pittsburgh Penguins.

Meanwhile, there was still the matter of raising the money to keep the team in Winnipeg. That task began on the morning of Monday, 10 June when Room 512 of the Marlborough Hotel was transformed into a makeshift office for the Manitoba Citizens Committee for the Jets, co-chaired by Jack McKeag and James Burns with Bob Graham acting as the spokesman. The general public was asked to buy membership shares for $25.00 for individuals and $100.00 for families, which would give shareholders first crack at season tickets, parking concessions and reduced ticket prices. Large businesses were approached to make interest-free Founders Loans to the non-profit corporation.

On the first day of business, the public answered the call of "Save the Jets" and gave a total of $106,000. Money from across the city and province continued to flow in and the total surpassed the $200,000 barrier on 18 June, but the corporate support was still not coming in. The public had responded generously but there was still $280,500 to be raised in the space of four days. Thursday, 27 June was the day that the group was waiting for when, at last, the corporate community got on the bandwagon. Aided by a last-minute $25,000 Founders Loan from an anonymous donor, the necessary total was reached. With $603,102.51 in their pockets, the Committee signed the papers at 4:30 p.m. the next day at Royal Trust. The Jets officially belonged to the people.

With the team's immediate future in Winnipeg secure and the roster retooled, the focus turned back to the ice, where the Jets got ready to open training camp at the Winnipeg Arena on 17 September as members of the expanded and reorganized WHA. Joining the Jets in the new Canadian Division were the Oilers, Nordiques, Toros, and Blazers, while the U.S.-based teams were split into two divisions. The Whalers, Crusaders, Cougars and Racers made up the Eastern Division and the Western Division featured the defending champion Aeros together with the Fighting Saints, Roadrunners, Michigan Stags and San Diego Mariners.

The Stags, as had been rumored late last season, had relocated from Los Angeles and the Jersey Knights/ New York Golden Blades franchise was purchased by new ownership and moved to Southern California to begin life anew as the Mariners. The Whalers also decided to pick up stakes and leave Boston for Hartford, Connecticut. They still kept the "New England" moniker, but their temporary home would be Springfield, Massachusetts until the new Hartford Civic Center was ready.

Pilous put his charges through a rigorous training camp and the Jets plodded through their exhibition schedule that included a home date against the NHL's Atlanta Flames on 29 September. Though the Jets lost by a score of 3-1, it marked the first time the Jets played an NHL opponent.

The NHL's Debut In Winnipeg

Though the Jets would eventually join the NHL for the 1979-1980 season, they played host to the Atlanta Flames on 29 September 1974 in their first matchup with an NHL team. Ron Ashton scored the Jets' only goal, but he would score only one regular season goal during his brief tenure with the Jets. Daniel Bouchard, the Flames' goaltender, would end his career as a member of the Jets in 1985-1986. Ironically, Bouchard's last appearance came against the Flames, and in his last game in uniform, he served as Daniel Berthiaume's backup as the Jets were eliminated in the playoffs by the Flames at the Winnipeg Arena.

Flames 3, Jets 1

First Period

Scoring – 1. Atlanta, Leiter (Brown) 9:52. 2. Atlanta, Leiter (Vail, Lemieux) 15:14.
Penalties – Miller, Wpg 1:04; Hextall, Atl 2:14; Richard, Atl 6:46; Ford, Wpg 10:48; Ketola, Wpg 14:03.

Second Period

Scoring – None.
Penalties – Vail, Atl, Ashton, Wpg (minors, majors) 2:41; Brown, Atl 14:54.

Third Period

Scoring – 3. Winnipeg, Ashton (Hornung, Woytowich) 9:36. 4. Atlanta, Lysiak (Bialowas, Richard) 11:47.
Penalties – None.

Goaltenders – Wakely, Larsson, Daley, Winnipeg; Bouchard, Atlanta.

Hull missed training camp and almost all the pre-season activities while he was skating with Team Canada in their eight-game series against the Soviet Union's national team. Unlike the series two years earlier, where only NHL players were allowed to represent Canada, the 1974 edition featured only WHA players. Bordeleau also missed a good deal of camp time, but his absence was for a different reason. After vowing in the off-season that hockey would come ahead of his farm, "Pepe" left the team with no explanation and was subsequently suspended for seven days. Later in the pre-season, Curt Larsson, one of the new arrivals, missed time due to a broken finger on his catching hand.

Bordeleau eventually rejoined the team, but just before the season, the Jets decided to part ways with Ted Hargreaves, another member of last year's squad. In deciding not to offer him a contract, the Jets stated in their official press release, "He performed strictly on heart and savvy and was well-respected for his attitude and personality." Days before the season opener, the Jets named Danny Johnson as their new captain, replacing the retired McDonald, while Hornung and Spring were appointed as assistant captains.

The new Jets opened the season on the night of Tuesday, 15 October in Vancouver, the same place where they had opened the season last year. Like the Jets, the Blazers were coming off a disappointing season and they had also made numerous off-season changes. Starting with their new coach, Winnipeg native Joe Crozier, who had coached the Buffalo Sabres for the last three seasons, the Blazers added goaltender Don "Smokey" McLeod from the Aeros along with centerman Ron Chipperfield, a star in the junior ranks with the Brandon Wheat Kings, defenseman Pat Price, the first overall selection in the WHA Amateur Draft, and veteran defenders Duane Rupp, Mike Pelyk and Paul Terbenche.

Before a crowd of 8,399 that included Annis Stukus, the Jets' former general manager, the Blazers carried the play in the first period, but it was the Jets who drew first blood and broke open a close game late in the second period with a dazzling display that carried the visiting Jets to a 6-2 victory. Six different Jets scored, including both Nilsson and Hedberg, and Joe Daley was particularly sharp in the early going after earning his first opening night assignment on the strength of an outstanding training camp.

The Jets returned to Winnipeg to battle the Oilers on Friday night, where a crowd of just under 8,000 paying customers made their way to the Arena on the chilly October evening to see their new and improved team. The Oilers came into town with relatively few changes from the team that edged the Jets out of third place last season. During the off-season, the Oilers had traded away high-scoring centerman Jim Harrison and veteran goaltender Jack Norris, but they added defenseman Barry Long from the Los Angeles Kings and youngster Mike Rogers, who was still days away from his 20th birthday. Rogers was coming off three seasons with the WCHL's Calgary Centennials, where he had racked up a total of 148 goals, including 67 one season ago.

The Jets assumed control of the game from the first minute and outskated their guests on their way to a comfortable 4-0 win. The Oilers, unable to skate with the Jets, resorted to the rough stuff to slow down the high-flying Jets, but to no avail. In making his second straight appearance in goal, Daley earned the shutout, but he was rarely called upon once the opening minutes of the game had passed.

Did You Know?

The night of 18 October 1974 marked the first appearance by Barry Long at the Winnipeg Arena to play against the Jets in a regular season game. Long would go on to play for the Jets in both the WHA and NHL and then he served in various off-ice capacities for the Jets, includinghead coach. Long coached the Jets during the 1984-1985 season, when they posted a 43-27-10 record, the best record they would achieve in 17 NHL seasons.

After their two-for-two start, the Jets had a full week before their next game in Toronto against the Toros, one of their new division rivals. For the third time in as many seasons, the Toros had a new home rink as they moved out of Varsity Arena in favor of the much more spacious Maple Leaf Gardens. The Toros made a number of key additions to the team that had come within a game of playing in the AVCO World Trophy final, including veteran NHL stars Frank Mahovlich and Paul Henderson, as well as Vaclav Nedomansky and Richard Farda, a pair of defectors from Czechoslovakia. Nedomansky was a star in his homeland and he defected with his family over the summer while they were vacationing in Switzerland. The Toros also added defenseman Jim Turkiewicz, whom they selected with the 12th overall selection in the Amateur Draft.

Despite needing a cortisone shot to dull the pain after injuring his back pulling fence posts on his farm during the week, Hull was able to play and opened the scoring with his first goal of the season. However, after the Jets controlled play in the first period, the Toros turned the tables in the second and third periods in front of a near-sellout crowd and handed the Jets a 3-1 defeat. The Toros raised their record to a perfect 5-0 to start their season and gave themselves an early four-point cushion atop the Canadian Division, while the Jets suffered their first defeat of the season.

Hull's Main Setup Man

> **Ulf Nilsson assisted on Bobby Hull's first goal of the season on 25 October 1974 in Toronto, the first of many assists he would record on the Golden Jet's goals. Hull would score a total of 303 regular season goals and 43 playoff goals as a member of the WHA Jets and no player recorded more assists on those goals than Nilsson did.**

The Jets returned home to begin a five-game home stand on Sunday night against the Stags. Besides a new moniker and a new coach in the person of former Kings and Red Wings bench boss Johnny Wilson, there were few differences between these Stags and last season's Sharks that had finished with the WHA's worst record. Despite lingering pain in his back, Hull joined his teammates in front of a crowd of 6,748 and though they held the upper hand all night long, Stags' goaltender Gerry Desjardins kept his team in the game. With only 15 seconds left in the second period, Nilsson broke a 1-1 tie with his third goal of the young season and the Jets scored three more times in the third period on their way to a 5-2 victory.

The second game of the home stand came on Wednesday night when the Jets welcomed the Roadrunners to Winnipeg for the first time. The visitors took advantage of a nervous Larsson, who was making his WHA debut after Daley had started the first four games of the season, and the Roadrunners took a 4-2 lead to the second intermission. The Jets didn't quit, however, and after the two teams traded goals early in the third period, the Jets struck twice in a span of 79 seconds to tie the game at 5-5. Hull completed his first hat trick of the season in the final minute of overtime to give the Jets a dramatic 6-5 come-from-behind victory.

The Jets opened the month of November with a Friday night engagement against the first-place 6-1-0 Toros, who had suffered their first defeat of the season two nights earlier at the hands of the Whalers in Springfield. The game would have almost assuredly sold out were it not for a clerical oversight that prevented 181 tickets from being sold, but the error was caught too late to register the historic first sellout to see the Jets when Gordie Howe wasn't in town. Those who did make it, however, got their money's worth as the Jets erased an early 1-0 deficit and pummeled their guests to the a tune of 10-1. Hull registered his second hat trick in as many games and Christian Bordeleau scored twice and added three assists in the victory that moved the Jets to within two points of the first-place Toros.

Come Sunday night, the 2-6-0 Stags were back for another visit, but this time around, the Jets poured it on early and often and left no doubt as to the game's outcome. The Jets hit double figures for the second consecutive game in routing the woeful Stags by a score of 11-3. Hull scored twice, giving him a total of eight goals in the last three games, and Ernie Wakely won in his first appearance of the season, stopping 25 shots for the victory that lifted the 6-1-0 Jets into a first-place tie with the Toros.

The Jets wrapped up their five-game home stand against the Fighting Saints in a rare Tuesday night game. An unusually large crowd numbering 8,133 made their way through the windy, November chill to see the Jets again get the early jump, but the Fighting Saints clawed their way back with two goals to narrow the Jets' lead to 3-2 at the end of the second period. The Jets continued to pepper Fighting Saints' goaltender Mike Curran, however, and their persistence paid off. The Jets scored three more times in the third period and held off their guests to win by a score of 6-4 before leaving for a two-game Western road trip.

On Saturday night, the Jets returned to Vancouver for their second visit in less than a month to do battle with the 4-6-0 Blazers. The two teams traded goals through regulation time and the Jets had a glorious opportunity to win in overtime, only to have Milt Black's shot go past "Smokey" McLeod after time had expired. The game ended in a 3-3 tie, but the Blazers were the better team and only Daley's exceptional goaltending allowed the Jets to escape with a point. The point came at a price, however, as Dan Spring sustained a shoulder separation and would be lost to the team for two weeks.

The Jets moved on to Edmonton to play the Oilers at the brand-new, $18-million, 15,000-seat Edmonton Coliseum, which was built in only nine months on a previously vacant lot that had once been home to Haywood Lumber. The Oilers opened their new home on Sunday with a 4-1 victory over the Crusaders and hoped to make it two-for-two against the visiting Jets on Wednesday night. Backstopped by veteran goaltender Jacques Plante, who was making his return to the ice after one season behind the Nordiques' bench, the Oilers got a hat trick from Ken Baird and they held off the Jets to win by a score of 5-3.

Pushed back into third place, the Jets returned home to begin a weekend home stand on the night of Friday, 15 November against the 4-9-0 Racers in their first-ever meeting with the expansion team. Before a good crowd of more than 7,700 fans, the Jets used two first period power-play goals to take a 2-0 lead and then broke the game open with three goals in just over two and a half minutes in the third period. Despite the 5-0 final score, Wakely was the star of the night as he stopped 39 shots for the shutout in only his second appearance of the season. The win pulled the 8-2-1 Jets to within three points of the first-place Toros, who were next on the Jets' schedule.

Before a sellout crowd at the Arena that included 501 fans who paid for standing room, the two early season contenders for supremacy in the Canadian Division locked horns for the third time this season on Sunday night. In a dramatic turnaround from their last visit, the Toros kept the Jets bottled up all night long and slowly pulled away from the frustrated home squad. Despite their best efforts, the Jets could only muster a late goal from Johnson in a 3-1 defeat that left them five points behind the division-leading Toros. To make matters worse, the Jets lost Anders Hedberg to a groin injury early in the game and they also lost Ron Ashton to a knee injury.

Did You Know?

The crowd of 10,578 on the night of 17 November 1974 was the largest that the Jets had in their seven seasons in the WHA and it was also the first sellout where Gordie Howe was not a member of the visiting team. All told, the Jets drew a total of 71 five-figure crowds over the course of seven WHA seasons, 16 of which came in the playoffs. The Jets posted a pedestrian 29-23-3 regular season record in those games, but they lost only once in the 16 playoff games where a five-figure crowd was on hand to cheer them to victory.

After suffering their first defeat of the season at home, the Jets were back on a plane bound for Edmonton to battle the Oilers again on Monday night. The Oilers, winners of their last six games, got the early jump on the Jets, but the visitors responded with three in a row, including two within a 28-second span to take a 3-1 lead. Unfortunately, the Oilers dominated the rest of the way and though Wakely, who had come off the bench to replace an injured Daley in the first period, performed admirably, it wasn't enough as the hometown Oilers cruised to another 5-3 victory.

The third-place Jets returned home and got back on the ice for a Wednesday morning skate before meeting the 5-7-0 Fighting Saints that evening for the second time this season. Still without Hedberg and Spring, the Jets were also without Daley, so they turned to Wakely in goal once again to put the brakes on their first two-game losing streak of the season. In front of just over 6,600 onlookers who had braved the windy conditions outside, Wakely responded with an outstanding effort and the Jets gave him all the offensive support he needed in a 3-1 win that kept the 9-4-1 Jets one point behind the second-place Nordiques and five points back of the first-place Toros. Hull scored two of the Jets' three goals to raise his season total to 17.

The Jets were back on the ice on Sunday night when the Roadrunners made their second appearance of the season at the Arena. Nearly 7,000 spectators who had endured the frigid temperatures outside watched as the visitors got on the board first, thanks to an early 5-on-3 power play. From there, the Roadrunners played a close-checking game and eventually wore down the Jets in a 3-1 win. The Jets could only manage 20 shots on Jack Norris, the former Oilers' goaltender, and Veli-Pekka Ketola's first period breakaway goal was the only one that beat him.

On Monday afternoon, the Jets took off for a pair of mid-week games starting Tuesday night in Indianapolis to visit the 4-15-0 Racers at the $20-million, 16,300-seat Market Square Arena. Still without Hedberg, Daley, and Spring, the Jets capitalized on a couple of power play chances to support Larsson, who faced 17 shots in the first period, and take a 2-0 lead to the intermission. From there, the Jets assumed control of the game and only the work of the maskless Andy Brown in the Racers' net kept the score down to 4-0. In making 39 saves, Larsson earned the shutout, marking the second straight time the Jets blanked the expansion Racers, who saw their losing streak stretched to eight games.

The next morning, the Jets flew to Cleveland to meet the Crusaders on Wednesday night in their new home, the $28-million, 19,000-seat Richfield Coliseum. Ernie Wakely returned to the nets to celebrate his 34th birthday, but he was treated rudely in the early going as the Crusaders took a 2-0 lead. The Jets kept pressing and eventually broke through against goaltender Gerry Cheevers, but the game went to overtime tied at 4-4. The Crusaders carried their strong third period into overtime and with 61 seconds left, referee Ron Ego made the evening's most controversial call when he sent Riihiranta off to the box for a tripping minor. Only six seconds were left on the clock when Jim Harrison, the former Oiler who had scored nine goals against the Jets over the past two seasons, lifted the puck over Wakely for his second of the night to give the Crusaders a heart-stopping 5-4 victory. Adding to the Jets' woes was more bad news on the injury front. The Jets lost Norm Beaudin in the second period to a back injury and Ketola had to leave on account of a knee injury. Though he didn't miss any ice time, Larry Hornung was favoring his knee all night after a first period collision with the Crusaders' Wayne Muloin.

The battered Jets flew home to begin a three-game home stand on Friday night against the Stags. A crowd numbering one short of 7,200 had braved the winter chill and saw both teams light up the scoreboard in a wild shootout that went right down to the final seconds as the Jets escaped with a 7-6 victory in the game that featured no fewer than 107 shots on goal. Hull scored four times to raise his season total to 23, feasting against a Stags team that showed some surprising resilience amid rumors of their imminent financial collapse. The game marked Spring's return to the lineup after he missed eight games thanks to a shoulder separation.

Did You Know?

On 29 November 1974, the Jets took 54 shots on the Stags goal and yielded 53 shots. Both marks would stand as single-game highs throughout their seven years in the WHA.

The 11-6-1 Jets opened the month of December on Sunday night when the Nordiques flew in for their first visit of the season. Led by new coach Jean-Guy Gendron and featuring celebrated rookie sensation Real Cloutier, the 12-7-0 Nordiques were off to the best start in franchise history and they held a one-point lead over the third-place Jets.

Before the start of the important divisional matchup, however, Ben Hatskin officially turned over the franchise to Bob Graham, President of Winnipeg Hockey Club Inc., during a center-ice ceremony that also included both Bobby Hull and Danny Johnson. All four posed for the camera while the certificate passed from Hatskin to Graham and songstress Vi Clift bellowed the words, "This team is your team ... this team is my team" to the 10,028 attendees celebrating the successful transfer of ownership.

On the ice, trainer Bill Bozak, known as "Ol' Magic Fingers" and "The Wizard of Gauze," got both Daley and Hedberg ready for action and both were in the lineup once referee Ron Harris dropped the puck. The Jets wiped out an early 1-0 deficit with three first period goals and Daley did the rest, making 28 saves and earning first-star honors in the 3-2 victory that vaulted the Jets into second place, six points behind the first-place Toros.

The Jets concluded their home stand with a Wednesday night engagement against the Aeros, marking the first meeting between the two teams since Gordie Howe & Co. had swept the Jets out of the playoffs back in April. The 16-8-0 Aeros came into town sporting the league's best record and they showed no signs of slowing down in the early part of the season after capturing their first WHA championship this past spring. The Jets had to contend with a formidable opponent without Christian Bordeleau, who had walked out on the team on Monday. At odds with Pilous, Bordeleau spent most of Sunday night's game on the bench and he subsequently asked for a trade.

Before the second consecutive five-figure crowd at the Arena, the Aeros tried to batter the Jets into submission, but it was the Jets who used two first period power-play goals to jump out to a 2-0 lead. The visitors persisted with their tactics and after tying the game late in the second period, they took the lead for good when Gordie Howe stole the puck from Hornung and put a backhand shot past Daley. The frustrated Jets could do little in response and the Aeros masterfully held on to their 3-2 lead the rest of the way and left Winnipeg with two points.

The 12-7-1 Jets left on a Thursday afternoon flight bound for Saint Paul to meet the Fighting Saints on Friday night to begin and end a one-game road trip. It didn't take long before the Jets lost two more key players, as Ulf Nilsson left the ice with a bruised shoulder and Hedberg reaggravated the same groin injury that had kept him out of action for six games. The Fighting Saints took advantage of their weakened guests and controlled most of the action en route to 4-2 victory despite a late charge from the Jets.

A Hat Trick With The Fisticuffs

At the end of the first period on 6 December 1974, Gord Gallant made a beeline for Bobby Hull and got him to drop the gloves for his third fight as a Jet. Hull previously fought Reggie Fleming of the Cougars on 22 December 1972 and traded punches with Ron Garwasiuk of the Sharks on 14 December 1973.

After the game, the Jets announced that they had traded the disgruntled Bordeleau to the Nordiques in exchange for 29-year-old defenseman Alain Beaule. The stockily built Beaule was in the midst of his ninth pro season and second with the Nordiques, after suiting up with five teams in three different minor leagues. Bordeleau was a fan favorite and a team leader during his tenure with the Jets, but the club had no choice but to trade him.

The Jets returned home on Saturday morning for a Sunday night game against the red-hot Cougars. Since their dreadful 2-11-0 start, the Cougars came into Winnipeg winners of seven of their last nine games, including their last five in a row. Fresh off an impressive 9-3 win over the Toros on Saturday night, they flew into Winnipeg to meet a Jets team without Hedberg, who had been forced to give in and rest his ailing groin. The Jets, however, would have Nilsson available, as well as the newly acquired Beaule on the blue line, wearing a jersey bearing the number 28.

In front of a crowd of 8,041, the Jets got off to a quick start, only to lose another player to the injury bug shortly after opening the scoring. Dan Spring hit the boards with the same shoulder he had dislocated a month before and left the ice in considerable pain. Led by the unlikely trio of Milt Black, Danny Johnson, and Norm Beaudin, the Jets still kept up the pressure on the visitors and grabbed a 4-1 lead that they took to the third period. From there, Daley stopped all but one of the 18 shots he faced the rest of the way and the Jets broke their two-game losing streak with a 5-2 victory that kept them one point back of the second-place Nordiques and six back of the first-place Toros. After the game, the Jets learned that Spring's shoulder, as feared, was again separated and that he could be lost to the team for a month.

On Monday afternoon, the Jets left for Indianapolis to kick off a three-game road trip on Tuesday night against the 5-21-0 Racers. The Racers had put an end to a league-record 13-game losing streak on Sunday night when they defeated the Mariners by a score of 5-3, but they still came into the contest with the WHA's worst record and had failed to as much as score a goal in two prior meetings with the Jets.

The Jets showed no mercy to their downtrodden hosts and jumped out to a 3-0 first period lead before the Racers responded with two quick goals of their own midway through the second to narrow the Jets' lead to a single goal. The spunky Racers kept the game close, but the Jets held on for an eventual 5-3 victory.

Two nights later, the Jets met the 7-17-1 Stags at Cobo Hall in Detroit for the first time. Last Saturday, the financially troubled Stags had been forced to trade one of their high-priced stars when they dealt Marc Tardif along with Steve Sutherland to the Nordiques in exchange for Pierre Guite, Alain "Boom Boom" Caron, and Michel Rouleau. Before an intimate gathering of 3,915 onlookers, the Jets opened the scoring five and a half minutes into the game, but it was the Stags who began to take the play to the visitors. After Daley came off the bench to replace an injured Larsson, the Stags tied the score late in the first period, then Guite scored his first two goals as a Stag in the span of 62 seconds early in the second period to give his new team a 3-1 lead. Guite completed his hat trick in the third period and the Stags handed the Jets an embarrassing 5-3 defeat.

The 14-9-1 Jets left Detroit in third place in the hotly contested Canadian Division, three points behind the Nordiques, but only four back of the Toros as they made their way to Houston for a Saturday night date with the Aeros to wrap up their three-game road trip. Hull opened the scoring with his 26th goal of the season, but after the Aeros tied the score late in the first period, they assumed control of the game and broke a 1-1 tie with three unanswered second period goals. Despite a late rally from the Jets, the

Aeros hung on and sealed the victory when Gordie Howe scored his second of the night and the 900th of his illustrious pro career with just over three minutes to play, sending the Jets down to their second consecutive 5-3 defeat.

After the game, while walking back to the hotel, two men approached Perry Miller and forced him at gunpoint to surrender his wallet, jacket, watch, shoes, and a ring that his late father had given him. Thankfully, the men fled without pulling the trigger. Miller and his teammates headed back to Winnipeg on Sunday morning for a game that evening against the Whalers.

Another five-figure crowd greeted the Jets as they took to the ice, but the Whalers opened the scoring while two men short. The Jets struck for two goals in 90 seconds to wipe out the deficit, but the Whalers were all over the Jets in the second period and regained the lead at 4-3. The Jets threw everything they had at the Whalers in the third period, but none of their 14 shots could beat goaltender Al Smith and the Jets lost their third consecutive game for the first time this season. To make matters worse, Hull suffered a sprained left knee in the game's final minute.

Next on the schedule was a pair of critical mid-week divisional meetings starting on Tuesday, 17 December at Maple Leaf Gardens against the Toros, who were without Frank Mahovlich, Bob Leduc and Brit Selby due to injury. Though the Jets were still without Hedberg and Spring, Hull was at least able to go despite the knee problem. The Golden Jet not only suited up, but scored twice in the first period to raise his season total to 29. His teammates did the rest in shutting down the high-flying Toros and the Jets went on to a 4-1 victory.

Still three points back of the second-place Nordiques, the Jets left for Quebec on Wednesday morning to do battle with the Nordiques that evening. A festive atmosphere filled Le Colisee and the Nordiques thrilled the crowd of 12,037 by scoring three times in the first period and easily handing the Jets a 5-1 defeat. Not only did the Jets suffer a humiliating defeat, but they lost Nilsson in the second period to an injured elbow. He had been hurt during last night's victory in Toronto, but the pain flared up so badly that he couldn't shoot or reach for the puck. In addition, the Jets faced Bordeleau for the first time as an opponent and he set up two of the Nordiques' five goals on the night to add further insult to the loss that put a five-point cushion between the two teams in the standings.

The 15-12-1 Jets returned home for a Sunday evening matchup with the Roadrunners and joining them was 27-year-old defenseman Thommie Bergman, formerly of the Detroit Red Wings. Bergman had signed with the Jets on Saturday for a reported salary of $90,000 after clearing waivers following his refusal to report to the Red Wings' AHL affiliate in Norfolk, Virginia. Like many of new teammates, the native of Munkfors, Sweden had been battling the injury bug and he was just coming off a groin problem.

Fortunately, Nilsson's elbow had healed enough during the time between games and Hedberg's groin was well enough for him to get back in the lineup, but Veli-Pekka Ketola had injured his knee in a collision with Hull during Friday's practice and would have to watch the game from the sidelines.

The crowd of 9,298 that made its way through the two inches of snow outside saw the Jets open the scoring a minute and a half into the contest, but the Roadrunners responded with two of their own before the first period was over. The Jets tied the score on Hull's 30th goal of the season early in the second period, but the opportunistic Roadrunners capitalized on their chances while the Jets could get no more past Gary Kurt in the Roadrunners' net. The end result was a disheartening 4-2 defeat that knocked the Jets down to fourth place, one point behind the Oilers and just two ahead of the cellar-dwelling Blazers.

On the day after Christmas, the Jets began a five-game road trip with their first appearance in Phoenix for a rematch with the Roadrunners. Bergman travelled with the team and would make his Jets debut, but to clear space on the roster, the Jets dealt Bob Woytowich to the Racers for unspecified future considerations. The trade of Woytowich had long been expected and he became the second original member of the squad to be traded this month.

Before a sellout crowd of 12,621, the two teams traded goals until Mike Ford's shot from the point beat Jack Norris and broke a 2-2 tie with just under nine minutes to play in regulation time. The Jets hung on and escaped with a 3-2 victory that lifted them back into third place and put an end to the Roadrunners' six-game winning streak.

Back To The Future

Many historians mark the Jets' debut in Arizona on 10 October 1996 when the relocated franchise defeated the San Jose Sharks by a score of 4-1 at America West Arena following 24 seasons in Winnipeg. However, the Jets played their first game in the Valley of the Sun on 26 December 1974 when they defeated the WHA Phoenix Roadrunners by a score of 3-2 at the Arizona Veterans Memorial Coliseum.

The road trip continued on Saturday night when the Jets made their first appearance in San Diego against the 15-15-1 Mariners. The Jets jumped out to a 2-0 lead, only to have the Mariners roar back to take the lead at 3-2. Hull's second goal of the night evened the score, but a minute and a half later, an ugly brawl began when Michel Rouleau started fighting with Curt Larsson while Bergman was pummeling Andre Lacroix. Kevin Morrison joined the altercation in Lacroix's defense and both benches emptied. The result was two ejections, a misconduct and four fighting majors. During the fracas, Rouleau pulled on Larsson's hair and nearly fainted when he saw that he had pulled off Larsson's wig instead. The game eventually resumed and Ron Ashton broke a 4-4 tie with only 68 seconds left in regulation time and Anders Hedberg's empty-net goal sealed a 6-4 victory.

Making It Count

Ron "Bam Bam" Ashton's goal at 18:52 of the third period on 28 December 1974 in San Diego proved to be the game-winner in a 6-4 Jets' victory over the Mariners. The goal would be his first and only one in major pro hockey.

One night later, the Jets were back on the ice in Houston against the Aeros. On the strength of a big second period, the Jets took a 3-1 lead to the final frame, but sadly, the travel-weary visitors ran out of gas and the Aeros took full advantage, scoring five times to post a 6-3 victory that put the brakes on the Jets' brief two-game winning streak.

The 17-14-1 Jets were not scheduled to make their first appearance of 1975 until Tuesday, 7 January, but during the break, they parted company with another original Jet when they dealt Ernie Wakely to the Mariners. Wakely was left as the odd man out in the three-headed goaltending logjam and the cash-strapped Jets found a willing trading partner in the Mariners. Wakely wanted a new deal from the Mariners in return for waiving the no-trade clause in his contract, but in the end, he agreed to the trade without the new contract. Under the terms of the deal, the Jets would receive no compensation from the Mariners if Wakely did not sign a new contract with San Diego, but if he did, the Jets would get the rights to any Mariners' player other than Andre Lacroix who was involved in a contract dispute within the next two years.

The Jets returned to game action at the Richfield Coliseum for the fourth of their five-game road trip. With them was Dan Spring, who was back in the lineup after a ten-game absence following his second shoulder separation of the season. The Jets shook off the rust after their lengthy layoff and scored the game's first two goals against a Crusaders team playing its third game with General Manager Jack Vivian behind the bench after the surprising dismissal of coach John Hanna on Saturday. The Crusaders turned the tables on the Jets in the second period and scored three times to take the lead, but Hedberg scored twice in the span of three and a half minutes late in the third to give the Jets a slim 4-3 lead. The lead held up until the final minute of regulation time when Rich Leduc put the puck past Daley in the middle of a goalmouth scramble to tie the score at 4-4. Both teams had their chances through overtime but neither team could score and the game ended in a draw.

The extended road swing came to a conclusion two nights later at Cobo Hall against the 12-25-3 Stags, who had become wards of the league since the Jets were last in Detroit. The Jets, along with each of the other WHA clubs, were on the hook for a monthly payment of $10,000 to keep the Stags afloat, but the Jets at least got their money's worth in the early going with two goals in the first five minutes of the game. Instead of putting their troubled hosts away, however, the Jets let up on the throttle and the Stags took full advantage by coming back from a 4-2 second period deficit to tie the score at 4-4. At one point, a frustrated Daley, in the middle of a 17-shot barrage in the middle frame, flung the puck over the glass behind him after making a save. The game went to overtime, when Steve West's shot went through Daley's legs and into the net to send the gathering of 3,125 die-hard fans home with a smile, while the sullen visitors boarded a plane bound for Winnipeg and a Friday night date with the Nordiques.

Stag-gering Out

The Michigan Stags' 5-4 overtime win over the Jets on the night of 9 January 1975 would be both their last win as the Stags and last appearance in Detroit. They played their last game on 18 January in a 2-1 loss at the hands of the Cleveland Crusaders at the Richfield Coliseum and five days later, the WHA announced that the team would be relocated to Baltimore for the remainder of the 1974-1975 season and be known as the Blades. The league would continue to operate the team and seek local ownership to purchase the franchise.

For the first time since before Christmas, the Jets made an appearance at the Arena where the first-place Nordiques were waiting for them. Undeterred by the four inches of snow, high winds and unseasonably bitter cold temperatures, a crowd of 10,067 was in attendance, the fifth five-figure crowd of the season. The Jets opened the scoring just two and a half minutes into the contest, but they proved to be no match for the Nordiques and goaltender Richard Brodeur as the visitors cruised to a 6-1 victory in a game that featured no fewer than six fights. The win enabled the Nordiques to extend their lead over the fourth-place Jets to a dozen points.

Two nights later, the Jets were scheduled to meet the Indianapolis Racers, but a major winter storm rolled into Winnipeg on Saturday. The winds reached 60 mph and 7½ inches of snow forced the airport to close for 34 hours, which not only kept the Nordiques from leaving Winnipeg, but it kept the Racers from reaching Winnipeg and, as a result, the game was postponed.

The First "White Out"

Though the "White Out" would later become a storied Winnipeg Jets tradition, the first "White Out" occurred on 12 January 1975, when the scheduled game between the Jets and the Indianapolis Racers was postponed on account of a snowstorm.

With his team in a tailspin, Rudy Pilous tried a new approach during Tuesday's practice. He had the Jets turn their sticks upside down during the session, but they were back in proper position when the Jets returned to game action on the night of Wednesday, 15 January against the Blazers. Despite a Booster Club giveaway of free sticks to the first 700 children, a season-low crowd of only 5,786 was on hand to see the lowly Blazers break a 2-2 tie with two third period goals and skate off with a 4-2 victory in a dull affair befitting a game featuring the division's bottom feeders. The Blazers not only broke their six-game losing streak at the Jets' expense, but they pulled even with the Jets in the standings, giving both teams an equal share of the Canadian Division basement. Losers of four of their last five games and still winless since the start of the new year, the Jets had some time between games to stew about their declining fortunes before their next game on Sunday night against the Crusaders.

During the break, there was still plenty of activity off the ice. The Jets attended a Thursday luncheon sponsored by the Manitoba Major Junior Hockey League's Charleswood Hawks, a team coached by Ab McDonald, their former captain. During the luncheon, Hull made headlines when he said, "my last dream is to see the two leagues together," in reference to a potential merger between the WHA and NHL. The Jets also made a roster move that day, assigning Ron Ashton to Roanoke of the Southern Hockey League, and recalling Randy Andreachuk from Roanoke.

On Friday, the Jets made one more roster move when they purchased the contract of 37-year-old Howie Young from the Roadrunners. In his 16th pro season, which included NHL stops with the Detroit Red Wings, Chicago Blackhawks and Vancouver Canucks, he was at odds with coach Sandy Hucul in Phoenix and was relegated to bench-warming duties. As a result, the Roadrunners sought to trade the popular Young, and they found three potential trading partners in the Racers, Cougars and Jets. Young was given the option and chose the Jets for the opportunity to play with Hull, his former roommate in Chicago. Though he had battled alcohol problems earlier in his career, he had been sober for nine years and he would bring a tough and vibrant personality into the Jets' locker room.

Forever Young

During his hockey career, Howie Young appeared in the movie None But The Brave, starring Frank Sinatra, and also appeared in Young Guns and Young Guns II after his playing days.

The Jets made more changes on Saturday when they shook up the front office. Pilous was effectively given Bill Robinson's job, while Robinson was made Chief Scout, reporting to Pilous. Though Pilous was still officially left with his coaching responsibilities, he would not be behind the bench and the coaching job effectively fell back to Hull. The explanation the Jets gave for the move was that the team needed more emphasis on building up depth on the roster and that, with the players grumbling about Pilous, a spark was needed with a coaching change.

Before the Jets got back on the ice on Sunday evening, the first general meeting of Winnipeg Hockey Club, Inc. took place that afternoon. Nearly 600 people were there to not only hear the announcement of the latest moves, but also that the Jets had received approval on Friday from the Government of Manitoba for a lottery. Jack Watts, chairman of the Jets' lotteries committee, told the gathering that tickets would cost $1 and the top prize would be $50,000. Jack Shields, chairman of the Jets' finance committee, informed the attendees that the projected operating losses that had been originally forecast at $50,000 were, in fact, only $5,700. The Jets would even have been running at a profit were it not for the $25,000 that the Jets and each of the other WHA clubs had had to contribute to keep the Stags afloat. In addition, 26 founders and 24 subscribers were elected by acclamation to the Board of Directors.

Board of Directors
Winnipeg Hockey Club, Inc.

Founders	Subscribers
Mr. Brian Aronovitch	Mr. R.S. Abbott
Mr. Neil Baker	Mr. Wm. Addison
Mr. Ivan Berkowitz	Mr. Aime Allaire
Mr. R. Bevis	Mr. Gary Bigwood
Mr. J.W. Burns	Mr. Bernard Christophe
Mr. J.A. Carson	Mr. Paul N. Duval
Mr. A.D. Cohen	Mr. Ted Foreman
Mr. Art Coulter	Mr. Ken Galanchuk
Mr. R.T. Curtis	Mr. John Gee
Mr. D.H. Gales	Mrs. Rose Glesby
Mr. R.G. Graham	Mr. Julian G. Klymkiw
Mr. Oscar Grubert	Mr. John B. Klumper
Mr. Ben Hatskin	Mr. Ken Kronson
Judge Ben Hewak	Mr. Howard O. Larke
Mr. A.R. Huband	Mr. E.J. Mazur
Mr. L.A. Landes	Mr. K.M. McLean
Mrs. W.A. Marr	Mr. L.O. Pollard
Mr. D.A. McCarthy	Mr. J.D. Raleigh
The Hon. W.J. McKeag	Mr. Charles R. Riess
Mrs. M.H. Nemy	Mrs. Anne Rogan
Mr. C.S. Riley	Mr. Ray Ross
Mr. D.S. Rogers	Mrs. Marguerite Scribner
Mr. W.E. Shields	Mr. David E. Smith
Mr. Gary J. Simkin	Dr. Gerry Wilson
Mr. Nestor W. Swystun	
Mr. J. D. Watts	

After a five-day break between games, the Jets and a gathering of 7,073 hardy fans welcomed the Crusaders to Winnipeg for their first visit of the season. Trailing 4-2 entering the third period, the Jets exploded with seven unanswered goals to post a 9-4 victory. Hull scored twice to give him 38 for the season, while Hedberg scored four times for his first hat trick as a Jet. Young contributed a goal in his Jets debut as the Jets put a decisive end to their five-game winless streak.

Did You Know?

The seven goals that the Jets scored in the third period on 19 January 1975 was the highest total that they would score in any single period in their seven years in the WHA.

On Tuesday night, Joe Daley, Lars-Erik Sjoberg, Bobby Hull, and Ulf Nilsson suited up for the West squad that defeated the East by a score of 6-4 in the WHA's third annual All-Star Game before 15,326 fans at the new Edmonton Coliseum. Hull scored once for the victorious West squad, but for the first time, he was there only as a player, since Bill Dineen of the defending champion Aeros was given the coaching responsibility.

The four All-Stars flew back to Winnipeg to rejoin their teammates for a Wednesday night game against the Racers for what was scheduled to be the Racers' second appearance of the home stand. Though there was another Booster Club giveaway of a free Nilsson button to the first 1,000 children, the crowd was held down to only 6,127 as the extreme cold was keeping an icy grip on the Manitoba capital. Hull opened the scoring late in the first period with his 39th goal of the season, but the maskless Andy Brown stood tall and kept the Jets from adding to their lead. Brown's teammates responded with two goals and they shut the Jets down the rest of the way. An empty-net marker in the dying seconds put the final nail in the Jets' coffin and they went down to a stinging 3-1 defeat.

Not only did the loss send the 18-18-2 Jets into sole possession of the Canadian Division cellar, but they lost Duke Asmundson to a season-ending injury. Early in the second period, Racers' defenseman Ken Desjardine had checked him into the boards and he fell awkwardly on his leg. After the game, it was confirmed that his leg was broken and that he would be lost for four months.

The Jets had no time to feel sorry for themselves as they hastily boarded a plane bound for Edmonton to play the Oilers on the night of Thursday, 23 January. The Oilers jumped out to a 3-0 first period lead and though the Jets made a game of it in the second, the Oilers pulled away with four more goals in the third to coast to a 7-3 victory. Blair MacDonald scored three times for the Oilers, while Mike Rogers added a pair in the rout. Hull scored twice for the Jets to lift his season total to 41, but it was far from enough as the Jets' record dipped below the .500 mark for the first time this season.

It was on to Vancouver for the reeling Jets, who wrapped up a grueling stretch of three games in three nights with a Friday night encounter against the Blazers. The Jets scored the game's first two goals, but the Blazers began to put on the pressure in the second period. The Blazers finally broke through against a stubborn Curt Larsson with a pair of third period goals that wiped out a 3-1 Jets' lead, sending the game to overtime. In the extra period, Butch Deadmarsh jammed the puck past Larsson for a 4-3 victory that sent the Jets down to their third defeat in as many nights.

Back home, the Jets' family grew by one on Sunday morning when Ulf and Barbro Nilsson welcomed their daughter Anna into the world. The proud father was on the ice that night with the rest of his teammates as they met the Aeros before the traditional sellout crowd at the Arena to see Gordie Howe. The Jets wasted a number of early power play opportunities early in the contest and the Aeros made them pay by scoring twice in the second period on their way to an eventual 3-1 victory. The loss put the last-place Jets six points behind the Blazers as they hit the road for four games starting Tuesday night in San Diego.

The scoring started early and continued at a furious pace throughout the contest. The Jets scored nine of the game's 16 goals, all against Ernie Wakely, their former teammate, and they captured the victory that put an end to their four-game losing streak. Hedberg scored three times for his second hat trick in just over a week, while Hull added a pair, which gave him 43 on the season. The action continued even after the game, where Alain Beaule and Perry Miller became involved in a fracas with some unruly Mariners fans. Fortunately, both players and the rest of their teammates were unharmed, and the Jets escaped Southern California and headed for Phoenix.

On Thursday night, the Jets continued their road trip against the Roadrunners, who scored three times in less than two minutes to grab a 3-1 first period lead. The Jets collected themselves and tied the score before the intermission, then they took the lead when Hedberg scored his second of the night early in the third period. The visitors used a solid team effort to keep the lead and Hull put the game away into an empty net as the Jets won by a score of 5-3.

The Jets moved on to Saint Paul to meet the Fighting Saints on Sunday night to begin the month of February. Moments before the game, former Michigan Stag Danny Gruen joined the team after the Jets signed the 22-year-old winger to a contract for the remainder of the season, along with an option for next season. Gruen had refused to follow the Stags to Baltimore when the franchise relocated just over a week ago and the Jets matched an offer from the Whalers to sign him. Gruen had tallied 10 goals and 16 assists in 34 games during the season and he had just returned after recovering from a knee injury. The Roadrunners and the Fighting Saints also had interest in Gruen, but the native of Thunder Bay, Ontario chose the Jets. In return for Gruen, the Jets offered Baltimore two players out of a list of 10 currently on their active roster.

Gruen had spent the last season in the Detroit Red Wings' organization and had signed a three-year deal with the Stags during the off-season. He was promised a car as a signing bonus, but after not receiving one, team management told him to go buy one and they would look after the payments. Those checks, along with his regular paychecks, either bounced or came back marked non-sufficient funds.

The crowd of 10,165, which included 97 members of the Jets Booster Club who traveled from Winnipeg, saw the Jets rally to tie the score after trailing by a pair in the third period. With the score tied at 4-4, the game went to overtime, when George Morrison knocked the puck out of mid-air and past Curt Larsson for his second goal of the night, giving the Fighting Saints a 5-4 victory. The overtime loss spoiled Larsson's 45-save performance in his finest game as a Jet, and again sent the enthusiastic and loyal boosters home disappointed.

The 20-22-2 Jets left for Cleveland on Tuesday to finish their road trip against the Crusaders on Wednesday night still in firm control of the Canadian Division's basement. The Jets shook off their Sunday night setback and controlled the first half of the game, but they only had a 1-0 lead to show for their efforts. Once the Crusaders tied the score late in the second period, however, they took over the play for the rest of the game and handed the Jets a 3-2 defeat. During the latter stages of the game, Joe Daley was visibly angry and his temper boiled over in the dressing room once the game was over. He told the *Winnipeg Free Press*, "I wouldn't play here again next season if they gave me the Richardson Building," and specifically called out Thommie Bergman as someone who "floats out there."

Six points back of the fourth-place Blazers and a whopping 24 points behind the first-place Nordiques, the Jets returned home to battle the Whalers on Friday night. Before the game, the Jets pared the roster, sending both Ron Snell and Randy Andreachuk to Roanoke. Snell balked at the assignment, so he was instead assigned to the Cape Codders of the North American Hockey League (NAHL). The demotions had come as a result of the recent acquisitions of both Danny Gruen and Howie Young. Prior to making his home debut as a Jet, however, Gruen had to shave his mustache before the game to comply with a long-standing club rule.

Buoyed by groups from across Manitoba and some who made the 350-mile trek from Regina, a crowd of 8,077 braved the winter cold to see the action, but the Jets did little in the opening minutes to warm their hearts. The Jets did bounce back, however, and Gruen's first goal as a Jet gave his new team a 4-3 lead early in the third period. Later in the period, the Whalers tied the goal on a soft shot that eluded Larsson and then won the game with a goal late in overtime to send the Jets down to their third consecutive defeat and seventh loss in their last nine games. The Jets gave it a solid effort, but they could not overcome a poor outing from Larsson to subdue the Eastern Division leaders.

The next night, the Jets moved on to Chicago for their first visit of the season to the International Amphitheater. Before the game, the Jets made yet another roster move, adding 21-year-old forward Robbie Neale. The Jets picked up the Winnipeg native from the Crusaders for future considerations and he was most recently playing in Cape Cod. Neale was in only his second year of pro hockey and had one goal and three assists in nine games with the Crusaders this season.

The Jets opened the scoring 23 seconds into the contest, but it was the Cougars, losers of nine of their last 10 games, who took over the game, scoring four times in the first period and adding a pair of goals in the second en route to a 6-3 victory. Not only did the Jets suffer their fourth straight loss, but they had lost Daley on account of a strained back muscle late in the second period when the Cougars' Rosaire Paiement fell on top of him. Daley remained in pain for several hours after the game and even had trouble breathing.

A season-low five games under the .500 mark, the Jets returned home for a Sunday night rematch with the Cougars. Daley's back wasn't feeling any better, so they made a call that afternoon to Terry Ross, a 23-year-old University of Manitoba student who had been playing for the St. Boniface Mohawks of the Central Amateur Senior Hockey League, to come and suit up as Larsson's backup. Ross had played in Austria last season after starring with the University of Winnipeg Wesmen. Ross had also previously attended the Atlanta Flames' training camp.

Despite the $2 discount offered to local hockey and ringette teams, along the unusual promotion of offering the same discount to anyone showing proof of U.S. citizenship, a smaller than normal gathering of 6,316 spectators watched as the Jets frittered away a 2-0 first period lead, only to get it back on Danny Johnson's goal in the latter half of the second period. From there, the Jets, backstopped by Larsson, held on and escaped with a 3-2 victory, barely putting an end to their four-game losing streak.

Did You Know?

Terry Ross, the Jets' backup goaltender on 9 February 1975, had a forgettable game on Saturday, 23 January 1971, while tending goal for the University of Winnipeg Wesmen. Ross and the Wesmen were on the wrong end of a 14-3 score when they faced the University of British Columbia Thunderbirds in front of gathering of around 1,500 at Thunderbird Arena. Ross faced a total of 60 shots during the game, including 30 in the third period when he yielded 10 goals. Ironically, two members of the Thunderbirds' roster, goaltender Ian Wilkie and centerman Bob McAneeley, would go on to play in the WHA and against the Jets.

The Jets had a few days to catch their breath before their next game on Wednesday, 12 February against the Toros. Despite their victory on Sunday night, the Jets were still eight points back of the fourth-place Blazers and 18 points behind the second-place Toros, led by new coach Bob Leduc, who had hung up the blades to take over for Billy Harris behind the bench. On the injury front, Daley's back was well enough for him to make the start, but this time, it was Larsson who couldn't go on account of a knee problem that would need off-season surgery. As a result, the Jets were again forced to turn to Ross as their backup goaltender and hope that Daley could make it through the game.

A good crowd of 7,773 fans turned out in spite of the extended cold spell and they saw the Jets roar back from a 4-1 second period deficit to tie the game at 4-4 before intermission. The Jets continued pressing in the third period only to have the Toros score three times in the first half of the period to extinguish the Jets' hopes of winning their second in a row.

On Valentine's Day, the Jets began another three-game weekend on Friday night against the Aeros. With the team not responding any better under Hull, Rudy Pilous decided to reassume the coaching duties and he was behind the bench for the first time since mid-January. Before the game started, however, the customary Gordie Howe sellout crowd saw Winnipeg city councillor C. John Gee and Manitoba Premier Ed Schreyer make hockey's elder statesman an honorary citizen of Winnipeg in an on-ice ceremony.

For the second straight game, the Jets fell behind early, but they stormed back and wiped out a 3-1 deficit to take a 4-3 lead to the third period. The Aeros fired 14 shots on the Jets' goal in the third period, but Larsson, making his return to the nets after having his knee artificially frozen, was the difference in holding the visitors off the scoreboard for the rest of the game. As time was expiring, Hull sped down the ice and fired a shot that went past Ron Grahame for his third of the night and his 50th goal in his 50th game. Wild celebrations ensued and even the Aeros offered their congratulations to the Golden Jet. More importantly, however, the Jets captured a much-needed 5-3 victory.

50 In 32

On 14 February 1975, Bobby Hull made history by scoring his 50th goal in his 50th game, but he actually scored in only 32 of the 50 games. During the streak, he scored against all of the other teams in the WHA at least once except for the Nordiques and his nine goals against the relocated Michigan Stags was the highest total of any opponent he faced. Stags' goaltender and good friend Gerry Desjardins yielded six goals, making him Hull's favorite victim, followed closely behind by Gilles Gratton and Jacques Plante, who each yielded five goals to the Golden Jet. He also scored twice against Ernie Wakely, who had started the season with the Jets, and only one of the 50 goals came into an empty net. Hull had one four-goal game, three three-goal games, and ten two-goal games as part of the 32 games he scored in.

Did You Know?

On 14 February 1975, Jetstakes tickets officially went on sale to the public. The tickets for the Jets lottery, available for $1 each, would have 14 winners matched with each of the 14 teams of the WHA at a drawing held on 10 May 1975. There would be a total prize pool of $50,000 distributed as follows:

Prize	Recipient(s)
$25,000	Ticket holder of the team winning the AVCO World Trophy.
$12,000	Ticket holder of the team that lost in the AVCO World Trophy final.
$2,500	Ticket holders of the two losing teams in the second round of the playoffs.
$1,250	Ticket holders of the four losing teams in the first round of the playoffs.
$500	Ticket holders of the six teams that did not qualify for the playoffs.

Manitoba Premier Ed Schreyer purchased the first ticket and Gordie Howe sold that ticket to him.

One night after the fanfare, the 22-26-2 Jets, who remained in firm control of the division basement, were back on the ice against the Crusaders at the Arena. Led by the line of Dan Spring, Veli-Pekka Ketola, and Danny Gruen, the Jets shook off an early Crusaders' goal and cruised to a well-earned 5-1 victory.

The Jets arrived at the Winnipeg International Airport on Sunday morning for their flight to Chicago, only to be delayed for seven hours before they could take off. Barely making it to the International Amphitheater in time for the game, the Jets scored three times in the first three minutes of play and held a 5-1 lead before the Cougars rallied for a pair of goals. However, they could get no closer and Danny Johnson sealed the 6-3 victory with his third of the night to collect his first hat trick as a Jet.

Proud owners of their first three-game winning streak since early November, the Jets moved on to Baltimore on Tuesday night to play the Blades for the first time since they were the Michigan Stags. The Jets overcame both an early second period 3-1 deficit and bad ice at the Baltimore Civic Center with four straight goals in a 5-3 victory. Anders Hedberg's goal with 2:47 left in the third period broke a 3-3 tie and stood up as the game-winner as the Jets kept the Blades still without a win since leaving Detroit.

The Jets returned to the Baltimore Hilton for some shut-eye before their Wednesday 6:15 a.m. wake-up call to head for home and begin a six-game home stand against the Oilers that evening. Still four points back of the fourth-place Blazers and five back of the third-place Oilers, but with a four-game winning streak in tow, the Jets wiped out an early 1-0 deficit and dominated their equally travel-weary guests as they went on to post a 4-1 victory that evened their record at 26-26-2. Though many of the 8,736 paying customers were late on account of a mixup on the starting time, they saw their team extend its winning streak to a season-high five games.

After a few days of rest, the Jets were back on the ice on Sunday, 23 February to entertain the Whalers before a crowd of 10,042 fans, marking the seventh time this season the Jets had drawn more than 10,000 to a game at the Arena. Though both teams had plenty of chances, the game became a battle of goaltenders as former roommates Joe Daley and Al Smith matched each other save for save. The Jets pressed hard in the third period to break the 1-1 deadlock, but Smith was at his best in the closing minutes of regulation time. Midway through the extra period, Tom Webster's shot rang off the inside of the goal post and past Daley to hand the Jets their first loss in six games.

Game three of the six-game home stand took place two nights later as the Fighting Saints made their last scheduled appearance of the season at the Arena for a rare Tuesday night home game. Unlike Sunday night's game, the goals came at a furious pace, but both teams split 12 goals down the middle and each club had to settle for a single point.

Still three points behind the fourth-place Blazers and four back of the third-place Oilers, the 26-27-3 Jets opened a weekend series on Friday night against the Mariners, who were making their first Winnipeg appearance since they called Cherry Hill home. Both teams battled right down to the wire, but the Jets took the lead for good when Hull scored his 55th goal of the season with just under three minutes to play in regulation time to break a 3-3 tie. From there, the Jets did a masterful job in holding off the Mariners to earn the 4-3 victory. In defeat, Wakely was outstanding in his return to Winnipeg, but though his 32-save performance earned him second-star honors, it was his former team that captured the two points before a crowd of more than 9,500 spectators.

The two teams went at it once again on Sunday night and opened the month of March before nearly 9,700 onlookers who had come to see the rematch. The Jets didn't let the bad Arena ice slow them down and they eventually took a 4-2 second period lead, but they let up in the third period and it cost them. The Mariners scored twice to tie the score and the game ended in a 4-4 tie after a scoreless overtime period. Wakely turned in another stellar performance that, this time, paid off in a single point for his new team. Despite the disappointing loss of a point, the tie lifted the Jets into a tie with the fourth-place Blazers to give them some company in the cellar of the Canadian Division.

The marathon home stand ended on Wednesday night with a visit from the Crusaders. Ulf Nilsson scored in each of the first two periods to give the Jets a 2-0 lead, only to have the Crusaders respond with two of their own to tie the score midway through the third period. The visitors had the Jets on the run, but the Jets picked up a fluky goal that gave them a one-goal lead that they made stand up as the game-winner. In the final minute, Hull sent a shot towards the empty Crusaders goal when goaltender Gerry Cheevers, who had been pulled for an extra attacker, left the bench to stop the puck. Referee Brent Casselman awarded the Jets a goal, making the final score 4-2 in the Jets' favor.

With the six-game home stand behind them, the Jets left town to begin a five-game road trip on Friday night in Phoenix. After the two teams split four first period goals, the Roadrunners took the lead for good in the second period and pulled away in the third to hand the Jets a 7-4 defeat. The Jets wasted an outstanding effort by Daley and two-goal performances from both Hull and Hedberg in suffering their first loss in five games. Hull's pair of goals raised his season total to 59.

The Jets moved on to San Diego to meet the Mariners on Saturday night, where they jumped out to a 2-0 first period lead, only to have the Mariners dominate the second period to take a 4-2 lead to the intermission. The Jets regrouped and got back in the game, but Norm Ferguson's goal with 8:15 to play in regulation time broke a 5-5 tie and Wakely shut the door on his former team to preserve a 6-5 Mariners' victory.

On Sunday night, the Jets finished off their three-game weekend with a date in Saint Paul against the Fighting Saints. Playing without Lars-Erik Sjoberg, who had finally succumbed to the effects of a shoulder injury he sustained against the Crusaders on Wednesday night, the Jets fell behind by a score of 5-2 early in the third period and looked to be well on their way to their third loss in as many nights. However, the exhausted visitors summoned some reserves and found the strength to rally and eventually tie the score on Veli-Pekka Ketola's marker with only ten seconds to play in regulation time. The Jets continued to press the issue into overtime, where Ketola scored his second of the night three minutes into the extra period to give the Jets a dramatic come-from-behind 6-5 victory.

The Jets moved on to meet the Whalers on Tuesday night in their inaugural appearance at the new Hartford Civic Center. After playing their home games in Springfield, Massachusetts earlier in the season, the Whalers moved into their new rink in January and a crowd of 10,507 saw the Jets draw first blood. As he had the last time the two teams met, goaltender Al Smith held firm and kept the Jets' lead to a single goal entering the second period. The Whalers then took control of the contest, and led by Fred O'Donnell's hat trick, they cruised to a 6-2 victory, handing the Jets their third loss in four games.

One night later, the Jets wound up their crippling five-game, 12-stop, cross-continent junket in Quebec against the first-place Nordiques. The Jets looked every bit like a team running on fumes, but they found the energy to come back from a 3-1 deficit to tie the game at 3-3. That's all they could muster, however, and the Nordiques scored the game's final two goals and skated off with a 5-3 victory that extended the margin between them and the fifth-place Jets to a virtually insurmountable 22 points. Aside from seeing the miserable road trip come to an end, the only bright spot for the Jets was Hull's two-goal performance that gave him 62 on the season, surpassing the old league record of 61 goals in a season, set by Danny Lawson of the then-Philadelphia Blazers in 1972-1973.

With only 14 games left in the regular season and five points in arrears of the last wild-card playoff position, the 29-31-4 Jets returned home to start a three-game home stand on Friday, 14 March in a rematch against the Nordiques. The Jets welcomed Sjoberg back into the lineup after a three-game absence and they proceeded to pepper Richard Brodeur in the Nordiques' net. Though Brodeur proved to be a formidable foe, Hull's 63rd goal of the season midway through the third period broke a 3-3 tie and gave the Jets an eventual 4-3 victory. The Jets fired a total of 51 shots at Brodeur and needed them all to send the standing-room-only crowd of 10,416 home happy.

On Sunday night, the Jets played host to the slumping Oilers, who were being coached once again by General Manager Bill Hunter after he had relieved Brian Shaw of his coaching duties just over a week ago. Shaw had reportedly lost 30 pounds since Christmas and had requested the change due to "severe strain and tension." Playing their third game in as many nights, the Oilers were no match for the Jets and the competitive phase of the game ended in the early minutes as the Jets routed their guests by a score of 10-1. The 31-31-4 Jets remained in the cellar, but they closed to within three points of the last wild-card playoff position. In addition to the victory, Hull completed his hat trick in the closing moments, giving him 66 goals on the season.

Did You Know?

Milt Black's goal that opened the scoring at 5:52 of the first period on 16 March 1975 would prove to be the last goal in North America for the original Jet. He would go on to play for Sodertalje SK in Sweden, where he tallied 28 goals in 66 games over the next two seasons. Ironically, while Black was in Sweden, he lived in Curt Larsson's house.

The Jets were off until Wednesday when the Blazers came calling for their second visit of the season. For the second straight game, a crowd of close to 10,000 spectators was on hand and they saw the Jets pick up right where they had left off on Sunday night. Five different scorers paced the Jets to a 5-1 second period lead before they eased up on the throttle and let the Blazers back into the contest. The Blazers managed to creep back to within a pair of goals, but the Jets, led by their top line of Hull, Nilsson, and Hedberg, pulled away in the third period with three more goals to put the game away. The 8-3 victory pulled the Jets even with the Blazers and kept them within three points of the Mariners, who held down the last wild-card playoff position. Larsson, who was making his second consecutive start in goal, aggravated his ailing knee, but he was able to finish the game and join his teammates for the start of another three-game weekend beginning Friday night in Hartford.

In front of a packed house at the Hartford Civic Center, Joe Daley held his team in the game in the early going. The Jets rebounded and broke open a 2-2 tie with four third period goals to claim a 6-3 victory, marking their first win in five tries this season against the Whalers. Hedberg scored three times to record his third hat trick of the season and Hull added one to raise his season total to 69.

The Jets moved on to Chicago to battle the 28-41-1 Cougars on Saturday night, where a season-high crowd of 7,504 turned out to see Hull for his last appearance of the season in the city he had once called home. It was Cougars, however, who instead put on a show in the first period. Both Daley and the Jets weathered the 23-shot barrage and erased a 1-0 deficit with two second period goals on their way to a 4-2 victory. Hull scored his 70th goal of the season to delight the Chicago fans as the Jets won their fifth in a row.

Farewell To The Windy City

On 22 March 1975, Bobby Hull played his last game in Chicago, a city where he starred for 15 seasons as a Blackhawk. Over the course of three seasons as a Jet, Hull scored a total of nine goals in Chicago and added eight more in Winnipeg against the Cougars.

Did You Know?

On 22 March 1975, Danny Johnson, the Jets' second captain and an original Jet, scored his last goal as a professional. Fittingly, the goal also proved to be the game-winner in the Jets' 4-2 win over the Chicago Cougars.

The two teams returned to Winnipeg for a Sunday night rematch before an overflow crowd at the Arena. The last standing room ticket was sold an hour before the game, leaving the people at the box office to have to turn fans away. Both teams showed signs of fatigue in the first period, but the action picked up as the game went on. With the score tied at 3-3 in the third period, Veli-Pekka Ketola put a rebound shot past Cougars' goaltender Dave Dryden with only 70 seconds to play in regulation time and the Jets held the fort the rest of the way for a 4-3 victory.

Riding high with a six-game winning streak under their belt, the Jets left to begin a three-game road trip in Indianapolis on Tuesday, 25 March in the hopes of keeping up the pressure on the Mariners and Fighting Saints, who held the two wild-card playoff positions. Hull's two first period goals got the Jets out to a 2-0 lead, but the 18-49-3 Racers continued to battle hard and shook off a pair of disallowed goals to eventually tie the score with a pair of goals that counted early in the third. The Racers dominated the third period, but they could get no more past Curt Larsson and the game went to overtime tied at 3-3. In the extra period, the Jets alertly capitalized on a pair of giveaways to score the game-winner and escape with a 4-3 win despite being badly outplayed in the latter stages of the game. The Jets' seventh consecutive victory kept them one point back of the Mariners and two back of the Fighting Saints, who had each won their games while the Jets were packing for Houston.

The Jets were back on the ice on Thursday night at the Sam Houston Coliseum. The Aeros held the visitors in check right from the outset and turned a close-checking game into a rout in the second half of the game. The Aeros scored twice in the second period and added five more in the third to make the final score 8-0, putting an abrupt halt to the Jets' season-high seven-game winning streak. The home crowd had even more reason to celebrate when Gordie Howe assisted on Jim Sherrit's third period goal to give him 2,000 points in his pro career. The win clinched first place in the Western Division for the Aeros and dealt a significant blow to the Jets' playoff hopes. The Jets left Texas four points behind the Fighting Saints and five behind the Mariners, with only six games left in the regular season to make up the difference.

Two nights later, the Jets met the Whalers in Hartford for the third time in 18 days to wrap up the three-game road trip. The Jets came out flat, but Joe Daley kept them in the game in the early going and his teammates got off the mat and completely turned the tables on the Whalers. The Jets scored four times in the latter half of the second period and poured it on with four more in the third period to take home a 9-3 victory. Hull scored three times to raise his season total to 75 and Perry Miller scored a pair to mark his first two-goal game as a Jet. More importantly, the Jets moved back to within three points of the Fighting Saints and kept themselves five back of the Mariners.

On Monday night, the Jets met the Racers at the Arena to make up the game that had been postponed in mid-January due to a snowstorm. Though the mercury outside dipped to a low of 15°-below to remind the 10,519 spectators of January weather, fortunately, snow wasn't a problem with the month of March hours from coming to a close. On the ice, the Racers concentrated their efforts to stop Hull, but the rest of the Jets picked up the slack and made easy work of the league's worst team, cruising to a 4-1 victory. Howie Young recorded a pair of goals for his third multi-goal performance in a Jets' uniform.

The Jets entertained the Blazers on Wednesday, 2 April in their second last home game of the regular season. Despite winning nine of their last 10 games, the Jets entered the contest still four points back of the last wild-card playoff position, but the Blazers, with nothing to play for but pride, stunned both the Jets and the sellout crowd of 10,361 by taking a 4-0 lead early in the second period. The Jets mounted a furious comeback and cut the deficit in half before the intermission, but Blazers' goaltender Don "Smokey" McLeod turned back all 17 Jets' shots in the third period and the 6-4 score held up. Anders Hedberg scored his 50th goal of the season in the disheartening defeat, but it was of little solace as the Jets' playoff chances suffered a catastrophic blow.

The season's last road trip started in Toronto on Friday night to kick off yet another stretch of three games in three nights. The Jets looked like anything but a team needing to win and before their largest crowd of the season, the Toros had their way with the visiting Jets. Larsson held his team in the game in the first period, but then the roof caved in and the goals poured in fast and furiously. When it was all said and done, the Jets were on the wrong end of a 7-1 blowout that could have been much worse than the score indicated. The defeat officially eliminated the Jets from post-season contention, giving them a long summer to contemplate what might have been. Not only did the Jets lose the game, but they also lost Gruen to a broken foot when he was hit by Hull's shot while screening Toros' goaltender Jim Shaw.

The Jets moved on to Quebec for their last road game of the season on Saturday night, where a crowd of 11,649 fans showed up to pay tribute to their Nordiques, who had not only qualified for post-season play for the first time, but had also claimed the Canadian Division title. The Nordiques put the crowd in even more of a celebratory mood when they jumped all over the visitors and took a 6-1 lead. The Jets rallied to make a game of it, but the Nordiques pulled away late in the third period to put any comeback hopes to rest. Though the game's outcome had long since been decided, Hull took a pass from Norm Beaudin in the final minute and fired a shot that beat Nordiques' goaltender Richard Brodeur for his 76th goal of the season, equaling the single-season record set in the NHL by Phil Esposito of the Boston Bruins four years earlier. The Jets were happy for Hull, and after the game, Brodeur brought a bottle of champagne across the ice to toast his accomplishment, but the 9-5 defeat was nothing to celebrate as the Jets got back on a plane to return home and finish their season on Sunday night against the Mariners.

Though their team was going to miss the playoffs for the first time in their history, an appreciative gathering of 10,410 fans welcomed the Jets home with a standing ovation. Before the opening faceoff, however, the Jets handed out their season-ending awards. Hull won the Co-Operators Credit Union trophy for being the leading scorer, Anders Hedberg won the Carling O'Keefe trophy for the best rookie and the Molson Cup for being the most frequent three star selection, Lars-Erik Sjoberg was awarded the Labatt's trophy for the most valuable player, and Ulf Nilsson won the Ben Moss STAG award for the combination of ability and sportsmanlike conduct.

When the game started, the two teams took turns lighting up the scoreboard, but the issue went to overtime tied at 5-5. The Jets tried their best to give their fans one last win before the summer ahead, but they couldn't break the deadlock and the game ended in a tie score. Hull did score one more to pass Esposito's record, but he couldn't catch the Mariners' Andre Lacroix for the WHA scoring title.

After the game, Jets' President Bob Graham presented Lacroix with a bottle of champagne in honor of his second WHA scoring title in three seasons, while the Jets packed their bags for a longer off-season than they anticipated. Despite the obvious disappointment of missing the playoffs, it was anything but a lost season. On the ice, the Jets did finish the regular season with a record of 38-35-5, an eight-point improvement over last season, but they made bigger strides off the ice. The community banded together to save the team and fans started coming to the Arena in droves. The Jets drew 13 crowds of 10,000 or more and they no longer needed Gordie Howe to pack the building. They had an exciting product that was in demand both in and outside of Winnipeg. There was still work to be done to make the Jets a championship contender, but a solid foundation was in place both on and off the ice.

Scores and Stats

1974-1975 Winnipeg Jets (38-35-5)

Regular Season

Date	Opponent	Score	Date	Opponent	Score
15 Oct	@Vancouver Blazers	6-2	24 Jan	@Vancouver Blazers	3-4*
18 Oct	Edmonton Oilers	4-0	26 Jan	Houston Aeros	1-3
25 Oct	@Toronto Toros	1-3	28 Jan	@San Diego Mariners	9-7
27 Oct	Michigan Stags	5-2	30 Jan	@Phoenix Roadrunners	5-3
30 Oct	Phoenix Roadrunners	6-5*	2 Feb	@Minnesota Fighting Saints	4-5*
1 Nov	Toronto Toros	10-1	5 Feb	@Cleveland Crusaders	2-3
3 Nov	Michigan Stags	11-3	7 Feb	New England Whalers	4-5*
5 Nov	Minnesota Fighting Saints	6-4	8 Feb	@Chicago Cougars	3-6
9 Nov	@Vancouver Blazers	3-3*	9 Feb	Chicago Cougars	3-2
13 Nov	@Edmonton Oilers	3-5	12 Feb	Toronto Toros	4-7
15 Nov	Indianapolis Racers	5-0	14 Feb	Houston Aeros	5-3
17 Nov	Toronto Toros	1-3	15 Feb	Cleveland Crusaders	5-1
18 Nov	@Edmonton Oilers	3-5	16 Feb	@Chicago Cougars	6-3
20 Nov	Minnesota Fighting Saints	3-1	18 Feb	@Baltimore Blades	5-3
24 Nov	Phoenix Roadrunners	1-3	19 Feb	Edmonton Oilers	4-1
26 Nov	@Indianapolis Racers	4-0	23 Feb	New England Whalers	1-2*
27 Nov	@Cleveland Crusaders	4-5*	25 Feb	Minnesota Fighting Saints	6-6*
29 Nov	Michigan Stags	7-6	28 Feb	San Diego Mariners	4-3
1 Dec	Quebec Nordiques	3-2	2 Mar	San Diego Mariners	4-4*
4 Dec	Houston Aeros	2-3	5 Mar	Cleveland Crusaders	4-2
6 Dec	@Minnesota Fighting Saints	2-4	7 Mar	@Phoenix Roadrunners	4-7
8 Dec	Chicago Cougars	5-2	8 Mar	@San Diego Mariners	5-6
10 Dec	@Indianapolis Racers	5-3	9 Mar	@Minnesota Fighting Saints	6-5*
12 Dec	@Michigan Stags	3-5	11 Mar	@New England Whalers	2-6
14 Dec	@Houston Aeros	3-5	12 Mar	@Quebec Nordiques	3-5
15 Dec	New England Whalers	3-4	14 Mar	Quebec Nordiques	4-3
17 Dec	@Toronto Toros	4-1	16 Mar	Edmonton Oilers	10-1
18 Dec	@Quebec Nordiques	1-5	19 Mar	Vancouver Blazers	8-3
22 Dec	Phoenix Roadrunners	2-4	21 Mar	@New England Whalers	6-3
26 Dec	@Phoenix Roadrunners	3-2	22 Mar	@Chicago Cougars	4-2
28 Dec	@San Diego Mariners	6-4	23 Mar	Chicago Cougars	4-3
29 Dec	@Houston Aeros	3-6	25 Mar	@Indianapolis Racers	4-3*
7 Jan	@Cleveland Crusaders	4-4*	27 Mar	@Houston Aeros	0-8
9 Jan	@Michigan Stags	4-5*	29 Mar	@New England Whalers	9-3
10 Jan	Quebec Nordiques	1-6	31 Mar	Indianapolis Racers	4-1
15 Jan	Vancouver Blazers	2-4	2 Apr	Vancouver Blazers	4-6
19 Jan	Cleveland Crusaders	9-4	4 Apr	@Toronto Toros	1-7
22 Jan	Indianapolis Racers	1-3	5 Apr	@Quebec Nordiques	5-9
23 Jan	@Edmonton Oilers	3-7	6 Apr	San Diego Mariners	5-5*

* - overtime

Scoring

Player	Regular Season									Playoffs								
	GP	G	A	Pts	PIM	+/-	PP	SH	Shots	GP	G	A	Pts	PIM	+/-	PP	SH	Shots
Ron Ashton	36	1	3	4	66		0	0	36									
Duke Asmundson	38	4	15	19	53		0	0	49									
Norm Beaudin	77	16	31	47	8		1	2	202									
Alain Beaule	54	0	14	14	24		0	0	36									
Thommie Bergman	49	4	15	19	70		3	0	85									
Milt Black	64	4	6	10	10		0	0	37									
Christian Bordeleau	18	8	8	16	0		0	2	52									
Joe Daley	51	0	1	1	6		0	0	0									
Mike Ford	73	12	22	34	68		3	0	205									
Jean-Guy Gratton	49	4	8	12	2		0	0	57									
Danny Gruen	32	9	12	21	21		3	0	64									
Anders Hedberg	65	53	47	100	45		20	0	271									
Larry Hornung	69	7	25	32	21		1	0	80									
Bobby Hull	78	77	65	142	41		27	0	556									
Danny Johnson	78	18	14	32	25		2	4	111									
Veli-Pekka Ketola	74	23	28	51	25		2	0	154									
Curt Larsson	26	0	1	1	4		0	0	0									
Perry Miller	67	9	19	28	133		0	1	99									
Robbie Neale	7	0	2	2	4		0	0	14									
Ulf Nilsson	78	26	94	120	79		7	0	147									
Hexi Riihiranta	64	8	14	22	30		2	0	102									
Lars-Erik Sjoberg	75	7	53	60	30		0	1	123									
Ron Snell	20	0	0	0	8		0	0	15									
Dan Spring	60	19	24	43	22		1	0	123									
Ernie Wakely	6	0	0	0	0		0	0	0									
Bob Woytowich	24	0	4	4	8		0	0	11									
Howie Young	42	13	10	23	42		2	0	81									

Goaltending

Goaltender	Regular Season									
	GP	Min	GA	GAA	Saves	Sv %	SO	EN	W	L	T
Joe Daley	51	2902	175	3.62	1375		1	0	23	21	4
Curt Larsson	26	1514	100	3.96	787		1	2	12	11	1
Ernie Wakely	6	355	16	2.70	197		1	0	3	3	0

Jets President Bob Graham **(above and at left)** was one of the leaders of the "Save the Jets" campaign in the summer of 1974.

LEFT: Bob Graham surveys the responses to a mail-in campaign asking fans to show their support for keeping the Jets in Winnipeg.

Jack McKeag **(right)** and James Burns **(far right)**, two more who also played significant roles in the "Save the Jets" campaign.

Dr. Gerry Wilson **(far left)** and Bill "Magic Fingers" Bozak **(left)**. It was Dr. Wilson, while studying in Stockholm, who urged the Jets to sign Anders Hedberg and Ulf Nilsson, along with many other Europeans. Bozak took over as the Jets trainer in 1974.

RIGHT: The four new Swedish arrivals for the 1974-1975 season. From left to right are Curt Larsson, Ulf Nilsson, Anders Hedberg, and Lars-Erik Sjoberg.

BELOW LEFT: More reinforcements from overseas, Hexi Riihiranta and Veli-Pekka Ketola from Finland.

BELOW RIGHT: Danny Johnson and Dan Spring

LEFT: Larry Hornung and Bobby Hull during the "Save the Jets" campaign.

RIGHT: Rudy Pilous

BELOW: More new arrivals in 1974-1975

(left to right) Perry Miller, Thommie Bergman, Danny Gruen, and Howie Young.

More new faces for 1974-1975:
TOP LEFT: Mike Ford
TOP MIDDLE: Ron "Bam Bam" Ashton
TOP RIGHT: Alain Beaule

ABOVE LEFT: Norm Beaudin, the original Jet.
ABOVE RIGHT: Bobby Hull at the bench.

TOP LEFT: Wakely battles with Rich Pumple while Duke Asmundson watches his back.

MIDDLE: Ernie Wakely does his magic against the Indianapolis Racers.

BOTTOM LEFT: Wakely covers up with Larry Hornung and Danny Johnson nearby.

BOTTOM RIGHT: Veli-Pekka Ketola puts a move on Ed Dyck of the Indianapolis Racers.

ABOVE: Curt Larsson fends off Robbie Ftorek of the Phoenix Roadrunners while Hexi Riihiranta has his goaltender's back.

LEFT: Bobby Hull is mobbed by his teammates.

BELOW: Anders Hedberg celebrates a goal against the Phoenix Roadrunners.

Season IV: 1975-1976 – The Payoff

Once the Aeros swept the Nordiques to claim their second consecutive AVCO World Trophy championship, the off-season officially got underway. After making great strides on and off the ice last season, the Jets began preparations for the 1975-1976 season seeking to build up their roster and turn an exciting and talented group of players into a winner. Though they had failed to qualify for the post-season play, the Jets garnered some prestigious post-season awards when Hull, despite not being named the most valuable player on his own team, was named the WHA's most valuable player for the second time in three seasons, and was also named to the league's First All-Star team. Anders Hedberg was named the WHA's rookie of the year and was also named as a Second Team All-Star.

As expected, the Chicago Cougars and Baltimore Blades promptly folded after the season and two expansion teams replaced them. The Cincinnati Stingers would finally ice a team after their inception in 1973 and the Denver Spurs were a last-minute addition to keep the league at 14 teams. In addition, the Blazers, after beginning life in Philadelphia, moved from Vancouver to Calgary and were renamed the Cowboys, with the 8,945-seat Calgary Stampede Corral serving as their new home rink. The Cowboys remained in the Canadian Division, while the Stingers joined the Crusaders, Racers and Whalers in the Eastern Division. The Spurs were placed in the Western Division with the Aeros, Fighting Saints, Roadrunners and Mariners.

In May, the Jets sent Rudy Pilous to Sweden on a recruiting trip and after six days, he returned with the signatures of right winger Willy Lindstrom and centerman Mats Lindh from Vastra Frolunda on Jets' contracts. The 24-year-old Lindstrom, who had spurned the Jets' offers last season, was a former truck driver in the Swedish Army who had trained as a mechanic. The scouts liked his aggressive and professional style while playing in Sweden. Lindh, the son of a lumberjack who would turn 28 before the start of the season, was a former classmate of Hedberg's and came with a reputation as a good skater and good stickhandler. Pilous also made overtures to Dan Labraaten, who ultimately decided to remain in Sweden, but left the door open to potentially joining the Jets at a later time.

The Jets re-signed Larry Hornung to a multi-year pact after he turned down a matching offer from the NHL's Kansas City Scouts. The Jets also acquired veteran defenseman Ted Green from the Whalers for future considerations. The 35-year-old native of the Winnipeg suburb of St. Boniface had one year left on his contract with the Whalers, but the Jets signed him to a new three-year deal. Green had been with the Whalers for the past three seasons after a distinguished career with the Boston Bruins.

The Jets made 10 selections in the third annual WHA Amateur Draft, but unlike last year, they didn't sign any of their draft choices. In early June, the Jets re-signed Perry Miller to a two-year contract for $34,000 per season, doubling his salary. The Detroit Red Wings showed an interest in Miller, but like Hornung, he chose to remain with the Jets. Miller had a tough time adjusting from defense to left wing this past season, but he handled the switch well. The Jets decided to part ways with Jean-Guy Gratton, Ron Snell, Ken Stephanson, and Milt Black. Both Gratton and Black were more members of the original squad to move on, while Stephanson hadn't played at all last season due to back problems.

Did You Know?

With the 166th overall selection in the 13th round of the 1975 WHA Amateur Draft, the Jets chose Swedish winger Bengt Lundholm of Leskands IF. Though they did not sign Lundholm at that time, six years later, as members of the NHL, the Jets signed him as a free agent and he played in 275 regular season games over the course of five seasons as a Jet.

Danny Johnson and Dan Spring were offered new contracts, but the Jets quickly broke off negotiations with Danny Gruen, The Red Wings offered him a three-year deal worth $55,000 per season, but he chose to sign with the Crusaders instead. After having been acquired from the Stags in mid-season, Gruen disappointed the Jets with his attitude and lack of toughness. Johnson, meanwhile, was hurt by the low offer from the Jets, which was contingent on making the team, and later in the summer he decided to retire. He turned down an offer from a team in Gothenburg, Sweden, and another from a club in Switzerland to be a playing coach so he could return to his jewelry store in Fort Frances, Ontario. The Jets offered Spring a one-year contract, but he wanted a three-year deal. Spring was willing to accept a two-year deal later in the summer, but the Jets didn't budge and they placed him on waivers.

The Jets also declined to offer Alain Beaule a contract, but Joe Daley mailed in his signed contract offer. The Jets added a pair of rearguards when they selected 29-year-old Randy Legge and 38-year-old Larry Hillman in the inter-league draft. Legge had played with the Stags/Blades franchise last season, while Hillman had been with the Crusaders for the past two seasons. Hillman was a veteran of six Stanley Cup championship teams and the Jets would be the 18th professional team to hold his playing rights since he first signed with the Detroit Red Wings on 5 March 1955. In the 1968-1969 season alone, he belonged to no fewer than five NHL clubs.

In late June, the Jets announced the signings of winger Bill Lesuk and centerman Peter Sullivan. The 28-year-old Lesuk had been a boyhood friend of Hornung's growing up in rural Saskatchewan and he'd picked up the nickname of "Tractor" because of his plodding style. The veteran of NHL stops in Boston, Philadelphia, and most recently with Washington, came to the Jets with a reputation as an excellent checker and hard worker that had earned him plenty of praise during his eight pro seasons.

Sullivan, a native of Toronto who was just days away from his 24th birthday, had spent the past three seasons in the Montreal Canadiens' organization playing for the Nova Scotia Voyageurs of the AHL. The slick stickhandler was fresh off a 44-goal, 104-point season and with nothing left to prove in the minors, he made the decision to sign with the Jets rather than wait and try to crack the deep Canadiens' lineup. Sullivan's father, Frank, was a member of the Canadian national hockey team that won the gold medal at the 1928 Olympics in St. Moritz, Switzerland, and he had also played football with the Toronto Argonauts. His six seasons with the Argonauts were highlighted by a Grey Cup championship in 1921.

Days after signing Lesuk and Sullivan, the Jets introduced a 46-year-old former glass blower, Bobby Kromm, as their new coach. Kromm had spent eight years being groomed in the Chicago Blackhawks' organization as the heir apparent to Billy Reay and had coached the Central Hockey League's (CHL) Dallas Black Hawks to the league final on five occasions, winning twice. For the previous four years, Kromm even managed the arena in Dallas in addition to his duties as coach and general manager of the team. During his time in Dallas, Kromm had had many NHL and WHA offers. The former skeptic of the new league, who had been among the many who had forecasted its quick demise, accepted the Jets' offer and signed a two-year contract that Jets' President Bob Graham hoped would be for a lifetime.

Pilous, who had been moved upstairs into the position of Director of Hockey Operations, had approached Kromm late last season about the Jets' coaching position. In addition to Pilous' endorsement, Kromm was also Hull's personal choice as Pilous' successor behind the Jets' bench, since Hull was familiar with Kromm from their time together in the Blackhawks' organization. Self-described as a demanding coach and a stickler for goals against, the cigar-smoking disciplinarian also had experience at the 1961 and 1963 World Championships that would undoubtedly help him work with hockey's most diverse and multicultural lineup.

Pat Kelly, coach and general manager of the Southern Hockey League's Charlotte Checkers; Jackie McLeod, coach and general manager of the WCHL's Saskatoon Blades; and Winnipeg native Jack Bownass, the former coach of the OHA's Kingston Canadians, were the other candidates for the job, but Kromm was the Jets' first choice.

Come mid-July, the Jets decided to withdraw their contract offer to Howie Young and Pilous sent him a letter to that effect. During negotiations, Young had asked that his $40,000 salary be doubled, while the Jets countered with a more modest increase of $10,000. Young didn't leave Winnipeg empty-handed, however, since the Booster Club had voted him the club's most popular player. To the Jets' surprise, there was a clause in his contract that paid him an additional $3,000 for the honor, which the Jets paid grudgingly.

To wind down the eventful summer, the Jets hired Norm Coston, the former promotion manager at the *Winnipeg Tribune*, as their Director of Media Relations, and they made arrangements to hold training camp in Europe. In the deal brokered by Dr. Gerry Wilson together with Pilous and Bill Robinson, the Jets expected to make $50,000 for spending most of September along with the Toros traveling across Finland, Sweden and Czechoslovakia, before returning to Winnipeg to begin the regular season.

Training camp opened on the last day of August with medicals at the Arena and skating at nearby St. James Civic Center before traveling overseas. Unfortunately, the Jets learned at the last moment that Peter Sullivan would have to stay behind on account of outstanding legal issues surrounding his signing. One of the conditions of the antitrust settlement was that WHA teams were unable to sign NHL players in their option year. Though Sullivan never signed his option, he was still in his option year and wasn't technically free to play for the Jets.

In Finland, the Jets defeated IFK by a score of 7-5 before more than 10,000 fans in Helsinki, then tied Tappara 3-3 in Tampere before a crowd of 8,695. They wrapped up their third game in four nights with a 4-3 loss at the hands of TSP in Turku before 4,797 spectators.

The Jets flew to Sweden, but their plane was struck by lightning on their way to Maimo. The plane landed safely and the team bused to Tyringe, where they spent three days before their next game on 17 September against the Swedish nationals in Stockholm. The Jets won by a score of 6-2 and two nights later, they defeated DIF-AIK Sodertalia by a score of 7-3, also in Stockholm. The Jets moved on to Gothenburg and handily defeated Leksand by a score of 8-2, then they edged Mats Lindh's and Willy Lindstrom's former team, Vastra Frolunda, by a score of 4-3, again in Gothenburg. The last game of their Swedish tour surprisingly featured two fights, as Ted Green battled Magnus Olsson and Perry Miller took on Tom Mellar.

Lightning Strikes Twice

Twelve seasons after the Jets' plane was struck by lightning, the Jets used "Lightning on Ice" as their marketing slogan. The front cover of the media guide featured players Jim Kyte, Dale Hawerchuk and Dave Ellett underneath a Canadian Forces airplane being struck by lightning.

Two nights later, the Jets faced the Czechoslovakian nationals and were routed by a score 6-1 before a crowd of over 14,000 in Prague. The Czechs completed the sweep the next night by defeating the Jets 3-1 before another gathering of more than 14,000 in Czechoslovakia's capital city.

After making the rounds across Europe, the Jets returned to North America to begin final preparations for the start of the regular season. The Jets named Lars-Erik Sjoberg as their new captain and also named Larry Hornung and Norm Beaudin as the assistant captains. Sjoberg became the first European captain in North American pro hockey and he was a fitting choice for his play on the ice and his leadership off the ice. He helped to convince each of his teammates to drop the personal bonus clauses in their contracts in favor of equal shares in one team bonus, payable at the end of November, January, and March if the Jets were in first or second place in their division at that time.

For the fourth time in as many seasons, the Jets began their regular season schedule on the road when they flew into Quebec to kick off a five-game road trip on Thursday, 9 October. Though the Jets made many changes in the off-season, the defending Canadian Division champions and AVCO World Trophy finalists from one season ago came into the game with most of their roster left intact. The Nordiques' most noteworthy addition was former Fighting Saints tough guy Gord Gallant, who was traded to the Nordiques following his scrap with coach Harry Neale over being fined for missing curfew.

Before a crowd of 9,732 that included Bob Graham, Jack McKeag, and Dr. Gerry Wilson, the Jets fell behind early, but they shook off the Nordiques' roughhouse tactics and scored four times to erase a 2-1 deficit. Marc Tardif's late goal narrowed the Jets' lead to two goals, but the Nordiques could get no closer and the Jets left Quebec with a 5-3 victory, marking their first win at Le Colisee in almost two years.

The Jets returned home for one night before leaving for Phoenix on Saturday to continue their road trip against the Roadrunners on Sunday afternoon. The team that had claimed the last wild-card playoff berth last season made three key additions to their lineup over the summer. The Roadrunners added Finnish defenseman Pekka Rautakallio, who, like Veli-Pekka Ketola, was both a native of Pori and played with Assat, his hometown team. They also signed Finnish winger Lauri Mononen, who scored 30 goals in 35 games with TPS Turku last season and domestic product Del Hall, who had spent the past four seasons in the California Golden Seals' organization. Though Hall had played in only nine games with the Golden Seals during that time, he was fresh off a 32-goal season with their farm team in Salt Lake.

After a scoreless first period, the Jets broke the ice with two second period goals. With the Roadrunners pressing in the third, the Jets added two more and coasted to a 4-0 victory. Hull scored his first two goals of the season and Ulf Nilsson added another to go with his pair on Thursday night to open the season.

The Jets left for Denver on Tuesday to meet the Spurs on Thursday, 16 October. Though technically an expansion team, the Spurs were able to take many of the players from the defunct Cougars in the expansion draft, as well as the dispersal draft that allocated the remaining Cougars and Blades. Despite the infusion of established players, however, the Spurs had suffered an embarrassing 7-1 defeat in their opening game last Wednesday at the hands of the Racers, who finished with the WHA's worst record last season.

Before only 2,500 onlookers at McNichols Arena, the Jets scored four times in the first five and a half minutes of the game and didn't look back as they routed the Spurs by a score of 7-3. Willy Lindstrom and Bill Lesuk each scored their first goals as a Jet and Curt Larsson, coming off knee surgery in the spring, picked up the win in his first start of the young season.

After making quick work of the hapless Spurs, the Jets moved on to San Diego to meet the Mariners on Saturday night in the fourth of their season-opening five-game road trip. The Mariners, who had been last season's AVCO World Trophy semi-finalists, came into the game with few changes to their lineup. Aside from re-signing Ernie Wakely, the Mariners' most noteworthy on-ice moves were trading 44-goal scorer Rick Sentes to the Cowboys in exchange for the rights to veteran minor league centerman Joe Noris and picking up John French from the Whalers for future considerations. Off the ice, the Mariners hired Ron Ingram as their new coach, replacing playing coach Harry Howell.

The goaltenders, former teammates Joe Daley and Ernie Wakely, shone in the early going, but it was Wakely who had the upper hand and the Mariners were able to scratch out a 2-1 lead going into the third period. From there, the Mariners held the Jets in check, limiting them to only five shots the rest of the way, and the Mariners handed the Jets their first defeat. On their way off the ice, the Mariners, led by Andre Lacroix, made a point of hanging around to taunt their vanquished guests before the Jets left to make a return trip to Phoenix to wrap up their road trip on Sunday night.

The Roadrunners capitalized on some shaky goaltending from Daley to take a 4-0 first period lead and though the Jets battled right to the end, it wasn't enough as the Jets suffered their second defeat in as many nights. The Jets did, however, welcome Peter Sullivan to their lineup for the first time after he had finally been legally freed to play, and he nearly scored a goal in his Jets debut. Though beaten, the 3-2-0 Jets boarded a plane in the knowledge that they were finally headed for home to play their first meaningful game at the Winnipeg Arena since April.

After making their way across Europe and North America, the Jets arrived in Winnipeg to settle down for an eight-game, three-week home stand. Their first opponent was the expansion Stingers, winners of two of their first three games despite the fact that, like the Jets, they had yet to play at home. Unlike the Spurs, their expansion cousins, the Stingers came in with a team built on a combination of free agency, trades and dispersal draft selections. Among their more prominent acquisitions were Rick Dudley, a 31-goal scorer with the Buffalo Sabres last season; Bryan Campbell, acquired via trade from Calgary; Gary Veneruzzo, selected in the dispersal draft off the Stags/Blades roster who was their leading scorer for two of the last three seasons; Pierre Guite, who had burned the Jets with a hat trick as a Stag last season; and Dennis Sobchuk, a 32-goal scorer with the Roadrunners last year. The Stingers hired former Sharks' coach Terry Slater to handle the duties behind the bench in their inaugural season.

After the Winnipeg Mass Pipe Band finished playing and Public Works Minister Russell Doern dropped the ceremonial first puck, the Jets finally opened the home portion of their regular season schedule before a crowd of 8,552 fans that included 5,200 season ticket holders. Just as he had done with the Sharks, the controversial Slater had his new team try to run the Jets out of the rink, but the Jets made the Stingers pay with three first period power-play goals and kept pouring it on in a 7-0 victory.

The two points, however, took a back seat to an incident late in the first period just after Veli-Pekka Ketola gave the Jets a 3-0 lead. Defenseman Ron Plumb went after Ketola, and Perry Miller joined the fray in defense of his teammate. The Stingers' Bernie MacNeil, a former Shark who had played under Slater in Los Angeles, also joined in and high-sticked Miller right in his eye. Miller dropped to the ice instantly and left the ice with double vision before going to the hospital. Curiously, MacNeil was not penalized, but, more importantly, after the game, the doctors determined that there was no serious damage to Miller's eye. The Jets and Hull, in particular, were fuming mad over the incident and with the Stingers' tactics during the game.

The Jets were off until Friday, 24 October when the Spurs flew into town coming off three straight road wins. As expected, the Jets were without Miller, whose eye was still on the mend, but Hull pulled himself out of the lineup as a personal protest against the increasing level of violence in pro hockey. Nonetheless, with Peter Sullivan taking Hull's place on the top line with Ulf Nilsson and Anders Hedberg, the Jets were all over the Spurs and they used three second period goals to propel themselves to a comfortable 5-2 victory. Sullivan connected for his second goal as a Jet and Hexi Riihiranta netted his first of the season after being switched from defense to left wing in training camp. Despite Hull's absence, the Jets raised their record to 5-2-0, which was good enough for sole possession of first place, two points ahead of the idle Nordiques.

Over the weekend, the Jets prepared to make do without Hull once again for their Sunday night game against the Roadrunners, but after returning from his oldest son's game on Sunday afternoon, Hull decided to put an end to his protest and rejoin his teammates in time for the game. Fittingly, it was Hull who opened the scoring early in the first period, but Daley stole the show with no fewer than 18 saves in the opening 20 minutes. The Jets continued to make the most of their chances and piled up a 5-0 lead, while Daley stopped all 39 shots he faced to earn first-star honors as well as his third shutout of the season.

Hull Got Action

In the days that followed Bobby Hull's return to the ice after sitting out one game to protest increasing levels of violence in pro hockey, most players, particularly his own teammates, were pleased to see him back, but they felt that he overreacted and shouldn't have taken this action unilaterally. When a player of Hull's stature sits out a game, however, people stand up and take notice, and Hull did succeed in drawing attention to the cause he was trying to support. For starters, Ben Hatskin, Jets' founder and CEO of the WHA, spoke out and made it clear that the league would be the first to react against coaches who condoned acts of violence. The league also required that the Stingers post a $1,500 bond to ensure there would be no violence in their upcoming games with the Jets and Nordiques. CBS sent one of its top newsmen, Dan Rather, to interview Hull and learn about the protest, and Ontario Attorney General Roy McMurtry instructed police in his province to lay charges against players involved in violent assaults during games. The amount of attention the issue attracted would not have been possible had Hull not decided to sit the game out, so, in exchange for one missed game against an expansion team that the Jets still won, some good for the sport as a whole came from of his actions.

Nine days after the incident that precipitated Hull's one-game strike, the Stingers came back to Winnipeg for a return visit on Thursday night. Not only was Hull in the lineup, but Miller, with the help of a specially fitted mask, also made his return. The game was considerably tamer than when the two teams had last met, but the game remained scoreless until late in the second period when the Jets erupted for two quick goals to take a 2-0 lead to the intermission. In the third period, the Jets added two more goals and cruised to a 4-0 victory as Daley earned his second consecutive shutout and third in his last four games. In the Jets' fourth straight win, Sullivan scored his third goal as a Jet just one day after attending his mother's funeral.

The fifth game of the Jets' season-opening, eight-game home stand came on Sunday night against the Nordiques to start the month of November. The Nordiques arrived in Winnipeg only two points behind the first-place Jets and, upon their entrance on the Arena ice, were greeted by a Booster Club sign in the north end that read "Quebec Nordiques – Welcome to Canada", in reference to the French-speaking province that perpetually threatens to break away from Canada. The Nordiques were also greeted by one of their former teammates in the person of 24-year-old winger Robert "Bobby" Guindon, who had paid his own way to Winnipeg 11 days ago asking for a tryout and received a five-game trial with the Jets. The former second-round selection of the Detroit Red Wings had spent the last three seasons with the Nordiques and had played in all 15 of their playoff games on their way to the AVCO World Trophy final last season.

The first five-figure crowd of the season saw a fast-paced game that went back and forth, but neither Daley nor Richard Brodeur in the Nordiques' goal could be beaten. The scoreless tie continued late into the third period, when tough guy Steve Sutherland's shot with 3:25 left to play in regulation time beat Daley and gave the visitors a 1-0 lead. The Jets gave it their all in the game's dying moments, but the score held, and the Nordiques were victorious in the early battle for division supremacy.

Did You Know?

Despite being scored upon late in the third period on 2 November 1975, Joe Daley had amassed a shutout streak that lasted for 228 minutes and 10 seconds. Between goals by Don Borgeson of the Denver Spurs at 8:25 of the first period on 24 October and by Steve Sutherland of the Quebec Nordiques at 16:35 of the third period on 2 November, Joe Daley did not allow a single goal. It was the longest shutout streak in Jets' history and the record survived not only through their WHA years, but also though 17 seasons of NHL play.

Bigwood's Big Shoes

The Booster Club sign in the north end on 2 November 1975 that read "Quebec Nordiques – Welcome to Canada" was put up by longtime President Gary Bigwood. He was among the most dedicated boosters and fans the Jets had and like many others in the Booster Club, he put in a lot of his own time behind the scenes as a volunteer and was said to be the Jets' best public relations man.

The native of St. Thomas, North Dakota became a hockey fan when he was living in Saint Paul in 1961 after spending two years at the University of North Dakota. He moved to Winnipeg in 1962 and worked for the Workmen's Compensation Board, but the U.S. Army drafted him in October 1963 and he served with the 1st Army Honor Guard in New York. Upon leaving he Army, he worked for Longines in New York and ITT in Denver before returning to Winnipeg in 1972.

Bigwood then took a job with Compu-Share Data Centre, where he was their Director of Marketing and he also served on the Board of Directors of the community-owned Jets in addition to holding down the presidency of the Booster Club. In September 1975, he traveled to Europe and spent three weeks with the team as they held training camp in Sweden, Finland and Czecholosvakia.

Two nights after suffering their first defeat in five games, the Jets hosted the Whalers for the first meeting of the season between the original WHA championship finalists. The Whalers, in their first full season in Hartford, came to Winnipeg with largely the same team that had lost its first-round playoff series to the Fighting Saints to prematurely end their season. Daley's former roommate, goaltender Al Smith, had retired, and they added the pugnacious Rosaire Paiement from the Cougars via the Spurs, as well as defenseman Gordie Roberts, who was a top prospect out of the junior ranks with the Victoria Cougars. Behind the bench, they were again led by their general manager, Jack Kelley, after coach Ron Ryan had suffered a dizzy spell while in Toronto late last season and had hit his head on a concrete floor. Though he was released from hospital, he was unable to resume his coaching duties.

The crowd of 7,989 that turned out in the unseasonably warm November evening saw a less spirited affair than Sunday night's game, but the Jets used a pair of second period goals from the top line to take a 2-0 lead to the third period. The Whalers responded with two goals in less than three minutes to tie the score and only Curt Larsson's outstanding work prevented the visitors from taking the lead. The game went to overtime, where the Jets rebounded and controlled play until Mike Ford's shot from the point four minutes into the extra period gave the Jets a 3-2 victory. The win enabled the 8-3-0 Jets to keep pace with the Nordiques as the two teams remained tied atop the Canadian Division.

The Jets didn't have a game on the schedule until Sunday, but the team participated in a Meet the Jets Social on Friday night at the Assiniboine Motor Hotel. At a cost of $5 per person, 200 fans had a chance to mingle with their heroes while munching on cold cuts and sipping coffee.

Back on the ice, the Jets played host to the Toros two nights after their social. The team that had lost to the Mariners in the first round of last season's playoffs added junior star Mark Napier, who was coming off a 66-goal season with the Toronto Marlboros, and rugged defenseman Jerry Rollins, who had racked up 473 penalty minutes split between the WCHL's Flin Flon Bombers and Winnipeg Clubs last season. The Toros lost goaltender Gilles Gratton to the St. Louis Blues and they made another coaching change, replacing Bob Leduc with former Maple Leafs' defenseman Bob Baun. Early returns on the Toros' off-season changes, however, were not positive, as the Jets' opponents flew into town with a 2-7-1 record, putting them firmly in control of the division basement. To add to their woes, the Toros were missing both Tom Simpson and Paul Henderson. Simpson was out with a knee injury and Henderson was suffering from a case of the flu.

The crowd of 10,255 saw the Jets dominate the first two periods and rack up a 5-0 lead after two periods. Only the work of goaltender Jim Shaw kept the score from being more lopsided, but the Jets let up in the third and though the Toros inched their way back into the game, Vaclav Nedomansky's hat trick had no effect on the outcome as the Jets made it to the finish line with a 5-3 victory.

With their record sitting at a lofty 9-3-0, the second-place Jets wrapped up the longest home stand in their history on Tuesday, 11 November against the Crusaders. Before the game, however, the Jets took an important step in securing their future when they signed Ulf Nilsson and Anders Hedberg to new contracts. After two weeks of negotiations with their lawyer and agent Don Baizley, Bob Graham obtained the signatures of both Swedish stars on identical contracts that would pay each of them around $600,000 over the course of the the current season and the next four. Nilsson and Hedberg began attracting the attention of the NHL, but the Jets took the proactive approach in making a long-term commitment to both of them.

Over the summer, the Crusaders added defenseman Bryan Maxwell, who had been a first-round selection of the Minnesota North Stars, winger Lyle Moffat, who had spent most of the last four seasons in the CHL, and 25-year-old Finnish star Juhani Tamminen, in addition to Danny Gruen, the former Jet. The Crusaders were another team that had made a coaching change in the off-season as they brought in Johnny Wilson, who had been behind the bench of the defunct Stags/Blades franchise last season.

The game remained close through the first two periods, but the Jets went to the intermission holding a slim 2-1 lead. The Crusaders, however, began to assert themselves in the third period and Gruen's goal three minutes in tied the score for the second time. The 2-2 score held until the final minute of regulation time, when Bergman was sent to the box for hooking. Eight seconds from overtime, Paul Shmyr's shot eluded Daley and, after the final seconds expired, the visitors celebrated their dramatic 3-2 victory. To add to their pain, the Nordiques had won in Saint Paul to pull six points ahead of the Jets, who left town for their first visit to Calgary on Thursday night.

The First "Battle of Alberta"

In the NHL today, there are few rivalries as intense as the one between the Calgary Flames and the Edmonton Oilers, but on the night of 11 November 1975, the first "Battle of Alberta" took place at the Stampede Corral between the Calgary Cowboys and the Edmonton Oilers. The Cowboys beat the Oilers by a score of 6-3 as Terry Caffery scored the winning goal in front of a crowd of 4,109 in Calgary.

At the Stampede Corral, the Jets took to the ice for their first road game in almost a month against a revamped Cowboys team playing in its third city in four seasons. In addition their relocation, the franchise had made a number of on-ice moves in the hopes of improving on their 37-39-2 record from a year ago as the Vancouver Blazers. After acquiring Rick Sentes from the Mariners, they traded Johnny McKenzie to the Fighting Saints for forwards George Morrison, Don Tannahill, defenseman Wally Olds and the rights to Joe Micheletti. After a slow start, the Cowboys came into the contest unbeaten in their last five games.

For the fourth straight game, the Jets got on the board first as they scored a pair in the span of 13 seconds in the first period, but the Cowboys tied the score with a pair of their own in the second. The Jets got those goals back in the first seven minutes of the third period and Joe Daley held the fort the rest of the way as the Jets claimed a 4-2 victory that pulled them back to within four points of the first-place Nordiques.

The 10-4-0 Jets were back at the Arena on Friday night to open a three-game home stand against the Oilers. Led by new former University of Alberta coach Clare Drake, the Oilers added goaltender Dave Dryden from the defunct Cougars and signed former Jet Dan Spring to bolster a lineup that had finished with a record of 36-38-4 last season, tied with the Blazers for last place in the Canadian Division.

Before a crowd of 8,561, the Jets completely controlled the game and though Dryden held up admirably under the onslaught, he could not save his team from suffering a 6-1 defeat. The listless Oilers could only muster 13 shots on Daley all night long, while the Jets fired 41 shots at Dryden. Bobby Hull and Peter Sullivan each scored a pair of goals to lead the Jets' attack as they moved to within two points of the Nordiques.

With a day between games to catch their breath, the Jets hosted the Racers on Sunday night. The league's worst team last season had added defenseman Pat Stapleton from the Cougars and centerman Reg Thomas from the Stags/Blades franchise during the off-season. After losing four of their first five games this season, the Racers had also made a coaching change when they replaced Gerry Moore with Jacques Demers, their director of player personnel.

Right from the start, the 4-9-0 Racers played in a defensive shell, but the Jets finally broke through with a goal late in the second period and added another early in the third. The Racers got one back, but Larsson and the Jets held firm and hung on for a 2-1 victory. Making only his third start of the season, Larsson earned first-star honors, getting the better of fellow Swede Leif Holmquist in the Racers' net.

The Jets wrapped up their 11th home game in their last 12 overall with a Tuesday night game against the two-time defending AVCO World Trophy champion Aeros, who were sporting a roster largely unchanged from a season ago. Before the game, however, the Jets had to say good-bye to Bobby Guindon. Though he made a positive impression with management during his tryout, which had been extended to eight games, they were forced to release him on account of lack of money in the budget.

Despite their recent struggles, the Aeros took it right to the Jets and opened the scoring late in the first period. Daley's superb goaltending kept the score at 1-0 until the third period, when Larry Lund scored his second of the game to double the visitors' lead. Sullivan's goal five minutes later brought the Jets back to life, but try as they might, they couldn't get the equalizer and the Aeros broke their three-game losing streak with a 3-2 victory.

The 12-5-0 Jets boarded a plane to begin a six-game road trip with a critical divisional showdown on Thursday night against the Nordiques. Hoping to narrow the gap between themselves and Quebec to two points, the Jets got off to a fast start but couldn't bury many of their chances and held only a 2-0 lead early in the second period. Left within striking distance, the Nordiques rallied for a goal late in the second period and another early in the third to tie the score and send the game to overtime. Just over a minute into the extra period, however, Ulf Nilsson sped past the defense and beat goaltender Richard Brodeur to give the Jets an exhilarating 3-2 victory.

With two points in hand, the Jets left Quebec the next morning bound for Cleveland to battle the Crusaders on Saturday night. Waiting for them at the Richfield Coliseum was a crowd of 15,621, the largest turnout for a WHA game this season. Sadly, the Jets looked anything like a team with the WHA's second best record and the Crusaders took full advantage, scoring four times in the first period and adding two more in the second to put the Jets down by a score of 6-0. The Jets countered with a pair of goals in the second and another in the third, but their mini-revival was far too late to make a difference and the Crusaders handed the Jets a humbling 6-3 defeat. Curt Larsson made only his fourth start of the season in goal and lost for the first time.

One night later, the Jets were back on the ice, this time in Hartford to meet the Whalers for their third game of the six-game road trip. The Jets came out much stronger and earned a 2-0 lead before two Whalers goals 16 seconds apart late in the second period tied the score at 2-2. Early in the third, however, Nilsson scored to put the Jets back out in front and they made the 3-2 score hold up to earn a weekend split.

The Jets enjoyed a bit of breather before their next game in Cincinnati on Wednesday, 26 November. The crowd lustily booed Bobby Hull on his entrance, but the Golden Jet answered all 7,839 of his critics with a goal in the first minute of play to get the Jets on the board first. The Stingers responded with two of their own in the span of 29 seconds, but the Jets took firm control of the game, scoring three more in the first period, three in the second, and four more in the third. Hedberg scored three times for his first hat trick of the season in the 11-3 whitewashing that put the Jets into a first place tie with the Nordiques. The Jets again silenced Stingers' coach Terry Slater, who had promised the Jets a physical beating after their last matchup. Instead, it was the Jets that administered the beating. The Jets didn't escape completely scott-free, however, as they lost Larry Hillman after he blocked a shot with his foot.

On Thursday, a Thanksgiving Day crowd of 12,028 filled Market Square Arena to see the Jets battle the Indianapolis Racers for the first time this season in the Indiana capital. For the third straight game, Hull opened the scoring, raising his season total to 11, but that's all the Jets could get past the tight-checking Racers, who scored two late second period goals to break a 1-1 tie and hand the Jets a 3-1 defeat. The Racers held the Jets to only 22 shots and beat the Jets for the first ever time at home. Larsson made a rare start in goal for the Jets and after deflecting the game-winning goal into his own net, he was flattened by the Racers' Ted Scharf and had to leave the game.

The Jets wound up the road trip with a stop in Toronto to meet the Toros on Friday night. Playing their third game in three nights, the Jets controlled play throughout the contest and finally pulled away with two third period goals that gave the Jets a 5-3 victory. Anders Hedberg's second goal of the game and his 18th of the season proved to be the game-winner as the 16-7-0 Jets returned home in sole possession of first place, two points ahead of the Nordiques.

Before an overflow Sunday night crowd of 10,222, which included more than 100 noisy members of the Saints Booster Shots, the Jets played host to the Fighting Saints for the first time this season to close out November. During the off-season, the Fighting Saints had acquired veteran forward Johnny McKenzie from the Cowboys and added longtime Maple Leaf Dave Keon to their lineup. They came into Winnipeg with a modest 10-8-1 record that was good enough for second place in the Western Division.

The Jets outclassed their guests in the first period and earned a 3-0 lead, but in the second, the Fighting Saints struck for two quick goals to get themselves right back into the game. Just over a minute later, however, Peter Sullivan had the Fighting Saints mesmerized in their own end and found Norm Beaudin, who scored his eighth goal of the season and effectively erased any comeback hopes. Larsson earned first-star honors in the 5-3 victory after being called on at the last moment to replace Daley, who had come down with a cold just before the game. The win kept the Jets one point ahead of the Nordiques and their first-place standing at the end of November allowed the team to collect on the first installment of their team bonus of $1,000 per player.

On Tuesday night, the Jets kicked off a three-game road swing in Denver to meet the troubled Spurs. Before a season-high gathering of 5,676 spectators who took advantage of an abundant supply of free tickets, the Jets overcame the bad ice at McNichols Arena to grab a 3-0 lead. Staring down a three-goal deficit and with rampant rumors of their imminent demise in the air, the Spurs didn't fold and they eventually tied the score with just 67 seconds to play in regulation time. The Jets rebounded and Hull, playing despite being at only 50 percent effectiveness, scored four minutes into overtime to rescue the two points and stay one point ahead of the Nordiques.

The Jets flew to San Diego the next day for a game on Thursday, 4 December against the Mariners. The Jets again took an early lead, but the Mariners matched the Jets goal for goal until Norm Ferguson's marker seven minutes into the third period put the Mariners in front for the first time in the game. Four minutes later, Hull scored his second goal of the night and the 800th of his pro career to tie the score at 4-4. The game appeared to be headed for overtime until Mats Lindh found Willy Lindstrom alone at the edge of the crease for the go-ahead goal that stood up as the Jets won their fourth in a row.

Answering a 5:30 a.m. wake-up call the next day, the 18-7-0 Jets left San Diego for Houston to meet the Aeros on Friday night. The Jets didn't make it in until 4 p.m., but they pulled themselves together in time for their first appearance at the Summit, the brand-new 14,900-seat home of the Aeros, which had hosted its first game just one month earlier.

Against considerable odds, the travel-weary Jets came out strong and Nilsson, who had successfully defended his title as the Jets' table tennis king the day before, gave the Jets a 3-1 lead midway through the first period. Aeros' goaltender Ron Grahame was knocked down on the play, and on the heels of another controversial Jets' goal earlier in the game, he became incensed and took his frustration out on referee Ron Asselstine. Grahame was ejected for his tantrum and had to be restrained by his teammates before leaving the ice. The Aeros narrowed the Jets' lead to 3-2 in the second period, but Asselstine soon became the center of attention once again when Gordie Howe first elbowed, then shoved the referee after being assessed a penalty for taking down Bill Lesuk. The elder Howe was ejected and irate fans began littering the ice with all sorts of debris. Asselstine and both linesmen then left the ice and the referee was in the shower when Hull, Kromm and Aeros' coach Bill Dineen convinced him to return.

The game eventually resumed and Hull's second goal of the game a minute and a half later extended the Jets' lead to 4-2. The two-goal lead held until the dying minutes, when the Aeros scored three times in the span of 83 seconds to pull off one of the greatest comebacks in hockey history and send the Jets home reeling with a crushing 5-4 defeat. Larry Hale scored his first goal of the season with only two seconds on the clock off a faceoff to Larsson's right, rewarding fans who had stayed around with a thrill that they would not soon forget.

The Aftermath

After the game on 5 December 1975 when he was assaulted by Gordie Howe, referee Ron Asselstine quit officiating briefly, but after meeting with WHA Vice-President Bud Poile, he decided to return, but by his choice, as a linesman. He was disciplined by the league for leaving the ice after the incident with Howe, but he went on to have a distinguished career as a linesman in the WHA and later, in the NHL, until his retirement in 1997. Asselstine did work another game as a referee when he was forced to substitute for referee Ron Ego, who came down with the flu prior to the game on 26 December 1976 between the Nordiques and Jets at the Winnipeg Arena.

For his part, Howe received only a two-game suspension for his actions in that game.

Off the ice, in 2007, Asselstine was awarded the Caring Canadian Award for his work with the Guelph Wish Fund for Children, an organization he founded in 1984 that grants wishes to ill, injured or disabled children.

Still three points ahead of the Nordiques, the Jets faced off against their closest divisional pursuers on Sunday night, hoping to put Friday night's collapse behind them. The Jets opened the scoring, but all the recent travel had caught up to them. The visiting Nordiques frustrated the Jets all night long and went on to post a 3-2 victory that narrowed the gap between the two teams to a single point.

With a couple of days rest to catch their breath, the Jets were back on the ice on Wednesday night to meet the struggling 8-15-2 Toros. For the sixth straight game, the Jets opened the scoring, but after the Toros replaced starting goaltender Mario Vien with Dave Tataryn, they got back into the game and took their first lead of the night late in the third period. The Jets responded quickly when Mike Ford tied the game a minute later, then Hull scored in the first minute of overtime on his seventh shot of the night to allow the Jets to escape with a 6-5 victory. Tataryn made only his fifth professional appearance and was playing on a tryout contract that paid him $100 per game if he dressed and an additional $100 if he played.

The next day, the Jets went through a light workout and gave Larsson a cream pie in his face as a present for his 31st birthday before returning to game action on Friday night against the 15-11-1 Cowboys. A late-arriving crowd of 8,376 made the trek to the Arena through the exceptionally bitter cold, high winds and snow only to be greeted by the sight of Bobby Leiter, the newest Cowboy, opening the scoring early in the first period. The Cowboys were the better team in the first half of the game, but Joe Daley kept them from extending their slim lead, then the Jets gradually turned the game around. Led by the "L" line of Mats Lindh, Willy Lindstrom, and Bill Lesuk, the Jets scored the next four goals on their way to a 4-2 win, putting five points between themselves and the Nordiques.

Did You Know?

Bobby Leiter joined the Cowboys 90 minutes before their game against the Jets on 12 December 1975 and opened the scoring at 6:46 of the first period. When he was last in Winnipeg on 29 September 1974, he scored two first period goals as a member of the Atlanta Flames in an exhibition game. Ironically, Leiter's last goal as a pro would also come against the Jets on 30 April 1976 in Game 4 of the Canadian Division final series.

The Jets moved on to Edmonton for a game on Sunday, 14 December against the Oilers in the first of a four-game road swing. The Jets dominated the contest from start to finish and only Chris Worthy's superb goaltending prevented an epic blowout, but the Jets still got enough past Worthy for a 3-1 victory. After the game, amid the overpowering stench of Kromm's traditional victory cigar in the dressing room, trainer Bill Bozak quickly became the most popular man in the room as the Jets licked their wounds. Unable to skate with their high-flying guests, the Oilers had decided to concentrate on extracting a physical toll instead and ice packs were as valued as gold bricks in the visitors' dressing room. Lindh suffered the most serious injury when he struck his head on in the inside of the glass above the door on the penalty box and broke his jaw. While his battered teammates left for Toronto, Lindh was forced to remain behind in an Edmonton hospital for one or two days.

Still recovering from their beating two nights earlier, the Jets, without Lindh, stepped onto the ice at Maple Leaf Gardens on Tuesday night to meet the Toros for the second time in less than a week. Before a crowd of 8,831, which included a number of Jets supporters, the game went back and forth but the issue wasn't settled until Hedberg took a pass from Hull, cut across the net, and fired a high shot past Tataryn with only 15 seconds left on the clock to give the Jets a 4-3 victory. Peter Sullivan scored twice in his hometown and Larsson made 40 saves to backstop the Jets to their fourth win in a row.

The next stop for the Jets was Le Colisee in Quebec for another showdown with the Nordiques on Thursday night. The Jets came roaring out of the gate and stormed out to a 4-1 lead, but the Nordiques slowly inched their way back into the game and tied the score at 4-4 early in the third period. With less than four minutes to play, Nordiques' defenseman Ric Jordan fired a shot from center ice that skidded along the ice and eluded Daley. The fluky goal stood up as the game-winner and the Nordiques climbed back to within three points of the first-place Jets.

The four-game road trip wound up on Saturday night at the Saint Paul Civic Center against the Fighting Saints. The Jets had a strong first period, but it was the Fighting Saints who took the early lead. The Jets rallied to tie the score at 2-2 late in the second period, but the Fighting Saints seized control of the game in the third and scored four times to send the Jets down to a 6-3 defeat. Wayne Connelly scored three times for the Fighting Saints and Fran Huck, the former Jet, scored the eventual game-winner in the decisive third period.

Both teams flew to Winnipeg for a rematch on Sunday night and the Fighting Saints picked up where they had left off in the third period the night before, coasting to a 3-1 victory. Only Daley's impressive 30-save outing prevented a more lopsided score in favor of the visitors, who had successfully played a hard-hitting physical game to slow down the Jets. Only because of the Nordiques' 11-7 loss in Cincinnati did the Jets end the weekend still in first place.

During the game, Fighting Saints' defenseman Rick Smith lost his stick over the boards and pleaded with a fan to throw it back on account of the team's financial problems. Bill Butters and Curt Brackenbury joined in and after they took swings at the fan with their sticks, three policemen intervened to restore order. Smith got his stick back and no one was penalized over the affair.

The Jets flew to Edmonton for one last game before the Christmas holiday in the hopes of busting out of a season-high three-game losing streak. They did just that, taking control from the outset and cruising to a 6-2 victory that wasn't nearly as painful as their last visit. Sullivan scored three times for his first hat trick as a Jet and Hull added two of his own for the 24-12-0 Jets, who returned home for the holiday three points ahead of the Nordiques.

On Friday night, the Jets were back on the ice for a Boxing Day matchup with the Cowboys. Hull's 23rd goal of the season late in the first period got the Jets on the board first, but goaltender Don "Smokey" McLeod was the star of the night and held his team in the game. Peter Driscoll's long shot from center ice early in the third period gave the visitors a 5-2 lead and though the Jets managed to put a couple of more past the stubborn McLeod, the Cowboys held on for a 5-4 triumph.

The next day, the Jets left for Calgary for a Sunday afternoon rematch with the Cowboys to start a five-game road trip. Goaltending was again the difference as Wayne Wood stopped 32 of 36 Jets shots, while the Cowboys pumped six of their 16 shots past Curt Larsson. Veli-Pekka Ketola recorded his first hat trick as a Jet, but it didn't prevent the Jets from dropping their fifth game in six outings. That, combined with the Nordiques' 6-1 victory in Toronto, knocked the Jets out of first place.

Game two of the road trip took place two nights later in Houston to close out 1975. In the afternoon, the Jets announced the acquisition of 27-year-old Calgary native Lyle Moffat from the Crusaders in exchange for Randy Legge, who the Jets had assigned to the Mohawk Valley Comets of the NAHL after picking him up in the off-season from the defunct Blades franchise. Bobby Kromm had become an admirer of Moffat when the two were on opposite sides in the CHL and when asked if there was one player on the Crusaders' roster he would like to have, he chose Moffat. Kromm described him as good skater and hard worker with a good attitude. As a youngster, Moffat was also an accomplished baseball player who once tried out with the Montreal Expos, but he didn't pursue his baseball aspirations any further because he had already committed to Michigan Tech on a hockey scholarship.

After a team meeting, the Jets took to the ice and, backed by a strong rebound outing from Larsson, they kept one step ahead of the Aeros all night long. The game went right down to the wire, but, unlike their last appearance at the Summit, there was to be no miracle comeback. The Jets hung on for a 5-3 win, marking their first victory in Houston since the 1973 playoffs. The win moved the Jets back into a first-place tie with the Nordiques, who had battled the Fighting Saints to a 4-4 draw in Saint Paul.

On New Year's Eve, the Jets returned home before leaving for Calgary on Friday for their third meeting with the Cowboys in eight days on Saturday night. The Jets bounced back from an early 2-0 deficit and outskated the Cowboys in the second period, scoring three times and adding a pair in the third for a 6-3 victory that snapped the Cowboys' five-game winning streak. Hull celebrated his 37th birthday with a goal and Joe Daley earned the victory, stopping 20 shots in his return after Curt Larsson had handled the starting assignment in the past two games.

The Jets moved north to meet the Oilers on Sunday night, where they dominated their listless hosts and pulled away with four third period goals in the 8-1 rout that extended the Oilers' losing streak to nine games. Despite a numb right arm after a vicious slash from Oilers' defenseman Al Hamilton, Peter Sullivan scored three third period goals to record his second hat trick in as many trips to Edmonton and Anders Hedberg chipped in with a pair as the Jets extended their lead over the Nordiques to four points. As the game wound down, the Edmonton fans turned their wrath on General Manager Bill Hunter by treating him to a potpourri of verbal abuse. The Oilers had been so bad of late that Hull went as far as to ask Rudy Pilous if there was something the Jets could do to help them out.

The five-game road trip came to a close two nights later with the Jets' third visit of the trip to Calgary. In the latest battle between very familiar opponents, the Cowboys used their size to knock the Jets off the puck at every turn and kept the Jets off the scoreboard while putting in five of their own past Larsson in the 5-0 whitewashing. Kromm called the defeat his team's worst game of the year, but the Jets could at least take comfort in the fact that they were flying home for an eight-game, three-week home stand.

A hardy crowd of 7,695 fans braved a blast of January cold to see the Jets in their first home game of the new year on Wednesday, 7 January against the Toros. The Jets looked like a completely different team than they had the night before as they blitzed the Toros with four first period goals and poured it on to humiliate their guests by a score of 8-2. Nilsson scored three goals and added two assists to lead the Jets' attack, while Moffat added his first goal since being acquired from the Crusaders. The win extended the Jets' divisional lead to six points over the idle Nordiques, while the Toros retained their hold of the Canadian Division basement.

Fergy's Road To Winnipeg

On the night of 7 January 1976, 37-year-old Vancouver native John Ferguson was named Head Coach and General Manager of the NHL's New York Rangers, replacing both Coach Ron Stewart and General Manager Emile Francis.

Ferguson would go on to lure both Anders Hedberg and Ulf Nilsson to New York in 1978, then after he was fired by the Rangers, he accepted the job as Vice President and General Manager of the Jets on 22 November 1978. After the Jets were admitted to the NHL, Ferguson held his post through nine full seasons until his dismissal on 30 October 1988.

With only marginal relief from the cold snap that had settled over Winnipeg, a season-low crowd of 7,404 turned out to witness the Indianapolis Racers' second visit of the season on Friday night. Those who filed through the doors were anything but entertained as the defensive-minded Racers slowed the game to a crawl. Mike Ford scored late in the third period to wipe out a 1-0 Racers' lead, but soon after getting out of the penalty box midway through overtime, Al Karlander beat Daley to a loose puck and put it into an unattended net to give the Racers an improbable 2-1 sudden-death victory that marked the Jets' first overtime defeat of the season.

The home stand continued on Sunday night as the Jets hosted the Ottawa Civics, who had been the Denver Spurs before their sudden relocation nine days before. The Civics had started their day with a 6:30 a.m. wake-up call in Phoenix and they didn't arrive in Winnipeg until 5 p.m., leaving precious little time before the start of the game two and a half hours later. Still wearing their Spurs uniforms, the Civics survived the first two periods and took a 5-3 lead early in the third, thanks to an unusually poor outing from Daley. While the crowd was treating Daley a chorus of Bronx cheers, the frustrated Jets pressed on and tied the score at 5-5 with a pair of goals two and a half minutes apart. The game went to overtime and though the Jets kept buzzing around the Civics' net, goaltender Lynn Zimmerman single-handedly kept the game tied, but Hedberg finally beat Zimmerman with only two minutes left to allow the Jets to take the two points in dramatic fashion. With the win, the 29-16-0 Jets restored their six-point lead over the Nordiques at the expense of the Civics, who had only one win to show for their first six games representing their new home city.

Though many of the Jets had a couple of days off between games, seven of them left for Cleveland the next morning to participate in the fourth annual WHA All-Star Game on Tuesday, 13 January. In front of a crowd of 15,491 at the Richfield Coliseum, Joe Daley, Thommie Bergman, Larry Hornung, Lars-Erik Sjoberg, Anders Hedberg, Bobby Hull, and Ulf Nilsson suited up for the Canadian squad, opposed by the best of the U.S.-based teams. Nilsson scored once as the Canadian team won by a score of 6-1.

The seven All-Stars had to hurry home to rejoin their teammates in time for a Wednesday night encounter with the Aeros, who had had four of their own players, along with Coach Bill Dineen, at the All-Star Game. The Jets were in complete control throughout and used a pair of goals in each of the second and third periods to knock off the Aeros by a score of 4-1 to pull eight points ahead of the Nordiques. Recently moved back to defense, Hexi Riihiranta was the Jets' best player and earned first-star honors and the Jets, as a team, held the Aeros to only 16 shots. On the other side of the Arena, a dejected Gordie Howe bemoaned being lustily booed by the crowd for elbowing and shoving referee Ron Asselstine more than a month ago. When he wasn't on the ice, Howe was repeatedly verbally abused by a number of fans seated behind the Aeros' bench.

Two nights later, the fifth game of the home stand saw the Oilers make their second appearance of the season in Winnipeg. Sadly, the Jets followed their impressive Wednesday night performance by playing down to the level of their opponents, and the Oilers encountered little resistance on their way to a 5-1 win. Lindh returned to the lineup for the first time in more than a month and was impressive despite still wearing a makeshift mask to protect his broken jaw, but the only other positive from a Jets perspective was Larry Hillman's first goal in two seasons and his first as a Jet.

The next day, the troubled Ottawa Civics franchise officially disbanded after a local group failed to raise the necessary capital to keep the team afloat. The team that started life as the Denver Spurs got off to a poor start on and off the ice in Denver and though the team was well received during its brief stay in Ottawa, the support wasn't enough to save the franchise.

On Sunday night, the Jets met the Whalers in the hopes of putting Friday night's embarrassment behind them. The Jets stormed out of the gate and held the upper hand from start to finish in an 8-0 rout. Hull scored three times on three different lines for his first hat trick of the season, while Daley stopped 26 shots to earn his fifth shutout as the Jets restored their six-point divisional lead over the Nordiques.

There was no game on Monday night, but the Jets made the trip downtown to the Winnipeg Convention Center for Vegas Nite, a fundraiser for the non-profit community ownership group. For a price $12.50 per person, Jets' supporters were treated to a night of dancing, entertainment, gambling, and a chance to win a potpourri of prizes that included a trip to Las Vegas, a 1976 Cadillac, two Jets season tickets, and a 14' aluminum Starcraft Sea Scamp. Mr. Elvin Fast won the Las Vegas trip, Mr. Yosh Ito won the Cadillac, Mr. Don Harman won the Jets season tickets, and Mr. Bert Todd won the boat. In addition, door prizes totaling $15,000 were awarded every half hour. It was a successful evening all around, despite problems caused by an overflow crowd.

Back on the ice, for the fifth time in a month, the 31-17-0 Jets again met the Cowboys as the marathon home stand resumed on Wednesday night. The Jets used two late second period goals to break a 1-1 tie and went on to a 4-1 victory that kept them six points ahead of the Nordiques. Filling in for Veli-Pekka Ketola, who was running a fever from a gum infection, Mats Lindh was the star of the game in another strong outing since his return to the lineup two games ago.

The season's second eight-game home stand came to a close on Friday night with another visit from the Oilers, who were making their second visit in a week. Coming off a 10-3 blowout defeat at home against the Cowboys on Tuesday night, Oilers' General Manager Bill Hunter assumed the coaching duties for the third time in four seasons, this time replacing Clare Drake. The injury-riddled Oilers jumped out to a 2-0 first period lead, but the Jets scored twice early in the second to tie the score at 2-2. After a half-hour intermission featuring some comedy acts, the Jets struck for two more in the first five minutes of the third period, causing Hunter to take his frustrations out on the concrete wall behind the bench. Hunter got the worst of that exchange and his team didn't fare any better as the Jets maintained their 4-2 lead for their sixth win of the home stand.

After the game, the Jets announced the acquisition of 37-year-old defenseman Gerry Odrowski from the Fighting Saints in exchange for the seldom-used Perry Miller. In his 16th season as a professional, Odrowski had NHL stints with the Detroit Red Wings, Oakland Seals and St. Louis Blues and WHA stops with the Sharks and Roadrunners before joining the Fighting Saints. A good puck handler and good skater that brought another steady veteran presence, the Jets had been interested in Odrowski for four seasons and he became available after a rift with coach Harry Neale. The Jets also welcomed back Bobby Guindon, whom they had released back in November over budgetary constraints, and signed him to a contract for the rest of the season.

Gerry Odrowski Fan Club

More than a dozen students at Ryerson College in Toronto once started a Gerry Odrowski Fan Club. Though none of them had ever met Odrowski, president George Mather and the group got banners ready in his honor and gave him a standing ovation when he first appeared in Toronto in November 1973. "We just figured here was a guy who had worked hard and never succeeded in anything sensational, and we'd honor him as our unsung hero," explained Peter Wilson.

The reinforced Jets began a seven-game road trip on Wednesday, 28 January in Saint Paul. Playing their first game away from Winnipeg in 22 days, Nilsson scored a pair of goals to stake the Jets to a 2-0 lead, but Miller burned his old team with a goal midway through the second period and his new teammates did the rest. Mike Walton and Paul Holmgren each scored a pair of goals as the Fighting Saints stormed back for a 6-2 victory that marked their third straight win over the Jets.

On Friday night, the Jets made their second and last regularly scheduled appearance of the season in Hartford. Odrowski made his Jets debut, but it was the big line, or the Hot Line, as the trio of Hull, Nilsson, and Hedberg had been dubbed, that stole the show as the Jets erased a 3-1 lead for an eventual 6-3 victory that left the Whalers awestruck. Hedberg and Hull each scored two goals, while Nilsson recorded five assists to help the Jets pull five points ahead of the red-hot Nordiques and allowed the Jets to collect their second $1,000-per-player bonus for being in first place at the end of January.

The Jets moved on to Cincinnati to continue the road trip, where 44 members of the Booster Club were waiting for them on Saturday afternoon at Stouffer's Hotel in downtown Cincinnati after a 23-hour trek from Winnipeg to Southern Ohio. The boosters, including Joe Playfoot, Daley's father-in-law, stood in the doorway and watched the players grab their bags and file in through a side door. Fortunately, the game that evening proved more enjoyable for both the boosters and their favorite team as, for the second straight night, the Jets wiped out a two-goal deficit on their way to a 5-2 victory. Lindstrom scored twice in the second period and the unheralded Duke Asmundson played a key role in the pivotal third period. Asmundson tied up a pair of Stingers' defenseman in front of goaltender Paul Hoganson on his first shift of the game, paving the way for Larry Hornung's eventual game-winner. He then followed up with a goal of his own on his third shift of the night, which put the game out of reach. The win came at a price, however, as Nilsson fell heavily behind the Stingers' goal in the first period and did not return after bruising his knee.

With their faithful entourage in tow, the Jets boarded a bus after the game for Indianapolis to battle the Racers on Sunday afternoon to begin the month of February. Playing their third game in fewer than three days, the Jets skillfully employed the same close-checking, defensive strategy used by the Racers and beat them at their own game. Peter Sullivan, who was replacing the injured Nilsson alongside Hull and Hedberg, scored the winning goal late in the second period as the Jets squeaked by with a 2-1 victory. Larsson made 38 saves to earn the win and he was at his best in the second period when he faced 22 shots and stopped all but one.

On Monday, the Jets left for Quebec in the hopes of extending their winning streak to four games and widening their seven-point lead over the second-place Nordiques on Tuesday night. On the heels of a vicious storm that left the area covered in snow and ice, a crowd of 12,152 turned out to see the latest battle between division contenders. The two teams traded goals until the Nordiques took the lead for the first time late in the second period and kept it despite a valiant effort on the part of the Jets to tie the score. Daley had a rare off night in the 5-4 defeat that kept the Nordiques within striking distance of the first-place Jets.

The 36-19-0 Jets moved on to Toronto the next day and had some time to catch their breath before their next game on Friday, 6 February against the Toros. The Jets jumped out to a 3-0 lead early in the first period, but scoring continued at a frantic pace as the youthful Toros came back time and again. Mark Napier's penalty shot goal late in the third period tied the score at 6-6, but the Jets got the last laugh. Just as they had in their last visit to Maple Leaf Gardens, the Jets scored in the game's final minute to take the lead for good. Mike Ford's blast from the point beat goaltender Les Binkley with only 55 seconds left on the clock and the Jets skated off with a 7-6 win to extend the Toros' winless streak to seven games. Nilsson scored once and added five assists in his second game back after missing Sunday afternoon's game in Indianapolis. Hedberg chipped in with two goals and two assists, and Bobby Guindon scored his first goal as a Jet. Larsson got the start in goal, but he was forced to leave after two periods after pulling a thigh muscle, leaving Daley to handle the goaltending chores for the third period.

Les Is More

The Jets last faced Les Binkley on 6 February 1976, but he would go on to work for the Jets after his playing days. Jets' General Manager John Ferguson hired Binkley, his former teammate with the Cleveland Barons, in December, 1978 as a scout, and Binkley would later succeed Bill Robinson as Chief Scout.

The last stop on the whirlwind road trip came on Saturday night at the Richfield Coliseum against the struggling Crusaders, winners of only two of their past nine games and without star goaltender Gerry Cheevers, who had left the team over a contract dispute and returned to the Boston Bruins. Still, it was the Crusaders who got off to a quick start, but the Jets picked themselves up and grew stronger as the game wore on. Three straight goals wiped out a 3-1 deficit and gave the Jets a brief 4-3 lead in the third period before the Crusaders tied the score with just over eight minutes to play in regulation time. Neither team could break the deadlock and the game ended in a 4-4 tie.

On the heels of their first tie of the season, the Jets awoke at 4:30 a.m. the next morning and hurried home for a Sunday night encounter with the Cowboys. After splitting six first period goals with their guests, the Jets seized control of the game in the second and pulled away with four goals. The third period belonged to the Cowboys, but they could do little to make a dent in the four-goal deficit and the Jets coasted to an 8-4 victory that kept them seven points up on the Nordiques.

The Jets were back in action on Wednesday night for another first-place showdown with the Nordiques at the Arena. In front of their eighth five-figure crowd of the season, the Jets came out on the wrong end of a 6-4 score as the Nordiques scored twice in the third period to break a 4-4 tie. Marc Tardif and Real Cloutier each scored twice for the visitors, who climbed back to within five points of the first-place Jets. Daley held his team in the game in the early going, but he could not spare the Jets their second defeat in eight games. Bobby Kromm lamented his team's poor play after the game, and the Jets' cause wasn't helped when Nilsson pulled some muscles in his right side. He played on despite the injury, but his effectiveness had been significantly limited.

On Sunday night, the Jets closed out their three-game home stand with another visit from the Toros, who were mired in a six-game losing streak and had been without a win for almost a month. The Jets took full advantage of the inexperienced Toros' defense and kept one step ahead of them all night long in the wild shootout. The game went right down to the wire, but the Jets escaped with their second straight 7-6 victory over the last-place Toros. Hedberg scored twice for the Jets and Nilsson picked up a pair of assists in shaking off the pulled muscles from Wednesday.

Still five points ahead of the Nordiques, the Jets left the next day for a game on Tuesday, 17 February in Edmonton. Winners of only three of their last 12 games, the Oilers proved to be a stubborn opponent and they took advantage of a shaky outing from Larsson to take a 4-2 lead midway through the third period. The Jets showed some resolve of their own and scored twice to tie the game. Hedberg narrowed the gap to a single goal less than a half minute after the Oilers' fourth goal, then Nilsson banked a shot off goaltender Dave Dryden's arm from behind the net to even the score with only 2:12 left to play in regulation time. After a cautiously played overtime, the two teams settled on a 4-4 tie. Rick Morris, a speedy winger who had spurned a contract offer from the Jets after the Ottawa Civics folded in mid-January, scored two shorthanded goals to lead the Oilers.

The Jets returned home for a game the next evening against the Roadrunners to begin a four-game home stand. Before the season's second-smallest crowd numbering 7,424, backstopped by Daley, the Jets built up a 3-0 lead and held off the industrious Roadrunners, who fought tooth and nail right to the end, for an eventual 4-3 victory. It was the line of Bill Lesuk, Veli-Pekka Ketola, and Norm Beaudin that proved to be the difference in holding off the Roadrunners in the game's final minute as the Jets raised their point total for the season to 82, one more than they had accumulated all of last season.

Two nights later, the home stand continued with the Jets' second game against the Oilers in less than a week. The Jets were the much better team for most of the night, but the Oilers again proved resilient and kept the score close. Sullivan scored the eventual game-winner in the final minute of the second period and Hull sealed the victory with his first goal in 12 days as the Jets won by a score of 4-2. It was Sullivan's 10th goal of the season against the Oilers and the victory clinched a playoff berth for the Jets with post-season play still seven weeks away.

After playing three games in four nights, the Jets had a few days before their next game on Wednesday night against the Crusaders. Wearing patches on their shoulders honoring the upcoming 1976 Olympic Games in Montreal, the Jets came stormed their way to a convincing 5-2 victory that flattered the visitors. Five different scorers did the damage in the complete team effort that again put them six points up on the second-place Nordiques.

The Oilers returned for their second visit in a week to round out the home stand on Friday night. Those among the late-arriving crowd of 8,225 saw the Jets again jump out to an early lead, but just as they had the week before, the Oilers hung around and made a game of it. The Jets, however, held on to the lead and Ketola scored the eventual game-winner late in the second period when he lifted Barry Long's stick off the puck and put a shot past goaltender Dave Dryden. The 4-3 victory was the Jets' fourth in a row and moved them eight points ahead of the Nordiques.

The schedule makers had left the Jets no time celebrate as they boarded a plane early the next morning for Quebec for their fifth and final regularly scheduled appearance of the season at Le Colisee. The Jets and Nordiques treated the crowd of 12,317 spectators to a thrilling contest befitting a matchup between the league's top two teams. After Rejean Houle's tying goal in the final minute, extra time was needed to settle the outcome. Two minutes into overtime, Larry Hillman's shot from the point landed in front of Lyle Moffat, who nudged it past goaltender Richard Brodeur and into the net to give the Jets a dramatic 4-3 victory. Though the Hot Line was held off the scoreboard, the foot soldiers took center stage and Joe Daley made 33 saves in a sparkling outing that widened the gap between the two clubs to 10 points.

On Leap Year Day, the Jets took to the ice at Maple Leaf Gardens for a Sunday matinee against the Toros to conclude another three-game weekend. Led behind the bench by assistant general manager Gilles Leger, who had replaced Bob Baun after the Toros' last visit to Winnipeg, the Toros took full advantage of a team playing its third game in as many days and bombed the visiting Jets by a score of 11-7. The lopsided defeat was a complete team effort in which the Jets left both Daley and Curt Larsson hung out to dry. Larsson played the last two periods and yielded seven goals on 30 shots.

The 44-21-2 Jets returned home and had a full week before their next game action, but they did have an off-ice function to attend on Friday night. The Booster Club held its third annual Awards Night at the International Inn, where more than 300 people were in attendance, including the entire Jets team. After Ken "Friar" Nicolson introduced the players and presented each of them with a trophy ashtray, Nilsson received his second consecutive most valuable award from the boosters, Ketola was named as the most improved Jet, Hedberg was selected as the most popular player, and Sullivan was the top rookie. The award winners each received a ceramic look-alike doll of themselves. Hull presented a $1,000 check to the Bobby Hull Scholarship Fund and the evening continued with dancing and socializing.

Over the weekend, the league lost another member when the Fighting Saints folded. The players had not been paid for February's games and the club had also missed a pay period in December. The remaining 14 players took a vote at the Minneapolis-Saint Paul Airport and elected not to continue playing, bringing an end to the franchise.

On Sunday night, the Jets were back on the ice against the Cowboys at the Arena. Before a crowd of 9,226 onlookers that included a contingent from Calgary, the Jets shook off the rust and peppered "Smokey" McLeod while playing a much tighter defensive game in their own end of the rink. The result was a 3-1 victory that restored their lead over the Nordiques to 10 points. Hull collected his 40th goal of the season and the third-place Cowboys, playing their fifth game in six nights, remained 12 points back of the Nordiques.

The Jets were back at the airport the next evening bound for Toronto once again to play a makeup game against the Toros on Tuesday night as a result of the Civics' demise. This time around, the Jets were much better and, led by Mats Lindh's pair of goals and another stellar outing from Hedberg, they handed the cellar-dwelling Toros a convincing 5-2 defeat. Only the outstanding goaltending of John Garrett kept the game closer than it should have been. Garrett, who was formerly with the Fighting Saints, signed with the Toros after leaving his original team last week along with former teammate Mike Walton before the team folded.

After a quick turnaround, the Jets were again in action on Wednesday night at the Arena against the Nordiques to open a pair of games against their closest divisional pursuers. The crowd of 10,251 who had come to see a hockey game, however, saw something quite different once the first period ended. With the Jets holding a slim 2-1 lead, Ulf Nilsson and Bill Prentice started shoving each other behind the Nordiques' goal, then Pierre Roy left the penalty box to elbow Nilsson in the face. Thommie Bergman grabbed Roy and the benches emptied. The police were eventually summoned on to the ice at the request of linesman Joey Dame as he tried to break up Mike Ford and Gord Gallant and it took six officers and all three officials to restore order. Four Nordiques were ejected and Lyle Moffat was the only Jet to receive a game misconduct. The Jets came out of it with three dislocated thumbs among the group. Moffat was sent to hospital and would have to stay overnight for observation after being decked by Charles Constantin. After the game resumed, the Jets answered the Nordiques' fists with goals and scored four times in each of the next two periods to come away with a satisfying 10-3 victory that put a dozen points between themselves and their pugilistic visitors.

The rematch took place on Friday, 12 March, but Daley was not able to make the start on account of two badly bruised ankles that he had sustained during Thursday morning's workout, leaving the goaltending chores to Larsson. The Jets did, however, have both Larry Hornung and Perry Miller back in their lineup. Hornung had been out for three games because of a rash, while Miller came back to the Jets after the Fighting Saints had folded. The Crusaders selected Miller in the dispersal of the remaining players, but they made no effort to sign him, and because the Jets had guaranteed Miller's contract, they brought him back to Winnipeg. Under the watchful eye of referee Bob Kolari, the two teams stuck to hockey, but Larsson had looked weak in letting in six of the first eight shots he faced during the first period, prompting Bobby Kromm to summon an injured Daley off the bench. The Jets gave it everything they had to recover from the deficit, which had reached six goals early in the second period, but they fell agonizingly short and went down to a 10-8 defeat in front of another five-figure crowd at the Arena. Willy Lindstrom scored his first hat trick as a Jet, but the Jets could only manage a split with their division rivals.

A Sunday night engagement with the fourth-place Oilers was next on the Jets' schedule and though the contest was considerably more subdued than the games had been against the Nordiques, the Jets jumped out to a 3-0 lead early in the first period and coasted the rest of the way in the 4-2 win. Lindh scored a pair for the victorious Jets, but they got a scare when Anders Hedberg limped off the ice in the third period with a sprained ankle.

The Jets wrapped up their eventful four-game home stand on Wednesday night with the sixth and final regular season visit from the Cowboys. Hedberg was on the sidelines with his ankle in a cast, but Daley rose to the occasion and held his team in the game against the determined Cowboys. Much to the delight of the enthusiastic gathering of 8,695, which included a group from Sioux Lookout, Ontario, the Jets eventually got rolling and scored three times before the Cowboys netted two of their own late in the third period. However, Daley and his teammates held firm over the final minutes and the 3-2 score held to give the Jets 100 points for the season, 14 more than the second-place Nordiques.

On Thursday morning, the Jets took off for a Friday night game in Edmonton. Daley again was the difference for the Jets, who played the Oilers to a scoreless tie through two periods. The Jets capitalized on a break to take the lead in the third, but the Oilers replied just 13 seconds later and grabbed the lead for good with only 4:21 to play when new acquisition Wayne Carleton scored directly off a faceoff. The 2-1 loss was only the Jets' third defeat in 13 games but they left Edmonton still a dozen points up on the Nordiques.

The next stop for the Jets before returning home was a Sunday afternoon game in Toronto. Despite Hedberg's absence, the Jets took the play to the Toros in the first two periods, but they were turned aside time and again by new arrival John Garrett. The Toros, meanwhile, gave their goaltender all the support he needed with five goals, including two from Vaclav Nedomansky, which put him over the 50-goal mark for the season, as the Toros kept their fading playoff hopes alive with a 5-2 victory. The Jets boarded a plane to return home with their second loss in a row for the first time since late December.

The Jets began their last home stand of the regular season when they hosted the Oilers on Wednesday, 24 March. Needing to win to keep ahead of the Toros for the last playoff position in the Canadian Division, the Oilers took a 2-1 lead to the third period, but Thommie Bergman's goal in the first minute of the third tied the score at 2-2. Though the Jets pressed hard for the go-ahead goal, they couldn't get any more past goaltender Dave Dryden and Tim Sheehy's second goal of the game with just over six minutes to play in regulation time was the difference as the Oilers beat the Jets for the second time in as many meetings.

With their lead atop the division dwindling and in the throws of a three-game losing streak, the Jets took to the ice on Sunday night against the Mariners. Up against a team playing its fourth game in as many nights — and whose players hadn't been paid in almost a month — the Jets used two first period goals from Hull and a four-point outing from Lindstrom to comfortably dispose of the Mariners by a score of 6-1. Though he didn't score, Hedberg returned to the lineup and played well in the much-needed victory that restored the Jets' lead over the Nordiques to eight points. At the game, former Jet Howie Young made his return to Winnipeg as an author, hawking copies of *Cowboy On Ice*, his life story, and sold dozens of copies to the crowd of 10,130 in attendance.

The Jets closed out both the month of March and their regular season home schedule with a visit from the Toros on Wednesday night. Before the game, however, the Jets handed out their traditional year-end awards. Anders Hedberg was named the most valuable player, Peter Sullivan took top rookie honors, while Joe Daley was honored for being the most frequent three star selection. In keeping with team policy regarding individual bonuses, Daley turned over the $500 check he received to charity. Once the game started, the Toros had their chances in the game's early stages to put the Jets in a hole, but the Jets kept the game close and the score was tied at 3-3 midway through the third period. With the chance to clinch first place on home ice at their fingertips, Hull took charge and scored twice within 75 seconds to break the deadlock and send the Jets on to a 5-3 victory. The two goals were his second and third of the night and raised his season total to 49, but more importantly, the top position in the Canadian Division belonged to the Jets.

With their position in the standings solidified, the Jets left on Thursday to begin the regular season's last road trip in Calgary on Friday, 2 April. The Jets went through the motions and offered little resistance in the 4-1 defeat that had no meaning for either team. Hedberg rested a sprained ankle, Ted Green sat the game out, and Larsson made the start in goal, giving Daley a rest before the playoffs.

The Jets moved on and travelled north to battle the Oilers on Sunday night. Earlier in the day, the Toros' 5-4 overtime loss to the Nordiques had allowed the Oilers to wrap up the fourth and final playoff position in the Canadian Division, setting up a first-round matchup between the Oilers and the first-place Jets. This game, however, still meant nothing to either team, but it was the Oilers who roared back from an early 2-1 deficit to grab a 5-2 win. Hull collected his 50th goal of the season in the second period, marking the fifth straight season he had reached that total, going back to his last season as a member of the Chicago Blackhawks.

Back in Calgary, the Jets took to the ice for their 81st and final regular season game on Tuesday night. They wrapped up their most successful campaign in style with a 5-3 victory that gave them a record of 52-27-2, good for 106 points. Hull picked up another hat trick, while Moffat added a pair to send the Jets to the playoffs on a winning note.

Returning home, the Jets opened the post-season on Friday, 9 April against the Oilers, who had finished with a regular season record of 27-49-5, 47 points behind the Jets. The overmatched Oilers again tried to intimidate the Jets, but the Jets responded with a flurry of goals and dominated the contest from start to finish. Seven different Jets scored in the 7-3 victory that gave the Jets the early lead in the best-of-seven series. Green had perhaps his finest game as a Jet and was named the game's first star.

Two nights later, the same two teams were back at the Arena for Game 2, but the Jets were not having the same early success as they had had on Friday night. The Jets fired shot after shot at the Oilers' goal, only to be repelled by the heroic effort of goaltender Dave Dryden. The Oilers made the most of their few opportunities against Larsson, who had replaced Daley early in the game. Midway through the first period, Daley was assessed a match penalty and ejected after delivering an over-the-head chop to the shoulder of Oilers' winger Rusty Patenaude. The Jets still led by a score of 4-3 late in the third period, but Tim Sheehy's goal with just under two minutes to play sent the game to overtime. Less than one minute into the extra period, Ulf Nilsson fired a slap shot from just inside the blue line that beat Dryden to give the Jets a 5-4 victory on their 62nd shot of the game. The goal was Nilsson's second of the contest and sent the Jets to Edmonton with a commanding 2-0 series lead.

Did You Know?

While the Jets were playing the Oilers on the night of 11 April 1976, one of the most violent incidents in hockey history was taking place at Le Colisee in Quebec City in Game 2 of the other Canadian Division series between the Calgary Cowboys and Quebec Nordiques.

Early in the first period, Cowboys' winger Rick Jodzio left the bench to hit the Nordiques' Marc Tardif across the face with a high stick. Jodzio proceeded to drop his gloves and pound Tardif in the head and face and an ugly brawl began. It took 20 police officers to restore order.

Tardif was taken to hospital and was ordered to stay overnight as a precaution. Jodzio was subsequently suspended indefinitely by the WHA and charged with causing bodily injury with intent to maim. Cowboys' coach Joe Crozier and Nordiques' tough guy Gord Gallant were each suspended for the rest of the series and both clubs were fined $25,000 for failure to control their personnel, while Nordiques' coach Jean-Guy Gendron and Cowboys' winger Danny Lawson were each suspended for Game 3. Bud Poile also tendered his resignation as the WHA's Vice-President in charge of hockey operations.

The Cowboys won the game by a score of 8-4.

In an ironic twist, less than a year later, Jodzio would file charges of aggravated assault against two opposing players as a result of fight in the lobby of the Erie County Fieldhouse on the night of Saturday, 26 February 1977. Jodzio, then with the Erie Blades of the North American Hockey League, filed the charges against Paul Stewart and Gary Jacquith of the Binghamton Dusters following the Blades' 7-3 victory over the Dusters.

The series resumed at the Edmonton Coliseum on Wednesday night for Game 3, where the Jets had to turn to Larsson once again in goal on account of the one-game suspension Daley had received for his match penalty on Sunday night. Backing up Larsson was 22-year-old amateur goaltender Andy Stoesz, who had been pulled from the Steinbach Huskies of the Central Amateur Senior Hockey League. Stoesz, a 10th round draft choice of the Toronto Maple Leafs last summer, had starred with the Selkirk Steelers of the Manitoba Junior Hockey League, and though Jets' scouts came away impressed after his performance against a West German team, he still had never played a pro game. The Jets jumped out to a 2-0 first period lead, but the Oilers rallied with two of their own in the second period. Midway through the third, Hull fired a hard shot that went off Dave Dryden's shoulder and into the net and the Jets held on for a 3-2 victory that put them one game away from a ticket to the next round. Larsson was sharp in goal and the Jets didn't miss a beat with Daley's suspension.

The Jets had a chance to wrap up the series in straight games and win their first playoff series in three years when they faced the Oilers on Friday night in Game 4. With Daley back in the nets, the Jets came out and showed the crowd of more than 13,000 spectators why they had finished so far ahead of their Oilers during the regular season. The determined Jets dominated the Oilers and broke open the game with five second period goals on their way to a convincing 7-2 rout, which gave them a four-game sweep of the series and a matchup against the winner of the Calgary-Quebec series. That heated matchup was decided on Sunday when the Cowboys won by a score of 6-4 in Quebec to take the series four games to one.

Sullivan Struck Oil

The Jets dispatched the Oilers in four straight games in the Canadian Division semi-final, but Peter Sullivan was one Jet who was unhappy to see the last of the Oilers for the 1975-1976 season. In 13 regular season games against the Oilers, Sullivan had scored 10 goals to go along with four assists; in four playoff games, he had scored twice and set up three others.

The Canadian Division final series began on Friday, 23 April with the Cowboys coming in to Winnipeg to play the Jets with a berth in the AVCO World Trophy final at stake. The Jets showed no sign of rust after a week between games and the Jets ran up a 6-0 score after the second period before letting up on the throttle in the third. Goaltender Don "Smokey" McLeod was not at his best and neither were his teammates, and the Jets took full advantage to gain the upper hand in the series with a comfortable 6-1 victory. Six different Jets scored in the rout, played front of a crowd of 10,069, the Jets' first five-figure crowd of the post-season.

Game 2 of the best-of-seven series took place on Sunday night, and things proved to be a little tougher. The Jets fought their way through an endless series of bad breaks and missed opportunities, but they persevered and Anders Hedberg beat McLeod early in the third to break a 2-2 tie. The score held and the Jets escaped with a 3-2 victory that gave them a 2-0 series lead.

The Jets left for Calgary on Tuesday afternoon where they would resume the series at the Corral on Wednesday night. The hometown Cowboys delighted the sellout crowd with three second period goals to take a 3-1 lead, but the Jets turned the tables in the third and replied with four of their own to take a 6-3 victory and a 3-0 lead in the series. Still playing with a heavily-taped ankle, Hedberg scored twice and added one assist in leading the Jets to their seventh straight playoff win.

Game 4 took place on Friday night at the Corral, where the Cowboys scored twice in a span of 40 seconds to take an early lead and they never looked back on their way to a 7-3 win to force a fifth game back in Winnipeg. The Cowboys held period leads of 3-1 and 5-2 and the Jets were not able to mount any serious comeback attempt like they had two nights earlier.

The series resumed on Sunday night at the Arena, where a crowd of 8,700 turned out to see the Jets try and finish off the Cowboys. Both teams played it close to the vest for two periods, but Hedberg's second goal of the game early in the third period got the Jets going and they didn't let up until the final buzzer. The Jets and their fans celebrated a 4-0 victory that put them in the AVCO World Trophy final for the second time in their four-year history. Though Daley faced only 17 shots on the night for the shutout, he was called upon to make many difficult saves and responded perfectly. After the game, Jets' founder and WHA CEO/Chairman of the Board Ben Hatskin presented Jets' captain Lars-Erik Sjoberg with the O'Keefe Cup, emblematic of the championship of the Canadian Division. Sjoberg carried the cup around the ice, giving the fans a look at the trophy that was originally handcrafted in London, England in 1883 and used as a punch bowl. Carling O'Keefe Breweries had purchased the cup the year before and Canadian artist Gordon Kring designed the trophy, which featured carvings from Antonio Galati and Anne Harris.

With the trophy in hand, the Jets retreated to their dressing room on the west side of the Arena to celebrate their series victory with three buckets of fried chicken. Their next task was to stay sharp while awaiting the winner of the Aeros-Whalers series that was due to start on Wednesday night at the Summit in Houston. Both teams were coming off long series and over the next 11 days, they would engage in another long series that went the distance. On 16 May, the Aeros beat the Whalers by a score of 2-0 and earned the right to host the Jets four nights later in defense of the WHA championship they had held for the past two seasons.

The AVCO World Trophy final opened on the night of Thursday, 20 May at the Summit with the defending champion Aeros, fresh off two grueling series against the Mariners and Whalers, meeting the Jets, who hadn't played for 18 days. With the championship on the line, however, both teams put on a show for the nearly 15,000 onlookers and, fittingly, the game went to the latter stages of the third period tied at 3-3. Despite being hampered by groin and hamstring pulls all season, Bobby Hull took a feed from Ulf Nilsson off the draw in the Aeros' end and got enough on a shot to beat goaltender Ron Grahame for his 10th goal of the post-season. The Aeros mounted a frantic rally to tie the score once again. They thought they had with just over a minute to play, only to have Joe Daley cover the puck on the goal line. From there, the Jets did a masterful job of holding the Aeros at bay and they skated off with a 4-3 victory and a 1-0 series lead.

While the Jets caught their breath after the nail-biter, Mike Ford left the next morning for his wedding to Lori Cole, which had originally been scheduled for the previous Saturday. Ford returned to the team in Houston on Sunday afternoon in time for the evening game, but Hexi Riihiranta had replaced him in the lineup and the newlywed was forced to watch Game 2 from the sidelines. The game itself was just as exciting Thursday night's affair and Daley and Ron Grahame were matching each other save for save. The action went back and forth, but it was Hull once again who broke the deadlock with a goal late in the third period. With only 1:54 left on the clock, the Golden Jet pounced on his own rebound and knocked it past Grahame to give the Jets a 5-4 lead. Hull's teammates made the lead hold up for a victory that put the Jets two wins away from their first AVCO World Trophy championship.

The Jets returned to Winnipeg on a charter plane that, ironically, made a stop in Kansas City. On the heels of published reports in February that Winnipeg was one of the six WHA cities being considered by the NHL as part of a potential merger arrangement, rumors had surfaced on Sunday that the Jets were going to replace the financially troubled Kansas City Scouts in the NHL.

After the scheduled stopover, the Jets touched down at the Winnipeg International Airport at 5 a.m. on Monday and Bobby Kromm had his charges on the ice for practice nine hours later. Sadly, during practice, Willy Lindstrom came around from behind the net and lost his footing and collided with Ted Green, who went down with a suspected twisted right ankle that was later diagnosed as broken. "The Seed" had been having an outstanding post-season, but the Jets would have to do without the respected veteran defender the rest of the way.

With Green watching as a spectator, the Jets were back in action on Tuesday night for Game 3. The crowd of 10,384 inside the sweltering-hot Arena greeted the Jets with a well-earned standing ovation and the Jets kept the fans on their feet with four first period goals. The Aeros were powerless to stop the onslaught and the 6-3 final score flattered the visitors, who were badly outplayed. Nilsson led the way offensively, scoring three times as the Jets took a 3-0 series lead and moved to within one win of the WHA's ultimate prize. Unfortunately, during the first period, the Jets suffered another injury when Duke Asmundson dislocated his shoulder, but he was able to play in the second and third with the shoulder tightly taped.

Two nights later, another sellout crowd was on hand to see the Jets put the final nail in the coffin of the defending champions and claim the AVCO World Trophy for themselves. The Jets came storming out of the gate and left no doubt as to their intentions, taking a 3-1 first period lead and blowing the game wide open with four more goals in the second period. With the crowd chanting "We're Number One", the Jets added a couple of more to make the final score 9-1 and complete the series sweep to capture their first championship. While Ben Hatskin and Jets' President Bob Graham presented the AVCO World Trophy to Lars-Erik Sjoberg for the traditional victory lap around the Arena, fans and players began their celebrations. The revelry was mildly tempered by Nilsson's absence, as the most valuable player of the playoffs was on his way to the hospital after being high-sticked by Andre Hinse late in the second period. His right eye was scratched and swollen and he would have to remain overnight as a precautionary measure. In addition, during the first period, Thommie Bergman became the second Jet in as many games to suffer a dislocated shoulder, when a frustrated Aeros' defenseman John Schella put his full body weight into a hit that also broke Bergman's shoulder blade. Playing with one arm, Bergman bravely finished the game and was there with his teammates to enjoy the post-game festivities. On Thursday afternoon, the Jets had signed him to a new three-year contract to ensure that would remain a Jet long after his recovery.

Outside the Arena, Portage Avenue was blocked all the way downtown with joyous fans honking their horns and the party continued into the next day. At noon, the Jets staged a victory parade that went down Portage Avenue and ended at Main Street, the same spot were Bobby Hull had signed the contract that gave both the Jets and the WHA instant credibility.

The championship was particularly meaningful for the five members of the original squad who had faced off against the New York Raiders at Madison Square Garden back on 12 October 1972. Bobby Hull, Joe Daley, Larry Hornung, Norm Beaudin, and Duke Asmundson were the last holdovers from that team and though Hull wasn't free to play for that first game, he had played a major role during the 1972-1973 season and for the next three that led up to the moment Jets fans had dreamed about for four years.

In capturing the AVCO World Trophy, the Jets had lost only one game in three playoff rounds and had they been dominant throughout the regular season, sharing the league's best overall record with the Aeros. They set a standard that would be tough to match and they had a short off-season ahead of them to reload and stay ahead of the rest of the league.

Scores and Stats

1975-1976 Winnipeg Jets (52-27-2)

Regular Season

Date	Opponent	Score	Date	Opponent	Score
9 Oct	@Quebec Nordiques	5-3	6 Jan	@Calgary Cowboys	0-5
12 Oct	@Phoenix Roadrunners	4-0	7 Jan	Toronto Toros	8-2
16 Oct	@Denver Spurs	7-3	9 Jan	Indianapolis Racers	1-2*
18 Oct	@San Diego Mariners	1-2	11 Jan	Ottawa Civics	6-5*
19 Oct	@Phoenix Roadrunners	5-6	14 Jan	Houston Aeros	4-1
21 Oct	Cincinnati Stingers	7-0	16 Jan	Edmonton Oilers	1-5
24 Oct	Denver Spurs	5-2	18 Jan	New England Whalers	8-0
26 Oct	Phoenix Roadrunners	5-0	21 Jan	Calgary Cowboys	4-1
30 Oct	Cincinnati Stingers	4-0	23 Jan	Edmonton Oilers	4-2
2 Nov	Quebec Nordiques	0-1	28 Jan	@Minnesota Fighting Saints	2-6
4 Nov	New England Whalers	3-2*	30 Jan	@New England Whalers	6-3
9 Nov	Toronto Toros	5-3	31 Jan	@Cincinnati Stingers	5-2
11 Nov	Cleveland Crusaders	2-3	1 Feb	@Indianapolis Racers	2-1
13 Nov	@Calgary Cowboys	4-2	3 Feb	@Quebec Nordiques	4-5
14 Nov	Edmonton Oilers	6-1	6 Feb	@Toronto Toros	7-6
16 Nov	Indianapolis Racers	2-1	7 Feb	@Cleveland Crusaders	4-4*
18 Nov	Houston Aeros	2-3	8 Feb	Calgary Cowboys	8-4
20 Nov	@Quebec Nordiques	3-2*	11 Feb	Quebec Nordiques	4-6
22 Nov	@Cleveland Crusaders	3-6	15 Feb	Toronto Toros	7-6
23 Nov	@New England Whalers	3-2	17 Feb	@Edmonton Oilers	4-4*
26 Nov	@Cincinnati Stingers	11-3	18 Feb	Phoenix Roadrunners	4-3
27 Nov	@Indianapolis Racers	1-3	20 Feb	Edmonton Oilers	4-2
28 Nov	@Toronto Toros	5-3	25 Feb	Cleveland Crusaders	5-2
30 Nov	Minnesota Fighting Saints	5-3	27 Feb	Edmonton Oilers	4-3
2 Dec	@Denver Spurs	4-3*	28 Feb	@Quebec Nordiques	4-3*
4 Dec	@San Diego Mariners	5-4	29 Feb	@Toronto Toros	7-11
5 Dec	@Houston Aeros	4-5	7 Mar	Calgary Cowboys	3-1
7 Dec	Quebec Nordiques	2-3	9 Mar	@Toronto Toros	5-2
10 Dec	Toronto Toros	6-5*	10 Mar	Quebec Nordiques	10-3
12 Dec	Calgary Cowboys	4-2	12 Mar	Quebec Nordiques	8-10
14 Dec	@Edmonton Oilers	3-1	14 Mar	Edmonton Oilers	4-2
16 Dec	@Toronto Toros	4-3	17 Mar	Calgary Cowboys	3-2
18 Dec	@Quebec Nordiques	4-5	19 Mar	@Edmonton Oilers	1-2
20 Dec	@Minnesota Fighting Saints	3-6	21 Mar	@Toronto Toros	2-5
21 Dec	Minnesota Fighting Saints	1-3	24 Mar	Edmonton Oilers	2-3
23 Dec	@Edmonton Oilers	6-2	28 Mar	San Diego Mariners	6-1
26 Dec	Calgary Cowboys	4-5	31 Mar	Toronto Toros	5-3
28 Dec	@Calgary Cowboys	4-6	2 Apr	@Calgary Cowboys	1-4
30 Dec	@Houston Aeros	5-3	4 Apr	@Edmonton Oilers	2-5
3 Jan	@Calgary Cowboys	6-3	6 Apr	@Calgary Cowboys	5-3
4 Jan	@Edmonton Oilers	8-1			

Playoffs

Date	Opponent	Score	Date	Opponent	Score
9 Apr	Edmonton Oilers	7-3	30 Apr	@Calgary Cowboys	3-7
11 Apr	Edmonton Oilers	5-4*	2 May	Calgary Cowboys	4-0
14 Apr	@Edmonton Oilers	3-2	20 May	@Houston Aeros	4-3
16 Apr	@Edmonton Oilers	7-2	23 May	@Houston Aeros	5-4
23 Apr	Calgary Cowboys	6-1	25 May	Houston Aeros	6-3
25 Apr	Calgary Cowboys	3-2	27 May	Houston Aeros	9-1
28 Apr	@Calgary Cowboys	6-3			

* - overtime

	Scoring																
	Regular Season								Playoffs								
Player	GP	G	A	Pts	PIM	+/-	PP	SH	Shots	GP	G	A	Pts	PIM	+/-	PP	SH	Shots
Duke Asmundson	72	5	11	16	19	1	0	0	50	13	3	2	5	11	2			
Norm Beaudin	80	16	31	47	38		2	0	155	13	2	3	5	10	-5			
Thommie Bergman	81	11	30	41	111	9	1	0	183	13	3	10	13	8	10			
Joe Daley	62	0	1	1	17		0	0	0	12	0	0	0	0		0	0	
Mike Ford	81	13	43	56	70	39	2	0	245	12	1	12	13	8	8			
Ted Green	79	5	23	28	73	32	0	0	61	11	0	2	2	16	6	0	0	
Bob Guindon	29	3	3	6	14	-7	1	0	26	13	3	3	6	9	7			
Anders Hedberg	76	50	55	105	48	60	9	6	271	13	13	6	19	15	16			
Larry Hillman	71	1	12	13	62	-3	0	0	67	12	0	2	2	32	2	0	0	
Larry Hornung	76	3	18	21	26	-6	1	0	50	13	0	3	3	6	1	0	0	
Bobby Hull	80	53	70	123	30	62	14	0	416	13	12	8	20	4	15			
Veli-Pekka Ketola	80	32	36	68	32	-4	8	0	339	13	7	5	12	2	7			
Curt Larsson	23	0	1	1	6		0	0	0	2	0	0	0	0		0	0	
Randy Legge	1	0	0	0	0	1	0	0	0									
Bill Lesuk	81	15	21	36	92	1	3	0	120	13	2	2	4	8	1			
Mats Lindh	65	19	15	34	12	7	4	0	99	13	2	2	4	4	-6			
Willy Lindstrom	81	23	36	59	32	4	5	1	151	11	4	7	11	2	9			
Perry Miller	47	7	6	13	41	8	1	0	42									
Lyle Moffat	42	13	9	22	44	3	4	0	61	13	3	3	6	9	-5			
Ulf Nilsson	78	38	76	114	84	65	7	3	152	13	7	19	26	6	15			
Gerry Odrowski	13	0	1	1	6	-8	0	0	13									
Hexi Riihiranta	70	1	8	9	26	0	0	0	38	4	0	4	4	5	7			
Lars-Erik Sjoberg	81	5	36	41	12	46	1	0	120	13	0	5	5	12	7	0	0	
Peter Sullivan	78	32	39	71	22	-4	5	0	161	13	6	7	13	0	7			

	Goaltending									
	Regular Season									
Goaltender	GP	Min	GA	GAA	Saves	Sv %	SO	EN	W	L	T
Joe Daley	62	3612	171	2.84	1600	0.903	5	0	41	17	1
Curt Larsson	23	1287	83	3.87	552	0.869	0	0	11	10	1
	Playoffs									
	GP	Min	GA	GAA	Saves	Sv %	SO	EN	W	L
Joe Daley	12	671	29	2.59			1	0	10	1
Curt Larsson	2	110	6	3.27			0	0	2	0

New faces for the 1975-1976 season:

TOP LEFT: Coach Bobby Kromm.
TOP RIGHT: Rudy Pilous sits at his desk in his new role as General Manager.

MIDDLE LEFT: Ted Green
MIDDLE CENTER: Bill Lesuk
MIDDLE RIGHT: Peter Sullivan

BOTTOM LEFT: Willy Lindstrom
BOTTOM CENTER: Larry Hillman
BOTTOM RIGHT: Bob Guindon

TOP LEFT: Mats Lindh wearing additional protection after returning from a broken jaw.

TOP RIGHT: Norm Beaudin and Perry Miller, each sporting additional facial protection. Miller was forced to wear a shield after being struck in the eye by Bernie MacNeil of the Cincinnati Stingers. The incident prompted Bobby Hull to stage a one-game strike against the increasing level of violence in pro hockey.

MIDDLE LEFT: Ulf Nilsson and Anders Hedberg buzzing around the net against the Minnesota Fighting Saints.

MIDDLE RIGHT: Anders Hedberg celebrates a goal against the Houston Aeros.

BOTTOM LEFT: Anders Hedberg tries to get away from Bruce Abbey of the Cincinnati Stingers.

TOP LEFT: Bobby Hull watches the action from the bench.

TOP RIGHT: Fans converge on the front doors of the Winnipeg Arena.

LEFT: Ulf Nilsson tries his luck with a shot against the Houston Aeros.

Scenes following the Jets' sweep of the Houston Aeros to capture to AVCO Cup in 1976:

ABOVE: Curt Larsson and Anders Hedberg shaking hands with the Aeros.

LEFT: Lars-Erik Sjoberg and Gordie Howe shake hands.

ABOVE: Lars-Erik Sjoberg accepts the AVCO Cup from Ben Hatskin.

RIGHT: The victorious Jets gather around the AVCO Cup.

BOTTOM LEFT: Bob Graham and Ben Hatskin shake hands with the coveted AVCO World Trophy in the middle.

BOTTOM RIGHT: Norm Beaudin, Lars-Erik Sjoberg, and Larry Hornung pose with the AVCO World Trophy.

TOP: Ben Hatskin, Bob Graham, Lars-Erik Sjoberg, and Bobby Kromm hold up the AVCO Cup in the Jets' dressing room.

LEFT: Anders Hedberg holds the AVCO World Trophy in the Jets dressing room.

BELOW: Anders Hedberg and linemates Ulf Nilsson and Bobby Hull pose with the O'Keefe Cup. In this shot, Nilsson's right eye still shows the effects of being high-sticked by Andre Hinse of the Houston Aeros in the last game of the championship series. Nilsson missed the post-game celebrations on account of the injury.

The Jets celebrate their WHA championship with a parade through downtown Winnipeg:

TOP: Fans converge near the Richardson Building at the corner of Portage Avenue and Main Street.

ABOVE: Lars-Erik Sjoberg accepts congratulations on his way down Portage Avenue while holding the AVCO World Trophy.

LEFT: Bobby Kromm accepts his award as Coach of the Year from The Hockey News.

Season V: 1976-1977 – A Trying Defense

Once the celebrations died down, it was time to get back to work for the defending AVCO World Trophy champions. Three days after the parade on 28 May, the Jets finally got Dan Labraaten's signature on a two-year contract. Labraaten, a native of Arvika, Sweden who was three months shy of his 25th birthday, had been coveted by the Jets for two years and might have signed last season, but twin brothers and Whalers teammates Christer and Thommie Abrahamsson had talked him out of it. The speedy winger, who had doubled as a public relations man with Swedish hockey equipment manufacturer Jofa, was scouted and signed by Dr. Gerry Wilson.

In early June, the Jets bid adieu to another member of the original 1972-1973 roster and one third of the Luxury Line when Norm Beaudin signed with SC Langnau in Switzerland. Though he had one year remaining on his Jets contract, the part-time salesman at Pan-Am Motors left with the Jets' blessing. His production had slipped from 103-point season he enjoyed in 1972-1973, but he made the successful transition to a checker and expert penalty killer and he was an inspiration to his teammates with his work ethic. Norm and his wife Linda, whom he had met on a blind date, held a farewell gathering at a suburban Charleswood hotel during the summer and he was given a hero's sendoff.

Lars-Erik Sjoberg underwent successful surgery on his heel to correct a problem that had hampered him for the past two seasons. Later in June, the WHA held an intra-league draft in which teams were allowed to select players from each other's rosters. Each team was allowed to protect only 12 skaters and two goaltenders, and as a result, the Jets were forced to leave Larry Hornung's rights exposed. The Oilers claimed Hornung, leaving only three members of the original 1972-1973 squad on the roster.

As expected, plenty of individual accolades came the Jets' way. Joe Daley, Ulf Nilsson and Anders Hedberg each earned a spot on the WHA First Team All-Star squad, and Hull was named a Second Team All-Star. Hull had been edged out from the First Team by league scoring champion and MVP Marc Tardif of the Nordiques. Bobby Kromm was also named the WHA's Coach of the Year.

The Jets mailed a contract off to Hexi Riihiranta and invited Bobby Guindon to training camp, but they lost both Larry Hillman and Duke Asmundson to retirement. Hillman went on to take a job in the Cowboys' front office as an assistant to Head Coach and General Manager Joe Crozier, while Asmundson took a job as the Fleet and Commercial Sales Manager for Columbia Tire in Winnipeg. Asmundson, the third original to leave the Jets during the off-season, had been used sparingly during his tenure, but in each of his four seasons as a Jet he had come to training camp having to earn a contract and had done just that. The gentle giant who had made his mark as a good checker and solid hitter also worked for the Jets in the off-season, visiting community clubs, appearing at speaking engagements, and occupying the Jets' booth at Manisphere, the annual agricultural fair held in and around the Arena.

Later in August, the Jets signed winger Kent Ruhnke and rugged defenseman Dave Dunn. Ruhnke had played for the University of Toronto on a Hockey Canada scholarship, where he earned an honors degree in Physical Education and a Bachelor of Education degree. Ruhnke had attended the Boston Bruins' training camp last year and after finishing his education, he had played two games with them at the end of the season. He then worked out with the Jets during the playoffs and after the season he had offers from both teams, but he chose to sign with the Jets. A native of Toronto who would turn 24 before the season, Ruhnke had set a Canadian college record for goals in a season the year before with 51 in just 43 games.

Dunn was a three-year NHL veteran who had played for both the Vancouver Canucks and Toronto Maple Leafs. He fit the Jets' need for a big defenseman who could clear traffic in front of the net. The Moosomin, Saskatchewan native was persuaded to put off retirement and signed a Jets contract the day after his 28th birthday.

There were changes once again around the league. The WHA went ahead with the same 12 teams that had finished the 1975-1976 season, but two of them changed addresses. The Toros relocated south to Birmingham, Alabama and the newly renamed Bulls would call the new 16,700-seat Jefferson County Civic Center home after three seasons competing with the Maple Leafs in Toronto. With the NHL's California Golden Seals moving to to take up residence near Cleveland in the Richfield Coliseum, the Crusaders were initially going to move to Florida, but they were later convinced to move west to Minnesota and occupy the vacant Saint Paul Civic Center. Like the last team that had played there, they would also take the name of Minnesota Fighting Saints. In addition, the Mariners franchise was saved one more time when Ray Kroc, owner of the McDonald's restaurant chain and the San Diego Padres baseball team, purchased the Mariners from the league. With all the teams in place, the league split them evenly into two divisions. The Jets, along with the Aeros, Mariners, Oilers, Cowboys and Roadrunners comprised the new Western Division, while the Nordiques, Bulls, Racers, Whalers, Stingers and Fighting Saints made up the Eastern Division.

On the heels of an ugly brawl between the Cowboys and Nordiques during the playoffs, the WHA had adopted new rules concerning fighting. There would be stiffer penalties for instigators, non-participants in a fight would be forced to retreat to their net or bench, and all teams were forbidden to use fighting in advertising or other promotions.

Though training camp would not begin until 12 September, many Jets were on the ice much earlier in preparation for the Canada Cup tournament that featured the best teams from Canada, Czechoslovakia, Finland, Sweden, the United States and the U.S.S.R. Hull joined the Canadian team, Sjoberg, Bergman, Hedberg, Lindstrom, Nilsson, and Labraaten were all with the Swedish team, while Ketola and Riihiranta represented Finland. In addition, Kromm was asked to be one of the assistant coaches for the Canadian team. Unfortunately, during a game between Canada and Sweden in Toronto, Darryl Sittler checked Bergman hard into the boards behind the Swedish net, dislocating the same left shoulder that was still weak after off-season surgery. More surgery would be required and it would leave Bergman unavailable until the end of November. Four days later, in a game in Quebec, Labraaten injured his knee, which would put him out of action for up to six weeks. Labraaten had battled injuries last season as well and was on the mend from a broken wrist and ribs that had kept him off the ice for two months.

Under the direction of Rudy Pilous with the help of Captain Dave Hunsinger of the Canadian Armed Forces, who was conducting a dry land workout program, the remaining players reported to training camp. Medicals were conducted at the Arena and practices were held at the nearby St. James Civic Center in preparation for the start of the exhibition schedule. Two NHL opponents were on the docket for the Jets, the first of which was a game on Friday, 24 September, in which the Jets defeated the Pittsburgh Penguins by a score of 5-3. On Sunday night, the Jets entertained the St. Louis Blues and the Jets won handily once again, but the 6-2 final score was the least of the Jets' concerns. Blues' enforcer Bob Gassoff, after serving a penalty for slashing Hull, got out of the box, made his way right for Hull and slashed him again, fracturing his wrist and putting the Golden Jet out of action for around six weeks.

The exhibition schedule continued on, but there were more fireworks on the agenda. During a game against the Oilers, defenseman Barry Long slammed Mats Lindh against the boards after Lindh had scored, which angered Kromm. A heated exchange between Kromm and new Oilers' coach Armand "Bep" Guidolin turned into a fight. The two men traded punches between the benches, but thankfully, no one was hurt. The pre-season games mercifully came to a conclusion without further incident, and it was at last time to being the regular season.

The Jets opened the defense of their AVCO World Trophy championship on Friday, 8 October at the Arena against the Cowboys, a team they had played 12 times during the regular season and another five times during the playoffs the year before. The Cowboys came into the season with a few changes to their lineup, but the Jets still had some unfinished business with their roster. Before the game that evening, they gave Guindon the good news that he had made the team and signed him to a contract for the upcoming season. Prior to the start of the game, in front of a crowd of only 7,502 that included nearly 5,000 season ticket holders, the Jets presented Winnipeg mayor Stephen Juba with a jersey bearing the number 20 on the back to honor the number of years he had been in office. Without Hull, Dan Labraaten, and Thommie Bergman, the Jets got off to a sluggish start, but Joe Daley kept the game scoreless until Willy Lindstrom scored a pair of second period goals to put the Jets out in front to stay. Kent Ruhnke added a third period goal in his first game as a Jet, but Daley was the star of the 4-1 victory, stopping 38 of the 39 shots he faced as the Jets won their third consecutive opener and raised their record in season-opening games to 4-1.

Rounding out the opening weekend was a visit from the Whalers on Sunday night. Behind the visitors' bench was the familiar face of Harry Neale, whom the Jets had last seen coaching the Fighting Saints before they folded in February. Neale had taken over the Whalers late last season and was embarking on his first full season in Hartford. Unlike Friday night's contest, the Jets came out strong and were one step ahead of the Whalers all night long. Veli-Pekka Ketola's goal midway through the first period broke a 2-2 tie and the Jets pulled away with two more goals in a 5-2 victory that was statistically close only because of the work of Whalers' goaltender Christer Abrahamsson. Nilsson scored twice for the Jets and added one assist in a particularly impressive performance.

After a breather, the Jets began their first road trip of the season in Edmonton on Friday night. In addition to Guidolin, the new coach and general manager who had scrapped with Kromm during the exhibition season, the Oilers had made many changes both on and off the ice after their loss to the Jets in the first round of last season's playoffs. New owner Nelson Skalbania had purchased the team from the controversial Bill Hunter and his group, putting an end to the fiery Hunter's stormy tenure that saw many players and coaches come and go with little success to show for his efforts. Guidolin, the former coach of the Boston Bruins and Kansas City Scouts, had brought in many new players over the off-season in the hopes of reversing the fortunes of a team that hadn't won a playoff series in their four seasons in existence.

The new Oilers, however, fared little better than their recent predecessors had against the Jets, as the visitors took over the game after an even first period and cruised to a 6-1 victory. Ruhnke scored twice while battling the flu to lead the Jets, and ironically, the best Oiler on the night was Larry Hornung, the former Jet.

After a 10-hour flight, the Jets were back on the ice one night later in the Valley of the Sun to battle the Roadrunners. Former NHL goaltender and coach of the Western Hockey League's Salt Lake Golden Eagles Al Rollins took over as the new coach behind the Roadrunners' bench, replacing Sandy Hucul, who had been named the WHA's coach of the year two seasons ago. Hucul had remained in Phoenix and took a job selling tires. On the ice, the Roadrunners had made few changes, trading Gary Veneruzzo to the Mariners and adding 29-year-old Finnish centerman Seppo Repo.

The Jets picked up right where they had left off and jumped out to a 3-1 lead after one period, but the Roadrunners tied the score in the second thanks to a couple of soft goals that prematurely ended Larsson's first start of the new season. The goaltending change didn't save the Jets in the third period, however, as the Roadrunners scored three times in just under three minutes on their way to a 6-4 victory.

On Sunday, 17 October, the Jets finished off their three-game weekend road trip with a visit to San Diego to play the Mariners. In addition to new ownership, the Mariners had made a few additions to their lineup that included high-scoring winger Gary Veneruzzo from the Roadrunners and defenseman Paul Shmyr, who had been the WHA's top rearguard last season when he was with the Crusaders. The Jets tried slowing the game down, but the strategy backfired as the Mariners held the lead for virtually the entire game and put the game away late in the third period to hand the Jets a 3-1 defeat. Before a crowd of 3,990 who had chosen the Jets/Mariners game instead of watching Game 2 of the World Series between the Reds and Yankees, the Jets could only a muster a franchise-low 14 shots on Ernie Wakely and Hedberg's third period goal was the only shot to beat him.

The Jets arrived back in Winnipeg on Frontier Flight 92 late the next afternoon in advance of their next game on Tuesday night against the Indianapolis Racers to kick off a seven-game home stand. The Jets opened up a close game with three second period goals and peppered Racers' goaltender Michel Dion with 45 shots on their way to a 6-1 win. Willy Lindstrom scored twice for the Jets, who had had their way with the normally defensive-minded Racers in front of a gathering of only 6,304 fans. Game 3 of the World Series and the fact that the Jets' game was shown on local television on a one-hour delay were major reasons for the lowest crowd at the Arena in nearly two years.

Next up for the Jets was a Friday night game against the Roadrunners for the teams' second meeting in less than a week. The Jets battled the Roadrunners even through two periods and Nilsson's goal seven minutes into the third gave the Jets a 3-2 lead, but the Jets were unable to put their guests away and the Roadrunners tied the score five minutes later. With just four and a half minutes to play, Robbie Ftorek scored off a two-on-one break to give the Roadrunners the lead for good. Goaltender Gary Kurt held the fort during the last minute of play to allow the Roadrunners to skate off with a 4-3 victory that pulled them into a three-way tie for first place with the Jets and Mariners. Anders Hedberg scored twice and added an assist for the Jets, and Dan Labraaten made an impressive debut in returning from the knee injury he had sustained in the Canada Cup tournament, but the Jets still lost for the third time in four outings.

Two nights later, the Jets welcomed the Birmingham Bulls for the first time since the former Toronto Toros and Ottawa Nationals moved to Alabama. The Jets rebounded from their disappointing showing on Friday night and turned in arguably their best performance of the season in the 7-1 whitewashing of the Bulls. Four third period goals erased all doubt as to the game's outcome and Lindstrom scored a pair in support of another solid outing by Daley that got the Jets back in the win column. Labraaten and Dave Dunn each scored their first goals as a Jet, but Ruhnke did not play for the second straight game and was diagnosed with mononucleosis, adding another member of the team to the sick bay.

The Jets didn't have another game until Friday, but the front office was in action on Monday, 25 October. Rudy Pilous called Mike Ford with the "good news" that he had been traded to the Cowboys for a second-round selection in next summer's Amateur Draft. The Jets offered the Cowboys a choice of three players and Head Coach and General Manager Joe Crozier chose Ford. The popular Ford was devastated by the news, but he had no choice but to pack up and head west to join his new teammates in Calgary.

The next day, the Jets picked up 27-year-old defenseman Barry Long from the Oilers. The Red Deer, Alberta native became the latest Oiler to be purged in their housecleaning, and he chose the Jets over three other WHA teams that had approached him. Long had been an All-Star last season had been voted as the Oilers' most valuable player and best defenseman two years ago. Like Ford, he was known for his hard, low shots from the point and had two seasons of NHL experience with the Los Angeles Kings before joining the Oilers. Long was originally a draft choice of the Chicago Blackhawks, and he had played three seasons for their farm team in Dallas that Kromm coached. Ironically, Kromm had taken a swing at Long during last season's first-round playoff matchup with the Oilers after Long skated by the Jets' bench hurling insults. Rather than take another swing at him, Kromm decided to pair Long with Lars-Erik Sjoberg, taking Ford's place alongside the Jets' captain.

The Jets made another roster move when they parted company with former Fighting Saints' defenseman Terry Ball, who had been in Winnipeg on a ten-game trial. Ball never actually got into a game for the Jets, though Kromm had wanted to give him a chance.

News of a very different nature preceded Friday night's game against the Oilers. The Jets announced that they would be heading for Moscow to compete in the prestigious Izvestia tournament. The Jets would leave for the Soviet Union on 13 December and return nine days later to become the first professional club to play as a team in the tournament that would also feature teams from Czechoslovakia, Sweden, Finland and the host U.S.S.R. The Nordiques had previously committed to represent the WHA, but after they backed out, the Soviets threatened to cancel the upcoming 14-game tour of WHA cities by the national teams of the U.S.S.R. and Czechoslovakia. The Jets stepped up to honor the league's commitment and save the tour for the benefit of their league brethren.

Back on the ice, the Jets treated a season-high crowd of 8,531 that included a busload from Altona, Manitoba, to an offensive explosion that included six goals in the first period as the Jets routed the Oilers by a score of 11-3. In an ironic twist of fate, Long made his Jets debut against his old team and scored on his first shot as a Jet, but the line of Ketola, Lindstrom, and Sullivan stole the headlines. Ketola scored three times, while Lindstrom added a pair and all told, the trio recorded 15 points on the night.

On Sunday night, the Jets hosted the Mariners for early-season supremacy in the realigned Western Division. The Jets stormed back from a 3-1 first period deficit with three goals in the second and blew the game open with two more 10 seconds apart in the third period. The Jets and the crowd of 7,958 got their Halloween treat with a 6-4 victory that gave the Jets a four-point cushion over the Mariners and kept them two points ahead of the second-place Aeros.

The home stand continued with a Tuesday night game against the Aeros, who were making their first appearance at the Arena since the Jets had captured the AVCO World Trophy at their expense back in May. Supported by stellar goaltending from Wayne Rutledge and a physical defense corps that kept the front of the net clear of traffic, the Aeros pulled into a first-place tie with the Jets with a 3-1 victory. Mats Lindh was the only Jet to score on Rutledge, who was named the game's first star with 36 saves to his credit.

The Jets wrapped up their home stand on Friday, 5 November with their first meeting against the new Fighting Saints. In addition to their relocation, the visitors had also made numerous other moves in the off-season that included bringing back many of the same players who were with the original Fighting Saints and hiring Glen Sonmor, who had coached the Fighting Saints in their inaugural season. Early returns were not positive for the 3-8-2 Fighting Saints and the Jets wasted no time in jumping all over their struggling guests. The Jets took a 3-0 lead by the time the game was seven and a half minutes old and the Fighting Saints could only respond with fisticuffs. In between fights, the Jets kept piling up the goals and had no trouble in picking up a 9-2 win that kept them tied for first place. Curt Larsson gave Joe Daley the night off and the seldom-used netminder had a relatively easy time and plenty of help to earn his first victory in only his second start of the season. The only downside of the evening was that Dave Dunn left the game in the first period after his second fight because of a broken jaw that could keep him out of the lineup for a month.

Bright and early the next morning, the Jets boarded a plane to take them to Cincinnati for a Saturday night game against the Stingers. The Jets held a slim 2-1 lead after two periods due mostly to Daley's stellar goaltending, but the roof caved in the third period and neither Daley nor any of his teammates could stop the onslaught. The Stingers scored no fewer than six times in the game's final 20 minutes, sending the Jets down to a 7-3 defeat. Jacques Locas scored three times for the winners in the decisive third period, leading the Stingers to their first victory over the Jets.

The 8-5-0 Jets turned around and returned home to complete the three-game weekend on Sunday night against the Oilers. Though they were understandably tired, the Jets broke open a close game with four second period goals and coasted to a 5-2 win that put them back into sole possession of first place, two points ahead of both the Aeros and Mariners. Daley again held his team in the game in the early going and the Jets' defense corps got an added boost with Thommie Bergman's return. Wearing a special piece of equipment designed by trainer Bill Bozak to protect his left shoulder, Bergman came back from his second surgery since Game 4 of last season's AVCO World Trophy final well ahead of schedule.

Two nights later, the Jets were back on the ice against the Whalers. The Jets were a little more refreshed, but the Whalers gave them all they could handle. The lead changed hands several times before Nilsson's goal with only 1:07 left in overtime gave the Jets a 5-4 victory. Making his second start in four games, Larsson wasn't always sharp, but he made several good stops in the overtime period to keep the game tied and set the stage for Ulf Nilsson's game-winning goal.

Next on the schedule for the Jets was a pair of games in Calgary, starting on the night of Thursday, 11 November at the Corral. The Jets grabbed a 2-0 lead before the game was three minutes old and took a 3-1 lead to the first intermission, but the red-hot Cowboys stormed back and tied the score during a wild six-goal second period. Warren Miller's goal late in the third period broke a 5-5 tie and Danny Lawson's empty-net marker put the finishing touches on a 7-5 Cowboys' victory that extended their winning streak to seven games. With Daley battling a cold and in Bobby Kromm's doghouse, Larsson made his second straight start in the Jets' goal and made 26 saves in a losing cause, while Mike Ford played his first game against his former team since being traded to the Cowboys just over two weeks ago.

The two teams went at it again on Sunday night. The Jets heeded Kromm's heated post-game criticism of their defensive work following Thursday night's loss and tightened up in their own zone, while Daley returned from a short exile and turned back all 31 Cowboys' shots in a 2-0 victory. Daley was especially sharp in the first period and his teammates gave him just enough support as the Jets pulled back into sole possession of first place, two points ahead of the Aeros.

With a split of their games in Calgary, the Jets returned home to meet the Nordiques for the first time this season. After being edged out of the Canadian Division title by the Jets last season, the Nordiques had gone down to the Cowboys in a series marred by the attack on Marc Tardif, the league's most valuable player, scoring champion and First Team All-Star. During the off-season, the Nordiques brought in former Pittsburgh Penguins' coach Marc Boileau to replace Jean-Guy Gendron behind their bench. The Nordiques also added former Crusaders and Winnipeg junior defenseman Paul Baxter as well as veteran NHL centermen Andre Boudrias and Paulin Bordeleau.

Before the first five-figure crowd of the season at the Arena, the former division rivals traded goals before the Jets blew the game open with five goals in the third period to hand the co-leaders of the Eastern Division an 8-4 defeat. The Jets scored three of their five third period goals while enforcer Curt Brackenbury was serving a major penalty for his attack on Labraaten, who had scored twice on the night. Hedberg also scored a pair of goals and added three assists to stay atop the league's scoring race.

The 12-6-0 Jets took their three-game winning streak back on the road to start another three-game weekend with a Friday night game in Hartford against the Whalers. After an even first period, the Jets scored three times in each of the next two periods to easily outpace their hosts and the Jets skated off with a 7-3 win. Hedberg scored twice for the second straight game and Nilsson scored one to go with three assists to widen their margin over the Aeros to four points.

Game two of the weekend tripleheader took place in Indianapolis, where the Jets came out on the wrong end of an 8-4 shootout. The Jets fell behind early and could not catch the Racers, who again played an uncharacteristically wide-open style. The Racers delighted the crowd of 11,718 by defeating the Jets for only the second time at Market Square Arena.

Back home, the Jets were on the ice merely five and a half hours after their return to Winnipeg on Sunday, 21 November to battle the Stingers. Another near-capacity crowd saw the Jets give it all they had, but after their hectic travel schedule, they had little left in the tank and it showed. The youthful Stingers out-skated the lethargic Jets and took a 3-0 lead to the third period. The Jets scored a pair of goals in the third to try and get back in the game, but Blaine Stoughton's goal midway through the period sealed the eventual 4-2 victory for the Stingers, who had beaten the Jets for the second time in as many meetings this season.

On Tuesday night, the Jets were in Quebec for their second game with the Nordiques in a week. The action started before the game, when both coaches traded punches during a meeting with referee Bob Kolari and WHA Chief-of-Officials Bob Frampton to explain the new rules to curb violence. Kolari and Frampton were able to separate the two, but not before Boileau's coat was torn. On the ice, there were more fisticuffs, this time involving players, but also plenty of goals. Real Cloutier's hat trick paced the Nordiques to a 5-2 lead and though the Jets rallied to narrow the gap to one goal, two late goals by the Nordiques made the final score 7-4 in the home team's favor. The Jets' third straight defeat dropped them into a first-place tie with the Aeros, their next opponent.

A first-place showdown was next on the Jets' schedule when they met the Aeros at the Summit on Friday night. Both teams battled hard, but the game's only scoring took place within a 32-second span in the second period when the Jets and Aeros split a pair of goals. By game's end, the Jets were battered and bruised, but they had held on for a 1-1 tie to maintain a share of the top spot in the Western Division.

The Jets returned home for a Sunday night date with the Roadrunners, where a crowd of 8,877, which included groups from as far away as Flin Flon and Altona, warmly greeted Hull, who made his first appearance of the regular season. Though still not fully recovered from the wrist injury, he was back in the lineup, but the Golden Jet's presence failed to inspire the rest of the team. Daley had to be at his best to keep the game tied at 3-3 through two periods, but two goals late in the third put the Roadrunners ahead to stay and the Jets went down for the fourth time in five games. After the game, Kromm called the 5-3 defeat one of the worst games the Jets ever played, but the Jets still remained tied with the idle Aeros for first place.

Two nights later, the Jets ended the month of November with a visit from the third-place Mariners, who came into Winnipeg only one point back of the Western Division co-leaders. After a quiet first period, the Jets turned the game into a rout with five goals in the second on their way to an 8-2 victory. Hedberg recorded his second four-goal game as a Jet and the reunited Hot Line accounted for six of the eight goals the Jets scored. The win kept the Jets in first place and allowed each player to collect the $1,000 bonus for being atop the division at the end of November, but the victory did come at a high cost. Lars-Erik Sjoberg left the ice with torn ligaments in his left knee and he would have to undergo surgery on Wednesday that would keep him on the shelf for at least two months.

Did You Know?

On 30 November 1976, the Jets announced that former defenseman Larry Hillman was suing them for $90,000. The suit alleged that the team owed him a contract for the 1976-1977 season, while the Jets countered that he was simply on loan from the former Cleveland Crusaders. As a condition of the loan, the Crusaders had paid more than half his $90,000 salary for 1975-1976 and when training camps opened in 1976, Hillman appeared on the protected list of the Crusaders, which subsequently became the Minnesota Fighting Saints.

Despite the lawsuit, after a year assisting Joe Crozier in Calgary, Hillman would go on to succeed Bobby Kromm as coach for the 1977-1978 season and lead the Jets to their second AVCO World Trophy.

Without their captain, the Jets left for Saint Paul to kick off another grueling three-game weekend on Friday night against the Fighting Saints. The Jets were joined by 46 members of the Booster Club who had made the trek aboard a Grey Goose bus driven by club director Rick Hohenstein. The extra fan support didn't help in the first period, however, as the Fighting Saints, riding high on a five-game winning streak, dominated the first period, but they only had a 2-1 lead to show for their efforts, thanks to Daley's stellar goaltending. The Jets turned the tables in the second period with three goals of their own and held on for a hard-fought 4-3 victory.

At 5:30 a.m. on Saturday, the Jets awoke to begin their trek east for a matchup with the Whalers in Hartford that evening. The Jets took full advantage of the struggling Whalers, who had been winners in only two of their last nine games, and they put the game out of reach with three goals in the third period on their way to a 6-2 victory. Six different scorers did the damage on the scoreboard as the Jets remained three points ahead of the second-place Mariners.

The Jets brought their busy weekend to a conclusion with a Sunday night game in Quebec. After a smartly played first period, fatigue caught up to the Jets and the Nordiques scored four times in the second to erase a slim 2-1 Jets' lead. Two late third period goals only made the score appear cosmetically closer as the Nordiques cruised to a 6-4 victory. During the game, Hull was booed by the crowd of 10,516 in response to his recent comments criticizing Nordiques' management and statements saying that the WHA would fold unless they merged with the NHL soon.

After a one-day break between games, the Jets were back in action on Tuesday night against the Roadrunners at the Arena. The Jets were much better than they had been two nights ago and used a complete team effort to post a 4-2 victory, their first win against the Roadrunners in four meetings. Miller was named the game's first star for his fourth two-goal game as a Jet and his first since Bobby Kromm had switched him back to his natural position of defense before the season. Rudy Pilous had made Miller a left winger when he first signed, but he had often looked out of place up front last season, prompting the change.

Wednesday, 8 December was supposed to be an off day for the Jets, but instead they had to fly to Calgary for a game with the Cowboys. The game was originally scheduled for Sunday, but the date was changed to accommodate an exhibition game with a touring Czechoslovakian team prior to the Jets' departure for Moscow the next day. The Cowboys were the better team for the first two periods, but they could only get one of their 25 shots past Daley. The Jets finally gave their beleaguered goaltender some support when Peter Sullivan and Bobby Hull scored less than a minute and a half apart late in the period to wipe out a 2-1 deficit. Hedberg's empty-net marker sealed the Jets' second consecutive 4-2 victory.

After playing their fifth game in six nights, the Jets returned home for a Friday night game against the Bulls in their last league game before the Izvestia tournament. The Jets threw everything they had at the visiting Bulls, but goaltender John Garrett stood tall and allowed his teammates to take a 4-1 lead to the second intermission. Like they had two nights earlier, the Jets broke through in the third period, but after narrowing the deficit to 4-3, Vaclav Nedomansky's long shot eluded Larsson, putting an end to the Jets' frantic efforts to tie the score. The 5-3 victory was the first road win for new Bulls coach Pat Kelly since taking over from Gilles Leger six games earlier. Kelly, who had coached in the minor leagues for 14 seasons prior to joining the Bulls, had been a candidate for the Jets' coaching job that eventually went to Kromm. Despite the loss, the Jets kept their five-point lead atop the division, though the second-place Mariners had three games in hand and would be playing them while the Jets were in Moscow.

Before leaving for the Soviet Union, the Jets had an exhibition game to play on Sunday afternoon against a Czechoslovakian national team starting a six-game tour of WHA cities in Winnipeg. Despite being without their best players, who were with the main national team in preparation for the Izvestia tournament, the Czechs broke the scoreless tie with four second period goals to take a commanding lead to the intermission. In the third period, however, the Jets completely turned the game around and blitzed the Czechs, dazzling the crowd of 10,023, the second-highest crowd of the season at the Arena. Sullivan scored the eventual game-winner with just under four minutes to play in the eventual 6-5 win that was also seen by a national television audience.

On Monday, 13 December, the Jets and a contingent of more than 100 of their supporters left for Moscow to compete in the tenth annual Izvestia tournament. It was sponsored by the Izvestia daily newspaper and had been held annually since 1967. Over the years, it had grown to become an unofficial prelude to the World Championship played in the spring.

The first professional team to play in the tournament had hoped to bring more players with them, but their WHA partners were not willing to help temporarily boost the shorthanded Jets' roster. Even after the Jets had agreed to step for the Nordiques on the trip, Quebec refused to part with Serge Bernier. Four other teams also refused the Jets' request for additional help. The Jets asked for Dennis Sobchuk from the Stingers, Mark Napier from the Bulls, Pat Stapleton from the Racers, and Thommie Abrahamsson from the Whalers, but the answer was negative each time. The Jets appealed to the league to force the issue, but they were again turned away. The only help the Jets got was the return of Dave Dunn, who played his first game in six weeks on Sunday afternoon with the aid of a face mask to protect his healing jaw.

The Stapleton Connection

At various times during the WHA years, Pat Stapleton was rumored to be headed for the Jets as a player and later as a general manager. He never worked for the Jets, but his son Mike signed with the Jets on 18 August 1995 and played 58 regular season and all six playoff games for the Jets in their last season before the franchise relocated to Arizona following the 1995-1996 campaign.

Nonetheless, the Jets touched down safely in the Soviet capital and after a three hour wait to get their luggage and clear customs, they had a couple of days to tour Moscow before their first game of the tournament against the Czechoslovakian national team at the Lenin Hockey Stadium. This Czechoslovakian team, unlike the one the Jets had just faced in Winnipeg, was comprised of the best the nation had to offer, but the Jets still battled them on even terms most of the way. The Jets rallied from a 2-0 first period deficit to tie the score, only to fall short at the end as the Czechs took the opening game by a score of 3-2 in a hard-fought contest. During the game, Soviet officials kept asking the Jets' vocal supporters to keep themselves quiet and tried to take their noisemakers away at one point, to no avail.

The next game was a Thursday afternoon matchup with the Swedish nationals. The Jets were not at their best and played out of character by trying to physically intimidate the Swedes. As a result, the Jets fell behind 4-1 and only a frantic late rally enabled them to salvage a 4-4 tie. Hedberg scored twice in the third period to lead the comeback effort against his countrymen.

> **Did You Know?**
>
> When the Jets met the Swedish national team on the afternoon of 16 December 1976 at the Izvestia tournament, they faced three players whom they would later acquire. Kent Nilsson signed with the Jets prior to the start of the 1977-1978 season, Bengt Lundholm signed with the Jets prior to the 1981-1982 season, while Stefan Persson was a Jet ever so briefly, but only on paper. Persson was acquired by the Jets late in the 1985-1986 season from the New York Islanders, but refused to report. The Islanders eventually returned the draft choice that the Jets had agreed to send as compensation for Persson.
>
> Five days later, the Jets played the Finnish national team, where they faced future Jet Markus Mattsson in goal. Mattsson signed with the Jets prior to the start of the 1977-1978 season and was one of the few holdovers to stay with the team when they joined the NHL two seasons later.

Three days later, the Jets took on the host Soviet team in a Sunday afternoon contest. The Jets fell behind the heavily favored Soviets, who scored three times in five minutes in the second period, but the Jets still gave them all they could handle. Three goals in the third period, however, could not erase a 5-1 deficit and the Jets went down to a 6-4 defeat. Hull scored twice for the Jets and Joe Daley was spectacular in a losing cause.

The Jets wrapped up their participation in the tournament two days later with a game against the Finnish national team. Though the Jets did not play well, two second period goals were all they needed to beat the Finns by a score of 2-1 to complete the four games with a record of 1-2-1. The Jets' only win of the tournament came at a cost, however, as Sullivan was struck by an errant puck above his right eye and required 30 stitches to close the wound. The Jets did get some small consolation when Daley was named the tournament's top goaltender and Hull played the role of ambassador to perfection, leaving a lasting positive impression on the Muscovites.

Having acquitted themselves honorably on the international stage, the Jets returned home for a Christmas party on Thursday and after the holiday, it was back to league action with a Boxing Day matchup against the Nordiques. A crowd of 10,335 was on hand to welcome the Jets, who had fallen back to third place during their absence, one point back of the second-place Aeros and seven back of the first-place Mariners. Hedberg got the Jets on the board in the game's first minute, but it was all downhill from there. The Jets were no match for the Nordiques, who made easy work of a team that had been half way around the world and back. Real Cloutier paced the visitors' attack in the 12-3 rout with three goals and four assists, which allowed him to pass Hedberg atop the league scoring race.

There would be no rest for the Jets, who had to go back on the road for a game in Houston two nights later. The Jets played the Aeros even through the fight-filled first period, but the second period belonged the Aeros, who scored three times to take a 4-1 lead. A gamely comeback effort fell short and the Aeros took the game by a score of 6-3, padding their margin over the third-place Jets to three points. After the game, Bobby Kromm was particularly harsh in his criticism of his players, but the effects of the overseas travel were coming home to roost.

The Jets moved on to San Diego for matchup with the first-place Mariners one night before New Year's Eve. Sadly, it was more of the same as the Jets fell behind by four goals early in the third period. Like they had done two nights earlier, they mounted a late charge, but the Mariners held on for a 4-3 victory. The Jets were only able to muster 15 shots against Ernie Wakely, their former teammate in the Mariners' goal, while Daley faced 42 shots and prevented a runaway score.

After the Jets returned to Winnipeg, frustrations came to a boiling point off the ice. On the heels of a team meeting in San Diego where players complained of Kromm's vitriolic criticism, both in public and in private, Rudy Pilous asked Kromm to watch the Jets' next game from the press box instead of from behind the bench. Though Kromm was less than pleased with what amounted to a one-game suspension, the Jets did indicate that he would resume his coaching duties at Monday's practice.

With the injured Lars-Erik Sjoberg handling the duties behind the bench, the Jets met the Aeros again for a Sunday matinee the day after ringing in the new year. The Jets responded to the off-ice shakeup and controlled the game throughout and also matched the physical Aeros hit for hit. The improving

Kent Ruhnke picked off an errant clearing pass to score the eventual game-winner in a 5-2 victory that pulled the Jets back to within a single point of the second-place Aeros. The win was the Jets' first in four meetings with the Aeros, but the injury bug hit the Jets one more time when a high stick from Gordie Howe caught Ulf Nilsson in the face and broke his nose.

On Tuesday night, the 19-15-1 Jets, with Kromm back behind the bench, faced off against the Indianapolis Racers, who trailed only the Nordiques in the Eastern Division standings. The visiting Racers kept the game close, but Bobby Guindon's goal off a two-on-one break midway through the third period was the difference in a 2-1 win. Goaltender Michel Dion was the best Racer on the night, but the Jets were able to get just enough past last season's controversial choice for the WHA's best goaltender to take the two points. Despite suffering a broken nose on Sunday afternoon, Nilsson was in the lineup playing with a wire cage, while Hull was also able to answer the bell after pulling his hamstring the day before.

The Jets were not done with their international exhibitions as a Soviet national team made its seventh stop of its eight-game tour in Winnipeg to battle the Jets on Thursday, 6 January. As had been the case in Moscow, the Jets were highly competitive against the Soviets, but two goals from Alexander Yakushev paced the Soviets to a narrow 3-2 victory. Sullivan was named the player of the game for the Jets, but Daley was the Jets' best player as he matched Soviet goaltender Vladislav Tretiak save for save. Nilsson, who was already dealing with a broken nose, pulled a stomach muscle during the game to add to his physical woes.

Returning to league action, the Jets hosted the Bulls on Sunday night. The Jets rewarded the 8,040 hardy customers that survived the bone-chilling cold outside with an efficient performance that earned the Jets a 4-1 victory, their third straight win against WHA opponents. Daley was again masterful while tending goal in the shadow of the Booster Club sign in the north end that read, "Jets Fans Enjoy Daley Nightly," and Veli-Pekka Ketola also had a particularly strong game. On the downside, the Jets lost Dave Dunn during the first period when he hobbled off the ice with a heel injury, becoming the second defenseman in as many days to fall victim to the ever-present injury bug. During Saturday's practice, Barry Long had suffered a cracked shoulder blade to add another member to the list of walking wounded.

The home stand came to a close on Tuesday night with the Roadrunners' fourth and final regularly scheduled appearance at the Arena this season. The Jets got off to a blazing-hot start and held a 6-0 lead by the midway point of the second period. From there, they had little trouble in taking a 9-2 win against the sliding Roadrunners. Dan Labraaten scored twice for the victors and Sullivan scored once to go along with three assists. Once again, however, the win came at cost as Willy Lindstrom sustained a suspected cracked cheekbone after being hit in the face in the third period. In addition, Hexi Riihiranta had been struck on the foot by a booming shot from Hull the day before and found out that he had a cracked bone. On a positive note, Long still played despite the pain from the cracked shoulder blade.

The Jets flew to Calgary for a game on Friday, 14 January at the Corral to play their first road game of the new year. Using their speed to their full advantage, the Jets easily skated past the Cowboys on their way to a 5-3 victory. Anders Hedberg led the Jets' attack with two goals that raised his season's total to 36, to go along with an assist on Sullivan's game-opening goal.

On Saturday morning, the Jets flew back home to attend the second annual Vegas Nite fundraiser that evening. Another overflow crowd filled the Winnipeg Convention Center for an evening's worth of entertainment and to try and turn a $12.00 ticket into one of many prizes, including two 1977 Pontiac Acadians, two trips to Las Vegas, a diamond ring, a pair of Jets season tickets, among others. Mr. Terry Zerawecki and Mr. Cal Johnston won the Acadians that were donated by McNaught Pontiac Cadillac Ltd.; Mr. Boris Balamatowski and Mr. Jan Stefanyk each won a Las Vegas trip; Mrs. C. Coz won the pair of Jets season tickets; and Mr. Perry Roitman won the diamond ring donated by Ben Moss Jewellers.

The next night, the Jets were back on the ice against the Stingers at the Arena. The Jets jumped out to a 2-0 lead before the game was six minutes old, but the Stingers kept pressing and the two teams went to the intermission with the score tied at 3-3. The Stingers took the lead for good in the second period and went on to hand the Jets their first defeat of 1977 by a score of 6-4. Gilbert Plains, Manitoba native Blaine Stoughton of the Stingers had his own cheering section in the stands and he responded by scoring four of the Stingers' six goals.

The Jets were off for a few days, but Kromm and six of his players headed for Hartford to participate in the annual All-Star Game on Tuesday, 18 January. Daley, Bergman, Hull, Nilsson, Hedberg, and Lindstrom represented the Western Division All-Stars, who went down to a 4-2 defeat at the hands of the best of the Eastern Division before a crowd of 10,337 at the Hartford Civic Center. Lindstrom scored once and set up the other West goal, earning him MVP honors for the Western squad. Ironically, the Eastern MVP was goaltender Louis Levasseur, whose contract had been recently purchased by the Oilers from the Fighting Saints after the second edition of the WHA's Saint Paul franchise had officially ceased operations the previous day.

After the All-Star break, the Jets' next game was a return visit from the Stingers on Friday night. The two teams traded goals through the first half of the game, but the Jets used two goals in the latter half of the second period to take a 5-3 lead to the intermission. Despite playing in Phoenix the night before, the Stingers again showed resilience and scored twice in the third period to send the game to overtime, but Hedberg's second goal of the game and league-leading 39th of the season at 3:57 of the extra period allowed the Jets to escape with a 6-5 win. After the overtime winner, in a fit of anger, Stingers defenseman John Hughes broke his stick over the crossbar and flung the shaft into the stands, narrowly missing a spectator. While the fan avoided injury, Hull was not so fortunate when he had collided with Nilsson in the second period. The Golden Jet suffered his second major injury of the season, a cut tendon above his right ankle that would put him out of the lineup for an extended period of time.

Sunday night saw the Cowboys' first visit since the home opener more than three months ago. The Jets got out to a 4-1 lead against a team playing its third road game in as many nights, but the Cowboys didn't quit and kept the game close. However, three goals in just over two minutes late in the second period put the game out of reach and the Jets ran away with a 10-5 victory, marking their seventh win in eight games. Ten different Jets scored in the game, including Hedberg, who scored his 40th of the season. The win enabled the shorthanded Jets to pull within three points of the second-place Mariners and four points of the first-place Aeros before taking off for a five-game road swing.

The road trip began on Tuesday, 25 January against the division-leading Aeros at the Summit. The Jets got on the board first with a pair of second period goals, but the Aeros got one back before intermission and added four more in the third to send the Jets down to a 5-2 defeat. Making his 17th straight start in goal, including all four games in Moscow, Joe Daley had a rare off night as the Jets fell six points back of the Aeros in the standings. Not only did the Jets lose the game, but they lost two more players to injury. Dan Labraaten suffered a slight separation of his left shoulder and Hedberg hurt his ribs during the game.

Down to 14 healthy skaters, the Jets left the next day for Birmingham to continue their road trip on Thursday night against the Bulls. Weakened by the loss of so many star players, the remaining Jets couldn't get anything past Bulls' goaltender John Garrett and they went down to a 3-0 defeat. It was the first time this season that the Jets were shut out and they suffered further humiliation late in the game as former Fighting Saints' enforcer Gord Gallant started a fracas that saw six players ejected with all of four seconds remaining on the clock.

In desperate need of healthy bodies, the Jets put out the call for two forwards playing in the Manitoba Central Amateur Senior Hockey League to join them in San Diego for their next game on Saturday night. Morris Mott of the Transcona Chargers and Jim Cole of the St. Boniface Mohawks were each signed to 10-game tryout contracts with permission from each of their respective teams. Mott had played three seasons with the NHL's California Golden Seals and had played last season with Vastra Frolunda in Sweden. Cole was on loan from the La Broquerie Habs of the Manitoba Eastern Hockey League and was the MEHL's leading scorer.

With their temporary reinforcements in the lineup, the Jets faced off against the Mariners in their third visit of the season to San Diego. The Jets stormed out of the gate, but this time, it was Ernie Wakely who turned them back, stopping 20 of 21 shots in the opening period while his teammates scored three times on Daley. Despite two goals from Lindstrom, the Jets couldn't make up the deficit and two goals from recently re-acquired Rick Sentes 26 seconds apart put the game out of reach. The 5-3 defeat was the Jets' third straight loss, which left them five points back of the Mariners and 10 behind the frontrunning Aeros. In his Jets and WHA debut, Mott received a black eye during a third period fight with Ray Adduono, but, fortunately, the Jets had no more serious injuries to contend with.

The Jets moved on to Phoenix for a Sunday night game against the Roadrunners, who came into the game on a three-game skid of their own. The Jets again started strong and held a 2-0 lead six minutes into the contest, but the roof caved in during a disastrous second period. Larsson's first start in nearly two months came to a premature end after he let in a couple of soft goals, but Daley fared no better and the seven-goal middle frame sent the Jets down to an eventual 8-5 defeat. Despite sore ribs, Hedberg returned to the lineup, but his presence couldn't prevent the Jets' fourth consecutive defeat. In the third period, Barry Long suffered a bruised hip to go along with his cracked shoulder blade in another injury the Jets could ill afford.

The road trip came to a conclusion two nights later in Edmonton as the Jets began the month of February. Battered and bruised, the Jets took their frustrations out on the Oilers and used a six-goal second period and routed their hosts by a score of 11-1. Playing with a broken rib and three others heavily taped, Hedberg scored four times as did Perry Miller, who set a WHA record for most goals in a game by a defenseman. The bruised hip and cracked shoulder blade didn't stop Long from suiting up for the first time as a visiting player in Edmonton and he chipped in with an assist against his former team.

Next up on the schedule was a pair of weekend games at the Arena, the first of which was a Friday night game against the Mariners. Before a crowd of 10,114 onlookers, the Jets broke open a 2-2 game with a dominating second period and rolled to an 8-2 victory that pulled them back to within five points of the Mariners. Shaking off problems with his ribs, Hedberg scored four times for the second straight game, raising his season total to 48 in only his 46th game.

Did You Know?

On the night of 4 February 1977, the Birmingham Bulls set a WHA attendance record when 17,489 spectators were on hand to see the Bulls defeat the visiting Quebec Nordiques by a score of 7-0. The main attraction, however, was not the game or the final score, but a booty of $5,000 in jewels that was given away to female patrons on "Diamond Night."

On Sunday night, the Jets welcomed the Cowboys for their third visit of the season to the Arena. Joining the Jets for the game was 32-year-old journeyman winger Ron Ward, who had found himself out of work with the demise of the Fighting Saints three weeks ago. Ward was a former 51-goal scorer with the New York Raiders in 1972-1973 and he had played with the Blazers and Sharks before joining the Crusaders in February 1974.

The Jets got off to a slow start, but they climbed back into the game in the second period and took the lead on Hedberg's 49th goal of the season. Soon after his goal, Hedberg had to leave the ice with a knee injury, but the Jets kept pressing and scored again to take a 4-2 lead to the intermission. Sensing the importance of a historic 50th goal to the team and its fans, Hedberg returned to the ice with his knee heavily taped by trainer Bill Bozak and with eight and a half minutes to play, he got the opportunity everyone was looking for. Bill Lesuk drew three Cowboys to him and fed a hobbled but wide-open Hedberg, who fired a wrist shot from the top of the faceoff circle past goaltender Gary Bromley. The crowd of 9,182 gave him a two-minute standing ovation and his teammates poured off the bench to congratulate him on scoring his 50th goal in his 47th game and the Jets' 49th game. The feat eclipsed the records set by Hull two seasons ago and Montreal's Maurice "Rocket" Richard in 1944-1945, but just as important, the goal restored the Jets' two-goal lead and it stood up as the game-winner. For good measure, Hedberg scored into an empty net with one second to play to seal the 6-4 victory with his 51st goal of the season as the Jets trimmed the margin between themselves and the Mariners to three points.

51 In 47

In scoring 51 goals in 47 games, Anders Hedberg scored at least once against each of the other 11 WHA teams, including the defunct Minnesota Fighting Saints. His favorite victim was the San Diego Mariners, against whom he scored 11 of his 51 goals. The Houston Aeros did the best job in containing the "Swedish Express," allowing Hedberg to score only once against them during his remarkable run. Hedberg used three four-goal games and one three-goal game to rack up his total. He scored in 34 of the 47 games he played in.

After the hoopla surrounding Hedberg's individual accomplishment died down, the Jets took off to begin a four-game road trip starting Tuesday night in Quebec. Unfortunately, Hedberg was not among those making the trip, because the knee he injured on Sunday night had to be fitted with a cast and he would be out for an estimated six weeks. The depleted Jets played a solid defensive game and took advantage of their limited opportunities to hand the Eastern Division leaders a 7-2 defeat in front of a crowd of 10,393. Ulf Nilsson picked up the slack for his injured teammates and the acting captain scored three times, while Curt Larsson made 28 saves in his first complete game since early December.

The 29-20-1 Jets traveled south to Hartford to meet the new and improved Whalers on Thursday night. The Whalers' lineup featured no fewer than six former Fighting Saints, most notably Dave Keon and Johnny McKenzie. The Jets couldn't repeat their success from Tuesday night's win in Quebec and they found themselves down 4-1 early in the second period. Kent Ruhnke and Peter Sullivan scored four minutes apart in the second to narrow the deficit to one goal, but they could come no closer and the Whalers took the game by a score of 6-3. Making his second start in a row, Larsson played well in a losing cause and Ruhnke recorded his second two-goal game of his brief pro career, but the Whalers were too strong for the Jets on this night.

The road trip continued the next evening in Cincinnati, where the Jets were badly outplayed by the Stingers all night long and only Daley's stellar goaltending prevented a more lopsided score. The Jets were shut out for the second time in the new year and the Stingers celebrated a 4-0 victory, disappointing a dedicated group of 35 boosters who had come from Winnipeg by bus for the games in Cincinnati and Indianapolis. The boosters didn't arrive until the end of the first period due to problems with a credit card after filling up at a gas station near Indianapolis, but in reality, they missed very little.

The Jets stayed over in Cincinnati the next day before moving on to Indianapolis to play the Racers on Sunday night to wrap up the road trip. Despite playing their third game in as many nights, the Racers alertly capitalized on some Jets miscues to take an early 3-1 lead, but the visitors tightened up and turned the game around. The Jets took the lead early in the second period and held on for a hard-fought 7-5 victory that wasn't secured until Miller's empty-net goal with 17 seconds to play. Nilsson again led the way for the shorthanded Jets with his second hat trick in four games, which included the game-winner early in the third period.

On Monday afternoon, the Jets returned to Winnipeg for a game on Tuesday, 15 February against the Cowboys, who were making their second visit in nine days to the Arena. Despite the fact that his shoulder was still too sore to put on a coat by himself, Labraaten played in his first game in three weeks and opened the scoring, but the Cowboys used their size to shut down the Jets the rest of the way. Lyle Moffat scored with seven and a half minutes to play in regulation time to enable the Jets to salvage a point in the eventual 2-2 tie. The point did allow the Jets to pull within six points of the Mariners, but they lost ground to the Aeros, who had increased their lead over the third-place Jets to eight points. The game also marked Lars-Erik Sjoberg's successful return to the lineup since injuring his knee at the end of November.

Two nights later, the Jets faced off against the Racers in a game that was originally scheduled to be played in early January, but had been rescheduled to accommodate the exhibition match between the Jets and the touring Soviet national team. The Jets used three second period goals in the span of 59 seconds to wipe out a 2-0 deficit and Veli-Pekka Ketola's empty-net marker in the final minute sealed the Jets' second victory in five days against the Racers. Mats Lindh scored twice to pace the Jets and Larsson was outstanding in earning first-star honors. Unfortunately, the Jets lost another player when Nilsson had to leave late in the game with a broken thumb.

With the entire Hot Line on the shelf, the Jets flew to Edmonton to begin a home-and-home series against the Oilers on Friday night. The Jets opened the scoring in the final minute of the first period, but the Oilers replied with three goals of their own and blunted the Jets attack for the rest of the game. Ron Ward scored his second goal as a Jet with just over seven minutes to play, but it wasn't enough to prevent the Oilers from taking the game by a score of 3-2.

The rematch took place back in Winnipeg on Sunday night, where a crowd of 8,745 saw the two teams slog through a dull affair, but the Jets scored twice in the third period to break a 2-2 tie. From there, Daley made the 4-2 lead hold up as the Oilers pressed to get back on even terms and the Jets earned a split of the two games. Ward scored the Jets' first two goals to give him three in his last two games and a total of four since signing with the Jets two weeks earlier.

The Aeros were the Jets' next opponent on Tuesday night, and the crowd of 9,594 spectators was treated to a much more spirited contest. The action was hot and heavy, but both Daley and Aeros' goaltender Wayne Rutledge matched each other save for save until the Jets scored twice in the third period to break a 1-1 tie. Despite a late goal off the stick of the Aeros' John Gray, the Jets prevailed by a score of 3-2 to pull into a share of second place and within six points of the first-place Aeros. In addition to Daley's heroics, Lindh had an excellent game and scored the game-winning goal with seven and a half minutes to play in the third period.

The Jets had little time to celebrate their victory as they left right after the game for a flight to Phoenix, where they met the Roadrunners on Wednesday night. The Roadrunners jumped out to an early 2-0 lead and though the Jets tied the score before the first intermission, they had nothing left in the tank for the rest of the game and the Roadrunners coasted to a 6-3 victory. Larsson made the start in goal and faced a 38-shot barrage with little help from his teammates. Frank Hughes scored four times for the Roadrunners, who won for only the second time in their last seven games.

A Kurt Response

On 23 February 1977, the Jets faced Phoenix Roadrunners' goaltender Gary Kurt for the last time. It was Kurt who had been in the nets for the New York Raiders on 12 October 1972 at Madison Square Garden in the Jets' first regular season WHA game. Kurt faced the Jets a total of 15 times and the Jets posted an 8-7-0 record in those games.

12 October 1972	Jets 6 at New York Raiders 4
5 November 1972	New York Raiders 1 at Jets 3
25 March 1973	New York Raiders 4 at Jets 8
11 March 1974	Jets 2 at Jersey Knights 10
30 October 1974	Phoenix Roadrunners 5 at Jets 6 (OT)
22 December 1974	Phoenix Roadrunners 4 at Jets 2
7 March 1975	Jets 4 at Phoenix Roadrunners 7
12 October 1975	Jets 4 at Phoenix Roadrunners 0
19 October 1975	Jets 5 at Phoenix Roadrunners 6
26 October 1975	Phoenix Roadrunners 0 at Jets 5
18 February 1976	Phoenix Roadrunners 3 at Jets 4
16 October 1976	Jets 4 at Phoenix Roadrunners 6
22 October 1976	Phoenix Roadrunners 4 at Jets 3
11 January 1977	Phoenix Roadrunners 2 at Jets 9
23 February 1977	Jets 3 at Phoenix Roadrunners 6

On Saturday night, the Jets met the Stingers in Cincinnati for the second time in just over two weeks and both Ulf Nilsson and Anders Hedberg joined them for the game. Nilsson's broken thumb was feeling well enough for him to play again and Hedberg had flown in from Winnipeg earlier in the day to play for the first time after a 10-game absence. The lead changed hands several times during the high-scoring affair, but the Jets scored four times late in the third period to turn a 6-4 deficit into an 8-6 victory. Lindstrom scored three times and despite yielding six goals, Daley had a fine outing in the Jets' goal, but the win that put the Jets into sole possession of second place again came at a price. During the first period, Thommie Bergman lost his balance in his own zone and separated his left shoulder and dislocated his thumb when he tried to brace himself while going hard into the boards. It was the same shoulder that had been dislocated during the Canada Cup in September and in Game 4 of the AVCO World Trophy final back in May, and the third dislocation in less than a year was expected to put an end to Bergman's season. In addition, Lars-Erik Sjoberg suffered a concussion after being slammed against the boards late in the game and had to remain in hospital while his teammates returned home.

Soon after their arrival back in Winnipeg, the Jets were right back on the ice where the Whalers were waiting for them after having played in Calgary on Friday night. Sjoberg rejoined his teammates and suited up for the game, but Nilsson's thumb flared up again and he was on the sideline with Bergman, who had his arm in a sling. The Whalers opened the scoring two minutes into the contest, but Sullivan scored twice to give the Jets the lead heading into the third period. However, the Jets let their slender lead slip away and Tom Webster's goal with just over seven minutes to play stood up as the game-winner in the 3-2 defeat. Though the Jets gave it a gamely effort on the heels of Saturday night's shootout, they played just well enough to lose.

There would be no rest for the Jets, who were back on the road for a Tuesday night game in Calgary to begin the month of March. The game was originally scheduled for 18 December, but it had been moved due to the Jets' participation in the Izvestia tournament. The weary Jets were no match for the Cowboys, who rolled to a 6-1 victory. Ron Chipperfield and Lynn Powis each scored twice for the victors, while Peter Driscoll contributed a goal and three assists in the winning cause. Miller's goal with 66 seconds to play was the only bright spot for the Jets, who denied Don "Smokey" McLeod a shutout.

The Jets quickly turned around and returned home to meet the Nordiques on Wednesday night at the Arena. A pair of goals from Lindstrom staked the Jets to a 2-0 lead after two periods, but the Nordiques scored three times in less than five minutes to take a 3-2 lead in the third. The Jets continued to press and Bobby Guindon's marker with less than three minutes to go tied the score. With time winding down in overtime, Ron Ward stole the puck from Nordiques' defenseman Paul Baxter and fed Hedberg out front, who beat Richard Brodeur for the dramatic game-winner. The 35-26-2 Jets were much improved over last night's disappointing outing and were full marks for the victory that put three points between themselves and the third-place Mariners. Unfortunately, the win again cost the Jets the services of a player when Ted Green had to leave the ice early after being struck on the knee from a shot off the stick of former Jet Christian Bordeleau.

The next morning, the Jets boarded a plane bound for Edmonton to play their fifth game in six nights. Led by new playing coach Glen Sather after Bep Guidolin announced before the game that he was devoting his full attention to the general manager's role, the Oilers scored three times in the second period to take a 4-2 lead to the third period, but the Jets found some reserves in their tank to mount a comeback. Goals from Barry Long and Perry Miller less than three minutes apart tied the score, but veteran Norm Ullman's goal late in the game gave the Oilers the lead for good and the Jets went down by a score of 5-4. A porous defense weakened by Green's absence and subpar goaltending from Larsson proved decisive in the Jets' third loss in their last four games. Not all the action, however, took place on the ice. After the game, Bobby Kromm climbed on top of a railing behind the bench and exchanged a few heated words with some fans before joining the team back in the dressing room.

Sather's Debut

Glen Sather made his coaching debut with the Oilers on 3 March 1977 in a 5-4 victory over the Jets. The win proved to be a foreshadowing of things to come when both teams joined the NHL for the 1979-1980 season. Sather's Oilers went on to dominate the Jets and Sather would face the Jets more often than any other coach during the 17 seasons the Jets played in the NHL.

The Jets dragged themselves back to the airport and took off for Phoenix, where they met they met the Roadrunners on Saturday night hoping to win for the first time in their four games in the desert. With Bobby Hull back in the lineup for the first time in more than a month, the Jets opened the scoring early in the second period, but three goals in the span of less than three minutes vaulted the Roadrunners into a lead they didn't relinquish. The listless Jets offered little resistance and the Roadrunners beat the Jets again, this time by a score of 4-1.

Back in Winnipeg, the Jets had a chance to catch their breath before their next game on Tuesday night against the slumping Mariners. The reunited Hot Line struck for two first period goals and Daley did the rest, stopping 42 shots in a scintillating performance to earn his second shutout of the season. The 5-0 victory put the Jets five points up on the Mariners, who saw their winless streak reach 10 games.

There was no game on Wednesday, but it was one of the busiest days in team history off the ice. In the afternoon, the Jets signed Fran Huck to provide some much-needed depth to an injury-ravaged lineup. Huck had last played for the Jets in the 1973-1974 season and he hadn't played in the WHA since the original edition of the Fighting Saints folded last year. He had spent this past season as a playing coach in Zurich, Switzerland and sent the Jets a letter asking for a chance to play and got his wish.

Late Wednesday night, the Jets consummated a long-rumored trade with the Cowboys when they sent Hexi Riihiranta and Veli-Pekka Ketola west in exchange for Mike Ford, 29-year-old speedster Danny Lawson, and the Cowboys' first-round draft choice in the upcoming amateur draft. Ford was no stranger to the Jets, having been with them earlier in the season before being traded to Calgary, and Rudy Pilous had coached Lawson when he played junior hockey in Hamilton. Lawson was a veteran of four NHL seasons before joining the Philadelphia Blazers, where he scored 61 goals in the 1972-1973 season. He had remained with the franchise after its moves to both Vancouver and Calgary and was the last holdover from the original Blazers squad before the trade. He was surprised when Pilous called him with the news that he had been traded to the Jets, but his skills were a good match for his new team and after the initial shock had passed, he warmed to the idea of joining the Jets.

For his part, Ford was surprised by the news, but overjoyed nonetheless, at the prospect of returning to the Jets, a team he had never wanted to leave in the first place. The former junior Jet didn't get very much ice time in Calgary and he had never felt comfortable in a Cowboys' uniform. The Cowboys had coveted Ketola for a long time and Coach and General Manager Joe Crozier welcomed him with open arms, but Riihiranta indicated that he would not report to the Cowboys, because he had a no-trade clause in his contract.

Once the dust settled on all the player movement, the Jets returned to game action on Friday, 11 March, ironically, against the Cowboys with all the principals involved except for Riihiranta, playing for their new teams for the first time. The Jets came out strong, but the scoreless tie wasn't broken until late in the second period when Hedberg scored his 56th goal of the season. The floodgates opened in the third and the Jets got three more on their way to a 4-1 victory. In addition to the traded players playing against their former teams, former Jet Larry Hillman handled the coaching duties for the Cowboys in place of Crozier, who had been called away to attend a club directors meeting.

A Sunday night game with the Oilers was next on the schedule, and the Jets scored early and often in a 9-3 rout in which the Jets made easy work of their guests. The Oilers were playing their fifth game in six nights and the Jets showed them no mercy, collecting their third straight victory with comparative ease. Eight different Jets did the damage on the scoreboard, including both Huck and Ford, who each scored for the first time since rejoining the Jets.

The Oilers remained in Winnipeg for a rematch on Tuesday, 15 March. The Jets' opponents were originally scheduled to be the Fighting Saints, but the league assigned the Oilers as the replacement after the Fighting Saints folded. The Jets picked up right where they had left off on Sunday night and scored three times on only five shots in the game's first four minutes. They added four more goals in the second period for a 7-0 win, their second consecutive blowout victory over the Oilers. Hedberg scored three times for his fifth hat trick of the season and Danny Lawson scored his first two goals as a Jet. While in Calgary, the budget-conscious Cowboys had told Lawson to stop taking slap shots because he was breaking too many sticks, but the restriction was lifted when he put on a Jets' uniform.

On Wednesday, the Jets sent Ron Ward to the Cowboys as compensation for Riihiranta's refusal to report to Calgary. Ward had been impressive during his brief tenure in Winnipeg, but since the Jets were on the hook for the remainder of Riihiranta's contract, financial considerations forced the Jets' hand. They offered Ward together with his high salary and the Cowboys gratefully accepted. The Cowboys became Ward's third team of the season and it would be his second time around with the franchise. Ward had played seven games with the Vancouver Blazers to start the 1973-1974 season before being traded to the Los Angeles Sharks.

The rest of the Jets left on Wednesday afternoon for a Thursday night game in Edmonton, marking their third straight meeting with the Oilers. Goaltender Ken Broderick was sharp in the first period to backstop the Oilers to a 2-1 first period lead, then his teammates took over the rest of the way. The Jets kept the game close, but the Oilers skated off with a 4-3 victory against a team that looked far less formidable than the group that had outscored the Oilers by a total of 16-3 over the past two games. During the first period, the Jets added one more injury to their season-long stockpile when Perry Miller stopped a shot from Wayne Connelly with the inside of his right foot and had to leave the game.

The Jets left Edmonton in the wee hours of the morning bound for Indianapolis, while Miller returned to Winnipeg for x-rays on his foot. The team didn't arrive in the Indiana capital until the afternoon, but they were on the ice a few short hours later at Market Square Arena against the Racers. Not only were the Jets without Miller, but Dave Dunn wasn't able to play because his equipment had been sent back to Winnipeg instead of Miller's, so the Jets only had four defensemen available for the game. Nonetheless, Hedberg led the Jets to a 4-2 lead after one period and they skillfully held on to the lead over the next two periods for a 7-5 win. The Jets' fifth win in their last six games was their 40th of the season and widened their lead over the third-place Mariners to 12 points while remaining a dozen points back of the division-leading Aeros.

On Saturday, the Jets left for Birmingham, where a large contingent of angry fans was waiting at the airport. They came out in force to show their displeasure toward Hull, who recently made comments about a potential WHA-NHL merger that didn't include Birmingham. Hull was treated no better at the rink on Sunday afternoon, but he answered them as only he could with the game-opening goal early in the first period. The Bulls, however, energized by a small but vocal gathering of 6,378 gave the Jets all they could handle and Dale Hoganson's goal late in the third gave them a 3-2 lead. With Daley on the bench in the game's final minute, Mike Ford blocked Mark Napier's shot headed for the unguarded net, then he fed Hull, who led a rush toward the Bulls' net. The Golden Jet drew three Bulls defenders towards him, then returned the puck to Ford, whose trademark hard shot beat goaltender John Garrett to tie the score with only 19 seconds to play. Ulf Nilsson completed the last-minute dramatics with a goal 95 seconds into overtime that gave the Jets a 4-3 victory.

Winners of six of their last seven games, the 41-29-2 Jets returned home for their fourth meeting with the Oilers in the span of nine days on Tuesday night. The Jets dominated the Oilers right from the outset and they piled up a 5-1 lead early in the second period, coasting to an 8-3 win. Danny Lawson scored two shorthanded goals and Anders Hedberg added a pair to give him 65 on the season. The Jets played without Perry Miller once again, and he was fitted for a cast on his injured foot. In attendance was 11-year-old Brenda Neiles, who was the Jets' 1,000,000th customer under public ownership. In her first game, she not only saw the Jets win to increase their lead over the Mariners to 14 points, but she received a dinner for two at the Winnipeg Inn, an autographed stick from the players and a Jets sweater.

The Jets had a few days before their next game on Sunday afternoon in Houston, where they hoped to keep the Aeros from wrapping up first place in the Western Division at their expense. One by one, the chippy Aeros led a parade to the box with a series of needless penalties and they paid dearly for it. The Jets scored four times with the man advantage and handed the Aeros their first loss at the Summit since mid-December, winning by a score of 5-3. Hull picked up his first hat trick of the season as the Jets kept their first-place hopes mathematically alive. Thommie Bergman bravely attempted a comeback from his third recent shoulder separation, but his shoulder again popped out in the game's first minute, putting him back on the shelf.

Both teams flew to Winnipeg for a rematch on Tuesday, 29 March at the Arena. The seventh five-figure crowd of the season saw the Aeros shut down the Jets in a complete reversal of Sunday afternoon's contest. The Hot Line was all but neutralized by the trio of Rich Preston, Terry Ruskowski and Morris Lukowich, who added three goals of their own in a 5-2 win that clinched first place for the Aeros. As a result, the Jets were assured of meeting the Mariners in the first round of the playoffs, while the Aeros would play either the Oilers or the Cowboys.

The Jets got right back on a plane where they flew to San Diego for a post-season preview on Thursday night at the San Diego Sports Arena. The Jets were the better team, but goaltender Ken Lockett stymied their attempts to widen their 2-0 lead. The Mariners then mounted a comeback and Joe Noris' second goal of the game on a sharp angle with only 26 seconds to play in regulation time gave the Mariners a 4-3 victory. The loss was the Jets' fourth in as many meetings with the Mariners in San Diego, while the Jets had won all four games played between the two teams in Winnipeg.

After wrapping up the month of March with a two-game losing streak, the Jets moved on to Birmingham for a Saturday night game against the Bulls, whose playoff aspirations had since been extinguished. The Bulls put on an early show in their last home game as they jumped out to a 3-0 lead, but the Jets stormed back with five of their own and held on for a 6-5 victory. Fittingly, after feeling the wrath of the fans during the Jets' last visit to Alabama, Hull led the comeback effort with two goals, while Hedberg scored the eventual game-winner, which gave him a total of 67 on the season. Miller also played for the first time since injuring his foot seven games ago, but Equipment Manager Kelly Pruden became the latest Jet to go down when he was mugged and missed the plane home.

With no time to rest, the Jets quickly flew back to Winnipeg to wrap up their regular season home schedule on Sunday night against the Cowboys, who remained deadlocked with the Oilers for the fourth and final playoff position in the Western Division. Before the game, the Jets presented their annual end-of-season awards and Joe Daley received the Labatt's Trophy as the most valuable player and also the Molson Three Star award, while Hedberg picked up the Ben Moss STAG award for the combination of ability and sportsmanlike conduct. Though they had little to play for, the Jets scored a pair of first period goals and did just enough for the rest of the game to hold off the desperate Cowboys to come away with a 6-4 victory.

On Monday night, the Jets were again in action in Edmonton for the season's last regularly scheduled encounter with the Oilers. Playing their third game in as many nights and with their playoff position secured, the Jets were easy pickings for the Oilers, who rolled to a comfortable 6-2 victory that put them two points ahead of the Cowboys in the race for the Western Division's last playoff spot.

The regular season game to a conclusion on Thursday night against the Cowboys, who had been eliminated from playoff contention by the Oilers' 6-4 victory over the Bulls on Wednesday night. A small turnout of 3,693 spectators saw the Jets break out to a 4-1 lead in the second period and skate off with a 6-4 win. Hedberg opened the scoring and finished his remarkable season with 70 goals, while Larsson made 29 stops in making his second straight start, giving Daley some much-needed rest before the start of the playoffs.

The Jets began the defense of their AVCO World Trophy championship on Sunday, 10 April as they hosted the Mariners in the first game of the best-of-seven Western Division semi-final. The Jets were dominant from the outset and built up a 4-0 lead that they guarded efficiently, taking the game by a score of 5-1. Having recovered from the myriad of injuries that plagued him all season, Bobby Hull led the Jets' attack with a pair of goals and at least one member of the Hot Line had a hand in four of the Jets' five goals. The Jets got a scare, however, when Ulf Nilsson left the ice after getting a knee in the thigh and the worry over his availability for Game 2 took the shine off the well-earned victory.

Two nights later, both teams were back on the ice for Game 2. Though Nilsson was in the Jets' lineup, the Mariners were the better team in the early going, but the score was still tied at 1-1 headed to the third period. Dave Dunn broke the tie a minute and a half into the third and goals from Miller and Hull made the final score 4-1 in the Jets' favor. Dunn, who had been frequently criticized by Bobby Kromm during the season for his play in his own end of the rink, had perhaps his finest game in a Jets' uniform and earned first-star honors as the Jets took a 2-0 series lead with them to San Diego for Games 3 and 4.

The series resumed on Saturday night in San Diego, where the Jets had the Mariners on the run for two periods and were full value for what appeared to be a commanding 4-1 lead. However, the Mariners were able to capitalize on some lucky breaks and fluky bounces to score four times in the latter stages of the game and get themselves back in the series with a 5-4 victory.

After having let one get away, the Jets had a chance to make amends one night later when the two teams went back at it for Game 4. The Mariners jumped out to a 3-1 first period lead, but the Jets rallied and the game was tied at 4-4 after two periods. The third period was played cautiously, but it was the Mariners who broke the tie when Norm Ferguson's power-play goal with only 70 seconds to play sent the Jets down to an eventual 6-4 defeat and to tie the best-of-seven series at 2-2. After the game, Bobby Kromm threw a plastic water bottle at referee Ron Ego and later kicked the door of the officials' room in his anger over the late penalty call to Mike Ford that ultimately decided the game, but nothing was going to change the end result. The Jets had to collect themselves and regroup on their way back to Winnipeg.

The Jets and Mariners faced off on Wednesday night at the Arena for a critical Game 5. Mats Lindh scored his first of the post-season early in the first period and Joe Daley did the rest, backing up a pre-game speech to his teammates where he vowed that one goal would be enough. Daley stopped all 25 shots he faced in a masterful performance, but, for good measure, the Jets added two more goals to make the final score 3-0.

The series shifted back to San Diego for Game 6 on Friday night, where the Jets hoped to eliminate the Mariners and advance to the next round. Unable to skate with the Jets, the Mariners resorted to the rough stuff, instigating a series of fights that culminated in an ugly incident prior to the third period. Ray Adduono butt-ended Ulf Nilsson under his right eye on his way back to the penalty box and after the subsequent brouhaha that saw Adduono and Nilsson fighting behind the stands, Kromm pulled his team off the ice for 10 minutes in protest. After play resumed, the Jets were unable to rebound from a 4-1 deficit and the Mariners took the game, sending the series back to Winnipeg for a deciding Game 7.

On Sunday night, the two teams were back in action to settle the series at the Arena for the right to play the Aeros in the Western Division final. Referee Bill Friday kept close tabs on the game and the Jets used their skill to overpower the Mariners right from the start. The competitive phase of the game ended early in the third period when Hull scored a pair of goals 31 seconds apart and the Jets cruised to a 7-3 victory that allowed them to take the series and advance to battle the Aeros.

The Jets left for Houston the next day to begin the best-of-seven Western Division final at the Summit on Tuesday, 26 April. The Aeros, who were well rested after disposing of the Oilers in five games, controlled play, but Daley kept his team in the game. Nilsson tied the score at 3-3 early in the third period with the Jets' second power-play goal of the night and there was no more scoring for the remainder of regulation time. In overtime, goaltender Ron Grahame came out to challenge an expected shot from Perry Miller, but instead of shooting, Miller fed Peter Sullivan at the side of the net. Sullivan put the puck in on a sharp angle for his second goal of the night, giving the Jets a 4-3 victory. Though his mind was back home where his wife Dorothy was overdue expecting the couple's first child, he and his teammates celebrated the win that gave them a 1-0 series lead.

Game 2 took place two nights later, but this time, the Aeros had an answer for Daley. The Aeros ran away with the game in a second period in which they scored five times, chasing Daley from the net after facing 32 shots and they tied the series with a 7-2 win. Mark Howe scored three times for the victorious Aeros, while his father Gordie added a pair in the victory that tied the series and pleased the audience of 9,533.

Both teams flew to Winnipeg to resume the series on Saturday night, the last day of April. Before the game, the Aeros had to scramble to replace some missing equipment that had been stolen out of their dressing room, but after piecing together what they had with some last-second replacements flown in from Houston, the Aeros were ready to face the Jets. The visitors again took the body at every opportunity, but the determined Jets shook off their hard-hitting guests and battled for a 3-1 lead that would have been more one-sided were it not for Grahame. The Aeros, however, didn't quit and they narrowed the deficit to one goal when they scored with only three seconds to play in the second period. In the third period, Gordie Howe's goal with less than five minutes remaining tied the score, but Sullivan again became the hero when he picked off a pass from Aeros' defenseman Poul Popiel and broke away to score the go-ahead goal with only 96 seconds to play in regulation time. The Jets held the fort and celebrated a 4-3 victory that put them ahead 2-1 in the series.

One night later, the two teams were in action once again and the Jets kept the heat on the Aeros. Paced by a particularly outstanding performance from Hedberg, the Jets racked up a 5-2 lead late in the second period. The proud Aeros chipped away at the Jets' lead, but Hedberg's third goal of the night off a two-on-one with Hull at his side put the game away and allowed the Jets to capture a 6-4 victory that moved them to within one game of a return trip to the AVCO World Trophy final. Hedberg was the first star, putting on a show for his mother, who had come all the way from Ornskoldsvik, Sweden, to be at the game.

The next day, the Jets flew to Houston for Game 5 on Tuesday night, but the Aeros masterfully slowed the game to a crawl and held the Jets in check. The game, however, still was tied early in the third period when Ted Taylor banked a shot off the back of Daley's leg and into the net to give the Aeros a slim 3-2 lead. The Jets had their chances, but the lead held up, allowing the Aeros to send the series back to Winnipeg.

On Thursday night, the two teams were back at the Arena for Game 6, where the Jets hoped to wrap up the series before an overflow crowd of 10,323 spectators, while the Aeros tried to change their luck by staying at a different hotel. After an evenly played first period, the Jets scored twice early in the second to expand their lead to 3-0 and the Jets were on their way. The Aeros valiantly tried to save their season, but they couldn't recover from the early deficit and the Jets won by a score of 6-3, taking the series four games to two. The fans serenaded the Aeros off to an early off-season and the Jets looked forward to their second AVCO World Trophy final in as many seasons.

The Jets' opponents would be the Nordiques, the new champions of the Eastern Division after they had dispatched the Racers in five games. The Jets and Nordiques had been rivals in the Canadian Division over the past two seasons and were very familiar with each other. Last season, the Jets narrowly edged out the Nordiques for top spot in the division and the two teams had split the six regular season meetings this year.

The fifth AVCO World Trophy final began in Quebec six days later on Wednesday, 11 May. The Nordiques had the better chances, but Daley stoned them time and again. The Jets scored twice in the second period to take a 2-0 lead and did a marvelous job of frustrating the Nordiques, who could only get within a single goal and the Jets took the opening game by a score of 2-1. In the final minute, with goaltender Richard Brodeur on the bench, Daley nearly scored when he shot the puck down the ice, but it came to a stop in front of the empty net.

Both teams enjoyed a bit of a break before Game 2 on Sunday night, where the Nordiques came out much more physical than they had four nights ago. The tactic paid off with four first period goals and, combined with some strong goaltending from Brodeur, the Nordiques were in total control and evened the series with a 6-1 victory. Enforcer Steve Sutherland scored three of his team's six goals and Dan Labraaten scored the Jets' only goal early in the third to spoil Brodeur's shutout bid.

After spending seven days in Quebec, the Jets returned home on Monday in preparation for the next two games of the series at the friendlier confines of the Arena. The combination of heat and humidity didn't make the Arena feel very friendly on Wednesday night for Game 3, but Daley kept his team close as the Jets struggled with both the conditions and the soft ice before blowing open a tight 2-1 game with four third period goals to take the game by a score of 6-1. Labraaten scored for the third straight game and added a pair of assists and his line with Lindstrom and Sullivan did most of the damage for the Jets.

Game 4 took place on Friday night under conditions inside the Arena that were slightly less uncomfortable than they had been for Game 3. In front of another five-figure crowd that included 100 fans from Quebec who had flown in for the game, the Jets took a 2-1 first period lead, but they sagged as the game wore on and the Nordiques seized control of the contest. Two Quebec goals in the second period gave the visitors a 3-2 lead and Serge Bernier's second goal of the game early in the third period effectively put the game away. Time expired and the Jets left the ice with a disappointing 4-2 defeat as the Nordiques tied the series at 2-2. During the second period, tempers had flared when Hull was pushed into Brodeur and though referee Bill Friday along with the two linesmen restored order on the ice, at the bench, Kromm had to be physically restrained and it took Huck, Larsson, and clubhouse manager Gabby Sanko to keep the coach under control.

With home ice advantage back in their favor, the Nordiques hosted the Jets on Sunday afternoon for Game 5 in front of a nationally televised audience watching on CBC. The Nordiques got back to the physical, intimidating style that had worked well for them in Game 2 and parlayed it into four first period goals that sent them on to an easy 8-3 victory. The Jets had failed to mount any serious comeback attempt and the win gave the Nordiques their first lead of the series, putting them one win away from their first WHA championship.

The Jets arrived back in Winnipeg on Sunday night and were back on the ice on Tuesday night for Game 6, needing to win to keep their hopes for a second consecutive AVCO World Trophy alive. Buoyed by a two-minute standing ovation from the encouraging crowd to start the game, the Jets turned the tables and took the play to the Nordiques. Four second period goals expanded the Jets' lead from 4-3 to 8-3 and they kept pouring it on until they had reached a dozen. Nordiques' coach Marc Boileau didn't see the entire 12-3 thrashing his team took after being ejected by referee Bill Friday in the third period, but the game was all but over by the time he returned to the dressing room. Hull scored three goals and Hedberg chipped in with a pair for the victorious Jets, who forced a Game 7 in Quebec on Thursday night.

For the first time in the five-year history of the WHA, a seventh and deciding game was necessary to decide the AVCO World Trophy winner and, ready or not, both teams faced off in front of another national television audience and an enthusiastic gathering of 11,461 at Le Colisee to play for the coveted championship. After a cautious and evenly played first period, the Nordiques scored two quick goals early in the second and J.C. Tremblay's long shot from center ice that eluded Daley sent the Nordiques off to the races. Two more goals before the intermission effectively sealed the game's outcome and the champagne began flowing in the stands. After playing out the string in the third period, Ben Hatskin presented Nordiques' captain Marc Tardif with the AVCO World Trophy amid the wild celebrations on and off the ice.

While Tardif made the rounds with the WHA's championship trophy, followed behind by a replica trophy with French inscriptions, the sullen Jets retreated to their dressing room. Considering all the adversity they had overcome all season long, however, making it that far was a major accomplishment for the Jets.

An incredible rash of injuries had hit the team and they had just completed their 111th league game, not to mention the Canada Cup games that many of the players had participated in. For those players, training camp had begun in early August and there had been precious few opportunities for any sort of respite during the season. As Hedberg would say later, "We had nothing left, we were done, beaten."

In the end, the Jets carried the title of league champion through the season most honorably and they fell a mere two periods short of recapturing the AVCO World Trophy. The Jets, however, remained very much a force to be reckoned with and they still had all the ingredients in place for another championship run next season.

Did You Know?

One of the members of the crowd at Game 7 of the AVCO World Trophy final on 26 May 1977 was Montreal junior prospect Robert Picard. Both the Nordiques and the Washington Capitals had selected him in their league's respective amateur drafts, but he opted to sign with the Capitals, where he spent three seasons. Picard went on to play for both the Jets and Nordiques after both clubs joined the NHL. His only full season with the Jets came in 1984-1985, when the Jets enjoyed their finest NHL season, finishing fourth overall in the 21-team league and winning their first NHL playoff series.

1976-1977 Scores and Stats

	Scoring																
	Regular Season								Playoffs								
Player	GP	G	A	Pts	PIM	+/-	PP	SH	Shots	GP	G	A	Pts	PIM	+/-	PP	SH	Shots
Thommie Bergman	42	2	24	26	37	3	0	0										
Jim Cole	2	0	1	1	0	-1	0	0										
Joe Daley	65	0	4	4	6		0	0		20	0	0	0	0		0	0	
Dave Dunn	40	3	11	14	129	-1	0	0		20	4	4	8	23	-7			
Mike Ford	22	3	14	17	20		0	0		20	3	13	16	12	7			
Ted Green	70	4	21	25	25	45	12	2		20	1	3	4	12	-4			
Bob Guindon	69	10	17	27	19	-12	3	0		20	4	4	8	9	-4			
Anders Hedberg	68	70	61	131	48	48	22	0		20	13	16	29	13	6			
Fran Huck	12	2	2	4	10	-1	0	0		7	0	2	2	6	-1	0	0	
Bobby Hull	34	21	32	53	14	16	7	0		20	13	9	22	2	6			
Veli-Pekka Ketola	64	25	29	54	59													
Dan Labraaten	64	24	27	51	21	-11	8	0		20	7	17	24	15	8			
Curt Larsson	19	0	1	1	4		0	0		1	0	0	0	0		0	0	
Danny Lawson	14	6	7	13	2		2	0		13	2	4	6	6	-1			
Bill Lesuk	78	14	27	41	85	23	2	0		18	2	1	3	22	-7			
Mats Lindh	73	14	17	31	2	-13	1	2		20	2	7	9	2	0			
Willy Lindstrom	79	44	36	80	37	-2	11	0		20	9	6	15	22	5			
Barry Long	71	9	38	47	54		4	0		20	1	5	6	10	-1			
Perry Miller	74	14	31	45	124	27	5	1		20	4	6	10	27	-6			
Lyle Moffat	74	13	11	24	90	-7	2	0		17	2	0	2	6	-6			
Morris Mott	2	0	1	1	5		0	0										
Ulf Nilsson	71	39	85	124	89	57	8	3		20	6	21	27	33	5			
Hexi Riihiranta	53	1	16	17	28	-1												
Kent Ruhnke	51	11	11	22	2	-12	0	0										
Lars-Erik Sjoberg	52	2	38	40	31	9	1	1		20	0	5	5	12	11	0	0	
Peter Sullivan	78	31	52	83	18	11	6	0		20	7	12	19	2	5			
Ron Ward	14	4	7	11	2													

Goaltending											
Regular Season											
Goaltender	GP	Min	GA	GAA	Saves	Sv %	SO	EN	W	L	T
Joe Daley	65	3818	206	3.24	1696		3	1	39	23	2
Curt Larsson	19	1019	82	4.83	463		0	2	7	9	0
Playoffs											
	GP	Min	GA	GAA	Saves	Sv %	SO	EN	W	L	
Joe Daley	20	1186	71	3.59			1	1	11	9	
Curt Larsson	1	20	1	3.00			0	0	0	0	

1976-1977 Winnipeg Jets (46-32-2)

Regular Season

Date	Opponent	Score	Date	Opponent	Score
8 Oct	Calgary Cowboys	4-1	21 Jan	Cincinnati Stingers	6-5*
10 Oct	New England Whalers	5-2	23 Jan	Calgary Cowboys	10-5
15 Oct	@Edmonton Oilers	6-1	25 Jan	@Houston Aeros	2-5
16 Oct	@Phoenix Roadrunners	4-6	27 Jan	@Birmingham Bulls	0-3
17 Oct	@San Diego Mariners	1-3	29 Jan	@San Diego Mariners	3-5
19 Oct	Indianapolis Racers	6-1	30 Jan	@Phoenix Roadrunners	5-8
22 Oct	Phoenix Roadrunners	3-4	1 Feb	@Edmonton Oilers	11-1
24 Oct	Birmingham Bulls	7-1	4 Feb	San Diego Mariners	8-2
29 Oct	Edmonton Oilers	11-3	6 Feb	Calgary Cowboys	6-4
31 Oct	San Diego Mariners	6-4	8 Feb	@Quebec Nordiques	7-2
2 Nov	Houston Aeros	1-3	10 Feb	@New England Whalers	3-6
5 Nov	Minnesota Fighting Saints	9-2	11 Feb	@Cincinnati Stingers	0-4
6 Nov	@Cincinnati Stingers	3-7	13 Feb	@Indianapolis Racers	7-5
7 Nov	Edmonton Oilers	5-2	15 Feb	Calgary Cowboys	2-2*
9 Nov	New England Whalers	5-4*	17 Feb	Indianapolis Racers	4-2
11 Nov	@Calgary Cowboys	5-7	18 Feb	@Edmonton Oilers	2-3
14 Nov	@Calgary Cowboys	2-0	20 Feb	Edmonton Oilers	4-2
16 Nov	Quebec Nordiques	8-4	22 Feb	Houston Aeros	3-2
19 Nov	@New England Whalers	7-3	23 Feb	@Phoenix Roadrunners	3-6
20 Nov	@Indianapolis Racers	4-8	26 Feb	@Cincinnati Stingers	8-6
21 Nov	Cincinnati Stingers	2-4	27 Feb	New England Whalers	2-3
23 Nov	@Quebec Nordiques	4-7	1 Mar	@Calgary Cowboys	1-6
26 Nov	@Houston Aeros	1-1*	2 Mar	Quebec Nordiques	4-3*
28 Nov	Phoenix Roadrunners	3-5	3 Mar	@Edmonton Oilers	4-5
30 Nov	San Diego Mariners	8-2	5 Mar	@Phoenix Roadrunners	1-4
3 Dec	@Minnesota Fighting Saints	4-3	8 Mar	San Diego Mariners	5-0
4 Dec	@New England Whalers	6-2	11 Mar	Calgary Cowboys	4-1
5 Dec	@Quebec Nordiques	4-6	13 Mar	Edmonton Oilers	9-3
7 Dec	Phoenix Roadrunners	4-2	15 Mar	Edmonton Oilers	7-0
8 Dec	@Calgary Cowboys	4-2	17 Mar	@Edmonton Oilers	3-4
10 Dec	Birmingham Bulls	3-5	18 Mar	@Indianapolis Racers	7-5
26 Dec	Quebec Nordiques	3-12	20 Mar	@Birmingham Bulls	4-3*
28 Dec	@Houston Aeros	3-6	22 Mar	Edmonton Oilers	8-3
30 Dec	@San Diego Mariners	3-4	27 Mar	@Houston Aeros	5-3
2 Jan	Houston Aeros	5-2	29 Mar	Houston Aeros	2-5
4 Jan	Indianapolis Racers	2-1	31 Mar	@San Diego Mariners	3-4
9 Jan	Birmingham Bulls	4-1	2 Apr	@Birmingham Bulls	6-5
11 Jan	Phoenix Roadrunners	9-2	3 Apr	Calgary Cowboys	6-4
14 Jan	@Calgary Cowboys	5-3	4 Apr	@Edmonton Oilers	2-6
16 Jan	Cincinnati Stingers	4-6	7 Apr	@Calgary Cowboys	6-4

Playoffs

Date	Opponent	Score	Date	Opponent	Score
10 Apr	San Diego Mariners	5-1	1 May	Houston Aeros	6-4
12 Apr	San Diego Mariners	4-1	3 May	@Houston Aeros	2-3
16 Apr	@San Diego Mariners	4-5	5 May	Houston Aeros	6-3
17 Apr	@San Diego Mariners	4-6	11 May	@Quebec Nordiques	2-1
20 Apr	San Diego Mariners	3-0	15 May	@Quebec Nordiques	1-6
22 Apr	@San Diego Mariners	1-3	18 May	Quebec Nordiques	6-1
24 Apr	San Diego Mariners	7-3	20 May	Quebec Nordiques	2-4
26 Apr	@Houston Aeros	4-3*	22 May	@Quebec Nordiques	3-8
28 Apr	@Houston Aeros	2-7	24 May	Quebec Nordiques	12-3
30 Apr	Houston Aeros	4-3	26 May	@Quebec Nordiques	2-8

* - overtime

New faces for 1976-1977:

TOP LEFT: Barry Long
TOP RIGHT: Kent Ruhnke
LOWER LEFT: Dave Dunn
LOWER RIGHT: Dan Labraaten

The WHA Jets took on NHL opponents as part of their exhibition schedule:

ABOVE: The Jets buzz around Pittsburgh Penguins goaltender Denis Herron.

BELOW: The Jets press the issue against the St. Louis Blues.

The Jets' 1976-1977 All-Stars:

ABOVE, Left to Right: Joe Daley, Thommie Bergman, Ulf Nilsson, Bobby Hull, Willy Lindstrom, Anders Hedberg, and Coach Bobby Kromm.

The Jets hosted national teams from the Soviet Union and Czechoslovakia:

ABOVE: Vladislav Tretiak and Joe Daley pose for a postgame shot.

LEFT: Bobby Hull exchanges gifts with a member of the Czechoslovakian team.

ABOVE: Willy Lindstrom breaks in on Michel Dion of the Indianapolis Racers.

BELOW: Dan Labraaten tries to put one in past an outstretched Ron Grahame of the Houston Aeros.

Season VI: 1977-1978 –
Another Crisis, Another Parade

Still stinging from the painful end to their season where they had come tantalizingly close to repeating as AVCO World Trophy champions, the Jets had to quickly turn their focus to next season. The first issue on their agenda was Coach Bobby Kromm, whose two-year contract had expired. However, according to reports published as early as last season's Canada Cup, he had signed to coach the Detroit Red Wings for the 1977-1978 season. During this past season, Kromm acknowledged the commitment he had made but he stated repeatedly that he wanted to stay with the Jets and had his lawyer try and to free him from that contractual obligation.

Come mid-June, the Jets finally gave up waiting and broke off negotiations with Kromm. In good faith, the Jets believed that he was going to get out of the deal he had made with the Red Wings. They even offered him more money than the $75,000 annual salary he was to be paid in Detroit, but in the end, the Jets realized that Kromm had a commitment elsewhere and they moved on. The next day, Red Wings' General Manager Ted Lindsay introduced Kromm as their new coach, while the Jets began looking for his replacement.

Around the league, the league quickly lost three teams when the Phoenix Roadrunners, San Diego Mariners and Calgary Cowboys each decided to cease operations and it appeared as though the Indianapolis Racers would soon join that group when the Indiana National Bank took control of the team's finances and began searching for new ownership. Meanwhile, merger talks between the WHA and the NHL that had been simmering late last season began to heat up over the summer. Under the proposed deal, the Jets, Whalers, Aeros, Stingers, Oilers, and Nordiques would each pay $2.75 million for an NHL franchise and each club would also have to pay an additional $500,000 to get out of the WHA.

Just as they did last season, the Jets garnered their share of post-season awards. Not surprisingly, Anders Hedberg, the league's leading goal scorer, led the way with his selection as *The Sporting News* WHA Player of the Year and as a WHA First Team All-Star, while Joe Daley and Ulf Nilsson were Second Team All-Stars. Daley had perhaps his finest season as a Jet, but he lost out on First Team honors to John Garrett of the Bulls.

On the ice, the Jets opted not to offer contracts to Curt Larsson and Mats Lindh. Perry Miller joined Kromm with the Red Wings, choosing to accept Detroit's offer of a two-year guaranteed contract for $45,000 per year over the Jets' offer of a one-year deal at the same salary, but that had a minor-league provision that would pay him only $20,000 per year if he was demoted. Miller had an excellent season for the Jets after going back to his natural position on the blue line and Kromm felt that Miller was his most consistent defenseman throughout the course of the season.

The Jets again participated in the Amateur Draft, but for the third straight year, they did not sign any of their selections. However, they did add a couple of players when they signed 22-year-old rugged defenseman Kim Clackson and budding Swedish star Kent Nilsson, who was still a couple of months away from his 21st birthday. Clackson had spent the past two seasons with the Racers, where he piled up 519 penalty minutes. The native of Saskatoon, Saskatchewan and former fifth-round draft choice of the Pittsburgh Penguins came with a reputation as a big hitter and tough competitor who looked out for his teammates on the ice. Clackson signed with a provision that he could go back to the Racers if the franchise could be rescued.

Kent Nilsson, no relation to Ulf Nilsson, had played last season for AIK in Sweden, where he tallied 30 goals and 47 points in only 36 games and won the Swedish league's scoring championship at the tender age of 18. Known for his hard shot, the former house painter in Stockholm had been drafted by the Atlanta Flames in the fourth round of last year's NHL Amateur Draft, but didn't sign with the Flames after attending their training camp because he had to return to the Swedish Navy.

In late July, the Jets introduced former defenseman Larry Hillman as their new coach at a press conference at the International Inn. With an abundance of experience as a player, but only one year of coaching experience as Joe Crozier's assistant in Calgary the season before, the Jets chose Hillman over

14 other applicants, including former Kings and Canucks coach Hal Laycoe, former Sabres coach Floyd Smith, former Blues coach Leo Boivin, as well as Pat Kelly and Jackie McLeod, who had been candidates for the job two seasons ago. In selecting Hillman, the Jets hoped that his low-key approach would be more effective than Kromm's fiery style. Kromm had alienated some players with his biting public criticism and though they would have continued to play for him, there were a number of players who were not saddened to see him move on.

Merger talks came to an end when the NHL narrowly defeated the proposal that would have seen the entry of six WHA teams, so the Jets and the rest of the league continued preparations for a sixth WHA season, albeit with fewer teams. The league also opted to do away with the two divisions and would instead group all of the remaining clubs together.

Former University of Minnesota defenseman Joe Micheletti became the newest addition to the Jets' roster when he signed a two-year contract. The 22-year-old Micheletti had spent the latter part of the season with the Cowboys, but the Oilers claimed that he was among the 13 players that they were awarded from the remains of the Cowboys' and Mariners' rosters when those teams folded.

The Jets solved their problem of lack of depth in goal when they signed former Cowboys' goaltender Gary Bromley to a one-year contract. The 27-year-old Edmonton native was perhaps best known to Jets' fans as the goaltender who had yielded Hedberg's 50th goal last season, but Bromley had been the Buffalo Sabres' number one goaltender three seasons ago, when he posted a 3.10 goals against average in 50 games. Last season, in a backup role, he appeared in 28 games with a 3.83 average on a Cowboys team that missed the playoffs. After contacting the Aeros and Racers, Bromley was a phone call away from accepting a job selling refinery equipment for a Calgary oil company, but the job fell through due to a slowdown in the oil business. The Jets initially pursued former Mariners' goaltender Ken Lockett, but the Jets were not willing to give him the two-year guaranteed contract he was seeking, so they turned their attention to Bromley. This was not the first time that Bromley had attracted the Jets' attention, as he was one of their selections in the 1973 Professional Draft.

Despite performing well late in the season after being acquired from Calgary, the Jets decided not to offer Danny Lawson a contract, but they did re-sign Bobby Guindon to a one-year contract and they also brought back Fran Huck, inking him to a deal for the remainder of the calendar year. The Jets also parted ways with Mike Ford, who subsequently signed with Vastra Frolunda in Sweden. Back in the fold was original Jet Larry Hornung, who again became Jets' property after the Mariners folded because the Jets had guaranteed his contract. Rudy Pilous attempted to place him elsewhere, but he ultimately remained with the Jets. The Jets made one more addition before leaving for training camp in Europe when they signed 20-year-old goaltender Markus Mattsson. The native of Suoniemi, Finland starred with Ilves Tampere of the Finnish league and had represented his country on the national stage, appearing in the Canada Cup, world championships and the Izvestia tournament that the Jets had participated in last December.

On the second day of September, the Jets and their entourage left for Sweden, but minutes before they stepped on the plane, they learned that the league awarded Micheletti's rights to the Oilers. Nonetheless, the rest of the team first flew to Copenhagen, then on to Stockholm and their home base at the Hotel Stadshotellet in nearby Sodertalje.

The Jets opened their exhibition schedule with a 4-1 victory over Timra IK in Sundsvall and followed it one night later with a 7-2 win in Skelleftea. In front of a sellout crowd of 5,247 in Anders Hedberg's hometown of Ornskoldsvik, the Jets racked up a 6-2 victory over MoDo before they flew to Finland for a game against IFK Helsinki. The Jets struggled and were fortunate to avoid defeat in the 6-6 tie. Former Jet Hexi Riihiranta set up a pair of goals and scored the goal that gave his team a 6-5 lead. After a return flight to Stockholm and a long bus ride to Leksand, the Jets looked bad in a 3-2 defeat. Moving on to Sodertalje, the Jets were again victimized by a former teammate when Curt Larsson stole the show in backstopping his team to a 5-2 victory.

After the game, Ulf Nilsson had to go to the hospital with a suspected torn muscle near his pelvic bone, but the Jets' fears were calmed when it turned out to be a stretched ligament in the groin area. The rest of the team made the two-hour trek to Orebro and got back on the winning track with an easy 9-2 win. Back in Stockholm, the Jets dropped a 7-5 decision to AIK Stockholm before winding up their Scandinavian tour with a 6-3 victory over Vastra Frolunda in Gothenburg.

The last few days had not been without anxious moments as the Jets were involved in a tussle over the Clackson signing. Since the Racers franchise was purchased by former Oilers owner Nelson Skalbania and would be operating this season, the league ordered Clackson to be returned to Indianapolis. The number of players on edge doubled when it was learned that Peter Sullivan might be sent to the Racers as compensation for Clackson. In the end, after a couple of days of wrangling, the Jets worked out a deal to send a combination of draft choices and cash to the Racers in exchange for Clackson.

The Jets' flight home was delayed three hours in Copenhagen causing them to miss their connection in Toronto, but the Jets arrived home safely. They were back on the ice two nights later for the North American portion of their exhibition schedule, which included five games against NHL opponents. The Jets defeated the North Stars by scores of 2-1 and 4-1, then swept a pair of games against the Blues by scores of 6-2 and 3-0. Three days before their league opener, former coach Bobby Kromm and the Red Wings visited the Arena and the Jets completed the sweep of the rival league with a 1-0 victory.

The sixth regular season for the Jets began on Wednesday, 12 October in Edmonton against the revamped Oilers. During the summer, Peter Pocklington had purchased the team from Nelson Skalbania and hired Larry Gordon to replace Bep Guidolin as the team's general manager. Glen Sather had retired as a player to become a full-time coach and the team added a number of players from the defunct Cowboys and Mariners to their roster, including defenseman Paul Shmyr and centermen Ron Chipperfield and Norm Ferguson.

The Oilers took the body effectively for the first two periods, but despite holding an edge in play, the game was tied at 2-2 at the second intermission. The Jets turned the game around and scored five times in the third period for a 7-3 victory. The win gave the Jets a 5-1 record on season openers and both Gary Bromley and Kent Nilsson had impressive debuts, but Bobby Hull was the star of the game. With a full off-season to recuperate from his injuries, the Golden Jet scored three times and was fully deserving of first-star honors. The Jets lost Ted Green during the second period with a pulled groin muscle, giving them flashbacks to the rash of injuries that had hit the team a year ago.

One night later, the Jets hosted the Nordiques for the first time since the epic AVCO World Trophy final the two teams had staged six months ago. The defending champions added goaltender Don "Smokey" McLeod and rugged winger Peter Driscoll from the Cowboys, but the team that had beaten the Jets in Game 7 was largely left intact. The Jets came out strong and built up a 3-0 lead, and though the Nordiques tried their best to mount a comeback, Daley blunted their efforts and the Jets held on for a 5-2 victory in their home opener. Kent Nilsson scored his first two goals as a Jet in another strong outing, but already without Green, the Jets lost another player to injury for the second straight game when Lindstrom suffered a hyperextended left knee in the second period.

Without both Green and Lindstrom, the Jets flew to Cincinnati for a Saturday night game against the Stingers. In addition to the presence of former Racers' coach Jacques Demers behind the bench, the Stingers had made some notable additions during the off-season, including Robbie Ftorek, the reigning WHA most valuable player, and Ernie Wakely, the former and original Jet. The Jets built up a 4-2 lead midway through the second period, but goals from Ron Plumb, last season's top defenseman in the WHA, and Rich Leduc late in the period tied the score at 4-4. The score held until the final minute of the third period when Lyle Moffat unleashed a slap shot from long range that rang off the inside of the goal past Wakely to give the Jets a 5-4 lead. The goal held up as the game-winner and the win raised the Jets' record to a perfect 3-0-0 to start the season. Markus Mattsson made 29 stops in his first league game as a Jet, making him the third Jets' goaltender in as many games to record a victory.

Back home one night later, the Jets entertained the Racers. Having narrowly avoided folding during the summer, the Racers had lost a number of players as well as their coach from the team that bowed out to the Nordiques in the Eastern Division final last season. Behind the visitors' bench was former Mariners' coach Ron Ingram, who had last been at the Arena at the conclusion of a hard-fought seven-game series in which his Mariners had lost to the Jets. Ingram saw his new team take an early lead, but it didn't last long as the Jets ran amok over the decimated Racers and routed them by a score of 9-1 in a game that was never competitive. Kent Ruhnke scored twice and added a pair of assists to lead the Jets' scorers, while Hull chipped in with a pair of goals to raise his season total to six in the team's fourth game.

The Jets were off until Friday, 21 October when they met the Whalers at the Arena. The Whalers had added Gordie Howe and sons Mark and Marty from the Aeros in the off-season and also welcomed back goaltender Al Smith, who had ended his retirement from hockey by giving up his job selling garbage cans in Toronto and was in goal facing Daley, his former roommate, once again. Kent Nilsson got the Jets on the board first early in the game, but the Whalers replied with three of their own before the end of the first period. The Jets dominated the second period, but Smith kept his team in front and the Whalers pulled away in the third while frustrating the Jets' comeback hopes at every turn. The Whalers took the game by a score of 5-2 and the Jets sent the vocal crowd of 10,330 home disappointed.

On the heels of their first loss of the season, the Jets sought to make amends when the Bulls came in for a Sunday night game. The Bulls had hired former Fighting Saints' coach Glen Sonmor as their bench boss during the off-season and Frank Mahovlich returned after missing most of the last season with a knee injury, but neither man could prevent the Jets from running up an early 4-0 lead or slow down the onslaught that followed. The Jets kept pouring it on and the final score of 10-3 that flattered the visiting Bulls. Hull scored three times and both Sullivan and Kent Nilsson scored twice each in the lopsided victory. After being signed to a 10-game tryout contract, 25-year-old winger Dave Kryskow made his on-ice debut. The former Cowboy played well, but he needed six stitches after being cut above his left eye by former teammate Paul Terbenche. Larry Hillman had recommended Kryskow to the Jets after coaching him last season in Calgary and Kryskow, ironically, had played for former Jets' coach Bobby Kromm in Dallas. Like Gary Bromley, his teammate in Calgary last season, the Jets had also selected Kryskow in 1973 Professional Draft, but did not sign him at that time.

On Wednesday night, the Jets were on the ice in Indianapolis for their third one-game road trip of the season. The Racers were much better than when the two teams had met 10 days earlier and two goals from Claude St. Sauveur 23 seconds apart early in the third period put the finishing touches on an eventual 5-3 win. St. Sauveur scored a total of three goals for the Racers and he was now fully healthy after being in a serious auto accident over a year ago in which he had suffered a broken collarbone, dislocated shoulder and a broken nose. Mattsson was called upon to make the start in goal at the last minute after Daley complained of back spasms and wasn't at his best in the loss that, combined with the Whalers' 7-1 win over Quebec, cost the Jets top spot in the eight-team league.

The 5-2-0 Jets returned home for a pair of weekend games starting Friday night against the Stingers. The Jets got off to a quick 2-0 lead and expertly held the Stingers at bay for the rest of the game to earn a 3-2 victory. Mattsson made his second straight start, but he was not severely tested for much of the night, while Hull opened the scoring, giving him 10 goals in eight games.

The Oilers were the visitors on Sunday night and despite winning only two of their first six games, they gave the Jets all they could handle right from the opening faceoff. Goaltender Ken Broderick took the edge off the Jets' attack with some fine saves and the scrappy Oilers kept on even terms with the Jets well into the third period. Hull then took matters into his own hands and scored twice late in the game to lead the Jets to a 5-2 victory that vaulted them over the idle Whalers and back into first place. Daley made a successful return after being bothered with back problems and Hedberg added a goal and an assist in the winning cause.

After a successful month of October, November began with the Jets' first multi-game road trip of the season, but Fran Huck was left behind after the Jets placed him on waivers. Huck's second stint with the Jets was not as successful as his first and the Jets decided to part company with him prior to the expiration of his contract at the end of December. The rest of the team was on the ice on Wednesday night in Edmonton in a rematch from Sunday night with the Oilers. The teams split four goals in the first period, but Ulf Nilsson's shorthanded goal late in the second proved to be the catalyst for the Jets, who scored three times in the third and came away with a 6-3 win.

The next day, the Jets moved on to Birmingham where their bus broke down on the way to their hotel, but they were back on the ice on Friday against the struggling Bulls, losers of their last seven games. The Bulls gave it a good effort, but Daley's outstanding goaltending and some well-timed goals allowed the Jets to leave Alabama with a 4-2 victory and keep them one point ahead of the Whalers atop the league standings. On the injury front, the Jets lost Green again when he bruised a tendon in his foot while blocking a shot during the game and Lars-Erik Sjoberg missed some time in the third period when he was getting stitched up after being cut between his eyes. Bill Lesuk filled in admirably on the blue line in the captain's absence while the Jets were holding on to their slim lead.

The three-game road trip wrapped up the next evening with the Jets' second visit of the season to Cincinnati. Like the Bulls the night before, the Stingers, losers of six of their first seven games, came into the game with troubles of their own, and Mattsson prevented them from capturing their second win of the season. The young Finn stopped all but one of the 39 shots he faced and the Jets gave him plenty of offensive support, pumping six goals past Ernie Wakely in a 6-1 victory.

The 10-2-0 Jets returned home for a bit of respite, but on Monday evening, the Jets' community ownership group held its annual meeting at the Winnipeg Convention Center. For the annual fundraiser, they decided to replace Vegas Nite with a $100 per plate dinner featuring NHL Players Association director Alan Eagleson as the keynote speaker. The members were also given an update on the Jets' worsening financial situation. The club's working capital had diminished and a new financing plan would be needed until the either the current arena was expanded or a new arena was built. One idea brought forward was to sell players' contracts to a limited company to attract investors for a tax shelter.

The topic of the contracts of Anders Hedberg and Ulf Nilsson was also discussed. Two years ago, each had signed a five-year contract with the salary for the first two years locked in, but in the third, fourth and fifth years, they each had the right to solicit offers from other teams. The Jets, however, had the right to retain each of them by making a matching offer that came within $20,000 per season of a higher offer that they might receive from another club.

Unfortunately for the Jets, the likelihood that they would receive a higher offer increased as a result of the fact that the NHL had recently made a ruling that allowed the pair of Swedish stars to freely negotiate with any NHL team. The Toronto Maple Leafs held Hedberg's NHL rights and the Buffalo Sabres owned Nilsson's rights, but both now could sell their services to the highest bidder.

Back on the ice, the Jets returned to game action on Wednesday, 9 November against the Aeros. Since the Jets had eliminated the Aeros in last season's Western Division final, the Aeros lost all three members of the Howe family to the Whalers, but they did pick up high-scoring centerman Andre Lacroix from the defunct Mariners to complement what was still a deep roster. The Jets used two quick first period goals to jump out front, only to have the Aeros reply with two of their own in short succession to tie the game before the intermission. The teams traded goals early in the second period, but an ineffective Jets' power play kept the game tied at 3-3 until Hull scored his first goal in three games eight minutes into the third to break the deadlock. From there, the Jets did an outstanding job of protecting their lead and the 4-3 score held up, putting the Jets back into first place, one point ahead of the surging Whalers. The Jets, however, lost Dave Dunn during the game with a pulled muscle in his rib cage. The Jets also announced that they had demoted the seldom-used Kent Ruhnke to the Binghamton Dusters of the AHL.

Two nights later, the Jets hosted the Nordiques in front of an overflow crowd of 10,357 at the Arena. The Jets had the better of the play, but third-string goaltender Jim Corsi prevented the Jets from expanding on their 2-0 second period lead. Buoyed by the play of their netminder, the Nordiques scored late in the second period, then added another marker early in the third to tie the score at 2-2. The game went to overtime, where the Jets had their chances, but Marc Tardif's second goal of the game ended the contest in the visitors' favor and also ended the Jets' six-game winning streak.

On Sunday night, the Jets welcomed back the Stingers, who brought newly signed veteran defenseman Pat Stapleton with them. The Jets again came out strong, but they only had a narrow 2-1 lead to show for a dominating first period. With the Jets holding on to their one-goal lead late in the third period, Rich Leduc's pass from behind the net went off Kent Nilsson's skate and past Mattsson to tie the score, then Blaine Stoughton scored with only 88 seconds to play in regulation time, allowing the Stingers to pull out an improbable 3-2 victory.

Losers of their past two games, the Jets left for Quebec to begin and end their fourth one-game road trip of the season on Tuesday night. For the first two periods, the Jets' fortunes appeared as bleak as they had when they last visited Quebec in May, but after Mattsson replaced Daley to start the third period, the Hot Line took charge and led the Jets back from a 6-3 deficit with three goals to tie the game. Early in overtime, however, the disgruntled Pierre Guite fired a high shot that beat Mattsson to give the Nordiques their second consecutive overtime victory over the Jets.

After the game, the sagging Jets boarded a bus for Montreal to catch a flight back to Winnipeg to battle the Bulls on Wednesday night. The 2-10-1 Bulls had flown into Winnipeg with a couple of new heavyweights in their lineup, having recently traded Vaclav Nedomansky and Tim Sheehy to the Red Wings in exchange for Steve Durbano and Dave Hanson, to go along with Gilles "Bad News" Bilodeau and Frank "Seldom" Beaton. Durbano had accumulated over 1,000 penalty minutes during parts of six NHL seasons, while Hanson had similar numbers scattered over the past three seasons, which he'd spent mostly in the minor leagues. Hanson was best known for his supporting role in the movie *Slap Shot*, featuring a failing minor-league team that resorted to fighting and goon tactics.

The still unsigned Dave Kryskow opened the scoring for his first goal as a Jet when his own rebound bounced in off his back, but it was a struggle the rest of the way for his teammates, who needed Dan Labraaten's goal late in the third period to escape with a 2-2 tie. Bromley faced only 18 shots on the night from the new-look Bulls, but he was called upon to make one key stop in overtime that could have won the game for the visitors.

The next day, the Jets were back on the road to start a three-game weekend in Hartford on Friday, 18 November. After Kent Nilsson opened the scoring, Hedberg's goal early in the third period gave the Jets a 2-0 lead, but the Whalers kept pressing and finally broke through against a stubborn Joe Daley. Two goals four and a half minutes apart tied the score, then Mike Antonovich capitalized on a careless giveaway from Kent Nilsson with just over four minutes to play to give the Whalers their first lead of the night. The Jets were unable to get the equalizer and the Whalers celebrated their 12th consecutive victory, which also expanded their lead over the Jets to six points. To make matters worse for the Jets, they lost two defensemen during the game to injury. Clackson suffered stretched knee ligaments and was expected to be out for a week, and Thommie Bergman had been cut in the face after being hit with Dave Keon's stick. The only bright spot on the night was the fact that the Jets were able to keep Gordie Howe from registering his 1,000th goal as a professional. Pro hockey's elder statesman came into the game stuck on 999 and both Daley and the Jets made him wait another day for the historic milestone goal.

With a five-game winless streak in tow, the Jets touched down in Indianapolis for a Saturday night engagement with the Racers. Before the largest crowd of the season at Market Square Arena, the hometown Racers doggedly kept after the Jets, but Kryskow's goal with just under four minutes to play finally put the Jets ahead to stay. The goal was the second of the night for Kryskow, who was playing on a four-game extension to his original tryout contract, and it lifted the Jets to an eventual 6-4 victory for their first win in 10 days.

The Jets boarded a plane headed for Winnipeg to wrap up the three-game weekend only to be told on their descent that the Winnipeg airport was closed due to a blizzard that had blanketed the city with several inches of snow. The plane was forced to turn around and land at the Minneapolis-Saint Paul airport, where the Jets would instead fly directly to Edmonton for their next game on Tuesday night.

After the Jets arrived safely in the Alberta capital, the Oilers completely dominated the first period, but Daley stood tall and stopped all but one of the 25 shots he faced in the opening frame. Hedberg's second goal of the game early in the second period actually gave the Jets a short-lived lead, but the Oilers would not be denied as they pumped three more past the beleaguered Jets' netminder on their way to a 4-2 win. In addition to having to deal with the pain of their fifth loss in seven games, the Jets lost a couple of more players to injury during the game. Lars-Erik Sjoberg popped a muscle in his lower ribs, while Bobby Guindon sustained a charleyhorse to go along with his sore knee.

The Jets finally returned home after for a breather before their next game on Sunday night, where the Bulls made their second visit to the Arena in 11 days. Ken Linseman scored the first period's only goal, but the Jets scored twice in the second to take the lead and Hedberg's goal seven minutes into the third made the score 3-1 in the Jets' favor. As the Jets were celebrating their goal, however, Linseman touched off a bench-clearing brawl when he hit Ulf Nilsson over the arm. Shoves were exchanged, then Beaton led the Bulls off the bench and Durbano followed suit. Once order was restored, five Bulls and two Jets were ejected and the multitude of other penalties kept the off-ice officials buzzing. When the game resumed 40 minutes later, with both teams playing with three skaters aside, the Bulls scored goals 48 seconds apart to tie the score and send the game to overtime. Three minutes into the extra period, Bob Stephenson put a backhand shot past Daley to give the Bulls a sickening 4-3 victory.

After bidding adieu to both the Bulls and the month of November, the Jets kicked off a three-game weekend with a return trip to Hartford on 2 December. The Whalers entered the contest without a win in their last five games after their 13-game winning streak was broken, but they had little trouble with the Jets, who offered little resistance. Slowly, but surely, the Whalers built up a 3-1 lead and sealed the victory with an empty-net goal in the game's final minute to send the Jets down to a 4-1 defeat. Without two defensemen, Kryskow was forced to take a regular shift on defense, but at least the Jets hadn't lost any more healthy bodies during the game. Kryskow was playing his first game armed with a contract for the rest of the season that he earned after his extended 14-game tryout. For the ninth consecutive game, Gordie Howe failed to score his 1,000th goal as a professional and his total stayed fixed at 999 for his distinguished career.

The reeling Jets moved on to Quebec for a Saturday night game against the Nordiques. They fell behind 3-0 in the first period and though they kept battling back, in the end, they played just well enough to lose and dropped a 6-5 decision to the Nordiques. As a result of their fourth consecutive defeat, the 12-10-1 Jets sank into third place in the league standings, two points back of the Nordiques and 10 behind the Whalers.

The three-game weekend came to a close with a Sunday night game against the Oilers at the Arena. Willy Lindstrom opened the scoring six minutes into the game, but the lead lasted only 51 seconds and the Oilers gleefully walked over the listless Jets to take a 3-1 lead. Dan Labraaten's goal late in the third period brought the Jets back to life, but it was a case of too little, too late, and the Jets went down to a 3-2 defeat.

On the heels of a stern lecture from Rudy Pilous after practice, followed by a players-only meeting, the Jets were back on the ice on Wednesday night against the Aeros. The Jets took out their simmering displeasure on their guests and made them pay with three first period goals on their way to a 5-2 victory that put an emphatic end to their five-game losing streak. Hull scored a pair for the Jets to give him 19 on the season and Ken Baird played his first game for the Jets after arriving the day before from Snow Lake, Manitoba. The 26-year-old gritty winger, who is also a diabetic, was the Oilers' last cut this season and he drove 500 miles to Winnipeg when Pilous called offering him a tryout. The Jets also won in spite of playing most of the game with only four defensemen, as Barry Long was put out of action in the first period as a result of a charleyhorse in his right leg.

The Jets made more player moves the next day when they claimed 28-year-old centerman Lynn Powis off waivers from the Racers. Like Baird, Powis had also played under Larry Hillman last year in Calgary and had two seasons of NHL experience under his belt before joining the Cowboys two years ago. In 14 games with the Racers this season prior to his release, Powis scored four goals and added six assists. The Jets also announced Larry Hornung's retirement, bringing an end to a distinguished pro career that had begun 11 years ago. Hornung was an original Jet and a member of their first championship team who had returned this season after splitting the previous season between the Oilers and Mariners. At times, he had been a target of some mean-spirited fans, but he kept his composure and made a positive contribution to the team in just over four seasons as a Jet.

The First "Ducky"

Most Jets fans will automatically associate the nickname "Ducky" with Dale Hawerchuk, the Jets' all-time leading NHL scorer who starred in a Jets' uniform for nine seasons. However, Lynn "Ducky" Powis became the first Jets' player to bear the nickname when the Jets claimed him on waivers from the Indianapolis Racers on 8 December 1977.

On Friday, 9 December, the Jets met the Stingers in a makeup from the game they had been scheduled to play almost three weeks ago but had been postponed because the Winnipeg airport was shut down due to a raging blizzard. Lars-Erik Sjoberg opened the scoring just 12 seconds into the game, but a pair of second period goals from Claude Larose wiped out the early lead. The Jets responded with a pair of their own and looked to have the game well in hand when defenseman Barry Melrose scored with just 63 seconds to play to tie the score. In overtime, Robbie Ftorek skillfully stationed himself between Thommie Bergman and Dave Dunn and knocked a bouncing puck past Gary Bromley to give the Stingers their second straight win in Winnipeg. The loss kept the Jets in third place, two points behind the Nordiques and a dozen back of the frontrunning Whalers.

Two nights after their gut-wrenching overtime defeat, the Jets hosted the struggling Racers, who were playing their third game in as many nights after dropping a 5-3 decision in Quebec on Saturday night.

The Jets were in no position to show any mercy to their guests and they gradually piled up a 6-0 lead before Rene Leclerc broke Bromley's shutout bid midway through the third period. The Racers' goal, however, proved to be little more than cosmetic and the game ended with the score 7-1 in the Jets' favor. Despite seeing limited ice time, Baird scored three times in front of a group of friends who had come from Snow Lake, but Ulf Nilsson was the star of the game with two goals and a pair of assists.

Having made a positive impression during his brief stay, Baird met with Rudy Pilous the next morning and both parties agreed on a contract to keep Baird a Jet for the rest of the season. The next night, Baird and his teammates wound up the five-game home stand with a game against a touring Czechoslovakian team. Like the team they had played in Winnipeg last year, the best Czech players were at the Izvestia tournament, but this Tuesday night affair was not simply an exhibition match because the game counted in the league standings. After a scoreless first period, the Jets seized control of the game with four goals in the second and the increasingly frustrated Czechs posed no real threat to the Jets' lead as the game wore on. The Jets went on to post a convincing 5-1 victory before a packed house at the Arena in which five different Jets scored, but the Hot Line was the dominant trio of the contest.

The Jets were off until Saturday, 17 December when they met the Whalers in Hartford for the first of a home-and-home series. The Whalers got on the board first two minutes into the game, but the Jets shook off the early goal and they ran up a 5-1 lead in the third period before two late goals from Jack Carlson narrowed the Jets' lead to 5-3. However, Kryskow's seventh goal as a Jet with two and a half minutes to play put the finishing touches on a 6-3 win, spoiling Gordie Howe's 2,000th game as a professional.

One night later, the same two teams were on the ice at the Arena for the rematch. It was more of the same as the Jets again took the play to the league-leading Whalers. The Jets used two goals late in the second period to break a 2-2 tie and they pulled away in the third to complete the impressive sweep by a score of 7-3. Anders Hedberg scored two goals and added two assists in earning first-star honors, but his linemate, Ulf Nilsson, had to leave during the first period after pulling a muscle in his hip. The pair of victories enabled the Jets to pass the Nordiques, who were in Moscow at the Izvestia tournament, and move to within eight points of the first-place Whalers.

Next on the schedule was a visit from a touring team from the Soviet Union on Tuesday night. Like the Czechs that had preceded them a week before, the nation's best players were competing at the Izvestia tournament and the group that was touring WHA cities was a younger team that was touted as the next top national team in waiting. The Jets continued on their hot streak and rolled to a 5-1 second period lead, then had to withstand a late Soviet rally for a 6-4 victory in a game that counted in the league standings. The win was the Jets' fifth straight and moved them to within six points of the Whalers.

Bright and early the next morning, the Jets began a trying day on their way to Houston for a game that evening. They left Winnipeg at 8 a.m. without Kent Nilsson, who had missed the plane, then after a stop at the Minneapolis-Saint Paul airport, they touched down in Chicago only to watch their connecting flight to Houston take off without them. Eventually, they got on a later flight, but they didn't arrive in Houston until 6:15 p.m. and had to be taken to the Summit under police escort.

The game itself began after a 45-minute delay and despite their travel woes and shortage of healthy bodies, the Jets played surprisingly well and managed to squeak out a 4-3 lead at the end of two periods. At that time, Kent Nilsson, who had to make his own way to Houston, rejoined his teammates, but in the third, the weary Jets shut down their attack and simply played it close to the vest in an attempt to hold on to their slim lead. The Jets limited the Aeros to only four shots in the final 20 minutes of play and they snuck out of Texas with an improbable 4-3 win.

The next day, the Jets made their way to Cincinnati in a far less eventful manner for a Friday night game against the Stingers before taking a break for the Christmas holiday. Having recuperated from their unwanted adventures two days before, the Jets stayed with the improved Stingers and Hedberg's pair of goals late in the second period put the Jets ahead to stay. Peter Sullivan's empty-net marker sealed the 6-4 victory and put smiles on their faces as they returned to Winnipeg only four points back of first place.

After spending Christmas at home with their families, the Jets prepared to meet the Nordiques on Boxing Day for their last league game prior to their upcoming trip to Tokyo to play the Soviet national team. The Nordiques had recently returned from Moscow, where they managed one tie in the four-game Izvestia tournament. One year ago to the day, the Jets had been in the same position and the visiting

Nordiques hammered the travel-weary Jets by a score of 12-3. This time around, the Jets returned the favor and laid a whipping on the Nordiques. The Jets had a 3-0 lead by the time the game was four minutes old and though they didn't reach double figures, the 9-4 rout was no less fitting. Hedberg scored four of the Jets' nine goals, enabling the Jets to take an eight-game winning streak with them to Japan.

The next day, the Jets took off for the Japanese capital to spend the next six days and play three games against the best team the Soviet Union had to offer. Unlike the past two international games the Jets had played in Winnipeg, the upcoming matches would not count in the league standings, and as a result, Larry Hillman insisted that the players treat this time as a vacation rather than as a business trip.

The Jets got settled in at the Takanawa Prince Hotel before the series' first game at the Yoyogi Arena the next day. The 11,300-seat arena was originally built as a swimming pool for the 1964 Olympic games, but it had since been converted to an arena where all three games between the two teams would be played. Inside, the rink had no glass along the sides and only netting at each end to protect spectators from stray pucks.

Before a crowd of around 6,500, the Jets took to the ice in the first of three matchups with what was arguably the world's best team. The Jets fell behind by a score of 2-0 in the first period, but they stormed back with three of their own to take the lead. The Soviets tied the score and later regained their two-goal lead in the latter stages of the second period, but the Jets kept the game close right to the end in the 7-5 defeat.

The second game took place the next day and the Jets again kept the game close, but the Soviets took the lead for good early in the second period and skated off with a 4-2 win. Lynn Powis scored his first goal since donning a Jets' uniform, but Gary Bromley was the Jets' best player and he was outstanding in a losing cause.

After some sightseeing with their families and a trip to the Canadian embassy, the Jets concluded the three-game series on New Year's Day. Joe Daley was scheduled to get the start in goal, but he had been hit on the left foot during the warmup and had to be taken to a hospital. Though x-rays later revealed no fracture, Bromley was called upon once again and only his stellar work prevented an embarrassing blowout. The Jets were thoroughly outplayed in the 5-1 defeat in which the score greatly flattered the Jets.

Despite going 0-for-3 in the series, the Jets, along with their delegation of over 100 others, enjoyed their trip and genuinely appreciated the first-class treatment they received in Japan. The Jets returned to Winnipeg, where they met the Soviets one more time in front of a packed house of 10,315 spectators at the Arena on Thursday, 5 January. Determined to make a better showing than they had in Japan, with the Hot Line leading the way the Jets stormed out to a 4-0 lead early in the second period. After Vladislav Tretiak replaced Aleksandr Sidelnikov in goal, the Soviets rallied for a pair before the period ended and added another early in the third. The Soviets pressed hard for the tying goal, but Hull put the game out of reach in the game's final minute, capping his hat trick and the Jets took the game by a score of 5-3.

Though it almost seemed anticlimactic on the heels of the thrilling victory over the mighty Soviets, the Jets flew to Edmonton to resume their league schedule the next night. The Jets took a 2-0 first period lead, and Bromley had to be at his best to keep the Oilers at bay in the second. The Jets were better in the third period and they captured a 4-1 victory that was their ninth straight in games that counted in the WHA standings. Ulf Nilsson scored a pair and added an assist to lead the Jets, while former Oiler Ken Baird scored once in his first game in Edmonton as a Jet.

On Top Of Old Smokey

On 6 January 1978, the Jets faced goaltender Don "Smokey" McLeod for the last time. McLeod's 39 regular season and 11 playoff appearances against the Jets were more than any other goaltender the Jets opposed during their seven seasons in the WHA. An original member of the Houston Aeros, McLeod had also faced the Jets as a member of the Vancouver Blazers, Calgary Cowboys, Quebec Nordiques, and the Edmonton Oilers.

The Jets returned home for a pair of games starting Sunday night against the Racers. Joined by 57 of their fans who had come from Indianapolis, the Racers hung tough despite playing their third game in as many nights. The Jets took the lead for good in the second period and shut the door on any comeback hopes the Racers may have entertained and the Jets held on for a 4-2 win. Goaltender Gary Inness made 30 stops to keep his team within striking distance, but it wasn't enough to extend the Racers' three-game winning streak or to prevent the Jets from extending their own winning streak to 11 games.

On Wednesday night, the Jets hosted the Bulls for the first time since late November, when the Bulls had instigated an ugly brawl. To make matters worse, referee Ron Ego had become ill before the game, leaving linesman Joey Dame to handle the head official's duties and Harvey Schmidt, a local minor official, was pulled out of the stands to fill in as a substitute linesman. As a player in 1963, Schmidt had been the captain of the Melville Millionaires and had competed against both Lesuk and Daley while they played junior hockey in Saskatchewan.

The game featured little of the extracurricular activity that had marred the last game between the teams and the Jets completely dominated the contest from start to finish. The Jets scored four times in each of the first two periods on their way to a satisfying 11-2 victory that moved them back to within four points of the first-place Whalers. The Hot Line led the Jets' attack once again, but everyone on the roster had a hand in the rout.

The next day, the Jets left to start a three-game weekend on Friday night in Houston. After missing most of the game the last time the Jets had been in Houston, Kent Nilsson opened the scoring with the first period's only goal, but the Aeros turned the game around and scored a three times in under two minutes in the second period. Kryskow scored late in the period, but the Jets could get no closer and their 11-game winning streak came to a halt with a 3-2 defeat. Ernie Wakely made 21 saves to backstop his team to the victory and won for the first time in six starts this season against his original WHA team. Wakely had lost all three starts he made against the Jets as a member of the Stingers and had been 0-for-2 since being traded to the Aeros in November.

The 24-13-1 Jets moved on to Indianapolis to play the Racers on Saturday night. The Racers had the Jets scrambling in the game's opening minutes, but after the visitors settled down, they wiped out a 3-2 deficit with a strong second period and the Jets went on to post a 6-3 victory. Lynn Powis scored his first league goal as a Jet in the first period, and ironically, it came against the team that had waived him earlier in the season.

Returning home, the Jets wrapped up the weekend with a visit from the Oilers on Sunday night. Both teams were playing their third game in three nights, and the Oilers had had an especially difficult time with travel connections getting to Winnipeg from Quebec, where they had dropped a 7-4 decision to the Nordiques the prior evening. The visitors eventually made it to Winnipeg, but the game had to be delayed for an hour and a half while the Oilers hastily got ready. The Jets took advantage of their harried guests by grabbing a 2-0 lead, but the Oilers gathered themselves and got back into the game. Regulation time ended with the score tied at 3-3, and in overtime Ron Chipperfield stole the puck from Powis and put a backhand shot past Bromley for the winning goal. The Jets also lost Ken Baird during the game with a mildly separated shoulder and played with only two goaltenders on their roster after shipping Markus Mattsson to the Nordiques. Larry Hillman had been going exclusively with the veteran tandem of Daley and Bromley, so the Jets sought to place Mattsson with a team where he could get some playing time. In exchange for Mattsson, the Nordiques covered half of the transfer fee the Jets paid to secure his release from the Finnish Ice Hockey Federation.

The league paused for its annual All-Star break as the defending champions met the best of the rest of the league at Le Colisee on Tuesday night. All three members of the Hot Line — Bobby Hull, Ulf Nilsson, and Anders Hedberg — along with Barry Long and Lars-Erik Sjoberg represented the Jets, but despite Hedberg's goal and one assist from each of Hull, Long, and Sjoberg, the Nordiques erased a 4-1 deficit and came back to win by a score of 5-4 before a crowd of only 6,413.

The Nordiques, together with the five All-Star Jets were in Winnipeg the next night for a game on Wednesday, 18 January at the Arena. The Jets had little difficulty in handling the injury-ravaged Nordiques and they coasted to a 5-1 victory in a game that ceased to be competitive early in the second period. Daley would have had his first shutout of the season were it not for a first period goal credited to Charles Constantin that appeared to hit the goal post on replay.

He Hits The Post, He Scores

Charles Constantin's apparent goal-post goal on 18 January 1978 would prove to be an ominous foreshadowing of a more infamous goal in Jets' history. During a playoff game on 7 April 1983, Paul Coffey of the Oilers rang a shot squarely off the goal post behind goaltender Brian Hayward, but goal judge Rick Lundgren ruled that it went in. Referee Kerry Fraser upheld the call made by the off-duty Los Angeles police sergeant, giving the Oilers a goal that broke a 2-2 tie. The Jets later tied the score, but Mark Messier's legitimate goal late in the third period proved decisive in the Oilers' tainted 4-3 victory.

In addition to Wednesday's victory on the ice, the Jets also received approval from the Winnipeg City Council to implement a proposal to sell $1.65 million worth of shares to the public as part of a $2.8 million refinancing scheme. The capital raised by selling the shares, priced at a minimum of $5,000 apiece, would be used, in part, to fund either an expanded or a new 16,000-seat arena. The vote, however, nearly failed as councillors were split down the middle, but Mayor Robert Steen's tie-breaking vote tipped the scales in the Jets' favor.

The refinancing proposal came on the heels of reports that the New York Rangers had offered both Hedberg and Ulf Nilsson contracts that would pay them $475,000 apiece for each of the next two seasons. The Jets had the right to match the offers, but they first needed to generate enough capital to continue running the club.

On Friday night, the Jets entertained the Whalers in a battle for first place. Anxious to wipe out the two-point differential between the league's top two clubs, the Jets scored twice early in the first period, but the Whalers kept nipping at the Jets' heels and Mark Howe's goal in the first minute of the third period tied the score at 4-4. The game went to overtime, where the Whalers had a glorious opportunity for the winning goal, but Ted Green made the diving save to keep the puck out of the net and the two teams had to settle for a draw.

The Jets were back on the ice on Sunday night against the Racers in their last home game before taking off for a season-high six-game road trip. Without Hedberg, who had returned to Sweden to attend his father's funeral, the Jets got on the board first, but the Racers battled hard and took the lead late in the second period thanks to a couple of glaring defensive gaffes by Jets' defenders. The Jets pressed for the equalizer in the third period, but they fell just short and the Racers broke their three-game losing streak with a 5-4 win over the disappointed Jets.

On Tuesday, the Jets left for Birmingham to begin the road trip. With Hedberg still in Swden and both Baird and Moffat nursing injuries, the Jets promoted Kent Ruhnke from Binghamton to rejoin the team. In 27 games with the Dusters since being sent down, Ruhnke had collected 10 goals and added 14 assists.

The next night, the Jets met the Bulls, who had been winners of three of their last four games. Using muscle instead of their fists, the Bulls banged the Jets around, kept them off balance all night long, and were in complete control of the game throughout. When it was all said and done, the Bulls sent the Jets off with a 6-2 defeat that kept them four points back of the first-place Whalers.

The Jets were licking their wounds the next day when they got a call from the league around noon. The Whalers had been scheduled to meet the Aeros that evening in Houston, but they couldn't get out of Cincinnati, so league officials asked the Jets to step in at the last minute and switch dates with the Whalers, who would honor the Jets' scheduled date in Houston on Saturday night. Aboard a 30-year-old two-engine propeller aircraft, the Jets flew to Houston and with the help of their second escort of the season from the Houston police, they arrived at the Summit to play the Aeros.

Armed with little else besides a pre-game meal of donuts and coffee, the Jets played a smart defensive game and the two teams battled to a scoreless draw through two periods. Each team scored once early in the third period and the game went to overtime, where youngster John Tonelli's slap shot got past Bromley to give the Aeros a 2-1 victory.

Back in Birmingham, the Jets met the Bulls on Saturday night for the second time in four days. Buoyed by Hedberg's return, the Jets raced out to a 5-2 lead, but after the Bulls had replaced second-string goaltender Wayne Wood with All-Star John Garrett, the game turned around. The Bulls proceeded to again physically manhandle the Jets and scored six unanswered goals to win by a score of 8-5, handing the Jets their fourth straight defeat.

With no time to rest, the Jets were in action one night later in Cincinnati. Relieved to escape the physical punishment of the Bulls, the Jets did what they did best and outskated the Stingers. The Jets piled up a 5-1 lead before the Stingers got back in the game with a pair of their own, but the Jets remained in control and cruised to an 8-4 win. Ruhnke and Kent Nilsson each scored a pair of goals for the winners, who put a merciful end to their four-game losing streak.

Two nights later, the Jets were in Quebec on the last day of January. It took the Jets all of 21 seconds to open the scoring and they continued to pour it on, showing no mercy to the Nordiques, who were missing no fewer than eight regulars from their lineup. Ulf Nilsson led the way for the Jets with three goals and an assist in the 7-2 victory that moved them back to within four points of the Whalers.

After a bit of a break, the Jets were off until their next game on Saturday night against the Stingers once again. The rested Jets pumped four first period goals past goaltender Michel Dion and racked up a 7-2 lead before the Stingers mounted a late rally that fell short and the Jets took their second straight game against the Stingers, this time by a score of 7-5. The Hot Line again led the way for the Jets, as one member of the line had a hand in five of the Jets' seven goals.

For the first time in two weeks, the Jets were back on the ice at the Arena, but without Dan Labraaten, who had to remain in a Cincinnati hospital with a suspected blood clot in his leg. They faced off against the Oilers in the Sunday night contest before a crowd of 9,485 who had turned out to welcome the Jets back. The Jets enjoyed a strong territorial edge in play, but goaltender Dave Dryden kept the game close until two late third period goals put the Jets in front to stay. The Oilers got one of the goals back, but the Jets held on long enough to preserve the 4-3 win that moved them to within two points of the league-leading Whalers.

Next on the schedule was a Wednesday night visit from the Bulls. Rather than return to the hard-hitting strategy that had resulted in a pair of wins in Birmingham, the Bulls instead tried to use their sticks to slow down the Jets. The visitors' tactics failed miserably as the Jets gleefully ran up the score in a 9-0 victory that pulled them even with the Whalers atop the league standings. Hedberg scored three times for the Jets and the Hot Line accounted for six of the nine goals the Jets fired past John Garrett into the Bulls' net. At the other end of the ice, Bromley made 19 saves to pick up his first shutout of the season and first as a Jet.

Two nights later, the Jets began a three-game weekend against the Stingers on Friday night. The Stingers were competitive, but, for the second straight game, the Jets ran up another lopsided score, thanks to some shaky goaltending from the pair of Norm LaPointe and Paul Hoganson. In the Jets' end, Bromley was outstanding and was the difference in the game. Bromley had made the start in place of Daley, who had gotten sick in the morning. The Jets skated off with a 10-2 win that was much closer than the score indicated and the two points enabled them to pass the idle Whalers and take sole possession of first place.

The next evening, the Jets were in Indianapolis to play the Racers, who had recently fired coach Ron Ingram. Led by new playing coach Bill Goldsworthy, the inspired Racers took a 2-0 lead in the first period, but they couldn't sustain the momentum and the Jets gradually assumed control of the game. The Jets scored four times against stubborn Racers' goaltender Gary Inness and earned a 5-3 victory, extending their winning streak to seven games. Kent Nilsson scored three times for his first hat trick as a Jet and Lynn Powis scored once again against his former team.

The three-game weekend game to a conclusion the next night in Houston, where the Jets came out flat, but they found enough energy to rally from a 3-0 deficit and eventually tie the score before Hedberg's goal with only 89 seconds to play before the end of regulation time put them ahead for the first time. The Jets made the goal stand up as the game-winner and they celebrated a hard-earned 6-5 win against a hungry Aeros team.

With their eighth consecutive victory in hand, the Jets returned home for a couple of days to catch their breath before Wednesday night's game against the Oilers at the Arena. Labraaten had returned to Winnipeg as well, but he was still undergoing treatment for phlebitis, a condition that results in the inflammation of a vein, which would likely put a premature end to his season. The Oilers had the Jets down 2-0 in the second period, but the Jets tied the score and later went ahead before the Oilers evened the score before the intermission. In the third, a pair of goals credited to Bill Lesuk that had gone in off the skates of Oiler defenders was the difference as the Jets squeaked out a 6-5 victory, extending their winning streak to nine games.

After the game, however, the Jets were briefed on some troubling off-ice news. The community ownership group had run out of money and they had to get a bank loan of $200,000 guaranteed by Ben Hatskin and the Simkin family, the team's former owners to whom $1.3 million was still owed, to be able to meet payroll.

The next day, while the Jets were on their way to begin a two-game road trip, the public was told the bad news at an afternoon press conference. In order to meet expenses for the rest of the season, the club's directors announced that they were seeking 40 loans of $10,000 each. Those loans would later be converted into limited partnerships after obtaining approval from the Manitoba Securities Commission to sell them. In addition, Winnipeg Enterprises Corporation, the Arena's landlord, agreed to defer collection of rent that was being paid at a rate of $2,500 per game or 5 percent of gate receipts.

Beyond the immediate need for cash, the team announced it would also seek permission from the WHA to pursue an NHL franchise without legal repercussions and ask the former owners to forgive the remaining debt. Since the community ownership group purchased the team, $500,000 of the debt was repaid together with an equal amount of interest, but a total of $1.5 million was still owed, including the $200,000 that the club had borrowed to meet payroll. Unless all parties agreed to those conditions, the title to the insolvent club would have to be returned to Hatskin and the Simkin family. The Jets were hoping that they could buy a struggling NHL team, such as the Cleveland Barons, and with the combination of the two teams, be ready to be an instant contender in the NHL.

With financial matters on the front burner back home, the Jets were back on the ice on Thursday, 16 February in Springfield, Massachusetts, the temporary home of the Whalers. Last month, the roof of the Hartford Civic Center had collapsed under the weight of a heavy buildup of snow just hours after a University of Connecticut basketball game. Miraculously, there were no injuries. Nonetheless, the Whalers were forced to find a new home until repairs could be completed and they chose to return to Springfield rather than accept an offer to use their original home, the Boston Garden.

On the ice, the Jets got off to a slow start, but they gradually got their legs underneath them as the game wore on. Bobby Guindon's goal early in the third period answered Ron Plumb's goal early in the second period and the game went to overtime tied at 1-1. Three minutes into the extra period, Willy Lindstrom picked off an errant pass from defenseman Gordie Roberts and fired a low shot that beat Al Smith for the game-winner. The 2-1 victory was the first overtime winner for the Jets this season after six defeats, and the Jets' 10th consecutive victory gave them a six-point lead over the second-place Whalers.

The Jets moved on to Cincinnati to play the Stingers on Saturday night. Anders Hedberg was the star of the night, scoring all four goals as the Jets blanked the Stingers 4-0, while Daley stopped 32 shots to pick up his first shutout of the season. The crowd of 5,839 shivered through the game at the Riverfront Coliseum as the Stingers complied with a federal request to curb their use of electricity and turned the heat off. Electrical power was at a premium as the U.S. was suffering under a coal miners' strike that had started in early December.

Back home, the Jets entertained the Nordiques on Sunday night to begin a four-game home stand. The Jets wiped out an early 1-0 deficit with two goals in the first period and sealed the game's outcome with two late third period goals 40 seconds apart for a 5-2 victory that extended the Nordiques' losing streak to seven games and allowed the Jets to extend their winning streak to a dozen games. Peter Sullivan, who had been centering a checking line all season, scored only his 12th and 13th goals of the season, while Hull added one to move to within six goals of 1,000 for his illustrious pro career.

On Wednesday, the Jets got some good news off the ice when the WHA freed all of its teams to seek an NHL franchise without fear of legal action from the league. The Jets and the other teams were granted the same concession that the Aeros had already received, but now, the Jets' task was to get a favorable response from the NHL.

That evening, the Jets began a pair of games against the Whalers in the hopes of putting some distance between themselves and their closest pursuers in the standings. The teams traded goals in each of the first two periods, but two third period goals from Lindstrom 28 seconds apart proved decisive in the 4-2 victory.

More important than the Jets' 13th consecutive victory, however, was the *Winnipeg Free Press* report the next day that a group of Winnipeg investors were negotiating to purchase the financially troubled Jets. The news couldn't have come at a better time with another pay period looming as well as Saturday's deadline to make a counter offer to Hedberg and Ulf Nilsson to keep them in Winnipeg.

Back on the ice, the Jets and Whalers went at it again on Friday night at the Arena. This time around, the Jets didn't leave it to the third period and they broke the game open with a three-goal first period on their way to an impressive 7-2 win that gave the Jets a 12-point cushion over the Whalers atop the league standings. Hedberg and Powis scored twice each and Hull chipped in with three assists in the Jets' 14th consecutive victory that set a new WHA record, eclipsing the previous mark of 13 set by the Whalers earlier in the season.

The Jets wrapped up their four-game home stand with a visit from the Aeros on Sunday night. The Jets got off to another quick start and though the Aeros hung tough, the Jets were too much for their guests and overwhelmed them in a 9-6 victory, extending their league-record winning streak to 15 games. Both Nilssons scored twice as did Hull, whose goals moved him to within three of the magic 1,000 plateau for his pro career. Unfortunately, the win came at a cost when Daley had to leave on account of a broken catching hand. Daley had made a glove save off Rich Preston and fell on his hand, causing it to snap and after the game, it was estimated that he could be lost to the team for a month.

At a Monday evening press conference, Jets fans got the best news of the season when a group of businessmen headed by Michael Gobuty announced that it would purchase the team. The group of eight investors told the gathering that they were putting up an initial investment of $700,000. Of that, $400,000 would be dedicated to operating the club for the remainder of this season, $200,000 would go to repay the loan guaranteed by the previous owners to meet the last payroll and $100,000 would represent the settlement of the remaining outstanding debt owed to Ben Hatskin and the Simkin family.

The investors also announced that they had made a counter offer to keep Anders Hedberg and Ulf Nilsson, but the matter of who the pair of stars would be playing for next season would be decided in the coming days by arbitrator Fred Dunsmore.

The initial five investors — Gobuty, Marvin and Barry Shenkarow, John Shanski, Jr., and Harvey Secter — presented their proposal to the community ownership group and insisted on the inclusion of Bob Graham, Dr. Gerry Wilson and Bobby Hull. They also made it clear that they would be trying to secure an NHL franchise for next season, and if they weren't successful, they would be offering the team back to the public corporation. If they were successful, they would need more investors, and, in that case, they also committed to repaying the loan from the City of Winnipeg that had been made to the community ownership group at a rate of $50,000 per year, upon the expansion of the current arena or the construction of a new facility.

Gobuty had been a Jets season ticket holder since 1972 and was the executive vice president of Victoria Leather, his family's company. In addition, Gobuty and Hull were close friends and Hull had recently been appointed as the vice president in charge of marketing for Victoria Leather. Marvin Shenkarow was the president of clothing manufacturer Sterling Stall and his brother Barry was a lawyer with the firm of Thompson Dorfman Sweatman. Shanski was the president of Sprague Distributors who had once played two games with the CFL's Winnipeg Blue Bombers, while Secter was the president of Ricki's, a Winnipeg-based chain of women's clothing stores.

Having secured their immediate needs off the ice, with Daley on the shelf for an extended period of time, the Jets needed a goaltender to serve as Bromley's backup, so the Nordiques sold Markus Mattsson back to the Jets. Mattsson floundered in Quebec and he had given up nearly seven goals per game in his six appearances as a Nordique. Nonetheless, the Jets had the luxury of a large lead and could likely make do with Bromley until Daley was ready to return.

On Wednesday, the first day of March, the Jets returned to Birmingham, the site where they had last lost a game more than a month ago. The Bulls again relied on the heavy hitting and the tactic worked just well enough to keep the Jets in check. Dave Hanson's goal early in the third period held up as the game-winner and the Jets went down by a score of 4-3, putting an end to their league-record 15-game winning streak.

The Streak

Between 29 January and 26 February, the Jets rattled off 15 straight victories, which stood up as a WHA record. They beat every other team in the league at least once during this stretch, which was even more remarkable considering the off-ice issues that arose during the streak. The Jets announced that they had run out of money and had to borrow funds to meet payroll and only when a hastily organized group of investors led by Michael Gobuty stepped forward in late February was their immediate future secured. Meanwhile, Anders Hedberg and Ulf Nilsson had received lucrative contract offers to play for the New York Rangers next season, which the Jets would have trouble matching and Bobby Hull was in pursuit of his 1,000th professional goal.

29 January 1978	Jets 8 at Cincinnati 4
31 January 1978	Jets 7 at Quebec 2
4 February 1978	Jets 7 at Cincinnati 5
5 February 1978	Edmonton 3 at Jets 4
8 February 1978	Birmingham 0 at Jets 9
10 February 1978	Cincinnati 2 at Jets 10
11 February 1978	Jets 5 at Indianapolis 3
12 February 1978	Jets 6 at Houston 5
15 February 1978	Edmonton 5 at Jets 6
16 February 1978	Jets 2 at New England 1 (OT)
18 February 1978	Jets 4 at Cincinnati 0
19 February 1978	Quebec 2 at Jets 5
22 February 1978	New England 2 at Jets 4
24 February 1978	New England 2 at Jets 7
26 February 1978	Houston 6 at Jets 9

Two nights later, the Jets were back at the Arena on Friday night against the Stingers to start another three-game weekend. The overflow crowd of 10,221 came to see if Hull could crack the 1,000-goal barrier, and he came within one when he opened the scoring midway through the first period, but the Jets did not score again for the rest of the evening. The Stingers took the lead for good in the second period and they put the game away in the third with three goals and surprised both the Jets and their fans by skating off with a 5-1 victory. Robbie Ftorek scored three times and added one assist to pace the Stingers' attack and goaltender Mike Liut stymied the Jets in only his second game back from knee surgery in December.

The Jets flew to Indianapolis for the second game of the weekend on Saturday night. The Jets used three goals in less than a minute and a half in the second period to grab a 4-2 lead, but they couldn't hold the lead during the goal-scoring extravaganza. Recent acquisition Blaine Stoughton's goal midway through the third period broke the 6-6 tie and propelled the Racers to an 8-6 victory. Mattsson's first appearance since being reacquired was anything but a success, but he had received no help from an unusually porous defense corps in front of him. The Racers, meanwhile, won their fourth straight game, while the Jets dropped their third in a row.

Back home on Sunday night, the Jets wrapped up their three-game weekend against the Aeros, who were also playing their third game in as many nights in addition to winding up a nine-game road trip. All night long, the specter of Hull's 1,000th goal was in the air, but the Aeros kept matching the Jets goal for goal until Larry Lund scored with just under eight minutes to play to give the Aeros their first lead. The Jets buzzed around the Aeros' net, but they couldn't get the equalizer and dropped a 4-3 decision that was their fourth straight defeat. Despite the loss, however, the Jets' margin atop the league standings remained at a dozen points over the second-place Whalers, who were also in the throws of a four-game losing streak.

On Tuesday night, the Jets held their annual fundraiser, this time with a $100 per plate dinner at the International Inn to hear NHL Players Association director Alan Eagleson speak. The proceeds from the event still went to the community ownership group, which had stated that the Jets would operate in the WHA for next season if the Gobuty group's attempt to secure an NHL franchise was unsuccessful. Dr. Wilson, who had recently returned from overseas, indicated that the Jets would have cooperation with teams in Sweden and Finland if they were forced to operate without a league for one season. He also said that the Jets were looking at adding a couple of players for the playoffs. One was Veli-Pekka Ketola, the former Jet, and the other was Swedish centerman Thomas Gradin, who had been a first-round draft selection of the Jets in 1976. As a player-coach, Ketola led Assat Pori, his hometown team, to the playoffs this season, and Dr. Wilson raved about Gradin, who had had an outstanding season with AIK in Stockholm.

The Jets returned to the ice on Thursday, 9 March with the Racers making their fifth and last appearance of the season at the Arena. One day after their five-game winning streak was broken, the Racers came out determined to start another streak. The visitors scored three times in the first half of the third period to take a 5-3 lead when the Jets rose from the ashes and turned the game around. Two goals less than a minute apart tied the game at 5-5, then Baird knocked Racers' goaltender Ed Mio out of the game with a hard hit on his shoulder. Just over a minute later, Bobby Guindon took a pass from Hull and fired a slap shot past Mio's replacement, Gary Inness, and the Jets held off the Racers for the remaining 35 seconds to claim a 6-5 victory.

The next day, the Jets regretfully announced that they were granting Thommie Bergman his release. When the Jets were facing a financial crisis, they told the players that they might not get paid for the rest of the season and that management would do its best to help any player who felt insecure about the current situation. Bergman was the only player who said that he did, so the Jets allowed him to buy his freedom from a contract that still had one season remaining in order to sign a new deal with the Red Wings. In going to Detroit, Bergman would rejoin his original team that he broke in with when he first came from Sweden to North America, and he would once again be playing for coach Bobby Kromm. The first Swedish player to make it in pro hockey in North America expressed regret over leaving his teammates and, all things being equal, he would have preferred to play in Winnipeg over Detroit, but he felt it was a decision he had to make. Bergman was having an excellent season and was finally fully healthy after sustaining multiple shoulder separations over the past year, but the Jets would have to move on without him.

Replacing him on the blue line was 25-year-old defenseman Mike Amodeo, who was playing in Sweden with Orebro IK. Dr. Wilson had recently approached Amodeo about the possibility of joining the Jets and the former Ottawa National and Toronto Toro was most agreeable. Amodeo had played four seasons for the Nationals/Toros franchise before his two seasons in Sweden. Amodeo was not the speediest defenseman to lace up a pair of skates, but his determination made him an effective defender, and he was regarded as the best defenseman playing in Sweden.

In addition to Amodeo's addition, the Jets recalled a couple of players from the AHL. Kent Ruhnke was summoned for his third tour of duty of the season, and the Jets also brought up 23-year-old defenseman Bill Davis from the Philadelphia Firebirds, where he had spent the season after starring at Colgate University. Davis had originally been drafted by the Pittsburgh Penguins in the 14th round of the 1974 NHL Amateur Draft and was picked up by the Jets last summer.

On Saturday night, the Jets were in Quebec to play the Nordiques, who were again being led by Maurice Filion after he replaced former coach Marc Boileau less than one season removed from winning the AVCO World Trophy. The Jets scored the only two goals of the first period, but after Serge Bernier's goal cut the Jets' lead in half early in the second, and with time winding down before intermission, Barry Long led a rush into the Nordiques' zone and fed Hull, who easily redirected the puck past Richard Brodeur and into the net. The goal not only restored the Jets' two-goal lead, but it gave the Golden Jet 1,000 for his pro career. The crowd of 10,313 gave Hull a lengthy standing ovation in honor of his historic accomplishment, and after the applause died down, the Jets continued scoring. They scored once more in the second and added three more in the third to take a 7-4 victory with them back to Winnipeg. Hull's goal was the most memorable of the night, but Kent Nilsson recorded his second hat trick of the season one month to the day after his first to lead the Jets offensively.

Most of the Jets flew back to Winnipeg for Sunday night's game against the Bulls at the Arena, but Kim Clackson had to remain in a Quebec hospital after sustaining a concussion during the game. The Bulls opened the scoring in the first period, but the Jets answered the goal before intermission and overcame the Bulls' rough tactics to take a 3-1 lead with two goals early in the third period. The Bulls got back in the game with a late third period goal, but with just over two minutes to play in regulation time, Ken Linseman started a fight on his way to the penalty box. During the ensuing melee, after Hull pulled Phil Roberto off a pile, Steve Durbano bolted off the bench and tackled Hull from behind, triggering the second bench-clearing brawl between the two teams this season. The chant of "Birmingham stinks" rang through the stands during the 23-minute episode that fortunately ended without any serious injuries. The remaining time expired and the Jets won by a score of 3-2, answering the brawling Bulls the best way they could.

On Monday night, the Booster Club held its annual Awards Night at the Winnipeg Inn. A sold-out gathering of more than 350 saw a sore Hull presented with a gold bracelet with a total of 21 diamonds, which represented each of his seasons in professional hockey. Kent Nilsson won the rookie of the year award, not only because of his 36 goals, but because he was the only rookie on the team. Barry Long was named as the team's most improved player, Bill Lesuk was presented with the unsung hero award, Ulf Nilsson took home most valuable player honors, and Anders Hedberg was chosen as the most exciting player.

The next day, the league came down with an iron hand and doled out discipline for Sunday night's brawl. As expected, Durbano received the harshest punishment. His third suspension of the season was 12 games in length and the league added a $500 fine along with a warning that his next suspension would be his last. The league also suspended both coaches, Ulf Nilsson, Ken Linseman and Serge Beaudoin each for one game to be served in the two teams' next meeting and fined a number of parties including Michael Gobuty, the Jets' new president, for making an obscene gesture near the Jets' bench.

The Jets' next game came on Wednesday, 15 March against the Oilers at the Arena. Before the game, the Jets formally recognized Hull's 1,000th professional goal with a ceremony that included his family, Winnipeg Mayor Robert Steen, and original Jets' General Manager Annis Stukus. Hull was showered with gifts that included an airline trip, a case of champagne, a bronze medallion and a gold ring. Hull's parents were also presented with a trip to Hawaii.

Once the game started, the Oilers gave it a good effort, but the injury-ravaged visitors could not stay with the Jets, who used three late third period goals to put the game out of reach. Hedberg and both Nilssons each scored a pair of goals in the 8-4 victory that moved the Jets closer to wrapping up first place, while the Oilers dropped their fifth in a row and remained ahead of only the Bulls, Stingers and Racers in the standings.

The two teams went at it again two nights later in Edmonton and a pair of first period goals from Hedberg less than a minute apart got the Jets out to a 2-0 lead, but the Oilers, energized by a full house of their own fans, didn't fold and dominated the rest of the contest. Norm Ferguson scored three times to put the Oilers ahead and Blair MacDonald's second goal of the game with just over seven minutes to play capped a 6-2 win. The Jets played with a number of players battling the flu and it showed on the ice, but they left Edmonton still a dozen points ahead of the Whalers.

Returning to Winnipeg, the Jets met the Nordiques on Sunday night before beginning a six-game road trip. The Jets overcame an early first period goal and built up a 4-1 lead three minutes into the second. The Nordiques fought back and narrowed the Jets' lead to one goal, but Willy Lindstrom's third period goal seconds after Serge Bernier left the penalty box restored the lead two goals. The Nordiques pressed hard to get back in the game, but Bromley withstood the 16-shot barrage in the final period and Long was particularly brilliant in support of his goaltender. The 5-3 victory inched the Jets closer to clinching first place and also snapped the Nordiques' three-game winning streak.

On Monday afternoon, the Jets held a press conference announcing that they had given up in their efforts to retain Anders Hedberg and Ulf Nilsson. The pair had officially signed with the Rangers on Saturday afternoon and for the next two seasons, they would each earn $600,000 US, figures that were much larger than what had been first reported. The new Jets' ownership could not afford to match the offers. Though both Hedberg and Nilsson liked Winnipeg, as did their families, and they had been treated very well during their time with the Jets, the money and the opportunity to compete at a higher level, combined with the uncertainty of the situation with both the Jets and the WHA were the main factors in their decision to accept the Rangers' offer.

Despite the stinging loss of the beloved pair of Swedes, the new owners assured the fans that there would be major league hockey in Winnipeg for the 1978-1979 season. However, because the NHL had turned a deaf ear to the Jets because of fears over more anti-trust litigation, the owners backtracked and said that they would continue in the WHA next season rather than offer the team back to the public ownership group.

Two nights later, the Jets were in Springfield for a Wednesday night game against the Whalers. The Jets did an outstanding job of keeping the Whalers in check and stayed in front for most of the game. Ulf Nilsson scored the eventual game-winner in the first minute of the third period and Long's empty-net marker in the game's final minute wrapped up a 5-3 victory. Hull scored twice and Hedberg set up three goals in the penalty-filled contest that moved the Jets to the edge of sealing first place in the league standings.

The Jets were off until Saturday night when they played the Bulls in Birmingham. Since most of the Bulls' heavyweights had been either suspended or injured, the two teams concentrated on hockey, and Hedberg shook off Frank Beaton, his shadow for the night, to score with just under nine minutes to play to break a 1-1 tie. Hedberg scored again into an empty net with 39 seconds left on the clock to put the finishing touches on a 3-1 victory in which Rudy Pilous handled the Jets' bench duties for the suspended Larry Hillman. The Jets had already clinched first place as a result of the Whalers' 1-0 loss at the hands of the Aeros the night before.

The next stop for the Jets was Houston and a Tuesday night game against the Aeros. The Jets started quickly but they fell apart just as fast. The Aeros were in total control for the rest of the night and all Gary Bromley could do was slow down the attack. Terry Ruskowski's goal early in the second period put the Aeros in front to stay and a pair of third period goals padded the Aeros' lead. A late goal from Ulf Nilsson proved meaningless in the 5-3 defeat that allowed the Aeros to extend their winning streak to three games.

Game number four of the six-game road trip took place in Indianapolis on Thursday night against the Racers, who had long since assured themselves of an eighth-place finish in the eight-team league. Ken Baird gave the Jets a 2-1 lead late in the first period and the Jets played it safe for the remainder of the game. Two third period goals put the game out of reach and this season's last meeting between the teams ended with a final score of 4-1 in the Jets' favor.

The Jets added some more depth for playoff time when they brought back Mike Ford and signed him to a contract for the rest of the season. Ford had spent this season with Vastra Frolunda in Sweden and was a co-proprietor of a sporting goods store in the Winnipeg suburb of Fort Richmond. He hopped on a plane and returned to North America to become a Jet for the third time.

Ford's new teammates were back on the ice on Saturday night in Quebec to ring in the month of April. After a scoreless first period, the Nordiques scored a pair of goals to take the lead and they added three more in the third to send the Jets down to a 5-2 defeat. Though the game meant nothing to the Jets in the standings, they did extract some measure of satisfaction from the contest when Kim Clackson broke Serge Bernier's nose during a first period fight, sending the pugnacious Bernier to the hospital.

The Jets wrapped up the road trip with their second visit to Houston in a week. This visit didn't start any better than their last appearance at the Summit had, as Daley gave up four goals in the first period in his return from a broken hand. The Jets battled back in the third period, but the early deficit was too much to overcome and the Aeros took the game by a score of 6-3.

Back home for the first time in over two weeks, the Jets hosted the Whalers on Thursday night. Before a full house of 10,303 spectators, the Jets scored four times in the first period and the visitors offered little resistance in the 7-4 Jets' victory. Seven different Jets scored in the game that again had no meaning for the Jets, but it did keep the Whalers from clinching second place. The win was the Jets' 50th of the season, marking the second time in three seasons the Jets had reached that plateau. Mike Amodeo made his Jets debut after arriving from Sweden, and Kent Ruhnke played for the first time since being recalled for the second time, having made the more than 1,500-mile trek from Binghamton to Winnipeg by car.

Playing out the string, the Jets flew to Edmonton for their last road game of the regular season on Friday night. The Jets were not sharp and only Daley's stellar goaltending prevented the Oilers from adding to their 4-2 first period lead. The score held through the rest of the game and the Jets quietly returned home to join Barry Long, Ted Green, and Bobby Hull, who had not made the trip to Edmonton.

Veli-Pekka Ketola was expected to arrive on Saturday to bolster the Jets' lineup, but after leading Assat Pori to the Finnish championship in the week before, he was told by Assat to stay in Finland to honor his contract that bound him until the end of the upcoming world championships. Ketola was deeply resentful over the last-second devlopment that kept him from rejoining the Jets, but both parties had little choice but to accept the news and move on.

The Jets completed their regular season schedule on Sunday night against the Aeros. With nothing to play for, both teams simply went through the motions before the Jets' third-straight five-figure crowd. The Aeros, however, got the better of the lethargic Jets and grabbed a 5-2 lead late in the second period. The Jets scored a pair to close the gap to 5-4, but there would be no more scoring and the Jets went down to defeat in their regular season finale. Lynn Powis scored twice in the loss and Amodeo tallied his first as a Jet and despite losing four of their last five games, the Jets still finished with a record of 50-28-2, the second best record in their six-year history.

After slogging their way through the latter stages of the regular season, the Jets began the first round of the playoffs on Friday, 14 April when they faced off against the sixth-place Bulls to open the first-round best-of-seven series. As the regular season wound down, the Bulls had edged the Stingers for the sixth and final playoff berth and their reward was a matchup with the first-place Jets. Though the Jets clearly had a more talented team than the Bulls, the Jets' concern entering the series was the two brawls that the Bulls had instigated in Winnipeg during the regular season.

The two teams traded goals in the game's first two minutes, then a few minutes later, Dave Hanson ripped the hairpiece off of Hull's head. Hanson escaped ejection because he didn't pull on real hair, but he and the Bulls didn't completely evade punishment. Hanson was given a major and a minor penalty and the Jets scored a pair of goals on the ensuing power play. Hull scored one of the goals after returning to a standing ovation while sporting a shiny red helmet covering his largely bald head. The Bulls, however, battled back and trimmed the Jets' lead to one on a disputed second period goal. Joe Daley claimed he had been tripped before the goal was scored and he was livid that referee Bill Friday did not call a penalty. Daley's rage eventually earned him a game misconduct, but Gary Bromley and the Jets held the Bulls off the scoreboard and they used five third period goals to turn a 4-3 nail-biter into a 9-3 blowout.

On Sunday night, the two teams returned to the Arena for Game 2. Prior to the start of the game, in a task they had normally handled in the last regular season home game, the Jets handed out their annual awards. Ulf Nilsson was the big winner as he received the top scorer, most valuable player and best all-around player awards. Kent Nilsson was named the top rookie and also received the award for most frequent three-star selections. Bromley was again in goal for the Jets on account of Daley's one-game suspension and $500 fine for his outburst midway through Friday night's game.

The Jets jumped out to a 3-1 lead before another ugly incident marred the evening. Late in the first period, Hanson and Phil Roberto had joined a fight between Kim Clackson and Gilles "Bad News" Bilodeau, sparking a melee that saw all four players ejected. Bilodeau was given an early trip to the showers for trying to knee Clackson, and Hanson made two trips across the ice to challenge the Jets' bench. Once the on-ice action resumed, the Jets scored a couple of power-play goals and they proceeded to run away with the game. The final score was 8-3 and the Jets had a 2-0 series lead to take with them to Alabama. Four of the Jets' goals had come with the man advantage as they made the Bulls pay for their embarrassing behavior. A sellout crowd of 10,401 spectators witnessed the game, one of whom was Stingers' defenseman Pat Stapleton, a rumored candidate to be the Jets' next general manager.

Two days later, the Jets left for Birmingham to play the third game of the series on Wednesday night. Unlike the first two games of the series, the Bulls dispensed with the theatrics and largely stuck to hard-hitting, physical hockey. The strategy worked well for the Bulls in the first period as they took a 2-0 lead and they would have enjoyed a larger lead were it not for Daley. Returning from his suspension, Daley made a number of key stops that kept his team in the game. The Jets rebounded in the second period with a pair of goals that tied the score, but the Bulls didn't stop and J.C. Stewart's goal late in the second restored the Bulls' advantage. Try as they might, the Jets couldn't get the equalizer in the third period and the Bulls celebrated a well-earned 3-2 victory and clawed their way back in the series. Over 8,500 fans in Birmingham were in attendance, along with former Manitoba Premier Ed Schreyer and Rangers'

General Manager John Ferguson, who was undoubtedly keeping an eye on two key members of next season's Rangers' roster.

The series continued with Game 4 on Friday night in Birmingham. The Jets were much stronger right from the outset and Anders Hedberg's goal 37 seconds into the game gave the Jets an early lead. After the Jets scored again in the first period, the Bulls cut the Jets' lead in half midway through the second, but the Jets answered with two goals in the span of 43 seconds to expand their lead to 4-1 and they never looked back. The determined Jets guarded their lead well and Hull's goal late in the third period finished off a 5-1 victory that put them one win away from eliminating the troublesome Bulls and advancing to their third consecutive AVCO World Trophy final.

Back in Winnipeg on Sunday night, the Jets and Bulls went at it for the fifth time in nine days. The Bulls opened the scoring, but the Jets plugged away and, slowly but surely, built up a 3-1 lead in the second period. Dunn's first goal of the post-season increased the Jets' lead to 4-1 in the first minute of the third and with the series virtually in the palm of their hand, they were not to be denied. Phil Roberto's goal midway through the third period gave the Bulls some semblance of hope, but Bobby Guindon's shorthanded marker with just 69 seconds to play salted away a 5-2 victory that gave the Jets one of their most satisfying series wins in their history. The Jets had beaten the Bulls' stable of goons with their sticks and skates rather than with their fists. After the game, Larry Hillman crossed the ice to shake hands with Bulls' coach Glen Sonmor, who instead, opted to retreat to the visitors' dressing room.

The Jets earned a bye in the second round of the playoffs as a result of being the highest-seeded surviving team and they would have some time off before competing for their second AVCO World Trophy championship. The Jets took advantage of that time to heal and recover from their encounter with the bruising Bulls and tried to stay in game condition while awaiting their next opponent. In the other first-round series, the Whalers disposed of the Oilers in five games, while the defending champion Nordiques defeated the Aeros in six games, setting the stage for a matchup between the respective winners in the next round. The Whalers put an end to the Nordiques' championship reign in the semi-final round by eliminating them in five games.

The best-of-seven AVCO World Trophy final series was set and the first two games would take place in Springfield starting on Friday, 12 May, then the series would shift to Winnipeg for the next three games. If necessary, Game 6 would be played in Springfield, and a deciding Game 7 would be played in Winnipeg.

Despite the long layoff, the Jets were ready to go from the drop of the puck in Game 1, but both Gary Bromley and Whalers' goaltender Louis Levasseur kept the game scoreless through two periods. Goals from Guindon and Peter Sullivan 22 seconds apart early in the third broke the deadlock and Guindon added his second of the period with just over six minutes to play to answer Larry Pleau's marker six minutes earlier. Sullivan scored into an empty net with 15 seconds to play to secure a 4-1 victory and take a 1-0 series lead.

Two nights later, the Jets and Whalers met again at the Springfield Civic Center for the second game of the championship series. With an even stronger and more determined effort than they'd had on Friday night, the Jets forechecked the Whalers into submission and breezed to a 4-0 second period lead. The Whalers mounted a third period rally, but it wasn't nearly enough to penetrate the Jets' lead and the game ended with the score 5-2 in the Jets' favor. Leading the charge for the visitors was the line of Guindon, Lesuk, and Lyle Moffat, while Dan Labraaten scored on a breakaway for his first goal since rejoining the team. Labraaten's season was thought to be over, as until recently and he was still having to suspend his leg for 10 hours a day to help the blood circulation, but he was back in action to help his team grab a 2-0 series lead and take it back to Winnipeg. The game's only blemish occurred in the third period when Amodeo crashed into the boards and had to be detained overnight at a local hospital with a sprained neck and fractured vertebrae.

After a five-day break, the series resumed on Friday night at the Arena. The time off did nothing to slow the Jets down and they blitzed the Whalers right from the opening faceoff. The Jets fired five goals past Al Smith before the game was eight minutes old and the Jets didn't even allow the Whalers to contemplate a potential comeback. The Jets finished off the rout with two third period goals, which put their total in double figures and they moved to within 60 minutes of the WHA's ultimate prize with a 10-2 thrashing. Lindstrom scored three times, while Lynn Powis and Kent Nilsson scored twice each in the scoring frenzy.

On the precipice of their second AVCO World Trophy championship, the Jets turned their eye to next year and announced over the weekend that they had secured the services of three key members of the team. Both Long and Labraaten eschewed offers from the Red Wings and agreed to four-year deals to stay with the Jets, while Bobby Guindon had signed a two-year deal a month ago, but the news had been kept under wraps. Detroit had offered Long a three-year contract that would have paid him $140,000 per year, but Gobuty upped the ante and Long agreed to a four-year contract worth a total of $650,000.

Come Monday night, it was time for the Jets to return their attention to the present and the fourth game of the AVCO World Trophy final. Anxiousness resonated through the crowd of 10,348 when the Whalers scored twice in the first period to take a 2-0 lead to the intermission, but the Jets settled some butterflies when they scored 12 seconds apart early in the second period to tie the score. Late in the second, Anders Hedberg tipped a Lars-Erik Sjoberg shot past Al Smith and early in the third, Hull finished off a three-way passing play with Hedberg and Ulf Nilsson for the eventual game-winner in what would prove to be the trio's last game together. The Whalers scored midway through the third to keep the premature celebrations on ice, but Daley made the lead hold up and Hedberg's empty-net goal with 32 seconds left wrapped up the 5-3 victory that gave the Jets a four-game sweep of the series and their second AVCO World Trophy in three seasons. Ben Hatskin presented the championship trophy to Sjoberg for the second time and the captain took the prized hardware for a lap around the ice to bring an outstanding season to a close.

Guindon was named the most valuable player of the playoffs for his inspirational and tireless efforts that had paid off with eight goals and five assists in only nine games. The "Golden Gorf" trailed only Hedberg and Ulf Nilsson in team scoring in the playoffs and the prospective restaurateur in his hometown of St. Jerome, Quebec more than earned his new contract.

The mood was certainly jubilant in the steamy Arena, but it was also bittersweet as it was the last time Jets fans would be treated to watching Hedberg and Nilsson in Jets uniforms. Both men had represented the Jets and Winnipeg in a first-class manner on and off the ice and no one wanted to see them leave. Nonetheless, most fans wished the pair nothing but the best in New York.

The traditional parade took place on the afternoon of Tuesday, 23 May in downtown Winnipeg along Portage Avenue to Memorial Boulevard, culminating in a luncheon at the Holiday Inn to celebrate the championship and bid adieu to the two men who had played such a major role in bringing two AVCO World Trophy championships to Winnipeg.

The Jets had been dominant throughout the season and iced arguably their best team ever, but the short off-season was at hand and a lot of work was ahead to reload the Jets' roster. Thanks to the new owners, however, there would at least be a next season, and life for the Jets would continue without Anders Hedberg and Ulf Nilsson.

Scores and Stats

1977-1978 Winnipeg Jets (50-28-2)

Regular Season

Date	Opponent	Score	Date	Opponent	Score
12 Oct	@Edmonton Oilers	7-3	18 Jan	Quebec Nordiques	5-1
13 Oct	Quebec Nordiques	5-2	20 Jan	New England Whalers	4-4*
15 Oct	@Cincinnati Stingers	5-4	22 Jan	Indianapolis Racers	4-5
16 Oct	Indianapolis Racers	9-1	25 Jan	@Birmingham Bulls	2-6
21 Oct	New England Whalers	2-5	26 Jan	@Houston Aeros	1-2*
23 Oct	Birmingham Bulls	10-3	28 Jan	@Birmingham Bulls	5-8
26 Oct	@Indianapolis Racers	3-5	29 Jan	@Cincinnati Stingers	8-4
28 Oct	Cincinnati Stingers	3-2	31 Jan	@Quebec Nordiques	7-2
30 Oct	Edmonton Oilers	5-2	4 Feb	@Cincinnati Stingers	7-5
2 Nov	@Edmonton Oilers	6-3	5 Feb	Edmonton Oilers	4-3
4 Nov	@Birmingham Bulls	4-2	8 Feb	Birmingham Bulls	9-0
5 Nov	@Cincinnati Stingers	6-1	10 Feb	Cincinnati Stingers	10-2
9 Nov	Houston Aeros	4-3	11 Feb	@Indianapolis Racers	5-3
11 Nov	Quebec Nordiques	2-3*	12 Feb	@Houston Aeros	6-5
13 Nov	Cincinnati Stingers	2-3	15 Feb	Edmonton Oilers	6-5
15 Nov	@Quebec Nordiques	6-7*	16 Feb	@New England Whalers	2-1*
16 Nov	Birmingham Bulls	2-2*	18 Feb	@Cincinnati Stingers	4-0
18 Nov	@New England Whalers	2-3	19 Feb	Quebec Nordiques	5-2
19 Nov	@Indianapolis Racers	6-4	22 Feb	New England Whalers	4-2
22 Nov	@Edmonton Oilers	2-4	24 Feb	New England Whalers	7-2
27 Nov	Birmingham Bulls	3-4*	26 Feb	Houston Aeros	9-6
2 Dec	@New England Whalers	1-4	1 Mar	@Birmingham Bulls	3-4
3 Dec	@Quebec Nordiques	5-6	3 Mar	Cincinnati Stingers	1-5
4 Dec	Edmonton Oilers	2-3	4 Mar	@Indianapolis Racers	6-8
7 Dec	Houston Aeros	5-2	5 Mar	Houston Aeros	3-4
9 Dec	Cincinnati Stingers	3-4*	9 Mar	Indianapolis Racers	6-5
11 Dec	Indianapolis Racers	7-1	11 Mar	@Quebec Nordiques	7-4
13 Dec	Czechoslovakia	5-1	12 Mar	Birmingham Bulls	3-2
17 Dec	@New England Whalers	6-3	15 Mar	Edmonton Oilers	8-4
18 Dec	New England Whalers	7-3	17 Mar	@Edmonton Oilers	2-6
20 Dec	Soviet All-Stars	6-4	19 Mar	Quebec Nordiques	5-3
21 Dec	@Houston Aeros	4-3	22 Mar	@New England Whalers	5-3
23 Dec	@Cincinnati Stingers	6-4	25 Mar	@Birmingham Bulls	3-1
26 Dec	Quebec Nordiques	9-4	28 Mar	@Houston Aeros	3-5
6 Jan	@Edmonton Oilers	4-1	30 Mar	@Indianapolis Racers	4-1
8 Jan	Indianapolis Racers	4-2	1 Apr	@Quebec Nordiques	2-5
11 Jan	Birmingham Bulls	11-2	4 Apr	@Houston Aeros	3-6
13 Jan	@Houston Aeros	2-3	6 Apr	New England Whalers	7-4
14 Jan	@Indianapolis Racers	6-3	7 Apr	@Edmonton Oilers	2-4
15 Jan	Edmonton Oilers	3-4*	9 Apr	Houston Aeros	4-5

Playoffs

Date	Opponent	Score	Date	Opponent	Score
14 Apr	Birmingham Bulls	9-3	12 May	@New England Whalers	4-1
16 Apr	Birmingham Bulls	8-3	14 May	@New England Whalers	5-2
19 Apr	@Birmingham Bulls	2-3	19 May	New England Whalers	10-2
21 Apr	@Birmingham Bulls	5-1	22 May	New England Whalers	5-3
23 Apr	Birmingham Bulls	5-2			

* - overtime

Scoring

Player	Regular Season									Playoffs								
	GP	G	A	Pts	PIM	+/-	PP	SH	Shots	GP	G	A	Pts	PIM	+/-	PP	SH	Shots
Mike Amodeo	3	1	1	2	0	3	0	0	4	7	1	3	4	19	-2			
Ken Baird	49	14	7	21	29		2	0		7	0	4	4	7		0	0	
Thommie Bergman	62	5	28	33	43	22	0	0	139									
Gary Bromley	39	0	1	1	4		0	0	0	5	0	0	0	2		0	0	
Kim Clackson	52	2	7	9	203	6	0	0	42	9	0	1	1	61	6	0	0	
Joe Daley	37	0	2	2	2		0	0	0	5	0	1	1	20		0	0	
Bill Davis	12	0	0	0	2	-9	0	0	9									
Dave Dunn	66	6	20	26	79	20	1	0	53	9	1	2	3	0	8			
Mike Ford	3	0	0	0	0	-5	0	0	6	2	1	0	1	0	-1			
Ted Green	73	4	22	26	52	19	2	0	88	8	0	2	2	2	4	0	0	
Bob Guindon	77	20	22	42	18	-1	0	4	127	9	8	5	13	5	9			
Anders Hedberg	77	63	59	122	60	60	17	6	290	9	9	6	15	2	5			
Larry Hornung	19	1	4	5	2	17	0	0	13									
Fran Huck	5	0	0	0	2	-2	0	0	4									
Bobby Hull	77	46	71	117	23	55	10	0	257	9	8	3	11	12	5			
Dave Kryskow	71	20	21	41	16	12	3	0	103	9	4	4	8	2	1			
Dan Labraaten	47	18	16	34	30	7	5	0	81	4	1	1	2	8	4			
Bill Lesuk	80	9	18	27	48	-4	0	0	85	9	2	5	7	12	9			
Willy Lindstrom	77	30	30	60	42	4	7	0	151	8	3	4	7	17	3			
Barry Long	78	7	24	31	42	10	1	1	159	9	0	5	5	6	11			
Markus Mattsson	10	0	0	0	0		0	0	0									
Lyle Moffat	57	9	16	25	39	-6	0	0	58	9	5	7	12	9	3			
Kent Nilsson	80	42	65	107	8	27	18	0	212	9	2	8	10	10	2			
Ulf Nilsson	73	37	89	126	89	41	7	3	180	9	1	13	14	12	5			
Lynn Powis	55	12	19	31	16		2	0		3	2	1	3	7	2			
Kent Ruhnke	21	8	9	17	2	9	0	0	26	5	2	0	2	0	-2			
Lars-Erik Sjoberg	78	11	39	50	72	60	0	1	133	9	0	9	9	4	8	0	0	
Peter Sullivan	77	16	39	55	43	-12	3	1	130	9	3	4	7	4	3			

Goaltending

Goaltender	Regular Season									
	GP	Min	GA	GAA	Saves	Sv %	SO	EN	W	L	T
Gary Bromley	39	2252	124	3.30	966	0.886	1	0	25	12	1
Joe Daley	37	2075	114	3.30	857	0.883	1	1	21	11	1
Markus Mattsson	10	511	30	3.52	227	0.883	0	1	4	5	0
	Playoffs									
	GP	Min	GA	GAA	Saves	Sv %	SO	EN	W	L	
Gary Bromley	5	268	7	1.57			0	0	4	0	
Joe Daley	5	271	13	2.88			0	0	4	1	

New faces for 1977-1978:

TOP LEFT: Ken Baird

TOP RIGHT: Kim Clackson

BOTTOM RIGHT: Lynn Powis

TOP LEFT: New coach Larry Hillman, one year removed from his last season as a player in which he was part of the Jets' 1975-1976 WHA championship team.

RIGHT: Markus Mattsson

BELOW: Gary Bromley

Season VII: 1978-1979 – New Owners, New Team, Same Result

Having captured their second AVCO World Trophy championship in three seasons, the Jets had their work cut out for them because of the two gaping holes in their roster left by the departure of Anders Hedberg and Ulf Nilsson to the NHL's New York Rangers. There was to be no soft landing for the new owners, who were embarking on their first season in charge of the team.

The reigning league champions, as expected, collected their fair share of post-season awards. Anders Hedberg and Ulf Nilsson were each named to the WHA First Team All-Star squad along with Lars-Erik Sjoberg, while Bobby Hull and Barry Long were selected as Second Team All-Stars. Sjoberg was honored as the WHA's defenseman of the year, and Kent Nilsson was named as the rookie of the year.

Michael Gobuty had a handshake agreement with Dan Labraaten on a four-year contract before the end of last season, but in early June, a snag occurred over the issue of a letter of credit to cover the first two years of the deal. Amid claims and counter-claims, negotiations continued, but Labraaten ultimately decided to accept the higher offer the Red Wings had originally made and signed a Detroit contract that would reunite him with Bobby Kromm, his former coach.

The Jets received another blow when Gary Bromley left to sign with the Vancouver Canucks, but the Jets did re-sign Mike Amodeo for the upcoming season. The ownership group took a major hit when Dr. Gerry Wilson resigned his position as Director of Team Operations and also relinquished his ownership position. With Gobuty and Barry Shenkarow taking an increasingly larger role in hockey operations, Dr. Wilson's position had become less influential and he opted to leave the organization.

Lyle Moffat signed a two-year contract with a club option for a third season, keeping him in the fold, and the Jets continued to negotiate with junior star Bill Derlago. The Jets offered the Birtle, Manitoba native a five-year deal worth $750,000, but he opted to sign with the Canucks, who had selected him fourth overall in the NHL Amateur Draft. The Jets also pursued Swedish centerman Thomas Gradin, but like Bromley and Derlago, he also decided to sign with the Canucks, where he would meet up with Dave Dunn, who had retired to become an assistant coach. In Vancouver, Dunn would work with Head Coach Harry Neale, who had jumped from the Whalers after his team lost in straight games to the Jets in the AVCO World Trophy final. Though it was a meaningless procedural move, the Racers secured Hedberg's WHA rights when they picked him in the second round of the inter-league draft.

Off the ice, Gobuty contacted John Ferguson about becoming the Jets' general manager. The Rangers had recently fired Ferguson, who ironically, had helped lure Hedberg and Nilsson to New York, but he said that he wasn't interested at the present time. The Jets also continued to talk with Pat Stapleton about the same job, but nothing materialized and Stapleton later signed on to become the coach and general manager of the Racers. Meanwhile, the Jets decided to bring coach Larry Hillman back for next season. Hillman's one-year contract had expired at the end of last season and after leading the Jets to the AVCO World Trophy championship, he was only given another one-year deal.

The Jets decided to turn their attention south to Houston in pursuit of new players for the upcoming season. After failing to secure an NHL franchise and on the heels of more unsuccessful merger talks between the two leagues, the Aeros' ownership had decided to cease operations. In early July, the Jets swooped in and purchased the remaining players the team still had under contract for a rumored price of $500,000. In a deal engineered by Gobuty and Barry Shenkarow, the Jets bought the rights to Terry Ruskowski, Rich Preston, Morris Lukowich, Andre Lacroix, Cam Connor, Scott Campbell, Don Larway, John Hughes, Paul Terbenche, Al McLeod, Steve West, and John Gray.

The league did not hold an Amateur Draft, but that didn't stop the Jets from dipping into the junior ranks and they signed winger Glenn Hicks, centerman Dale Yakiwchuk and defenseman Paul MacKinnon, each of whom were still months removed from their 20th birthday. Hicks was a second-round selection of the Red Wings who had scored 50 goals with the Flin Flon Bombers last season, while Yakiwchuk had scored 32 goals and piled up 312 penalty minutes with the Portland Winter Hawks. A second-round choice of the Montreal Canadiens, Yakiwchuk was a physical force who frequently stood up for his teammates. Rounding out the trio was MacKinnon, a second-round selection of the Washington Capitals, who had excelled as a stay-at-home defenseman with the Peterborough Petes.

Regrettably, a number of the foot soldiers from the last season's championship squad had moved on. Dave Kryskow retired, and Ken Baird, Lynn Powis, and Kent Ruhnke had each signed to play in West Germany, but Bill Lesuk signed on to stay with the Jets for the upcoming season. The Jets sold the rights to John Hughes, Don Larway and Al McLeod to the Racers, and the Jets traded Andre Lacroix to the Whalers for future considerations. Lacroix, one of the most outspoken players against the influx of European players in North American pro hockey, had a clause in his contract that prevented him from being traded to a Canadian team, so the Jets were forced to deal him to a team south of the border. He was entering the third year of a seven-year, $100,000 per season contract that had been guaranteed by former Mariners' owner Ray Kroc. In addition, Cam Connor signed with Montreal, though the Jets claimed that Connor was their property, while Connor countered that he had a no-trade contract that was breached when the Jets had purchased it from the defunct Aeros.

In mid-August, Winnipeg City Council voted in favor of a bare bones plan to expand the Winnipeg Arena at a cost of $3.5 million. The enlarged facility would be able to seat 15,000, the minimum number required to make the Arena NHL-ready. The seating capacity of just over 10,000 had been a significant reason why the NHL turned Ben Hatskin away in 1971 and it remained a thorn in the side of the community ownership group as they watched their working capital dwindle away.

Less than three weeks before the start of training camp, the Jets held a press conference at the International Inn to announce the signings of Lukowich, Ruskowski, Campbell, and Preston to new contracts. Lukowich, Ruskowski and Campbell each signed five-year contracts, while Preston signed a three-year contract.

The 22-year-old Lukowich, a native of Speers, Saskatchewan, was coming off a 40-goal season with the Aeros and had chosen to sign with the Aeros over the Penguins two seasons ago because of the opportunity to play with Gordie Howe. This time around, despite a comparable offer from the Penguins, the speedy winger signed a $120,000 per year deal with the Jets so he could stick with linemates Ruskowski and Preston. Known for his tenacity and dedication, Lukowich had spent three seasons in junior hockey with the Medicine Hat Tigers before signing with the Aeros.

Gobuty persuaded Ruskowski, the Aeros' captain last season, to sign a $130,000 per year contract from the Jets and to turn down a lucrative offer from the Chicago Blackhawks. The 23-year-old native of Prince Albert, Saskatchewan was coming off four seasons in Houston where he had also partnered with Larway, his teammate in junior hockey with the Swift Current Broncos, in a record store. An aggressive player who was known for being good in the corners, Ruskowski was a fan favorite in Houston and had a reputation as an excellent fighter when called upon. Ruskowski centered a line with Lukowich and Preston that had had the task of shutting down the Hot Line last season and their work helped the Aeros to be the only team with the distinction of posting a winning record against the Jets.

Campbell was a former first-round selection of the St. Louis Blues, but he had opted to sign with the Aeros for the past season after three years of junior hockey with the London Knights. The 21-year-old Toronto native's biggest asset was his size and the imposing defenseman had spent most of the time in his own end of the ice. Campbell signed a new $95,000 per year deal and joined his former teammates as part of the remade Jets roster.

Though Preston had an existing contract, like his former Aeros teammates, he still signed a new pact with the Jets, one that would pay him $90,000 per year. The 26-year-old native of Regina, Saskatchewan had racked up a total of 105 goals over the course of four seasons with the Aeros after spending four years at Denver University. A complete, all-around player and well-conditioned athlete, Preston excelled in both ends of the ice. He had played the right side with Ruskowski and Lukowich on the Aeros' top line, while also being a reliable penalty killer who had chipped in with eight shorthanded goals over the past two seasons. In high school, Preston was an outstanding quarterback, but he chose hockey over football so he could further his education. His father, Ken, was the former general manager of the CFL's Saskatchewan Roughriders and also acted as his agent in negotiations with the Jets.

Training camp opened on 17 September with the obligatory medicals before the team hit the ice as a group for the first time. One week later, the season got off to an ominous start when Lars-Erik Sjoberg tore his Achilles tendon against the St. Louis Blues during the Jets' first exhibition game. The 2-2 draw at the Arena meant nothing in comparison to the prospect of being without their captain for several months. Two nights later, Morris Lukowich sustained a slight concussion and suffered a cracked bone in his shoulder during a 5-3 loss to the Colorado Rockies at the Arena.

The New York Rangers came into Winnipeg for a pair of games and beat the Jets by scores of 5-2 and 7-4. Fittingly, former Jet Ulf Nilsson was the first star in both games. The Jets tied the Minnesota North Stars 5-5 and beat them by a score of 6-5 before finishing the pre-season schedule with a game against the Oilers.

Peter Sullivan was the Jets' best player during training camp, but Paul Terbenche was the biggest surprise to come out of camp. One of the forgotten group that the Jets had purchased from the Aeros, the diminutive 33-year-old rearguard had spent most of the last season in the minor leagues before the Aeros purchased his contract from the Bulls late in the season. While still in the minors, however, Terbenche went down to block a shot and was struck under the right eye. His cheekbone was shattered and a prominent plastic surgeon in Houston had had to rebuild the right side of his face. He made a successful return from the devastating injury and played in all six post-season games for his new team. The Jets had originally planned to trade Terbenche during the off-season, but they decided to hang on to the veteran of three full NHL seasons who had played one season with the Blazers and two more with the Cowboys before being picked up by the Bulls. Terbenche had played for Hillman during his last season in Calgary and had also played for former Jets' coach Bobby Kromm 10 years earlier when the two were in Dallas.

The new Jets officially began the defense of their championship on the evening of Friday, 13 October in Birmingham to kick off a three-game weekend. During the off-season, the Bulls had replaced coach Glen Sonmor with John Brophy and had cleaned out most of the goons on their roster who had embarrassed both the league and the game. In their place, the Bulls signed a host of underage junior players that included goaltender Pat Riggin; defensemen Craig Hartsburg, Rob Ramage and Gaston Gingras; and forwards Michel Goulet and Rick Vaive. The Bulls also picked up original Jet Ernie Wakely to team up with the young Riggin between the pipes.

The Bulls scored the first period's only goal, but the Jets responded with two quick goals early in the second to grab their first lead of the season. The energetic young Bulls, however, continue to buzz around the Jets' goal and it took them all of 24 seconds to tie the game at 2-2. After trading goals early in the third period, Louis Sleigher's goal with just under nine minutes to play gave the Bulls a 4-3 lead. In the final minute, with Joe Daley on the bench in favor of the extra attacker, Lukowich scored his first goal as a Jet with just six seconds left on the clock to send the game to overtime. In the extra period, the Bulls pressed on, but Bill Lesuk's weak backhand shot found its way past Riggin to give the Jets a 5-4 sudden-death victory. The Jets had been outplayed by a considerable margin all night long, but Daley nearly single-handedly kept the Jets in the game and allowed them the chance to pull off the late-game heroics that improved their record in season-opening games to a near-perfect 6-1-0.

The Jets moved on to Indianapolis one night later to play the Racers. Led by new coach and general manager Pat Stapleton, the Racers added three former Aeros to their lineup and they made headlines when junior star Wayne Gretzky signed a personal-services contract with owner Nelson Skalbania. The 17-year-old centerman had scored 70 goals and added 112 assists last season in junior hockey with the Sault Ste. Marie Greyhounds and despite his tender age, he had nothing left to prove at the junior level but was still a year away from being eligible for the NHL draft.

The Racers put on a show in front of a crowd of 11,721 curious onlookers, but Markus Mattsson kept the Jets on even terms through two periods and the Jets took the lead for good early in the third when Kent Nilsson stole the puck and fed Willy Lindstrom for the go-ahead goal. Nilsson scored himself later in the period to double the Jets' lead and Sullivan's empty-net marker capped the scoring in the 6-3 win.

Did You Know?

With 39 seconds remaining in the first period on 14 October 1978, Kent Nilsson set up Bobby Hull for his second goal of the season, which tied the score at 2-2 before intermission. It was Hull's 303rd regular season goal as a WHA Jet and it would prove to be his last. After two more games, Hull left the team and later announced his retirement. Hull did make a brief return in the 1979-1980 season after the Jets were admitted to the NHL and he scored four goals in 18 games before being traded to the Hartford Whalers, where he finished his career.

On Sunday night, the Jets wrapped up their hectic weekend with a visit from the Stingers in their home opener. Led by new coach Floyd Smith, who had been a candidate for the Jets' coaching position before they had selected Hillman as Kromm's replacement, the Stingers joined the Bulls and Racers in supplementing their roster from the junior ranks when they signed Mike Gartner, who was still a couple of weeks shy of his 19th birthday. Though the Jets were the home team, the Stingers were the more rested of the two clubs as the Jets had spent most of the day on planes and in airports and hadn't made it back to Winnipeg until three hours before the game.

Nonetheless, before a gathering of over 8,500 that included a record-high 7,600 season ticket holders, the Jets scored the first period's only goal, but their lack of jump became evident as the game wore on. The Stingers used their speed to take control and Rick Dudley's goal early in the third period gave the visitors a 4-2 lead. The Jets summoned what little energy they had and Lesuk's goal later in the period brought them back to within one, but they could get no closer and the Stingers handed the Jets a 4-3 defeat to spoil the first of a four-game home stand.

After a couple of days between games, the Jets were next in action on Wednesday, 18 October against the Whalers for their first meeting of the season against the team they had defeated in the AVCO World Trophy final. Over the off-season, the Whalers had brought in former Aeros' coach Bill Dineen to replace Harry Neale, who had left to coach the Vancouver Canucks and they added Andre Lacroix from the Aeros via the Jets. Lacroix was coming off a 113-point season in Houston, marking his sixth consecutive season where he recorded 100 points or more. The Whalers had also picked up star goaltender John Garrett to team up with Al Smith, who had been the WHA's top goaltender last season and also a First Team All-Star.

The Jets opened the scoring, but it was the Whalers who eventually took charge of the game and broke a 2-2 tie with two third period goals. Trailing by two goals, the Jets rallied and Peter Sullivan's goal with just under four minutes to play narrowed the deficit to one before Kent Nilsson's shot from the point in the final minute of regulation time made it through a maze of bodies and into the net to tie the score at 4-4. Neither team could break the tie in overtime and the game ended in a draw. Lukowich scored twice for the Jets, who still had two wins and a tie to show for their first four outings despite a sluggish start.

The home stand continued on Sunday night with the Oilers' first visit of the season. Over the course of the summer, the Oilers had added some veterans with NHL experience when they signed defenseman Claire Alexander and centerman Stan Weir and traded for winger Bill Goldsworthy, who had finished last season as the playing coach of the Racers. The Jets were without Bobby Guindon on account of an ear infection, and Terry Ruskowski, due to persistent knee and hand injuries in addition to a sprained ankle, but then Larry Hillman got a rude surprise 40 minutes before the game. Just before the Jets were about to go out for the warmup, he was told that Bobby Hull would not be available for personal reasons. There were reports that the Golden Jet was not even in Winnipeg, but in Toronto selling leather goods.

Despite playing their third game in as many nights, the Oilers took it to the shorthanded Jets and racked up a 4-0 lead before Steve West's first goal as a Jet late in the second period got the Jets on the board. The goal failed to lift the Jets and the Oilers added two more in the third and the Jets meekly went down to a 6-2 defeat that left both Hillman and his players exasperated. The humiliating loss dropped the Jets' record to 2-2-1 that left them in fourth place in the seven-team league.

The Jets had a little time to stew over Sunday night's outing before returning to the ice on Wednesday night against the Bulls. Though both Ruskowski and Guindon were back, the Jets announced on Wednesday morning that Hull had been granted a temporary leave of absence from the team to deal with personal and family matters. Once the game began, the Jets started slowly, but they gradually built up a lead against the young Bulls and put the game away with three third period goals and handily won by a score of 7-2. Lindstrom scored twice to answer Hillman's recent criticism of his play, but neither Ruskowski nor Guindon could finish the game. Ruskowski turned his ankle, and Guindon was struck beside the right eye by an errant clearing attempt from Mike Amodeo.

The next afternoon, the Jets left to begin another three-game weekend on Friday night in Springfield against the Whalers, but not before making a roster move. The Jets assigned Yakiwchuk to the Philadelphia Firebirds of the AHL to join fellow Jets' property Bill Davis in the hopes of allowing the inexperienced youngster the chance to develop at the minor league level. Without Yakiwchuk or Guindon, whose sight was still impaired from Wednesday night's mishap, the Jets grabbed an early 2-0 lead and stayed ahead of the persistent Whalers the rest of the evening. The Jets' best outing of the young season culminated in a well-deserved 6-4 victory as they continued their recent mastery over the Whalers. Kent Nilsson scored twice and was particularly outstanding, while Ruskowski led by example, playing with a badly sprained ankle. Twice during the game, he had to be helped off the ice, but he managed to get through the game. In addition, Glenn Hicks scored his first goal as a Jet and Rich Preston added a pair of goals.

One night later, the Jets moved on to Indianapolis to meet the struggling Racers, winners of only one of their first six games. The Racers battled hard and used Ed Mio's stellar goaltending to stay on even terms through two periods, then with the score still tied at 2-2 late in the third, Blaine Stoughton finished off a three-on-one break to give the Racers the lead. Mio and his teammates made the lead hold up and the Jets went down to a 3-2 defeat in a game they should have won easily.

The rematch took place on Sunday night in Winnipeg, and both teams showed the effects of playing three games in as many nights. Nonetheless, the Jets overcame a 2-1 first period deficit and scored twice in the second to take a 3-2 lead. With eight and a half minutes to play in regulation time, however, Claude Larose's goal tied the score and the game went to overtime. The Racers sensed a rare opportunity for a second win in a row and only an exceptional display of goaltending from Joe Daley prevented any further scoring. The game ended with the score tied at 3-3 and Daley's 34 saves earned him first-star honors. In addition to almost losing the game in overtime, the Jets lost Barry Long, their interim captain, during the extra period when he was struck on the knee. The game marked the debut of the Winnipeg debut of the much-ballyhooed Wayne Gretzky, but he didn't see much ice time since the Racers were concerned about his play in his own end of the rink.

The sagging 4-3-2 Jets had a few days to recover before their next game, but on Wednesday evening, the Jets received more bad news when Gobuty formally announced Hull's retirement. Hull had looked good during the exhibition schedule and in the first four league games, but after taking an abrupt leave of absence, he opted to make the leave permanent by retiring. He did, however, leave the door open for a potential return and said that if he did return, it would be with the Jets. Hull did not attend the press conference, but he had this to say in an interview with Mickey Redmond of ON-TV in December 1979:

"I wasn't feeling that badly physically, but I just couldn't get involved in the game the way I wanted to, you know the way I play the game and that's 100 percent all the time and I just couldn't get motivated to the point where I could go out there in front of the fans and give them everything they deserve so I decided that maybe it was about time that I called it quits."

Having not played since Sunday night, the Jets returned to game action on Friday, 3 November in Edmonton, the day after the Oilers had pulled off a coup by purchasing Gretzky, Peter Driscoll and Ed Mio from the Racers for the princely sum of $850,000. The Racers were nearing the end of their financial rope, while the Oilers saw an opportunity to improve their team and were able to make the large monetary payment to pry Gretzky out of Indianapolis. The Jets were rumored to be in the mix as well, but having already spent a large amount to acquire the former Aeros, they were not in a good position to match the Oilers' offer.

The Jets got the early jump against the reinforced Oilers, but it didn't take long before the Oilers responded in kind four minutes later and they added a pair in the second period to take a 3-1 lead. The Jets rallied and scored a pair of their own, tying the score at 3-3 on Sullivan's goal with just over six minutes to play in regulation time. The Jets kept the pressure on the Oilers in overtime, but it was Driscoll, in his Oilers' debut, who beat Markus Mattsson six minutes into the extra period to give his new team a sudden-death 4-3 victory. Gretzky also scored in his first game as an Oiler in front of a crowd of 11,762 that saw the Jets' winless streak reach three games.

The Jets returned home for a Sunday night encounter with the undermanned Racers, who had flown into Winnipeg after a pair of games against the Whalers in successive nights. The Racers had enough left in their tank to take a 2-1 first period lead, but the Jets rose up and put the visitors down with two quick goals midway through the second and added three more in the third for a decisive 6-2 win. Sullivan and Ruskowski scored twice each for the 5-4-2 Jets, who pulled into sole possession of fourth place in the tight league standings, three points back of their next opponent, the first-place Nordiques.

Did You Know?

> Mark Messier of the Alberta Junior Hockey League's St. Albert Saints joined the Indianapolis Racers for a five-game tryout that began on 5 November 1978 in Winnipeg against the Jets. Though Messier did not record a point in this game, as a member of the Edmonton Oilers, he would go on to feast on the Jets after both teams joined the NHL. Only teammates Wayne Gretzky and Jari Kurri scored more points against the NHL Jets than Messier during regular season play.

Two nights later, the Jets began a three-game road swing in Quebec to play the Nordiques for the first time this season. The Nordiques, led by former Racers' and Stingers' coach Jacques Demers, had welcomed back some injured players to their lineup this season, added promising youngsters Richard David and Daniel Geoffrion, and also reacquired defenseman Dale Hoganson. The Jets stood on Mattsson's shoulders to hold their own against the red-hot Nordiques and the two teams went to the second intermission with the score tied at 1-1. Early in the third period, Amodeo pounced on his own rebound to score his second goal in as many games and Mattsson did the rest to make the lead stand up, giving the Jets a 2-1 victory.

The next day, the Jets flew to Birmingham to play the Bulls on Thursday night. The goals came early and often and the Bulls scored four of the six first period markers. The Bulls scored two more in the second period in the wide-open affair and though the Jets valiantly tried to mount a third period comeback, they fell just short and the Jets went down by a score of 6-5. Joe Daley was not sharp in the Jets' fifth loss of the season and neither were his teammates in the game's early stages.

The Jets wrapped up the road trip with a game in Cincinnati on Friday night. The Jets spent the entire night under siege by the Stingers, but Mattsson single-handedly prevented the Stingers from running up the score. In the second period, the Jets scored a pair of goals to wipe out a 2-0 Stingers' lead, but Mattsson could only hold the fort for so long and the Stingers regained the lead in the third. The listless Jets offered little in response and the Stingers skated off with a 3-2 victory. In addition to losing the game, Ruskowski reinjured his hand when he fought Chuck Luksa late in the second period.

Returning home, the 6-6-2 Jets entertained the Nordiques on Sunday, 12 November. The Nordiques had come into Winnipeg without former Jet Christian Bordeleau, who had announced his retirement earlier in the day. Following Norm Beaudin's departure for Switzerland and Hull's retirement, Bordeleau was the last active member of the Luxury Line that had propelled the Jets to the league finals in their first season. Bordeleau had been battling injuries and combined with his commitments to his farm, he made the decision to call it a career.

Before a near-sellout crowd, the Jets took a 2-1 lead late in the first period, but the Nordiques bounced back and grabbed a 4-3 lead with two goals late in the second period that included Serge Bernier's second of the night with just two seconds left before intermission. In the third period, after Alain Cote gave the Nordiques a two-goal lead, the Jets mounted a late rally that again came up short and the Nordiques took the game by a score of 6-4. In losing their fourth straight game, the Jets fell below the .500 mark for the first time in over three and a half years.

Amid discontent and lack of unity in the dressing room, a rift between Larry Hillman and some players, and troublesome trade rumors circling overhead, the fortunes of the fourth-place Jets took another hit when Daley fell ill and missed Monday morning's practice while visiting the doctor. He wouldn't be able to available for Wednesday night's rematch in Quebec, so the Jets frantically began hunting around for a goaltender to serve as Mattsson's backup. The next day, the Jets turned to 24-year-old Harvey Stewart, who had been playing with the East Kildonan-Elmwood Millionaires of the Central Amateur Senior Hockey

League in addition to his day job at Weldwood of Canada, a Winnipeg wholesale plywood distributor. Five seasons ago, Stewart and Kim Clackson had been teammates with the Flin Flon Bombers, and the Los Angeles Kings had subsequently drafted Stewart in the seventh round of the NHL Amateur Draft. After failing to crack the Kings' lineup, Stewart played two seasons in the minor leagues and he had also had an unsuccessful tryout with the Cleveland Barons.

In addition to being without Daley, the Jets flew to Quebec without Bill Lesuk, who was attending the funeral of a close friend and neighbor in nearby Birds Hill, and Ted Green, who was being rested for the pair of upcoming weekend games. The Jets gave it a better effort, but the Nordiques were on top of their game and would not be denied, quashing the Jets' comeback attempts on their way to an eventual 5-2 victory.

Carrying a four-game losing streak with them, the Jets returned home to entertain the Stingers on Friday, 17 November. The Jets stormed out of the gate and took their anger out on the Stingers, racking up a 5-2 lead early in the second period. The Stingers didn't quit, but neither did the Jets, and they put a merciful end to their losing streak with an impressive 10-6 win. Morris Lukowich scored four times and added an assist to lead the Jets and the crowd of 8,166 responded with chants of "Luke, Luke" in honor of the former Aero. Stewart again served as Mattsson's backup in place of Daley, who remained bed-ridden with a flu virus.

On Sunday night, the Jets hosted the crumbling leftovers of the Racers franchise. Late last week, the Racers purged more salary and talent from their roster when they jettisoned Rich Leduc and Kevin Morrison. The pair was traded to the Nordiques for the right to switch positions in the next three WHA drafts, in effect, giving them away. To their credit, the Racers who were left behind made a game of it for two periods, but the Jets broke a 2-2 tie with three goals in the third and won by a score of 5-2.

After sweeping the pair of weekend games, the Jets had a couple of days off until their next game on Wednesday, 22 November in Springfield against the Whalers. Back home, however, the Jets held a press conference that morning at the Viscount Gort Hotel to end a month's worth of speculation by announcing the hiring of John Ferguson as their general manager. The Rangers had fired the 40-year-old Ferguson during the off-season and Michael Gobuty instantly began pursuing him aggressively until he finally relented and accepted the Jets' offer. During his playing days, Ferguson had spent eight seasons with the Montreal Canadiens, where he had acquired a reputation as a hard-nosed tough guy. After his retirement as a player, Ferguson had been an assistant to Head Coach Harry Sinden for Team Canada in the 1972 series against the Soviet Union and he had returned to the game when the Rangers hired him in January 1976 as their coach and general manager. Ferguson held the dual roles until the end of the 1976-1977 season when he delegated the coaching responsibilities to former Denver Spurs' coach Jean-Guy Talbot. Ferguson had helped lure both Anders Hedberg and Ulf Nilsson to the Rangers late last season before being fired.

Ferguson signed a five-year contract with the Jets and was given the title of Vice President and General Manager, effective immediately. Unlike past holders of the general manager's title, however, Ferguson was given the full powers that went with it. He was given complete control of hockey operations, on and off the ice, and all the current members of the hockey administration, including Larry Hillman and Rudy Pilous, would now be reporting to Ferguson.

In Springfield that night, Ferguson's new team fell behind 3-0 in the first period and passively went through the motions in a 5-2 defeat. The win was the Whalers' first against the Jets in nearly a year and the loss sent the Jets under the .500 mark once again and they remained in a fourth-place tie with the Oilers, one point ahead of the sixth-place Bulls.

The 8-9-2 Jets flew to Indianapolis for a game the next evening with the Racers. The Racers again proved stubborn and they tested Mattsson often in the early going, but their competitive fires dimmed after the Jets scored twice 51 seconds apart in the second period to break a 1-1 tie. With little fanfare, the Jets went on and claimed a 5-1 victory in front of a loyal gathering of 7,181 fans at Market Square Arena. The Racers saw their winless streak reach nine games, while the Jets won for the third time in four games.

The next day, the Jets flew to Quebec for a Sunday night game against the Nordiques. Playing in front of their new boss for the first time, the Jets played smartly in their own end and used a late first period goal and an early second period marker to take a 2-0 lead. Nordiques' defenseman and Winnipeg native Paul Baxter scored twice four minutes apart later in the second, but the Jets shut the Nordiques down the rest of the way. There was no more scoring through the rest of regulation and overtime and the game ended in a 2-2 tie.

Upon their return to Winnipeg, Ferguson announced his first move when he hired 44-year-old Marc Cloutier as the Executive Director of Business Operations. Like Ferguson, Cloutier was a veteran of the Canadiens' organization, where he had served for six seasons as their Sales and Promotion Manager, Director of Public Relations, and Assistant to the President. Cloutier had been in the real estate business with his brother when Ferguson called and offered him the job with the Jets.

The Jets also replaced public address announcer Donn Kirton with Bob Bell, their Executive Director of Marketing and Administration. Kirton's rendition of "Here Come the Jets" when the Jets stepped on the ice had become a familiar trademark that most fans enjoyed, but he had also been prone to mispronouncing players' names. Earlier this season, Rob Ramage of the Bulls had shouted at Kirton after hearing his name mispronounced following a penalty call. Kirton was nonetheless a dedicated fan who had first become involved with the team when he teamed with CJOB radio colleague Peter Warren in the Save the Jets campaign. Kirton's broadcasting career had begun more than 27 years ago, most of which was spent with CJOB, the radio home of the Jets.

On Wednesday night, the Jets hosted the Whalers on John Ferguson Night. Before the game, Bob Banman, Manitoba Minister of Fitness of Recreation, and Winnipeg Mayor Robert Steen joined Gobuty to introduce Ferguson to the crowd and welcome him to Winnipeg. Once the ceremony concluded, the Jets proceeded to put on a show for Ferguson and the 8,394 paying customers and were full marks for their two-goal second period lead, which would have been much larger were it not for John Garrett in the Whalers' goal. Andre Lacroix scored late in the third period to bring the Whalers back to within one goal, but Lukowich scored his second of the game with an empty-net marker in the final minute to salt away a 4-2 victory. In addition to Lukowich's pair of goals, Kent Nilsson recorded three assists and was named the game's first star.

The month of December began with a Friday night game against the Stingers at the Arena. The game started with the drop of the puck at center ice from linesman Joey Dame, who was elevated to the referee's role for the night because Peter Moffat had been stranded in Fort Wayne, Indiana on account of a snowstorm. The Jets fell behind early, but they stormed back with four straight goals to take a 5-3 lead early in the third period. The Stingers responded with one of their own a minute and a half after the Jets' fifth goal, then Reg Thomas's goal with just under four minutes to play tied the score. The game appeared to be headed for overtime when Mike Gartner put a rebound over a prone Daley to give the Stingers a 6-5 lead with just 25 seconds left on the clock. That was not nearly enough time for the Jets to respond and they could only watch as the Stingers snatched the last-minute victory from under their noses. Daley made his first start since recovering from a severe case of the flu and faced 44 shots in the losing cause.

The next day, the disheartened Jets left for Quebec to battle the Nordiques on Sunday night for their fifth meeting in four weeks. The game began the way Friday night's game had ended for the Jets as the Nordiques ran up a 4-0 lead seven minutes into the first period. The Jets clawed their way back into the game, but the tying goal remained elusive through the third period and Curt Brackenbury's empty-net goal with 20 seconds left on the clock sealed a 5-3 win for the hometown Nordiques.

After a bit of a break, the Jets' next game took place on Thursday night in Indianapolis against the woeful 4-16-2 Racers. The Jets had little trouble building up a 4-0 lead before the game was 12 minutes old and though the overwhelmed Racers managed to trim the Jets' lead to 6-4 early in the third period, they had no miracle comeback in them and the Jets scored three more times to post a 9-4 victory. The only blemish on the game for the Jets came when Kent Nilsson was struck in the face by a hard shot off the stick of Blaine Stoughton. Nilsson sustained a broken nose and a fractured cheekbone, and his left eye had been nearly swollen shut.

Off the ice, reports of further talks with the rival NHL surfaced once again. The Jets, along with the Stingers, Oilers, Whalers and Nordiques submitted expansion proposals to the NHL, but any decision on whether or not they would accept the WHA teams was put off until January.

The Jets flew back to Winnipeg on Friday and awaited the Nordiques for a Sunday night encounter with the league leaders. A pair of first period goals from Real Cloutier got the Nordiques out in front, but the Jets answered with three goals in just over two minutes in the second period to take the lead. The Nordiques regained the lead before the intermission, but Peter Sullivan's third period goal got the Jets back on even terms. Neither team could score for the remainder of regulation time and overtime settled nothing, so the game ended in a 4-4 tie. Sullivan's goal was his 18th of the season, which was two more than he had had all of last season when he was centering a checking line. Despite making 33 saves, Daley had an off night, and the gathering of 8,862 critics in the stands did not hesitate to express its displeasure with the work of the last remaining original Jet.

In more off-ice news, Ferguson continued to build up the Jets' organization with the hiring of scouts Mike Doran and Les Binkley. Doran was assigned to cover the NHL, Ontario Hockey Association and international leagues, while Binkley, a former NHL and WHA goaltender, was given the task of covering the WHA, AHL, and IHL. Binkley, a former teammate of Ferguson's with the Cleveland Barons, was also to serve as a goaltending coach.

On Monday, 11 December, the Jets made a pair on-ice moves when they assigned Steve West to the Rochester Americans of the AHL and recalled Dale Yakiwchuk from the Philadelphia Firebirds. The 26-year-old West, one of the lesser-known names among the group the Jets had picked up from the Aeros, had been the Central Hockey League's scoring champion two seasons ago and he had tallied 32 points last season with the Aeros, but he had only one goal with the Jets so far this season. Regrettably, Yakiwchuk didn't get much playing time with the Colorado Rockies' farm team in Philadelphia, because Rockies' players were given preference, but the Jets nonetheless hoped for a bit of spark from the move.

The Jets were off until Thursday night when they played host to a touring team from the Soviet Union in a game that counted in the league standings. The Soviet team that had been advertised as the second best national team pumped four goals by Mattsson in the first period on only five shots, but the Jets still went to the second trailing by only two goals. Sullivan scored early in the second period as the Jets got stonger in the latter stages of the game, but they could get no more past goaltender Vladimir Myshkin, who had replaced ineffective starter Sergei Babariko. The Jets ran out of steam and also ran out of time and the Soviets took the game by a score of 4-3.

Friday was another day of off-ice headlines when John Ferguson fired Rudy Pilous. The last man to hold the title of general manager had been with the Jets since the beginning of the 1974-1975 season and had been behind the bench for most of that year before moving into the front office. Though Pilous held a lofty title, unlike Ferguson, he had never been given a matching level of authority. Ferguson thought that Pilous was overqualified as a scout and since the Jets had a new general manager, there was no room in the organization for Pilous.

That same day, the WHA lost another franchise when the troubled Racers announced that they were ceasing operations as of midnight. The league was left with six teams and though the Racers' demise caught few by surprise, it was a most sad day for the Racers' loyal following in and around Indianapolis. The Racers had begun as an expansion team in 1974-1975 and won the Eastern Division title the next season. Financial problems nearly doomed the franchise after the 1976-1977 season, but in the end, their rescue had only postponed their eventual downfall.

That evening, the Jets played an exhibition game against a touring Swedish national team at the Arena. Before a gathering of just over 6,000 onlookers, the Jets and the best Swedes not at the Izvestia tournament went through the motions, but Nilsson's late third period goal broke a 3-3 tie and gave the Jets a 4-3 triumph in a contest that looked every bit like a meaningless exhibition game. The event's only real drama took place before the game at the International Inn, where nine members of the Swedish team were trapped in an elevator for 40 minutes.

Two nights later, the Jets returned to league play with a Sunday night visit from the struggling Stingers, who came into Winnipeg without a win in their last six games. The Jets grabbed a 2-1 lead in the first period and tripled their lead with two more goals in the second. The Stingers kept the Jets on their toes, but Mattsson was the difference in keeping the Jets in front and Lesuk's pair of third period goals provided the necessary insurance in the 6-3 victory. Lukowich also scored twice for the Jets, who evened their record at 12-12-4 and pulled back into a fourth-place tie with the Oilers.

The Jets' last game before the Christmas holiday took place on Friday night in Edmonton. The Jets opened the scoring with a pair of early first period goals, but the Oilers kept up the pressure on the visiting Jets and took their first lead of the game late in the second. The Jets responded with a pair before intermission and Lukowich's second goal of the game seven minutes into the third gave the Jets the lead for good. Mattsson made the one-goal lead stand up and the Jets left Edmonton with a well-earned 5-4 win, putting the brakes on the Oilers' three-game winning streak.

After the holiday, the Jets were back on the ice on Boxing Day for a rematch against the Oilers at the Arena. The Jets charged out to a 5-1 lead after two periods, but after the Oilers scored a pair of quick goals early in the third, the Jets slammed the door on their guests and went on to post a 5-3 victory. Kent Nilsson scored a pair of pretty goals to dazzle the crowd of 10,355, who saw the Jets win their third in a row.

One night later, the Jets were back in Edmonton to battle the Oilers for the third time in six days. The Jets rallied from a 3-1 deficit to tie the score in the second period, but Dennis Sobchuk's goal early in the third period put the Oilers back in front. This time it was the Oilers who clamped down in their own end and they limited the Jets to only three shots in the third period. Bill "Cowboy" Flett's goal late in the third doubled the lead and the game ended with the final score of 5-3 in the Oilers' favor.

The Jets returned home and they were back on the ice on Friday morning at the Arena for an intra-squad game and hockey clinic for the benefit of more than 3,800 youngsters who had made their way through Thursday's snowfall to see their heroes. The next evening, the Jets hosted Moscow Dynamo, a team comprised of members of the police force, border patrols and the feared KGB, the Soviet Union's national security agency, in an exhibition game. The Jets put on a good show for the crowd of around 8,200 and earned a convincing 6-4 victory in the last of four games for Dynamo against WHA teams before they played a three-game series against the WHA All-Stars the following week in Edmonton. Larry Hillman used the opportunity give Daley his first game action in almost three weeks and he shook off the rust to backstop his team to the win.

Two nights later, the Jets played a touring second-tier Czechoslovakian national team on New Year's Day, but unlike the game against Dynamo, this game did count in the league standings. Before a small, but vocal crowd of 6,243 spectators, the Jets broke a 1-1 tie with a pair of second period goals and coasted into the third period with a 3-1 lead. The Czechs cut the Jets' lead in half with eight and a half minutes to play, but the Jets still looked to have the game well in hand as time wound down. Only seconds were left when the Czechs buzzed around the Jets' goal for one last desperate attempt to tie the score. The Czechs did score, but too late, as the green light behind Daley lit up, indicating that time expired instead of the red light that normally signaled a goal. However, inexperienced Czechoslovakian referee Vladimir Subrt ruled that the puck crossed the goal line before time ran out, infuriating both the Jets and their fans. The angry Jets dominated overtime, but they couldn't get the winning goal and the game ended in a 3-3 tie.

The 14-13-5 Jets seethed after the game over the lost point due to Subrt's controversial call, but replays later showed that the head official had indeed been correct. Meanwhile, it was time for the league's annual All-Star break, and Larry Hillman, along with Markus Mattsson, Barry Long, Morris Lukowich, and Peter Sullivan, flew to Edmonton to represent the WHA in a three-game series against Moscow Dynamo. Lukowich scored two goals and Sullivan added another over the three games, all won by the All-Stars, and Mattsson played the final two games, making a total of 36 saves.

After the break, the Jets were back in action on Sunday, 7 January against the Nordiques. Both teams showed the effects of the lengthy layoff, but the Jets had got enough energy back in their legs to take a 2-1 lead in the first period and Sullivan took a feed from Paul Terbenche to score early in the second to extend the lead to 3-1. Serge Bernier brought the Nordiques back to within one goal with an early third period marker, but the Jets played it smart in their own end to make the 3-2 lead hold up the rest of the way. Long was a bulwark on the Jets' blue line and he earned his first-star selection in leading the Jets to their fourth win in six games.

On Tuesday night, the Jets hosted the Oilers in a game where the Racers had originally been scheduled to be the opponent. The Oilers got the early jump on the Jets, but goals from Rich Preston and Nilsson in the waning minutes of the first period tied the game at 2-2. The teams traded goals in the second period and neither team could score in the third, sending the game to overtime. Six and a half minutes into the extra period, Nilsson took a feed from Terry Ruskowski in front of the Oilers' net and fired a wrist shot past goaltender Ed Walsh to give the Jets a 4-3 victory, much to the delight of the crowd of 8,229 who had braved the January cold to see the game. The two points enabled the Jets to vault over the slumping Stingers into third place and moved them three games over the .500 mark before embarking on a four-game road trip.

The Jets left for Birmingham the next day to play the first of two against the Bulls on Friday night. During their connecting flight from Chicago to Atlanta, they hit an air pocket and suddenly dropped several hundred feet, but they landed safely and made it to Birmingham in time to battle the sixth-place Bulls, who had entered the game trailing the third-place Jets by only four points. The feisty Bulls came out flying, but it was the Jets who made the most of their limited opportunities and scored three times on only 11 shots in the first two periods. Trailing by a score of 3-0 going into the third, the Bulls didn't quit, but Mattsson turned them away time and again to backstop his team to a 3-1 victory. Mattsson stopped all but one of the 37 shots he faced and his solo act enabled the Jets to extend their modest winning streak to three games.

In Saturday night's rematch, the Jets were more ready to play and this time, they were fully deserving of their 2-0 first period lead. The Jets expertly held the Bulls in check and Nilsson's goal late in the third period sealed their second consecutive 3-1 victory to keep the Bulls in the basement of the league standings.

After sweeping the pair of games in Birmingham, the Jets moved on to Springfield to complete the three-game weekend against the Whalers on Sunday night. The Jets jumped out in front for the third straight game and just as they had on Saturday night, they played exceptionally well in their own end of the rink in defense of their lead. The Whalers managed a goal in each of the second and third periods, but the Jets would not be denied as they went on to a 4-2 win that moved them to within a point of the second-place Whalers.

Before their next game, the Jets picked up 24-year-old centerman Roland Eriksson. The tall, lanky native of Storatuna, Sweden had accumulated two goals and 12 assists this season with the Vancouver Canucks before being placed on waivers by the NHL club. Eriksson had begun his pro career two seasons earlier when he chose to sign the Minnesota North Stars instead of the Jets and scored 25 goals in his first year with Minnesota. He finished third in the balloting for the rookie of the year award, but his production had fallen off slightly the following year and he subsequently signed with the Canucks. Ironically, the speedy Eriksson had played left wing during the 1976 Canada Cup on a line with former Jets Anders Hedberg and Ulf Nilsson.

Eriksson joined his new teammates in Edmonton for a Tuesday night game against the Oilers. The Jets had little energy left in the tank after their grueling three-game weekend and they had to rely on Mattsson to hold them in the game. The young Finn was solid, but he didn't get much support, enabling the Oilers to edge the Jets by a score of 3-1. Ron Chipperfield scored twice for the victorious Oilers, who got just enough past Mattsson to put an end to the Jets' five-game winning streak.

One night later, the two teams faced off against each other once again in the rematch at the Arena. The Jets rallied to wipe out a 2-0 first period deficit, but in the second, the Jets looked no better than they had on Tuesday night. The Oilers scored three times in the second period and added another in the third to hand the Jets a 6-3 loss. Eriksson scored twice for his first two goals as a Jet, but his teammates turned in another sub-par effort. Daley made his first start in over a week, but he was pulled after yielding five goals on 14 shots.

The Jets picked up the pieces and returned to the ice on Friday, 19 January against the Stingers to begin their second consecutive three-game weekend. John Gray scored a pair of goals 56 seconds apart in the first period to get the Jets off on the right foot, but it was all downhill from the second period on. The Stingers scored twice in the second and blew the game open with five more in the third to send the Jets down to an embarrassing 7-2 defeat, much to the disgust of the 8,695 spectators at the Arena who paid to see the game. Robbie Ftorek scored four times to lead the Stingers, who won their third in a row and pulled to within one point of the Jets, whose hold on third place became increasingly fragile.

On Saturday night, the Jets took on the first-place Nordiques in Quebec. The game became a rout from the early stages and the Nordiques scored five times in the second period to remove all doubt as to the outcome. The only bright spot on the otherwise disastrous evening came early in the third period when Lukowich spoiled goaltender Jim Corsi's shutout bid. The game mercifully ended with a score of 10-1 in favor of the Nordiques, who handed the Jets their fourth consecutive defeat.

Both teams flew to Winnipeg for the rematch on Sunday night as the Jets prepared for their eighth game in 10 nights. Having hit rock bottom on Saturday night, the Jets rolled up their sleeves and came out ready to work. The two teams split a pair of first period goals, but the Jets scored twice 34 seconds apart in the second to take a two-goal lead and shut down the Nordiques the rest of the way to grind out a 3-1 win. Lesuk was masterful in shadowing high-scoring winger Real Cloutier and Mattsson backed up his teammates with an exceptionally strong outing after giving up a soft goal in the first period.

The next day, the Jets lost one of their best leaders when Ted Green announced his retirement. Citing problems with his arthritic knees, Green listened to the doctors and grudgingly ended a distinguished 20-year career in which he had been an integral part of two Stanley Cup and three AVCO World Trophy winning teams. Green was an intense competitor who had recovered from a serious head injury he sustained in a 1969 stick-swinging incident to remain one of the most respected rearguards in the game. After his arrival in Winnipeg in 1975, he had led the Jets to their two AVCO World Trophy championships and he had been one of the biggest supporters on the team of the European players. Despite the physical problems, he had entered the season determined to play, but in the end, the five knee operations and the wear and tear on his body over his long career took their toll and forced his hand.

While Green packed his gear and turned his focus to running the Carman Motor Inn, his former teammates left for Cincinnati to begin another four-game road swing on Wednesday night. The Jets scored three times in the second period to erase a 2-1 deficit and added another marker in the third to take a 5-2 lead. The game looked to be comfortably in the Jets' hands until the Stingers rose from the ashes and scored twice 10 seconds apart to get back in the game. The Stingers continued to swarm around the Jets' goal until Bill Gilligan put one past Markus Mattsson with only 16 seconds left on the clock, tying the game in dramatic fashion. In overtime, the Stingers kept up the pressure and only a couple of outstanding saves by Mattsson enabled the Jets to escape with a 5-5 tie.

The next stop on the road trip was a Saturday night engagement in Quebec, where the Jets had suffered their worst defeat of the season just one week earlier. The Jets rebounded from Wednesday night's collapse and took a 2-0 first period lead, only to have the Nordiques respond with a pair of their own, tying the game with only three seconds left before the second intermission. In the third period, the Jets maintained their resolve and held the Nordiques at bay until Guindon, the former Nordique, set up Lyle Moffat for the go-ahead goal with just over four minutes to play. The Jets made the lead hold up and sealed the 4-2 victory with an empty-net marker in the final minute. Lesuk, the newest assistant captain following Green's retirement, did another excellent job holding Real Cloutier in check, and Joe Daley earned his first victory in over two weeks by making 31 saves.

The Jets moved on to Springfield on Sunday night and played the Whalers even through the first period, but they were blitzed in the decisive second period when they gave up six goals. The Jets didn't quit, but they fell short in the end and went down by a score of 8-6 in the wild shootout. Mattsson had an off night in the Jets' goal, and his teammates were equally poor in their own end of the rink as the Jets went down for the first time in four games.

Two nights later, the same two teams again faced off in Springfield, where the Whalers again had the upper hand. The Whalers took a 4-0 lead in the second period, and though the Jets rallied to make a game of it, the Whalers maintained control of the contest and handed the Jets a 5-2 defeat to sweep the pair of games.

The next evening, the Jets were back home and on the ice on Wednesday night against the Oilers to wrap up the month of January. The Jets fell behind 2-0 in the first period, but after a tongue-lashing from John Ferguson between periods, the Jets responded in the second with three goals and added three more in the third to break a 3-3 tie on their way to a 6-3 victory. Nilsson and Lukowich scored twice each in the comeback win that moved the Jets to within two points of the league-leading Nordiques.

The Jets added another reinforcement to their roster when they brought in goaltender Gary Smith on a tryout. Days short of his 35th birthday, Smith had been out of work since the Racers had folded in mid-December and he called the Jets from his home in Lake Tahoe, Nevada asking for a job. Smith was a well-travelled NHL veteran, having played for the Oakland/California Seals, Chicago Blackhawks, Vancouver Canucks, Washington Capitals, and the Minnesota North Stars before signing with the Racers in September. Smith had posted a 5.51 goals against average without a victory to his credit in 11 games for the Racers, but he had a much more impressive track record in past seasons. His best year came in 1974-1975 when he played in 72 games, leading the Canucks to the Smythe Division title. Smith picked up the nickname of "Suitcase" because of the many stops in his career, and also went by "Axe," a handle he acquired for his liberal use of the goal stick to clear traffic from the front of his net. The Ottawa native also came with a reputation for being a good puck handler and for his eccentric behavior on and off the ice.

On Friday, 2 February, the Jets and Oilers went at it again at the Arena and the Jets picked up right where they left off on Wednesday night. They scored the game's first two goals and held the Oilers down for the rest of the evening. When the game ended, the Jets were full marks for a 4-2 victory that gave them a share of first place with the Nordiques. Sullivan scored a pair of goals and the Jets limited the Oilers to only 21 shots on Mattsson, who was far less busy than he had been two nights earlier. The only blemish on the night occurred in the third period, when Gray had to be taken off the ice on a stretcher after a whiplash and he had to spend the night in hospital.

The well-rested Stingers flew in to play the Jets on Sunday night at the Arena. Before the game, the Stingers were jolted by the news that winger Rick Dudley had been sold to the Buffalo Sabres and the Jets didn't help their state of mind by jumping out to a 3-1 first period lead. The Jets continued to pour it on and Daley was solid in thwarting any potential comeback hopes the Stingers may have entertained. The game ended with the final score of 8-1 in favor of the Jets, who kept pace with the Nordiques atop the league standings. Nilsson scored three times in the rout and Sullivan chipped in with a pair to lead the Jets' attack.

Dudley's Return

The Stingers sold Rick Dudley to the Buffalo Sabres prior to their game against the Jets on 4 February 1979, but Dudley would later return to Winnipeg as a Jet. On 12 January 1981, the Jets claimed Dudley off waivers from the Sabres and he finished the season in a Jets' uniform, scoring five goals in 30 games. The next season, Dudley spent seven games in the AHL before retiring.

Winners of their last three games, the Jets played host to the Bulls on Wednesday night in the Bulls' first visit to the Arena since late October. Both teams played it close to the vest, but the opportunistic Jets scored in each of the first two periods to take a 2-0 lead to the third and they held on for a 3-2 victory. Lukowich scored two of the Jets' three goals to raise his season total to 41, but, more importantly, the two points enabled the Jets to take sole possession of first place, one point ahead of the Whalers and two ahead of the Nordiques.

The next day, the 25-19-6 Jets left for Cincinnati and made their way through a major snowstorm to begin a five-game road trip on Friday night. The Stingers scored three times in the first period to seize control of the contest and the Jets offered little resistance in an eventual 4-0 defeat. Mike Liut only had to make 18 saves to become the first goaltender to blank the Jets this season, while Daley played admirably well in a losing cause.

The Jets moved on to Springfield for a first-place showdown with the Whalers on Saturday night. The Whalers scored the first period's only goal and they blew open a tight game in the second. The Jets took chances to try and get back into the game, but goaltender Al Smith answered each challenge and the Whalers countered with three goals in the third period to turn the game into a rout. The 7-2 defeat bumped the Jets out of first place and it was their third straight loss at the Springfield Civic Center.

On Sunday, the Jets returned to Cincinnati to play the Stingers again on Wednesday, 14 February. The Jets rebounded nicely off the pair of disappointing defeats and jumped out to a 3-0 first period lead. From there, the checkers shone and when the Stingers were able to break through, Mattsson replied with a big save. The end result was a 5-1 victory that put the Jets back into first place, one point ahead of the Whalers, who lost by a score of 7-4 to the Bulls in Springfield.

Two nights later, the Jets continued their road trip in Birmingham against the Bulls, who were returning from a four-game road trip. After a scoreless first period, the Jets dominated the second, but they only had a 1-0 lead to show for their efforts, thanks to the stellar work of goaltender Pat Riggin, who had withstood the 19-shot barrage largely unscathed. In the third, the Bulls capitalized on a couple of mistakes by the Jets to snatch the lead away and the Jets could not get the equalizer, allowing the Bulls to make off with a 2-1 win.

The Jets finished up their road trip on Saturday night with their third trip to Cincinnati in just over a week. Lukowich opened the scoring in the game's first minute, but the Stingers both outskated and outscored the tired Jets. The Stingers ran up a 5-2 lead late in the third period and though the Jets fought back at the end, they fell just short and the Stingers took the game by a score of 6-4. Lukowich scored again in the third period for his second of the night and 44th of the season, but it didn't prevent the loss that knocked them back into a second-place tie with the red-hot Oilers.

The next evening, the Jets were back on the ice at home against the Whalers. The Jets kept the game close through two periods, but the Whalers scored twice in the first half of the third period to extend their 2-1 lead to 4-1. The harder the Jets tried to get back in the game, the more chances they left for the Whalers, who added three more goals to make the final score 7-1. On their way out, many of the 9,426 spectators turned their attention to Larry Hillman and were calling for his dismissal in the wake of the Jets' fifth loss in their last six games.

On Tuesday night, the Jets were back in Cincinnati one more time, marking their fourth visit to the Queen City in 12 days. The game was evenly played through the midway point of the third period, but the Stingers broke a 2-2 tie with three goals in the span of four and a half minutes and the Jets passively went through the motions for the remainder of the game. The 5-2 defeat was the Jets' fourth straight loss and combined with the Oilers' victory over the Whalers, the Jets fell back into third place, only two points ahead of the fourth-place Nordiques in the standings.

The Jets returned home in time for a game the following evening against the Whalers. The Jets busted out of their malaise and took it to the Whalers, using a pair of goals in each of the second and third periods to post a convincing 5-2 victory. Morris Lukowich and Steve West scored twice, while Daley made 32 saves during a strong outing in making his second straight start in the Jets' goal. West was playing his second game since both he and Bill Davis were recalled from the AHL.

The next day, the Jets left for Birmingham to play the Bulls on Friday night. The Bulls came out flying and scored five goals in the first period, then added four more over the next two periods to make the final score 9-1. The Jets were every bit as bad as the score indicated, and both Daley and Mattsson were treated as rudely by their own teammates as they were by the Bulls. Davis' first period shot from the point went in off Serge Beaudoin for the Jets' only goal and his first goal as a Jet, but there was nothing else from this game to celebrate from a Jets' perspective.

In Springfield the next day, the Jets held a team meeting to discuss their sagging fortunes before returning to the ice on Sunday night against the Whalers. Making amends for their bad outing in Birmingham, the Jets, to a man, were much better and showed a strong competitive spirit. The Jets took the lead for good when Lukowich scored in the final minute of the second period and after splitting four goals in the third, Sullivan's empty-net marker with 40 seconds left in regulation time sealed a well-earned 7-5 victory. Lukowich's third goal of the game and 50th of the season proved to be the game-winner as the Jets stayed above the .500 mark and moved one point ahead of the fourth-place Nordiques in the logjam atop the league standings.

Club 50

With a hat trick against the Whalers on 25 February 1979, Morris Lukowich raised his goal total for the season to 50, making him only the third player in Jets' history to score at least 50 goals in a season. Bobby Hull scored 51, 53, 77, and 53 goals in each of his irst four seasons as a Jet, and Anders Hedberg scored 53, 50, 70, and 63 goals in his four seasons in Winnipeg.

Joe's Last Win

Joe Daley stopped 34 shots as the Jets defeated the Whalers by a score of 7-5 in Springfield on 25 February 1979. The win was Daley's 167th regular season victory as a Jet and it would prove to be his last. However, his 167 regular season and 30 playoff wins would each stand as WHA records. Ironically, the victory would also be the last for Jets' coach Larry Hillman, who was fired two days later after the Jets were beaten by a score of 5-2 at the hands of the Birmingham Bulls.

The Jets returned to Winnipeg on Monday afternoon to open a pair of home games on the night of Tuesday, 27 February against the Bulls. The two teams traded goals in the first period, but the Bulls took control of the game in the second period against a Jets team that again showed little energy or passion. The Bulls took a 3-1 lead to the intermission and added another nine minutes into the third before Nilsson brought the Jets back to within a pair. That was the last goal that Wakely would give up, however, and the former Jet put the finishing touches on an excellent outing as his newest team completed a 5-2 victory, marking their third straight win against the Jets to the disgust of the 7,671 paying customers.

Immediately after the game, on the heels of the Jets' eighth loss in their last 11 games, Ferguson fired Hillman and the former coach then broke the news to the players. The Jets had initially hired Hillman after parting ways with the fiery Bobby Kromm and the team responded positively to Hillman's more serene, laid-back style last season, but molding the revamped roster together with the former Aeros proved to be a considerably more formidable task. Ultimately, the players didn't perform up to expectations, and Hillman paid the price with his job.

In a press conference later in the evening in his office, Ferguson announced that 43-year-old Thomas Ballantyne McVie, better known as Tom, would be taking over as Hillman's replacement. Ferguson had hired McVie on Monday and was going to have him scout NHL teams for the time being, but he decided instead to hand McVie the coaching reins right away instead of elevating assistant coach and former Jets player Bill Sutherland. Ferguson had brought in Sutherland back in December to work alongside Hillman, and now he would be working alongside McVie.

McVie came to the Jets after two and a half seasons behind the bench of the expansion Washington Capitals, where he had finished second in the balloting for the coach of the year award in 1976-1977 to Scotty Bowman of Montreal. As a player, he was a veteran of 18 minor league seasons and got into coaching late in his playing career, eventually working his way up the ranks to the NHL. The native of Trail, British Columbia and the son of a miner had met Ferguson at an early age when the two were defense partners on their lacrosse team and they remained friends even as their careers took different paths. As a coach, McVie was known as a stern disciplinarian who worked his teams hard and ensured that they would be in top-notch condition. McVie also had a Winnipeg connection since his wife, the former Arlene MacFarlane, a one-time member of the Ice Follies touring figure skating show, was born in Winnipeg.

Led by their new coach, the Jets were back on the ice on Friday night against the Whalers. Kent Nilsson opened the scoring less than two minutes after the drop of the puck, but the lead didn't last long and the Whalers had their way with the wilting Jets, who hadn't looked any better than they had on Wednesday night. Despite missing a number of key players from their lineup, the Whalers cruised to a 4-1 victory before a near-capacity crowd of 9,795 that wasn't any more impressed with the Jets under McVie than they had been with Hillman behind the bench.

Did You Know?

On 2 March 1979, the Jets lost to the New England Whalers by a score of 4-1 at the Winnipeg Arena. The game not only marked the debut of new coach Tom McVie behind the Jets' bench, but it was also the last time the Jets would face Bill Dineen, who was then coaching the Whalers. Dineen had been the Aeros' coach for all six seasons of the franchise's existence before signing with the Whalers to begin the 1978-1979 season. He had faced the Jets in both regular season and playoff competition more often than any other coach during their seven seasons in the WHA.

McVie put his players to work over the next few days before their next game in Birmingham on Tuesday night. Gary Smith got his first start in net for the Jets and promptly gave up three goals in the first period, but the Jets rallied with two late goals to shrink the Bulls' lead to 3-2 before intermission. Willy Lindstrom's goal early in the second tied the game and the Jets stayed in the game with a much more representative effort, but the Bulls scored early in the third period to take the lead for the third and final time and went on to a 5-4 victory. The loss was the Jets' second in as many games under McVie's command and they fell under the .500 mark once again. In addition to losing the game, the Jets also lost John Gray during the second period with a shoulder separation, putting him on the shelf indefinitely.

The next evening, the Jets met the Stingers in their seventh and final visit of the regular season to Cincinnati. This time, the Jets got off to a quick start and scored the only three goals of the first period. The Stingers tried battling back, but the Jets didn't buckle under the pressure and captured a 5-3 win. Nilsson's hat trick led the way offensively, and Mattsson made 32 saves for the Jets, who won for the first time in four games and for the first time under McVie. The win enabled the fourth-place Jets to move back to within two points of the third-place Whalers and seven points of the first-place Oilers.

Upon their return the Winnipeg, the relief of their victory in Cincinnati was quickly tempered when the Jets, along with the Nordiques, Oilers and Whalers, found out that the NHL had narrowly turned down their expansion proposal. The NHL was originally supposed to vote on the matter back in January, but they had opted to defer the issue until their March meeting in Key Largo, Florida. The proposal called for each of the four teams to pay a total of $6 million for entry into the NHL and to pay off the remaining WHA teams, but the vote fell just short of the ¾ majority needed to pass. The Toronto Maple Leafs, Montreal Canadiens, Vancouver Canucks, Los Angeles Kings and Boston Bruins were reported to be the teams that cast the dissenting votes that killed the proposal.

The vote by the NHL Board of Governors surprised most people in the hockey world and left the four rejected WHA teams and their fans nothing short of outraged. In Winnipeg, the community's anger was directed at Molson Breweries, owners of the Canadiens.

The Jets terminated Molson's sponsorship of the nightly Three Star Awards and removed Molson's name from the Three Star Room in the basement of the Winnipeg Arena. The brewery had furnished the room and the Jets subsequently offered to buy the furniture from them. Winnipeggers also did their part and stopped purchasing Molson's products en masse to show support for the Jets.

Come Sunday night, the Jets switched their focus back to the ice and began a five-game home stand against the Nordiques, who flew in to play their third game in as many nights. With a spirited effort in defiance of the NHL's rejection, the Jets jumped all over the Nordiques and ran up a 4-0 lead before the visitors countered with a pair of goals two minutes apart. The determined Jets pressed on and turned the game into a rout early in the third period, delighting the crowd of 9,675 with a 7-2 victory. The biggest cheer of the night, however, came in the third period when the announcement was made inviting fans to remain seated after the game for the selection of the three stars. Fans in the crowd had noticed that the former title sponsor's name was conspicuously absent from the announcement and with their applause, they enthusiastically endorsed the Jets' decision to cut ties with Molson's.

After the game, history was made when Sheree Walder, a sportscaster with University of Manitoba radio station CJUM, visited the Jets' dressing room, becoming the first female reporter to tread down the path that had been traditionally a male-dominated field. Players were surprised to see her and they were forced to scramble for towels to cover themselves.

The next day, reports came out that the boycott of Molson's products was having a real effect on the brewery's bottom line and that, not coincidentally, the NHL announced that there would be more merger talks scheduled later in the month. Meanwhile, the WHA had begun preparations to continue on without the NHL and it announced that all six teams were committed to the league for next season. The league also began looking at the possibility of an expansion to 10 teams with a European division and an interlocking schedule with the North American teams.

The Jets also brought in 19-year-old junior defenseman John Gibson for a tryout. His size had given him a commanding presence on the blue line of the Niagara Falls Flyers, but the team had suspended him after a disagreement with coach Bert Templeton. In addition to his size, Tom McVie was also impressed with his shot during his first workouts with the team.

The Jets and Nordiques went at it again on Wednesday, 14 March at the Arena, but the Nordiques took full advantage of the rest and turned the tables on the Jets right from the outset. The Nordiques scored twice early in the first period to grab a 2-0 lead, while goaltender Jim Corsi rebounded from an off night on Sunday and kept his team in front. The Jets broke through and tied the game with a pair of second period goals, but early in the third period, the Jets gave up a crushing shorthanded goal that proved to be the game-winner. Alain Cote picked up the puck after it bounced over Kent Nilsson's stick and he took off down the ice and beat Mattsson to make the score 3-2 in favor of the Nordiques. Serge Bernier's goal with just five and a half minutes to play sealed the win and the Nordiques earned a split of the back-to-back series with a 4-2 victory. The Jets, to their credit, gave it a good effort, but they played just well enough to lose.

The third of five straight home games took place on Friday night with the Stingers providing the opposition. The Jets had little trouble in staking themselves to a 4-0 lead by the midway point of the game, but the Stingers fought back in the third period and nearly tied the score. However, the Jets hung on to their lead and Rich Preston's empty-net marker in the final minute of the game preserved an eventual 5-3 victory. The Jets' third win in their last four games moved them to within three points of the third-place Whalers and allowed them to keep pace with the first-place Oilers, who remained eight points ahead of the Jets.

The Jets wound up the weekend with a Sunday night visit from the Bulls. Both teams slogged through the first two periods, but the Jets turned it on in the third period and Bill Lesuk's goal three minutes in broke a 2-2 tie. Roland Eriksson added an insurance marker late in the period and the Jets persevered to emerge with a 4-2 win. The unheralded Paul Terbenche fearlessly threw himself in front of a number of Bulls' shots during the game and was the defensive star for the Jets, who held the Bulls to only 20 shots. The most entertaining part of the otherwise dull game took place behind the Bulls' bench, where a fan got into an altercation with coach John Brophy. A nearby police officer had to restrain Brophy several times, but no one was hurt in the affair.

On Monday evening, the Jets were on hand at the Booster Club's sixth annual Awards Night at the Winnipeg Inn. Ken "Friar" Nicolson, the voice of the Jets, was the Master of Ceremonies for the evening where a number of players were honored. Markus Mattsson was chosen as the rookie of the year, Peter Sullivan was named the team's most improved player, Lukowich was selected as the most exciting player, Terbenche was tabbed as the unsung hero, and the most valuable player award went to Terry Ruskowski. More than 400 people were on hand for the $20 per plate dinner and festivities, including original Jet Norm Beaudin and his wife, Linda.

While representatives of the two leagues were meeting in Chicago to reconsider the expansion proposal, the Jets hosted the league-leading Oilers on Wednesday night. The Jets looked sluggish from the outset and the Oilers capitalized on every mistake the Jets made. The visitors scored four times in the second period to blow the game wide open and two third period goals from the Jets did nothing to affect the game's outcome. After the final buzzer, the Oilers celebrated a 7-4 victory in their last regular season visit to Winnipeg that widened their lead over the fourth-place Jets to 10 points. One casualty from the game was referee Peter Moffat, who had suffered a broken jaw after a first period collision involving a linesman, Paul Terbenche, and John Hughes of the Oilers. Moffat was taken to nearby Grace Hospital, while linesman Ron Asselstine took over as the referee for the rest of the game.

Off the ice, talks between the two leagues continued to heat up in Chicago over the next day. After much bickering between and within both camps, a proposal passed that would allow for the Jets, Oilers, Nordiques, and Whalers to become members of the NHL for next season and bring an end to the seven-year run of the WHA. The Jets would be placed in the Smythe Division along with the Oilers, Chicago Blackhawks, St. Louis Blues, Vancouver Canucks and Colorado Rockies and the new 21-team NHL would regain its monopoly on major pro hockey. The news was met with a combination of relief and jubilation among the four future NHL teams, but entry into the more established league came at a steep price.

In addition to the high financial price, which included a $6 million franchise fee to join the NHL and $1.5 million per team to buy out the Stingers and Bulls and wind up the WHA, the existing NHL teams would be allowed to reclaim any player on a WHA roster that they had rights to. The four WHA teams would be allowed to protect two skaters and two goaltenders and could retain any player whose rights were not held by an NHL team, but all four clubs, including the Jets, would have their rosters decimated. No fewer than 14 members of the current Jets' roster had their rights held by an NHL team and the Jets would be left in the unenviable position of having to choose which four players to protect to begin their new NHL franchise with.

Jets players whose rights were held by an NHL team

Player	NHL Team
Scott Campbell	St. Louis Blues
Kim Clackson	Pittsburgh Penguins
Joe Daley	Minnesota North Stars
Glenn Hicks	Detroit Red Wings
Bobby Hull (retired)	Chicago Blackhawks
Barry Long	Detroit Red Wings
Morris Lukowich	Pittsburgh Penguins
Paul MacKinnon	Washington Capitals
Markus Mattsson	New York Islanders
Kent Nilsson	Atlanta Flames
Rich Preston	Chicago Blackhawks
Terry Ruskowski	Chicago Blackhawks
Paul Terbenche	Colorado Rockies
Steve West	Washington Capitals
Dale Yakiwchuk	Montreal Canadiens

After the dust settled on the groundbreaking news out of Chicago, the Jets returned their focus to hockey and flew to Edmonton for a rematch with the Oilers on Friday, 23 March. The Jets again fell behind early, but despite some sloppy play in their own end of the ice, they kept the score within reach and they scored twice late in the second period to tie the game at 4-4. In the third, Ruskowski broke the deadlock with just 83 seconds to play before the end of regulation time and Lukowich completed his hat trick with 10 seconds left to complete a come-from-behind 6-4 victory that left the fourth-place Jets three points back of both the Nordiques and Whalers. Smith made his second start as a Jet and stopped 36 shots to earn his first victory as a Jet and first of the season after 14 appearances.

Back home, the Jets welcomed a touring Finnish national team on Sunday afternoon at the Arena. The game didn't count in the standings, but the Jets still pulled out a 4-3 overtime win over the Finns, who had finished their three-game swing of WHA cities with a win and a pair of losses.

The Jets' next league game came on Wednesday night when they played the Stingers for the 15th and final time during the regular season. The Jets were porous in their own end in the early going, but Gary Smith kept them in the game with some key stops and Long scored late in the second period to give the Jets the lead for good. Preston and Lukowich added third period markers to widen the lead and the Jets went on to post a 6-3 win. Lukowich's third period goal was his second of the game and gave him 59 on the season for the victorious Jets, who moved to within a single point of the third-place Whalers. The Stingers, meanwhile, remained only two points ahead of the Bulls in the race for the fifth and final playoff position as both clubs continue to battle right to the end of their last season.

Winners of their last three games, the Nordiques flew in to meet the Jets on Friday night at the Arena on the day that the NHL officially put its stamp of approval on the admittance of both teams along with the Oilers and Whalers for next season. The crowd of 10,194 began the evening by giving the returning Lars-Erik Sjoberg a standing ovation. It was Sjoberg's first game action since rupturing his Achilles tendon in late September and after resuming skating in early January, he was at last able to rejoin his teammates as they headed down the home stretch before the start of the playoffs.

The two teams proceeded to put on a show and they kept up the hectic pace for the entire evening, but the first goal didn't come until the second period when Nordiques' sharpshooter Real Cloutier beat Smith, who was making his third straight start. At the other end of the rink, Nordiques' goaltender Richard Brodeur was masterful and he turned aside all 35 shots he faced to make Cloutier's goal stand as the game-winner. The 2-0 defeat was disheartening for the Jets, but it wasn't for a lack of effort. Sjoberg showed no ill effects in his first game and Smith also played well in the losing cause.

In addition to Sjoberg's return, the game marked the pro debut of 22-year-old St. Malo, Manitoba native Rich Gosselin. The Jets had brought Gosselin in for a tryout after he finished his 27-goal season in Switzerland. As a junior, the dimunitive Gosselin had starred for the Flin Flon Bombers, where he had scored 67 goals three seasons ago. The Montreal Canadiens took notice and selected him in the seventh round of the 1976 NHL Amateur Draft, but he went overseas to play in Switzerland instead.

Both teams flew to Quebec for the back end of the home-and-home series on Sunday night to open the month of April. This game was another wide-open affair, but unlike Friday night's goaltenders' duel, the first period featured seven goals, four of them belonging to the Jets. The Jets added three more in the second period while shutting down the Nordiques the rest of the way to capture a 7-3 victory that vaulted them over the Whalers and into third place. Lukowich and Lindstrom each scored a pair for the Jets and Smith finished his fourth consecutive start despite being speared by former Bull Gilles "Bad News" Bilodeau in the third period. Fittingly, Bilodeau left with a knee injury after Scott Campbell jumped him in coming to the defense of his goaltender.

The 35-32-6 Jets returned home for the first of a three-game home stand on Wednesday night against the struggling Whalers. With new coach Don Blackburn at the helm, the Whalers scored the only two goals of the first period, making the Jets look like the team that had dropped their last four games. Hostilities boiled over in the second period as three fights broke out, but the Whalers got the only goal and took a 3-0 lead to the third period. The Jets rebounded and Lindstrom's pair of goals made a game of it, but it was a case of too little, too late, as the Whalers went on to a 4-2 win that allowed them to leapfrog over the Jets and regain sole possession of third place. Smith sat out what would have been his fifth start in a row because he had missed a team meeting earlier in the day. He was expecting a ride from a teammate, who had forgotten to pick him up, and as a result, Tom McVie had him in street clothes while Mattsson and Daley dressed as the two goaltenders.

At a press conference the following afternoon, the Jets and Molson Breweries announced a new sponsorship agreement. The deal would guarantee the Jets around $3.5 million over the next six years in exchange for their exclusive advertising and promotional rights. The Jets and Molson had quickly renewed their ties after the Molson-owned Canadiens decided to reverse their stance and vote in favor of the proposal to have the Jets join the NHL next season.

Back on the ice, the Jets hosted the Bulls on Friday night. Just as they had two nights earlier, the Jets fell behind 2-0 in the first period, but Ernie Wakely stymied their efforts to claw back into the contest in the second. Peter Sullivan scored early in the second, but that was the only goal the original Jet gave up and the Bulls pulled into sole possession of the fifth and final playoff position with a 2-1 victory. The Jets, meanwhile, remained one point back of the third-place Whalers in the race to avoid a best-of-three preliminary round series with the fifth-place finisher, likely to be either the Bulls or the Stingers.

The home stand ended with another critical matchup against the Whalers on Sunday night. Once again, the Jets were quickly looking up at a 2-0 deficit, but they scored three times to take the lead by the midway point of the first period. Kent Nilsson scored his second of the game early in the second, but the Whalers replied with two of their own to send the game to the third tied at 4-4. The Jets didn't let up and Morris Lukowich's second of the game early in the third gave his team the lead for good. Bill Lesuk's late goal sealed an eventual hard-earned 6-4 win that put them back into third place and assured them of a place in the WHA's last post-season.

The Jets flew to Edmonton for a Tuesday night game with the Oilers, who had wrapped up first place as a result of the Nordiques' loss on Monday night. The Jets jumped all over the Oilers and Lindstrom's goal four minutes into the third period gave the Jets a commanding 5-1 lead. The Oilers sprang back to life and three goals from teenage star Wayne Gretzky shrank the Jets' lead to one goal, but the Jets hung on and prevailed by a score of 6-4 to stay one point ahead of the Whalers. Lukowich scored twice and added an assist, while Smith recorded three assists, tying a WHA record for goaltenders, and also won his fifth game since seizing the starting job a short time ago.

On Wednesday night, the Jets were back at the Arena for a game against the Bulls, who came into the game deadlocked with the Stingers for the final playoff position in each of the two teams' final season. The desperate Bulls fought for their playoff lives, but the Jets matched their effort every step of the way. Both goaltenders kept the score down to a goal apiece through the first half of the game, but Rich Preston picked off an errant pass from defenseman Rob Ramage late in the second period and scored to put the Jets in front for good. The 2-1 lead held up and the win enabled the Jets to move three points ahead of the Whalers in the struggle for third place.

The Jets' last regular season WHA home game took place on Sunday, 15 April against the same Bulls, who had returned to Winnipeg after splitting a pair of games against the Oilers in Birmingham. The Jets entered the game still clinging to a one-point bulge over the Whalers, but the level of urgency for the visiting Bulls was far more critical. The Bulls needed to win and have the Nordiques beat the Stingers that evening in order to squeak into the post-season and prolong their team's existence for another day.

Before the game, the Jets handed out their traditional individual year-end awards. Markus Mattsson received the trophy from Carling O'Keefe for being the top rookie, Kent Nilsson was given the award from Ben Moss Jewellers for the best combined athletic ability and sportsmanship, and Morris Lukowich earned the Molson Three Star Award for the most three star selections. Original Jet Dunc Rousseau, the first Jet to wear number 12, was on hand to present the award to Lukowich, the last WHA Jet to wear the number. Capping the ceremony was the presentation of the Labatt's trophy for the most valuable player award to Terry Ruskowski. The crowd of 10,094 gave the Jets' inspirational leader and former Aero a standing ovation for his award, and then it was time for the game to get underway.

The Jets got the early jump on the Bulls, but the visitors, facing the prospect of their permanent elimination, didn't succumb to the pressure and they erased a 4-2 Jets' lead with two quick goals in the latter stages of the second period. Neither team could break the tie in the third, sending the game to overtime, where Smith made a couple of big saves to keep the contest going. Late in the extra period, Bulls' coach John Brophy contemplated pulling goaltender Ernie Wakely in favor of the extra attacker, but the opportunity was lost when Sullivan sent a shot between Wakely's legs to end both the game and the Bulls franchise.

The 5-4 overtime victory, combined with the Whalers' loss in Edmonton later in the evening, secured third place for the Jets and a first-round playoff matchup with the second-place Nordiques. The Whalers, meanwhile, would meet the Stingers in a best-of-three preliminary round for the right to play the first-place Oilers. Despite losing to the Nordiques, the Stingers clinched the final playoff berth thanks to the Jets' win over the Bulls.

On Wednesday night, the Jets were in Edmonton to play in the WHA's last regular season game and the Jets left a few players at home for the game that had no meaning other than for historical significance. The Ottawa Nationals had hosted the then-Alberta Oilers on 11 October 1972 and six and a half years later, the Oilers hosted the Jets to wrap up the WHA's seventh and final regular season.

Right from the early stages of the game, the Oilers had their way with the Jets, who offered only feeble resistance to what became an onslaught. Tempers boiled over as often as the Oilers pumped goals past the helpless combination of Daley and Mattsson, culminating in a stick fight between Lukowich and Steve Carlson. Both players were ejected and Lukowich had to be held back from carrying the fight to the Oilers' bench on his way off the ice. Even the coaches got into the act when they got into a shouting match.

Warmup For The Main Event

Jets' coach Tom McVie verbally sparred with Oilers' coach Glen Sather on 18 April 1979 in the last regular season WHA game, but less than five months later, McVie was involved in a more serious incident with an opposing coach.

On 6 November 1979, the Jets made their first visit to Atlanta to meet former Jet Kent Nilsson and the Flames at the Omni. In the third period, with the Flames leading by a score of 8-0, a brawl erupted and McVie removed his coat, tie and false teeth before attempting to climb over the glass partition between the benches to get at Flames' coach Al MacNeil. Arena security officials restrained McVie, who was ejected along with eight players following the fracas. The NHL subsequently suspended McVie for three games and fined him $500.

Nilsson, whose rights were reclaimed from the Jets following the 1978-1979 season, scored twice and added an assist against his former team and Gary Smith gave up six goals in the first two periods before being relieved by Pierre Hamel to start the third period.

The game ended in a 9-3 defeat, leaving the Jets with a record of 39-35-6, their worst record in four seasons. The Jets had, however, won four of their last five games and they proved that they could both beat anyone and be beaten by anyone in what was an up and down season. Sjoberg was back and healthy and Smith gave the Jets some solid goaltending as the regular season wound down.

Off-ice events dominated the next few days as the Jets prepared to open the playoffs in Quebec on Monday, 23 April. The World Hockey Players Association threatened a strike over the issues of pay and scheduling for the playoffs. The owners offered $7,000 to each player on the eventual championship team, down from the $10,000 that the Jets had received last season, and the players balked over the length of the post-season schedule. The strike was averted when the league agreed to shorten the schedule, but the Jets also had to fret about Lukowich's potential availability as a result of the incident last Wednesday night with Steve Carlson. Fearing the loss of their 65-goal scorer to a suspension, the Jets were relieved to learn that Lukowich would only be fined and not suspended. Lukowich received a $1,200 fine as the instigator, while Carlson was fined $500.

The Jets made another addition to their roster before the start of the series with the Nordiques when they inked 23-year-old winger John Markell to a multi-year contract. Markell had racked up 31 goals and 49 assists in 42 games while playing for Bowling Green State University and the native of Cornwall, Ontario would be available to suit up for the playoffs, if needed. Markell had spent four seasons at Bowling Green, where he left as their all-time leading point scorer with 102 goals and 134 assists.

After a break, the Jets opened their first round best-of-seven series in Quebec on Monday night. The two teams traded goals 29 seconds apart in the first period, but the Jets took control of the contest in the second with five goals to take a 6-2 lead to the intermission. The Nordiques scored late in the third period, but the game was well in hand and the Jets won the opening game by a score of 6-3. Bobby Guindon, last season's playoff MVP, scored twice and added an assist in the winning cause in which his team simply showed a greater desire and work ethic. The game cost Scott Campbell one of his front teeth when Gilles "Bad News" Bilodeau butt-ended him in the mouth late in the third period. With his team hopelessly out of the game, Bilodeau spent much of the third period trying to run the Jets out of the building, but though he inflicted a physical toll, the Jets still skated off with a 1-0 series lead.

Game 2 took place two nights later and the determined Jets once again jumped all over the Nordiques from the drop of the puck. The Jets scored three times in each period and used a complete team effort to bludgeon the Nordiques by a score of 9-2 that left the home team in a state of shock. Eight different scorers did the damage for the Jets, who again shook off Bilodeau's antics to grab a 2-0 lead in the series going back to Winnipeg.

On Friday night, the series resumed at the Arena before a lower-than-expected crowd of 8,209, caused by the need for people to leave the city to help fight the rising Red River floodwaters south of Winnipeg. The water had risen so high that Manitoba Premier Sterling Lyon was forced to order the evacuation of the entire Red River Valley. The Jets struggled in the early going against a more formidable foe this time around, but the Jets hung around and the game was tied at 4-4 headed to the third period. Preston scored his second of the game in the first minute of the third and the Jets held on to the slim lead until they exploded for three goals in the span of 48 seconds to turn a tight game into a rout. Lindstrom's empty-net marker late in the period closed the scoring in the 9-5 victory that gave the Jets a 3-0 lead in the series and put them one win away from their fourth consecutive trip to the AVCO World Trophy final. McVie's trademark of having his teams in top-notch condition paid off, as the Jets were the more energetic of the two teams in the decisive third period.

With an enthusiastic gathering of 10,169 behind them at the Arena, the Jets were back on the ice on Sunday night for Game 4 in the hopes of completing the sweep of the best-of-seven series with the Nordiques. The Jets left nothing to chance and came out firing on all cylinders and broke through against a stubborn Richard Brodeur with three second period goals on their way to a 6-2 thrashing that wasn't as close as the score indicated. Lindstrom scored twice and added an assist to earn a first-star selection and he finished the four-game series with six goals and three assists. McVie made history when he was named the third star of the game for his work in bringing the team together at the right time. It was the first time a Jets' coach had been named one of the game's three stars.

The Jets celebrated their series victory in a low-key fashion with a couple of cases of beer and waited patiently for their opponent in the last WHA final. The Whalers needed all three games of the best-of-three preliminary round series to eliminate the Stingers and advance against the Oilers in a best-of-seven series. The Oilers prevailed, but despite the 15-point difference between the two teams in the regular season standings, it took the maximum number of games to decide the outcome.

Nearly two weeks after sweeping the Nordiques, the Jets were back in action in Edmonton on Friday, 11 May to defend their AVCO World Trophy championship against the Oilers in Game 1 of the best-of-seven final series. Despite their long layoff, it was the Jets that got the early jump and they grabbed a 2-1 lead after the first period. The Oilers were much stronger in the second period, but Gary Smith shut the door to make the slim lead hold up. Rich Preston's second goal of the game late in the third period provided a little breathing room and the Jets took the opening game by a score of 3-1.

Two nights later in Game 2, it was Oilers' goaltender Dave Dryden's turn to shine as he held the Jets off the scoreboard for the first two periods and the Oilers went to the third period owners of the game's only goal. Undaunted, the Jets pressed on and tied the score early in the third only to have the Oilers regain their lead three minutes later. The Jets would not be denied, however, as Lukowich tied the game with eight minutes remaining and Lindstrom scored his eighth goal of the playoffs with four and a half minutes left to grab a 3-2 lead that they didn't relinquish. The Jets outlasted the Oilers in the pivotal third period to stake their claim to a 2-0 series lead going back to Winnipeg. The win was the Jets' 12th straight in post-season play, dating back to the first round of last year's playoffs when they had defeated the Bulls in five games.

On Tuesday night, the Jets were back on the ice at the Arena for Game 3 of the WHA's last championship series. Lukowich got the Jets on the board five minutes into the game with his sixth goal of the playoffs, but the Oilers replied with a barrage of their own. The Jets managed to keep the game close, but four goals in the third period from the Oilers emphatically put down any thoughts of a quick end to the series. The 8-3 defeat was by far the Jets' worst outing of the post-season and to make matters worse, they also lost Terry Ruskowski early on due to a shoulder injury.

Game 4 took place one night later inside the steaming-hot Arena, but unfortunately, Ruskowski was not among the participants. Still suffering the effects of a banged-up shoulder, Ruskowski was forced to watch from the sidelines as the Jets and Oilers plodded their way through the unseasonable mid-May heat that reached as high as 81° earlier in the day. The two teams traded goals in the first period, but the Oilers scored the only goal in the second and they took a 2-1 lead to the second intermission. In the third, the Jets had more jump than the sagging Oilers and they took advantage with two goals four minutes apart to grab the lead. Smith and his teammates made the lead stand and the 3-2 victory gave the Jets a 3-1 stranglehold on the series and moved them to within one game of their second consecutive WHA championship.

The series moved back to Edmonton for Game 5 on Friday night, where a crowd of 13,308 was in attendance to give the Oilers a boost in the hopes of keeping the series alive. The Oilers dominated from the outset and all doubts as to the game's outcome ended in the first period. Four goals in the opening frame got the Oilers out to an early lead and they kept scoring by the bushel load until the game ended. The final score was 10-2 and Tom McVie lifted Gary Smith in favor of Joe Daley midway through the game to spare him any more humiliation. Ron Chipperfield scored five times and added an assist to lead the Oilers to the victory that forced a Game 6 in Winnipeg.

One That Got Away

Brandon, Manitoba native Ron Chipperfield scored five goals against the Jets on 18 May 1979 in Game 5 of the AVCO World Trophy final. Ever since entering the league with the Vancouver Blazers in 1974, Chipperfield had been long sought after by former general manager Rudy Pilous and his name surfaced frequently in trade rumors when the Blazers had moved to Calgary. Cowboys' Coach and General Manager Joe Crozier, however, steadfastly refused to part with Chipperfield and the Oilers signed him shortly after the Cowboys folded at the conclusion of the 1976-1977 season.

Chippperfield had been a fourth-round selection of the Blazers in the 1974 WHA Amateur Draft and the former 90-goal scorer with the Brandon Wheat Kings tallied 153 goals in 369 WHA games over five seasons. His best season came in 1975-1976 when he scored 42 goals and had 41 assists in 75 games as a member of the Cowboys. Against the Jets, he scored a total of 29 regular season goals and added nine more during two playoff series.

During the summer of 1977, Chipperfield's career nearly ended prematurely when he was hospitalized in Winnipeg with a rare disease that causes inflammation in the joints of the legs. He eventually recovered, but his career did not last much longer. He remained with the Oilers after they joined the NHL, but he was traded to the Nordiques late in the 1979-1980 season and he quickly wound up in Italy, where he played for three seasons before retiring.

On Sunday night, the same two teams were back in action at a considerably less steamy Winnipeg Arena for the critical Game 6. Back in the Jets' lineup was Ruskowski, who made a courageous return after a two-game absence. The Jets' inspirational leader was still feeling the effects of his injured shoulder, but he was determined to tough it out to be there to support his teammates. He did just that in the first period, setting up both goals as the Jets grabbed a 2-0 lead. In the second period, the Jets doubled their lead with two quick goals, then they chased goaltender Dave Dryden after Barry Long's shot from outside the faceoff circle gave the Jets a 5-0 lead. The proud Oilers scored a pair in response, but Kent Nilsson's goal early in the third period squashed their comeback hopes and the Jets went on to a 7-3 victory that secured the last AVCO World Trophy championship. Willy Lindstrom scored twice to give him a total of 10 for the playoffs, but it was Rich Preston who was selected among a host of worthy candidates as the most valuable player of the post-season. For the third time, Lars-Erik Sjoberg skated to center ice to accept the AVCO World Trophy and, with his jubilant teammates not far behind, he made the victory lap in front of 10,195 spectators.

The Jets' third AVCO World Trophy championship in seven seasons, along with two more appearances in the finals, cemented their status as the dominant team of a league that had just played its last game. The last team functions were another parade down Portage Avenue through the heart of downtown, followed by a luncheon at the Winnipeg Inn, just a stone's throw away from the corner of Portage and Main, where Bobby Hull signed the contract that gave life to the new league. Uncertainty loomed as far as how badly the Jets' championship roster would be raided by the NHL over the summer, but nonetheless, the Jets and their fans savored the moment and looked forward to the day that the Jets would bring another championship to Winnipeg.

Scores and Stats

1978-1979 Winnipeg Jets (39-35-6)

Regular Season

Date	Opponent	Score	Date	Opponent	Score
13 Oct	@Birmingham Bulls	5-4*	20 Jan	@Quebec Nordiques	1-10
14 Oct	@Indianapolis Racers	6-3	21 Jan	Quebec Nordiques	3-1
15 Oct	Cincinnati Stingers	3-4	24 Jan	@Cincinnati Stingers	5-5*
18 Oct	New England Whalers	4-4*	27 Jan	@Quebec Nordiques	4-2
22 Oct	Edmonton Oilers	2-6	28 Jan	@New England Whalers	6-8
25 Oct	Birmingham Bulls	7-2	30 Jan	@New England Whalers	2-5
27 Oct	@New England Whalers	6-4	31 Jan	Edmonton Oilers	6-3
28 Oct	@Indianapolis Racers	2-3	2 Feb	Edmonton Oilers	4-2
29 Oct	Indianapolis Racers	3-3*	4 Feb	Cincinnati Stingers	8-1
3 Nov	@Edmonton Oilers	3-4*	7 Feb	Birmingham Bulls	3-2
5 Nov	Indianapolis Racers	6-2	9 Feb	@Cincinnati Stingers	0-4
7 Nov	@Quebec Nordiques	2-1	10 Feb	@New England Whalers	2-7
9 Nov	@Birmingham Bulls	5-6	14 Feb	@Cincinnati Stingers	5-1
10 Nov	@Cincinnati Stingers	2-3	16 Feb	@Birmingham Bulls	1-2
12 Nov	Quebec Nordiques	4-6	17 Feb	@Cincinnati Stingers	4-6
15 Nov	@Quebec Nordiques	2-5	18 Feb	New England Whalers	1-7
17 Nov	Cincinnati Stingers	10-6	20 Feb	@Cincinnati Stingers	2-5
19 Nov	Indianapolis Racers	5-2	21 Feb	New England Whalers	5-2
22 Nov	@New England Whalers	2-5	23 Feb	@Birmingham Bulls	1-9
23 Nov	@Indianapolis Racers	5-1	25 Feb	@New England Whalers	7-5
26 Nov	@Quebec Nordiques	2-2*	27 Feb	Birmingham Bulls	2-5
29 Nov	New England Whalers	4-2	2 Mar	New England Whalers	1-4
1 Dec	Cincinnati Stingers	5-6	6 Mar	@Birmingham Bulls	4-5
3 Dec	@Quebec Nordiques	3-5	7 Mar	@Cincinnati Stingers	5-3
7 Dec	@Indianapolis Racers	9-4	11 Mar	Quebec Nordiques	7-2
10 Dec	Quebec Nordiques	4-4*	14 Mar	Quebec Nordiques	2-4
14 Dec	Soviet All-Stars	3-4	16 Mar	Cincinnati Stingers	5-3
17 Dec	Cincinnati Stingers	6-3	18 Mar	Birmingham Bulls	4-2
22 Dec	@Edmonton Oilers	5-4	21 Mar	Edmonton Oilers	4-7
26 Dec	Edmonton Oilers	5-3	23 Mar	@Edmonton Oilers	6-4
27 Dec	@Edmonton Oilers	3-5	28 Mar	Cincinnati Stingers	6-3
1 Jan	Czechoslovakia	3-3*	30 Mar	Quebec Nordiques	0-2
7 Jan	Quebec Nordiques	3-2	1 Apr	@Quebec Nordiques	7-3
9 Jan	Edmonton Oilers	4-3*	4 Apr	New England Whalers	2-4
12 Jan	@Birmingham Bulls	3-1	6 Apr	Birmingham Bulls	1-2
13 Jan	@Birmingham Bulls	3-1	8 Apr	New England Whalers	6-4
14 Jan	@New England Whalers	4-2	10 Apr	@Edmonton Oilers	6-4
16 Jan	@Edmonton Oilers	1-3	11 Apr	Birmingham Bulls	2-1
17 Jan	Edmonton Oilers	3-6	15 Apr	Birmingham Bulls	5-4*
19 Jan	Cincinnati Stingers	2-7	18 Apr	@Edmonton Oilers	3-9

Playoffs

Date	Opponent	Score	Date	Opponent	Score
23 Apr	@Quebec Nordiques	6-3	13 May	@Edmonton Oilers	3-2
25 Apr	@Quebec Nordiques	9-2	15 May	Edmonton Oilers	3-8
27 Apr	Quebec Nordiques	9-5	16 May	Edmonton Oilers	3-2
29 Apr	Quebec Nordiques	6-2	18 May	@Edmonton Oilers	2-10
11 May	@Edmonton Oilers	3-1	20 May	Edmonton Oilers	7-3

* - overtime

Scoring

Player	Regular Season									Playoffs								
	GP	G	A	Pts	PIM	+/-	PP	SH	Shots	GP	G	A	Pts	PIM	+/-	PP	SH	Shots
Mike Amodeo	64	4	18	22	29	-1	0	0	62									
Scott Campbell	74	3	15	18	248	5	0	0	108	10	0	2	2	25		0	0	
Kim Clackson	71	0	12	12	210	-6	0	0	32	9	0	5	5	28		0	0	
Joe Daley	23	0	1	1	2		0	0	0	3	0	0	0	0		0	0	
Bill Davis	5	1	2	3	0	-2	0	0	4									
Roland Eriksson	33	5	10	15	2	-5	3	0	55	10	1	4	5	0				
John Gibson	9	0	1	1	5	1	0	0	6									
Rich Gosselin	3	0	0	0	0	-1	0	0	1									
John Gray	57	10	15	25	51	-7	6	0	91	1	0	0	0	0		0	0	
Ted Green	20	0	2	2	16	-7	0	0	13									
Bob Guindon	71	8	18	26	21	-12	0	0	130	7	2	1	3	0				
Glenn Hicks	69	6	10	16	48	-2	0	0	59	7	1	1	2	4				
Bobby Hull	4	2	3	5	0	1	1	0	12									
Bill Lesuk	79	17	15	32	44	-14	0	0	106	10	1	3	4	6				
Willy Lindstrom	79	26	36	62	22	7	11	0	206	10	10	5	15	9				
Barry Long	80	5	36	41	42	-2	0	0	180	10	2	3	5	0				
Morris Lukowich	80	65	34	99	119	26	16	0	278	10	8	7	15	21				
Paul MacKinnon	73	2	15	17	70	-3	0	0	81	10	2	5	7	4				
Markus Mattsson	52	0	1	1	4		0	0	0									
Lyle Moffat	70	14	18	32	38	-14	0	1	89	10	3	1	4	22				
Kent Nilsson	78	39	68	107	8	1	8	0	279	10	3	11	14	4				
Rich Preston	80	28	32	60	88	-5	6	1	177	10	8	5	13	15				
Terry Ruskowski	75	20	66	86	211	13	6	1	138	8	1	12	13	23				
Lars-Erik Sjoberg	9	0	3	3	2	-1	0	0	15	10	1	2	3	4				
Gary Smith	11	0	3	3	2		0	0	0	10	0	0	0	0		0	0	
Peter Sullivan	80	46	40	86	24	-6	9	2	220	10	5	9	14	2				
Paul Terbenche	68	3	22	25	12	-1	0	0	58	10	1	1	2	4				
Steve West	18	3	11	14	6	6	1	0	24	6	2	3	5	2				
Dale Yakiwchuk	4	0	0	0	0	1	0	0	1									

Goaltending

Regular Season

Goaltender	GP	Min	GA	GAA	Saves	Sv %	SO	EN	W	L	T
Joe Daley	23	1256	89	4.30	606	0.872	0	0	7	11	3
Markus Mattsson	52	2990	181	3.63	1363	0.883	0	3	25	21	3
Gary Smith	11	626	31	2.97	248	0.889	0	1	7	3	0

Playoffs

Goaltender	GP	Min	GA	GAA	Saves	Sv %	SO	EN	W	L
Joe Daley	3	36	3	4.86			0	0	0	0
Gary Smith	10	563	35	3.73			0	0	8	2

The Jets purchased a number of contracts from the defunct Houston Aeros after the 1977-1978 season:

TOP LEFT: Terry Ruskowski
TOP MIDDLE: John Gray
TOP RIGHT: Morris Lukowich

MIDDLE LEFT: Steve West
MIDDLE CENTER: Paul Terbenche
MIDDLE RIGHT: Glenn Hicks
BOTTOM RIGHT: Scott Campbell

ABOVE LEFT: Paul MacKinnon **CENTER:** Joe Daley, the last original Jet still with the team in 1978-1979. **RIGHT:** Kent Nilsson

More new faces for 1978-1979:

LEFT to RIGHT:
Mike Amodeo,
Dale Yakiwchuk
Rich Preston
and Roland Eriksson

ABOVE: Game action against the Birmingham Bulls with Glenn Hicks and Peter Sullivan swarming around the Bulls' net.

Epilogue

The last AVCO World Trophy champions garnered relatively few individual post-season awards. Kent Nilsson took home the Paul Deneau Trophy for being the WHA's most gentlemanly player, while Morris Lukowich was named a WHA Second Team All-Star.

Upon the conclusion of the AVCO World Trophy final, work began on expanding the Winnipeg Arena to add 5,200 seats. The roof was raised to add balconies on the east and west sides, while the south wall also had to be pushed back to accommodate additional seating. Steel had been ordered back in December and construction crews had their work cut out for them to make the new 15,000-seat facility ready by October in time for the Jets' first NHL game.

On the ice, the challenges were even greater. In June, as feared, NHL clubs did claw back virtually all of the players they had rights to and the Jets were only able to protect two skaters and two goaltenders. The Jets elected to protect defenseman Scott Campbell and winger Morris Lukowich as the two skaters and Markus Mattsson as the lone goaltender. The decision to protect Campbell, in particular, ahead of Terry Ruskowski or Kent Nilsson became very controversial and one that General Manager John Ferguson undoubtedly agonized over, but it was clear that the Jets would not be icing anything close to a championship-caliber team in the coming season regardless of the choices they made.

NHL clubs plucked Kent Nilsson, Terry Ruskowski, Rich Preston, Glenn Hicks, Barry Long, Kim Clackson, and Paul MacKinnon off the Jets' roster and left them left with an assorted collection of castoffs that the Jets, Oilers, Whalers and Nordiques reluctantly picked over in the NHL Expansion Draft. The Jets did retain the rights to the retired Hull and picked up a few former Cincinnati Stingers, but the new Jets roster was not impressive.

Nonetheless, the future looked bright for the new NHL franchise. The Jets had already sold more than 10,000 season tickets, and Ferguson continued to build up the organization to major league standards after years of operating subject to tighter financial constraints and with a different management structure under community ownership.

The Jets were bottom feeders in their first two seasons in the NHL, but they rose from being the worst team in NHL history to a break-even record and a second-place finish in the realigned Norris Division in their third NHL season. Though they made a quick exit from the playoffs, it looked as though the Jets were on their way back to again being a championship contending team in the near future.

The Stanley Cup contender that Ferguson had promised to deliver never materialized. In the 1984-1985 season, the Jets finished fourth overall in the 21-team NHL, only to meekly bow out in four straight games to the Edmonton Oilers in the second round of the playoffs and the Jets would never reach those heights again. Eternal mediocrity came to define the Jets franchise and it would continue long after Ferguson's dismissal on the day before Halloween in 1988. The team that had won three championships in seven WHA seasons also became known for its playoff futility. Over the course of 17 NHL seasons, the Jets won only two playoff series and never won as much as a single game beyond the first round of post-season play.

Amid the failures, the staunchly loyal Jets fans were treated to many shining individual moments. Stars like Dale Hawerchuk and Teemu Selanne dazzled many an Arena crowd, and the double-overtime marker from Dave Ellett that beat the Oilers in the 1990 playoffs will never be forgotten in the Manitoba capital.

The financial pressures as a small market team in the growing NHL began to take their toll. Two decades of calls for a new arena went unanswered and the Jets' ownership put the club up for sale. A last-ditch effort was launched to purchase the club and keep it in Winnipeg and though local businessmen banded together and ordinary citizens opened their wallets as they had in 1974, in the end, it wasn't enough. The Jets were sold to Richard Burke and Steven Gluckstern during the 1995-1996 season and they announced that Phoenix, Arizona would be the new home of the Jets next year.

On the afternoon of 28 April 1996, the Jets went down to the Detroit Red Wings at the Arena by a score of 4-1 and lost the best-of-seven Western Conference quarterfinal four games to two. After 625 WHA games and 1,400 more in the NHL, 24 seasons of Jets hockey had come to an end.

In the desert, the Arizona-based team continued to lose money and it was no more successful on the ice than it had been in Winnipeg. The new team missed the playoffs in seven of its first 12 seasons and the franchise declared bankruptcy following the 2008-2009 season. The former Jets franchise remains in Phoenix as of this writing, and in 2011 an unrelated NHL franchise began play in Winnipeg.

The franchise's soiled NHL legacy in and out of Winnipeg, however, cannot wipe away the standard of excellence that the Jets had established in the WHA. Ben Hatskin partnered with a group of pioneers that had risked millions of dollars to start a new league in defiance of many critics. The Jets led the way in revolutionizing the game when they molded a collection of North American and European players into a fast-skating, close-knit team that was among the best the game had to offer. They became the best of the WHA and they won with class and dignity. Winnipeg hockey fans will be forever indebted to all of them, and we owe it to them to never forget one of the best teams in hockey history.

Part II - Records and Miscellany

The Players

Player	Seasons played with jersey number in brackets
Mike Amodeo	1977-1978 (2), 1978-1979 (2)
Bob Ash	1972-1973 (3), 1973-1974 (3)
Ron Ashton	1974-1975 (10)
Duke Asmundson	1972-1973 (21), 1973-1974 (21), 1974-1975 (21), 1975-1976 (21)
Ken Baird	1977-1978 (26)
Norm Beaudin	1972-1973 (11), 1973-1974 (11), 1974-1975 (11), 1975-1976 (11)
Alain Beaule	1974-1975 (28)
Thommie Bergman	1974-1975 (2), 1975-1976 (2), 1976-1977 (2), 1977-1978 (2)
Milt Black	1972-1973 (19), 1973-1974 (19), 1974-1975 (19)
Frank Blum	1973-1974 (27)
Christian Bordeleau	1972-1973 (7), 1973-1974 (7), 1974-1975 (7)
Wally Boyer	1972-1973 (8)
Gary Bromley	1977-1978 (30)
Brian Cadle	1972-1973 (20)
Scott Campbell	1978-1979 (7)
Kim Clackson	1977-1978 (5), 1978-1979 (5)
Jim Cole	1976-1977 (21)
Steve Cuddie	1972-1973 (6)
Joe Daley	1972-1973 (1), 1973-1974 (1), 1974-1975 (1), 1975-1976 (1), 1976-1977 (1), 1977-1978 (1), 1978-1979 (1)
Bill Davis	1977-1978 (7), 1978-1979 (25)
Dave Dunn	1976-1977 (8), 1977-1978 (8)
Roland Eriksson	1978-1979 (19)
Mike Ford	1974-1975 (3), 1975-1976 (3), 1976-1977 (5), 1977-1978 (24, 23, 21)
John Gibson	1978-1979 (14)
Rich Gosselin	1978-1979 (27)
Jean-Guy Gratton	1972-1973 (16), 1973-1974 (16), 1974-1975 (16)
John Gray	1978-1979 (16)
Ted Green	1975-1976 (6), 1976-1977 (6), 1977-1978 (6), 1978-1979 (6)
Danny Gruen	1974-1975 (18)
Bob Guindon	1975-1976 (7), 1976-1977 (18), 1977-1978 (18), 1978-1979 (18)
Jim Hargreaves	1973-1974 (6)
Ted Hargreaves	1973-1974 (8)
Anders Hedberg	1974-1975 (15), 1975-1976 (15), 1976-1977 (15), 1977-1978 (15)

Glenn Hicks	1978-1979 (15)
Larry Hillman	1975-1976 (16)
Bill Holden	1973-1974 (28)
Larry Hornung	1972-1973 (5), 1973-1974 (5), 1974-1975 (5), 1975-1976 (5), 1977-1978 (24)
Fran Huck	1973-1974 (25), 1976-1977 (7), 1977-1978 (25, 19, 16)
Bobby Hull	1972-1973 (9), 1973-1974 (9), 1974-1975 (9), 1975-1976 (9), 1976-1977 (9), 1977-1978 (9), 1978-1979 (9)
Danny Johnson	1972-1973 (17), 1973-1974 (17), 1974-1975 (17)
Veli-Pekka Ketola	1974-1975 (12), 1975-1976 (12), 1976-1977 (12)
Dave Kryskow	1977-1978 (26,16,19)
Dan Labraaten	1976-1977 (21), 1977-1978 (21)
Curt Larsson	1974-1975 (24), 1975-1976 (30), 1976-1977 (30)
Danny Lawson	1976-1977 (11, 12)
Randy Legge	1975-1976 (7)
Bill Lesuk	1975-1976 (17), 1976-1977 (17), 1977-1978 (17), 1978-1979 (17)
Mats Lindh	1975-1976 (19), 1976-1977 (19)
Willy Lindstrom	1975-1976 (20), 1976-1977 (20), 1977-1978 (20), 1978-1979 (20)
Barry Long	1976-1977 (3), 1977-1978 (3), 1978-1979 (3)
Morris Lukowich	1978-1979 (12)
Paul MacKinnon	1978-1979 (24)
Markus Mattsson	1977-1978 (35), 1978-1979 (35)
Ab McDonald	1972-1973 (14), 1973-1974 (14)
Perry Miller	1974-1975 (8), 1975-1976 (8), 1976-1977 (25)
Lyle Moffat	1975-1976 (22), 1976-1977 (22), 1977-1978 (22), 1978-1979 (22)
Morris Mott	1976-1977 (11)
Robbie Neale	1974-1975 (10)
Kent Nilsson	1977-1978 (11), 1978-1979 (11)
Ulf Nilsson	1974-1975 (14), 1975-1976 (14), 1976-1977 (14), 1977-1978 (14)
Gerry Odrowski	1975-1976 (8)
Lynn Powis	1977-1978 (19)
Kelly Pratt	1973-1974 (24)
Rich Preston	1978-1979 (21)
Hexi Riihiranta	1974-1975 (6), 1975-1976 (18), 1976-1977 (5)
Garth Rizzuto	1972-1973 (15), 1973-1974 (15)
Dunc Rousseau	1972-1973 (12), 1973-1974 (12)
Kent Ruhnke	1976-1977 (23), 1977-1978 (23)
Terry Ruskowski	1978-1979 (8)
John Shmyr	1972-1973 (22)
Lars-Erik Sjoberg	1974-1975 (4), 1975-1976 (4), 1976-1977 (4), 1977-1978 (4), 1978-1979 (4)

Gary Smith	1978-1979 (30)
Ron Snell	1973-1974 (20), 1974-1975 (20)
Dan Spring	1973-1974 (22), 1974-1975 (22)
Ken Stephanson	1973-1974 (10)
Peter Sullivan	1975-1976 (10), 1976-1977 (10), 1977-1978 (10), 1978-1979 (10)
Bill Sutherland	1972-1973 (10), 1973-1974 (27)
Cal Swenson	1972-1973 (18), 1973-1974 (18)
Paul Terbenche	1978-1979 (23)
Gord Tumilson	1972-1973 (28)
Ernie Wakely	1972-1973 (30), 1973-1974 (30), 1974-1975 (30)
Ron Ward	1976-1977 (11)
Steve West	1978-1979 (26)
Bob Woytowich	1972-1973 (2), 1973-1974 (2), 1974-1975 (2)
Dale Yakiwchuk	1978-1979 (14)
Howie Young	1974-1975 (7)
Joe Zanussi	1972-1973 (4), 1973-1974 (4)

Team Records

Blowouts

The Jets had been on both ends of many a lopsided score over the years. Following are the games that represent their largest margins of victory and defeat.

Largest Margins of Victory

Regular Season

Date	Opponent	Score
1 Feb 1977	@Edmonton Oilers	11-1
16 Mar 1975	Edmonton Oilers	10-1
1 Nov 1974	Toronto Toros	10-1
8 Feb 1978	Birmingham Bulls	9-0
11 Jan 1978	Birmingham Bulls	11-2
17 Mar 1974	New England Whalers	10-1
10 Feb 1978	Cincinnati Stingers	10-2
14 Nov 1972	Los Angeles Sharks	8-0
16 Oct 1977	Indianapolis Racers	9-1
3 Nov 1974	Michigan Stags	11-3
29 Oct 1976	Edmonton Oilers	11-3
18 Jan 1976	New England Whalers	8-0
26 Nov 1975	@Cincinnati Stingers	11-3

Playoffs

Date	Opponent	Score
24 May 1977	Quebec Nordiques	12-3
19 May 1978	New England Whalers	10-2
27 May 1976	Houston Aeros	9-1
25 Apr 1979	@Quebec Nordiques	9-2
14 Apr 1978	Birmingham Bulls	9-3
23 Apr 1976	Calgary Cowboys	6-1
16 Apr 1978	Birmingham Bulls	8-3
16 Apr 1976	@Edmonton Oilers	7-2
18 May 1977	Quebec Nordiques	6-1
24 Apr 1977	San Diego Mariners	7-3
10 Apr 1977	San Diego Mariners	5-1
27 Apr 1979	Quebec Nordiques	9-5
29 Apr 1979	Quebec Nordiques	6-2
20 May 1979	Edmonton Oilers	7-3
21 Apr 1978	@Birmingham Bulls	5-1
20 Apr 1973	Houston Aeros	5-1
2 May 1976	Calgary Cowboys	4-0
9 Apr 1976	Edmonton Oilers	7-3

Largest Margins of Defeat

Regular Season

Date	Opponent	Score
27 Jan 1974	@Minnesota Fighting Saints	2-12
19 Dec 1973	@Houston Aeros	0-10
26 Dec 1976	Quebec Nordiques	3-12
20 Jan 1979	@Quebec Nordiques	1-10
11 Mar 1973	Cleveland Crusaders	2-11
27 Mar 1975	@Houston Aeros	0-8
11 Mar 1974	@Jersey Knights	2-10
23 Feb 1979	@Birmingham Bulls	1-9
7 Nov 1973	@New England Whalers	2-9
15 Feb 1974	@Minnesota Fighting Saints	1-7
26 Feb 1974	@Quebec Nordiques	1-7
18 Apr 1979	@Edmonton Oilers	3-9
18 Feb 1979	New England Whalers	1-7
6 Jan 1974	@Houston Aeros	1-7
4 Apr 1975	@Toronto Toros	1-7

Playoffs

Date	Opponent	Score
13 Apr 1974	@Houston Aeros	1-10
18 May 1979	@Edmonton Oilers	2-10
26 May 1977	@Quebec Nordiques	2-8
28 Apr 1977	@Houston Aeros	2-7
29 Apr 1973	@New England Whalers	2-7
22 May 1977	@Quebec Nordiques	3-8
15 May 1977	@Quebec Nordiques	1-6
15 May 1979	Edmonton Oilers	3-8
30 Apr 1976	@Calgary Cowboys	3-7
8 Apr 1974	Houston Aeros	2-5
2 May 1973	New England Whalers	4-7
6 May 1973	@New England Whalers	6-9

We Want Ten

When the Jets would start running up the score, once their total would get to nine goals, the chant of "We Want Ten" would begin echoing off the walls of the Winnipeg Arena. Following are the games in which the fans got their wish, and also when the scoreboard reached double digits on the opposite side. The Edmonton Oilers and Cincinnati Stingers were the victims of a 10-goal barrage three times each, more than any other team, while the Jets were victimized three such times by the Quebec Nordiques.

For

Regular Season

Date	Opponent	Score
17 Mar 1974	New England Whalers	10-1
1 Nov 1974	Toronto Toros	10-1
3 Nov 1974	Michigan Stags	11-3
16 Mar 1975	Edmonton Oilers	10-1
26 Nov 1975	@Cincinnati Stingers	11-3
10 Mar 1976	Quebec Nordiques	10-3
29 Oct 1976	Edmonton Oilers	11-3
23 Jan 1977	Calgary Cowboys	10-5
1 Feb 1977	@Edmonton Oilers	11-1
23 Oct 1977	Birmingham Bulls	10-3
11 Jan 1978	Birmingham Bulls	11-2
10 Feb 1978	Cincinnati Stingers	10-2
17 Nov 1978	Cincinnati Stingers	10-6

Playoffs

Date	Opponent	Score
24 May 1977	Quebec Nordiques	12-3
19 May 1978	New England Whalers	10-2

Against

Regular Season

Date	Opponent	Score
11 Mar 1973	Cleveland Crusaders	2-11
19 Dec 1973	@Houston Aeros	0-10
27 Jan 1974	@Minnesota Fighting Saints	2-12
11 Mar 1974	@Jersey Knights	2-10
29 Feb 1976	@Toronto Toros	7-11
12 Mar 1976	Quebec Nordiques	8-10
26 Dec 1976	Quebec Nordiques	3-12
20 Jan 1979	@Quebec Nordiques	1-10

Playoffs

Date	Opponent	Score
13 Apr 1974	@Houston Aeros	1-10
18 May 1979	@Edmonton Oilers	2-10

Friday The 13th

The Jets played only three times on Friday the 13th, winning twice and losing the other. Here are the games they played on that infamous date:

Date	Opponent	Score
13 Oct 1972	@Minnesota Fighting Saints	4-3
13 Jan 1978	@Houston Aeros	2-3
13 Oct 1978	@Birmingham Bulls	5-4 (OT)

The Terrible Trifecta

On 26 occasions, the Jets had to play three games in as many days. To make matters worse, the Jets had to travel to a different city for each one of the three games in all but two of those stretches. Following are all these three-game stretches that the Jets endured.

	Date	Opp	Result	Date	Opp	Result	Date	Opp	Result	W-L-T
1.	8 Nov 1972	@Que	2-3	9 Nov 1972	@Ott	4-1	10 Nov 1972	Min	1-5	1-2-0
2.	22 Jan 1975	Ind	1-3	23 Jan 1975	@Edm	3-7	24 Jan 1975	@Van	3-4	0-3-0
3.	7 Feb 1975	NE	4-5	8 Feb 1975	@Chi	3-6	9 Feb 1975	Chi	3-2	1-2-0
4.	14 Feb 1975	Hou	5-3	15 Feb 1975	Cle	5-1	16 Feb 1975	@Chi	6-3	3-0-0
5.	7 Mar 1975	@Phx	4-7	8 Mar 1975	@SD	5-6	9 Mar 1975	@Min	6-5	1-2-0
6.	21 Mar 1975	@NE	6-3	22 Mar 1975	@Chi	4-2	23 Mar 1975	Chi	4-3	3-0-0
7.	4 Apr 1975	@Tor	1-7	5 Apr 1975	@Que	5-9	6 Apr 1975	SD	5-5	0-2-1
8.	26 Nov 1975	@Cin	11-3	27 Nov 1975	@Ind	1-3	28 Nov 1975	@Tor	5-3	2-1-0
9.	30 Jan 1976	@NE	6-3	31 Jan 1976	@Cin	5-2	1 Feb 1976	@Ind	2-1	3-0-0
10.	6 Feb 1976	@Tor	7-6	7 Feb 1976	@Cle	4-4	8 Feb 1976	Cal	8-4	2-0-1
11.	27 Feb 1976	Edm	4-3	28 Feb 1976	@Que	4-3	29 Feb 1976	@Tor	7-11	2-1-0
12.	15 Oct 1976	@Edm	6-1	16 Oct 1976	@Phx	4-6	17 Oct 1976	@SD	1-3	1-2-0
13.	5 Nov 1976	Min	9-2	6 Nov 1976	@Cin	3-7	7 Nov 1976	Edm	5-2	2-1-0
14.	19 Nov 1976	@NE	7-3	20 Nov 1976	@Ind	4-8	21 Nov 1976	Cin	2-4	1-2-0
15.	3 Dec 1976	@Min	4-3	4 Dec 1976	@NE	6-2	5 Dec 1976	@Que	4-6	2-1-0
16.	1 Mar 1977	@Cal	1-6	2 Mar 1977	Que	4-3	3 Mar 1977	@Edm	4-5	1-2-0
17.	2 Apr 1977	@Bir	6-5	3 Apr 1977	Cal	6-4	4 Apr 1977	@Edm	2-6	2-1-0
18.	2 Dec 1977	@NE	1-4	3 Dec 1977	@Que	5-6	4 Dec 1977	Edm	2-3	0-3-0
19.	13 Jan 1978	@Hou	2-3	14 Jan 1978	@Ind	6-3	15 Jan 1978	Edm	3-4	1-2-0
20.	10 Feb 1978	Cin	10-2	11 Feb 1978	@Ind	5-3	12 Feb 1978	@Hou	6-5	3-0-0
21.	3 Mar 1978	Cin	1-5	4 Mar 1978	@Ind	6-8	5 Mar 1978	Hou	3-4	0-3-0
22.	13 Oct 1978	@Bir	5-4	14 Oct 1978	@Ind	6-3	15 Oct 1978	Cin	3-4	2-1-0
23.	27 Oct 1978	@NE	6-4	28 Oct 1978	@Ind	2-3	29 Oct 1978	Ind	3-3	1-1-1
24.	12 Jan 1979	@Bir	3-1	13 Jan 1979	@Bir	3-1	14 Jan 1979	@NE	4-2	3-0-0
25.	19 Jan 1979	Cin	2-7	20 Jan 1979	@Que	1-10	21 Jan 1979	Que	3-1	1-2-0
26.	16 Feb 1979	@Bir	1-2	17 Feb 1979	@Cin	4-6	18 Feb 1979	NE	1-7	0-3-0

Sunday's The Day

The Jets played more games on Sunday than on any other day of the week. During the regular season, the Jets were also the most successful on Sundays, while Friday was their most successful day of the week in the playoffs. Following is a breakdown of the Jets' record by day of the week.

Day of Week	Regular Season					Playoffs			
	Games	W	L	T	Pct.	Games	W	L	Pct.
Monday	9	2	6	1	0.278	3	2	1	0.667
Tuesday	82	45	31	6	0.585	8	5	3	0.625
Wednesday	91	46	41	4	0.527	11	8	3	0.727
Thursday	45	23	20	2	0.533	7	5	2	0.714
Friday	121	62	54	5	0.533	15	11	4	0.733
Saturday	53	27	24	2	0.528	4	1	3	0.250
Sunday	154	97	51	6	0.649	22	16	6	0.727

By The Month

The Jets enjoyed success in almost every month they played, but their best month of the regular season was October, when they got each of their seasons off to a good start. They tailed off with the onset of winter, but they warmed up with the rising temperatures. April was the only month of the regular season where the Jets posted a losing record, but their playoff record in April was stellar. Following is a listing of how the Jets fared in each month of the year.

Month	Regular Season					Playoffs			
	Games	W	L	T	Pct.	Games	W	L	Pct.
October	62	39	19	4	0.661				
November	101	50	44	7	0.530				
December	87	45	40	2	0.529				
January	90	49	36	5	0.572				
February	95	58	32	5	0.637				
March	93	51	40	2	0.559				
April	27	10	16	1	0.389	41	29	12	0.707
May						29	19	10	0.655

Monsters of Maroons Road

Though the Jets were known more for their hockey skills, there were a number of nights where fisticuffs and penalties dominated the headlines. Following are the top such games the Jets were involved in during their time in the WHA.

Date	Opponent	Score	PIM	Breakdown
12 Mar 1978	Birmingham Bulls	3-2	198	Birmingham 19 minors, 1 major, 4 misconducts, 3 game misconducts Winnipeg 10 minors, 1 major, 5 misconducts, 1 game misconduct
10 Mar 1976	Quebec Nordiques	10-3	184	Quebec 11 minors, 6 majors, 3 misconducts, 4 game misconducts Winnipeg 6 minors, 6 majors, 1 misconduct, 1 game misconduct
27 Nov 1977	Birmingham Bulls	3-4 (OT)	170	Birmingham 15 minors, 4 majors, 2 misconducts, 5 game misconducts Winnipeg 10 minors, 2 majors, 2 game misconducts

Date	Opponent	Score	PIM	Penalties
16 Apr 1978	Birmingham Bulls	8-3	156	Birmingham 13 minors, 2 majors, 3 misconducts, 1 match penalty, 2 game misconducts Winnipeg 5 minors, 2 majors, 3 misconducts, 1 game misconduct
28 Dec 1976	@Houston Aeros	3-6	129	Winnipeg 8 minors, 3 majors, 1 misconduct, 1 game misconduct Houston 9 minors, 4 majors, 2 misconducts, 2 game misconducts
5 Nov 1976	Minnesota Fighting Saints	9-2	120	Minnesota 13 minors, 4 majors, 2 misconducts, 1 game misconduct Winnipeg 7 minors, 4 majors, 1 misconduct
29 Oct 1976	Edmonton Oilers	11-3	120	Edmonton 6 minors, 3 majors, 4 misconducts Winnipeg 4 minors, 3 majors, 3 misconducts
22 Apr 1977	@San Diego Mariners	1-3	104	Winnipeg 9 minors, 5 majors, 1 game misconduct San Diego 8 minors, 5 majors, 1 game misconduct
10 Jan 1975	Quebec Nordiques	1-6	104	Quebec 7 minors, 6 majors, 2 misconducts Winnipeg 5 minors, 6 majors
28 Dec 1974	@San Diego Mariners	6-4	01	Winnipeg 6 minors, 3 majors, 1 game misconduct San Diego 7 minors, 4 majors, 2 misconducts, 1 game misconduct

Best Periods

Following is a listing of the most goals scored by the Jets in an individual period in both regular season and playoff competition:

Regular Season

Date	Opp	Score	Pd	Goals
19 Jan 1975	Cle	9-4	3	7
29 Oct 1976	Edm	11-3	1	6
16 Oct 1975	@Den	7-3	1	6
1 Feb 1977	@Edm	11-1	2	6
29 Mar 1974	Hou	7-5	3	6
4 Mar 1978	@Ind	6-8	2	5
17 Mar 1974	NE	10-1	3	5
12 Oct 1977	@Edm	7-3	3	5
10 Feb 1978	Cin	10-2	1	5
7 Dec 1973	Tor	7-4	2	5
16 Feb 1975	@Chi	6-3	1	5
26 Feb 1977	@Cin	8-6	3	5
30 Nov 1976	SD	8-2	2	5
16 Nov 1976	Que	8-4	3	5
12 Mar 1976	Que	8-10	2	5
1 Nov 1974	Tor	10-1	1	5
13 Mar 1977	Edm	9-3	2	5
3 Nov 1974	Mic	11-3	3	5

Playoffs

Date	Opp	Score	Pd	Goals
19 May 1978	NE	10-2	1	6
16 Apr 1976	@Edm	7-2	2	5
14 Apr 1978	Bir	9-3	3	5
15 Apr 1973	Min	8-5	2	5
23 Apr 1979	@Que	6-3	2	5
27 Apr 1979	Que	9-5	3	5
24 May 1977	Que	12-3	1	4
24 May 1977	Que	12-3	2	4
24 May 1977	Que	12-3	3	4
18 May 1977	Que	6-1	3	4
12 May 1978	@NE	4-1	3	4
14 Apr 1978	Bir	9-3	1	4
25 May 1976	Hou	6-3	1	4
28 Apr 1976	@Cal	6-3	3	4
27 May 1976	Hou	9-1	2	4

Conversely, following is a listing of the most goals scored against the Jets in an individual period in both regular season and playoff competition:

Regular Season

Date	Opp	Score	Pd	Goals
30 Jan 1977	@Phx	5-8	2	7
26 Dec 1976	Que	3-12	1	7
27 Jan 1974	@Min	2-12	2	6
7 Nov 1973	@NE	2-9	1	6
28 Jan 1979	@NE	6-8	2	6
6 Nov 1976	@Cin	3-7	3	6
12 Mar 1976	Que	8-10	1	6
11 Mar 1974	@Jer	2-10	2	5
19 Dec 1973	@Hou	0-10	3	5
18 Feb 1979	NE	1-7	3	5
29 Feb 1976	@Tor	7-11	3	5
19 Oct 1975	@Phx	5-6	1	5
20 Jan 1979	@Que	1-10	2	5
27 Mar 1975	@Hou	0-8	3	5
29 Dec 1974	@Hou	3-6	3	5
19 Jan 1979	Cin	2-7	3	5
23 Feb 1979	@Bir	1-9	1	5
11 Mar 1973	Cle	2-11	3	5

Playoffs

Date	Opp	Score	Pd	Goals
26 May 1977	@Que	2-8	2	6
2 May 1973	NE	4-7	3	5
28 Apr 1977	@Hou	2-7	2	5
13 Apr 1974	@Hou	1-10	1	5
6 May 1973	@NE	6-9	1	5
15 May 1979	Edm	3-8	1	4
18 May 1979	@Edm	2-10	1	4
15 May 1977	@Que	1-6	1	4
13 Apr 1974	@Hou	1-10	3	4
18 May 1979	@Edm	2-10	2	4
15 May 1979	Edm	3-8	3	4
10 Apr 1973	@Min	4-6	1	4
29 Apr 1973	@NE	2-7	1	4
22 May 1977	@Que	3-8	1	4

Take A Shot

Following are the games in which the Jets had their highest shot totals:

Regular Season

Date	Opp	Score	Shots
29 Nov 1974	Mic	7-6	54
7 Jan 1973	@Min	6-2	53
4 Nov 1973	Que	8-2	51
14 Mar 1975	Que	4-3	51
19 Jan 1975	Clev	9-4	50
5 Nov 1974	Min	6-4	50
3 Nov 1972	NY	6-9	49
3 Mar 1974	Que	8-6	49
11 Jan 1976	Ott	6-5 (OT)	49
12 Mar 1976	Que	8-10	49
24 Feb 1974	Chi	3-1	49

Playoffs

Date	Opp	Score	Shots
11 Apr 1976	Edm	5-4 (OT)	62
29 Apr 1979	Que	6-2	50
14 Apr 1978	Bir	9-3	48
9 Apr 1976	Edm	7-3	48
8 Apr 1973	Min	5-2	47
25 Apr 1976	Cal	3-2	45
6 May 1973	@NE	6-9	44
16 Apr 1978	Bir	8-3	44
24 May 1977	Que	12-3	42
11 Apr 1973	@Min	3-2 (OT)	41
20 Apr 1977	SD	3-0	41

Conversely, these are the games in which the Jets yielded the most shots:

Regular Season

Date	Opp	Score	Shots
29 Nov 1974	Mic	7-6	53
9 Mar 1974	@Chi	4-5 (OT)	52
4 Apr 1975	@Tor	1-7	52
27 Jan 1974	@Min	2-12	51
12 Mar 1975	@Que	3-5	50
22 Mar 1975	@Chi	4-2	50
18 Nov 1974	@Edm	3-5	50
2 Feb 1975	@Min	4-5 (OT)	50
15 Feb 1974	@Min	1-7	49
20 Feb 1974	@Edm	1-4	49
6 Nov 1976	@Cin	3-7	49

Playoffs

Date	Opp	Score	Shots
13 Apr 1974	@Hou	1-10	44
15 Apr 1973	Min	8-5	42
18 May 1979	@Edm	2-10	41
24 Apr 1973	@Hou	4-2	40
26 Apr 1977	@Hou	4-3 (OT)	38
28 Apr 1977	@Hou	2-7	38
8 Apr 1974	Hou	2-5	35
19 Apr 1978	@Bir	2-3	35
11 Apr 1973	@Min	3-2 (OT)	34
15 May 1977	@Que	1-6	34

Following are the individual periods in which the Jets had their highest shot totals:

Regular Season

Date	Opp	Score	Pd	Goals
2 Apr 1977	@Bir	6-5	1	27
29 Oct 1972	Hou	5-3	3	25
12 Mar 1976	Que	8-10	2	25
29 Nov 1974	Mic	7-6	1	24
5 Nov 1974	Min	6-4	2	24
4 Nov 1973	Que	8-2	3	24
26 Dec 1972	Chi	3-2	2	23
4 Apr 1978	@Hou	3-6	3	23
28 Mar 1973	@Chi	4-3 (OT)	2	22
18 Feb 1975	@Bal	5-3	3	22
16 Nov 1973	Edm	3-1	2	22

Playoffs

Date	Opp	Score	Pd	Goals
11 Apr 1976	Edm	5-4 (OT)	1	24
11 Apr 1976	Edm	5-4 (OT)	3	21
14 Apr 1978	Bir	9-3	1	21
10 Apr 1977	SD	5-1	2	20
24 Apr 1977	SD	7-3	1	19
9 Apr 1976	Edm	7-3	1	18
8 Apr 1973	Min	5-2	2	17
20 Apr 1977	SD	3-0	3	17
24 May 1977	Que	12-3	2	17
8 Apr 1973	Min	5-2	1	17
23 Apr 1978	Bir	5-2	1	17
29 Apr 1979	@Que	2-6	1	17
9 Apr 1976	Edm	7-2	3	17
6 May 1973	@NE	6-9	1	17
27 Apr 1979	Que	9-5	1	17
29 Apr 1979	Que	6-2	3	17

Conversely, following are the individual periods in which the Jets yielded their highest shot totals:

Regular Season

Date	Opp	Score	Pd	Goals
22 Nov 1977	@Edm	2-4	1	25
22 Mar 1975	@Chi	4-2	1	23
30 Dec 1976	@SD	3-4	3	22
15 Oct 1978	Cin	3-4	2	22
1 Feb 1976	@Ind	2-1	2	22
28 Jan 1975	@SD	9-7	2	21
8 Mar 1975	@SD	5-6	2	21
20 Feb 1974	@Edm	1-4	2	21
3 Dec 1976	@Min	4-3	1	21
6 Feb 1976	@Tor	7-6	2	21
27 Jan 1974	@Min	2-12	2	21
18 Nov 1974	@Edm	3-5	2	21
29 Nov 1974	Mic	7-6	3	21

Playoffs

Date	Opp	Score	Pd	Goals
28 Apr 1977	@Hou	2-7	1	21
15 Apr 1973	Min	8-5	3	20
24 Apr 1973	@Hou	4-2	1	19
13 Apr 1974	@Hou	1-10	3	18
13 Apr 1974	@Hou	1-10	1	18
28 Apr 1976	@Cal	6-3	2	17
11 May 1977	@Que	2-1	2	17
18 May 1979	@Edm	2-10	1	16
26 Apr 1977	@Hou	4-3 (OT)	1	15
20 Apr 1977	SD	3-0	1	14
8 Apr 1974	Hou	2-5	1	14
16 Apr 1977	@SD	4-5	3	14
12 May 1978	@NE	4-1	3	14
19 Apr 1978	@Bir	2-3	2	14
21 Apr 1978	@Bir	5-1	3	14
15 Apr 1973	Min	8-5	2	14
3 May 1973	NE	4-3	3	14
23 Apr 1979	@Que	6-3	1	14

Venues Jets Visited

Aside from the Winnipeg Arena, where the Jets played all of their home games, following is a listing of the most popular venues where the Jets played their road games. Topping the list in both regular season and playoff competition is Le Colisee in Quebec City, followed closely behind by the Edmonton Coliseum.

Regular Season

Venue	# of Games
Le Colisee	29
Edmonton Coliseum	28
Market Square Arena	18
Riverfront Coliseum	18
Jefferson County Civic Center	15

Playoffs

Venue	# of Games
Le Colisee	6
Edmonton Coliseum	5
The Summit	5
Sam Houston Coliseum	4
Boston Garden	3
San Diego Sports Arena	3

Individual Records

Pulling The Goaltender

When trailing by one or two goals late in the third period, teams customarily pull their goaltender in favor of a sixth attacker to put on extra pressure to tie the score. The Jets used this tactic with some success, as they scored seven times with their goaltender on the bench. In five of those instances, the Jets not only tied the score, but they went on to win in overtime.

Date	Opponent	Scorer	Time	Score
10 February 1973	@Los Angeles Sharks	Dunc Rousseau	19:53	6-5 (OT)
22 March 1973	Alberta Oilers	Norm Beaudin	19:44	1-1 (OT)
11 April 1973	@Minnesota Fighting Saints	Bill Sutherland	19:15	3-2 (OT)
9 March 1975	@Minnesota Fighting Saints	Veli-Pekka Ketola	19:50	6-5 (OT)
20 March 1977	@Birmingham Bulls	Mike Ford	19:41	4-3 (OT)
13 October 1978	@Birmingham Bulls	Morris Lukowich	19:54	5-4 (OT)
18 October 1978	New England Whalers	Kent Nilsson	19:41	4-4 (OT)

The Hot Line

The "Hot Line," comprised of Bobby Hull, Ulf Nilsson and Anders Hedberg, was one of the best lines in hockey history, and certainly the best trio the Jets ever had. The following is a listing of their best games and a breakdown of their individual performances.

Date	G-A-P	Opponent	Score	Goaltender(s)	Hull	Nilsson	Hedberg
19 Jan 1975	6-8-14	Cleveland Crusaders	9-4	Gerry Cheevers	2 G, 3 A	3 A	4 G, 2 A
30 Nov 1976	5-9-14	San Diego Mariners	8-2	Ernie Wakely	1 G, 4 A	5 A	4 G
6 Feb 1976	4-9-13	@Toronto Toros	7-6	Jim Shaw/Les Binkley	1 G	1 G, 5 A	2 G, 4 A
30 Jan 1976	4-9-13	@New England Whalers	6-3	Christer Abrahamsson	2 G, 2A	5 A	2 G, 2 A
26 Nov 1975	5-7-12	@Cincinnati Stingers	11-3	Norm Lapointe/ Serge Aubry	1 G, 3A	1 G, 3A	3 G, 1 A
15 Nov 1977	5-7-12	@Quebec Nordiques	6-7 (OT)	Jim Corsi	1 G, 3A	2 G, 2A	2 G, 2A
4 Feb 1977	5-7-12	San Diego Mariners	8-2	Ken Lockett	---	1 G, 5 A	4 G, 2A
7 Mar 1975	4-8-12	@Phoenix Roadrunners	4-7	Gary Kurt	2G, 2A	4A	2G, 2A
30 Oct 1974	4-8-12	Phoenix Roadrunners	6-5 (OT)	Gary Kurt	3G, 2A	4A	1G, 2A
8 Feb 1978	5-6-11	Birmingham Bulls	9-0	John Garrett	1G, 1A	1G, 4A	3G, 1A
22 Mar 1977	5-6-11	Edmonton Oilers	8-3	Louis Levasseur	1G, 3A	2G, 2A	2G, 1A
28 Jan 1975	5-6-11	@San Diego Mariners	9-7	Ernie Wakely	2G, 2A	4A	3G
25 Feb 1975	4-7-11	Minnesota Fighting Saints	6-6 (OT)	Mike Curran	1G, 2A	1G, 2A	2G, 3A
19 Mar 1975	4-7-11	Vancouver Blazers	8-3	Don McLeod	2G, 2A	1G, 3A	1G, 2A
11 Jan 1978	4-7-11	Birmingham Bulls	11-2	Wayne Wood/ John Garrett	2G, 1A	4A	2G, 2A

The Heave-Ho

Following is a listing of the Jets who were tossed out of a game by the means of either a game misconduct or match penalty. Lyle Moffat and Ulf Nilsson were given the boot three times each during regular season play, leading the Jets, while Joe Daley was ejected twice during the playoffs, the only two-time offender in post-season play.

Player	Date	Opp
Dunc Rousseau	19 Nov 1972	@LA
Garth Rizzuto	28 Jan 1973	@Ott
Thommie Bergman	28 Dec 1974	@SD
Bobby Hull	28 Jan 1975	@SD
Lyle Moffat	10 Mar 1976	Que
Lyle Moffat	28 Dec 1976	@Hou
Veli-Pekka Ketola	27 Jan 1977	@Bir
Lyle Moffat	27 Jan 1977	@Bir
Ulf Nilsson	27 Jan 1977	@Bir
Dave Dunn	4 Feb 1977	SD
Perry Miller	18 Feb 1977	@Edm
Kim Clackson	23 Oct 1977	Bir
Peter Sullivan	22 Nov 1977	@Edm
Ulf Nilsson	27 Nov 1977	Bir
Willy Lindstrom	27 Nov 1977	Bir
Barry Long	11 Dec 1977	Ind
Ulf Nilsson	12 Mar 1978	Bir
Scott Campbell	19 Nov 1978	Ind
Rich Preston	27 Dec 1978	@Edm
Kim Clackson	9 Feb 1979	@Cin
Peter Sullivan	27 Feb 1979	Bir
Scott Campbell	11 Mar 1979	Que
Terry Ruskowski	18 Apr 1979	@Edm
Morris Lukowich	18 Apr 1979	@Edm

Player	Date	Opp
Joe Daley	11 Apr 1976	Edm
Ulf Nilsson	22 Apr 1977	@SD
Joe Daley	14 Apr 1978	Bir
Kim Clackson	16 Apr 1978	Bir
Scott Campbell	25 Apr 1979	@Que
Lyle Moffat	18 May 1979	@Edm

Best Individual Performances

Following is a listing of the best individual scoring performances recorded by Jets players in both regular season and playoff competition:

Regular Season

Player	Date	Opp	G	A	Pts
Bobby Hull	15 Feb 1973	@Chi	4	2	6
Perry Miller	1 Feb 1977	@Edm	4	2	6
Anders Hedberg	4 Feb 1977	SD	4	2	6
Anders Hedberg	19 Jan 1975	Cle	4	2	6
Veli-Pekka Ketola	29 Oct 1976	Edm	3	3	6
Anders Hedberg	6 Feb 1976	@Tor	2	4	6
Ulf Nilsson	4 Feb 1977	SD	1	5	6
Ulf Nilsson	6 Feb 1976	@Tor	1	5	6
Morris Lukowich	17 Nov 1978	Cin	4	1	5
Anders Hedberg	1 Feb 1977	@Edm	4	1	5
Christian Bordeleau	12 Oct 1972	@NY	4	1	5
Bobby Hull	4 Nov 1973	Que	4	1	5
Bobby Hull	18 Jan 1976	NE	3	2	5
Bobby Hull	30 Oct 1974	Phx	3	2	5
Bobby Hull	20 Jan 1974	Jer	3	2	5
Ulf Nilsson	7 Jan 1976	Tor	3	2	5
Christian Bordeleau	1 Nov 1974	Tor	2	3	5
Christian Bordeleau	25 Mar 1973	NY	2	3	5
Anders Hedberg	25 Feb 1975	Min	2	3	5
Bobby Hull	3 Nov 1974	Mic	2	3	5
Anders Hedberg	16 Nov 1976	Que	2	3	5
Willy Lindstrom	29 Oct 1976	Edm	2	3	5
Bobby Hull	19 Jan 1975	Cle	2	3	5
Bobby Hull	15 Mar 1974	Van	2	3	5
Bobby Hull	8 Mar 1973	@Que	1	4	5
Norm Beaudin	12 Jan 1973	Cle	1	4	5
Bobby Hull	30 Nov 1976	SD	1	4	5
Ulf Nilsson	8 Feb 1978	Bir	1	4	5
Ulf Nilsson	4 Feb 1978	@Cin	1	4	5
Ulf Nilsson	30 Nov 1976	SD	0	5	5
Ulf Nilsson	1 Feb 1977	@Edm	0	5	5
Fran Huck	20 Jan 1974	Jer	0	5	5
Ulf Nilsson	30 Jan 1976	@NE	0	5	5

Playoffs

Player	Date	Opp	G	A	Pts
Norm Beaudin	15 Apr 1973	Min	3	4	7
Bill Sutherland	15 Apr 1973	Min	2	4	6
Anders Hedberg	1 May 1977	Hou	3	2	5
Anders Hedberg	24 Apr 1977	SD	2	3	5
Ulf Nilsson	1 May 1977	Hou	1	4	5
Willy Lindstrom	19 May 1978	NE	3	1	4
Anders Hedberg	22 May 1978	NE	2	2	4
Christian Bordeleau	14 Apr 1974	@Hou	2	2	4
Bobby Hull	24 Apr 1977	SD	2	2	4
Kent Nilsson	19 May 1978	NE	2	2	4
Anders Hedberg	24 May 1977	Que	2	2	4
Peter Sullivan	24 May 1977	Que	2	2	4
Rich Preston	25 Apr 1979	@Que	1	3	4
Mike Ford	27 May 1976	Hou	0	4	4
Ulf Nilsson	24 May 1977	Que	0	4	4
Terry Ruskowski	20 May 1979	Edm	0	4	4
Lars-Erik Sjoberg	14 Apr 1978	Bir	0	4	4
Bobby Hull	15 Apr 1973	Min	0	4	4

Conversely, following is a listing of the best individual scoring performances recorded against the Jets in both regular season and playoff competition:

Regular Season

Player	Date	Opp	G	A	Pts
Real Cloutier	26 Dec 1976	Que	3	4	7
Marc Tardif	24 Mar 1974	@LA	4	1	5
Danny Lawson	2 Apr 1975	Van	3	2	5
Reg Thomas	20 Nov 1976	@Ind	3	2	5
Real Cloutier	12 Mar 1976	Que	3	2	5
B.J. MacDonald	23 Jan 1975	@Edm	3	2	5
Ron Buchanan	11 Mar 1973	Cle	3	2	5
Real Cloutier	23 Nov 1976	@Que	3	2	5
Real Cloutier	20 Jan 1979	@Que	2	3	5
George Morrison	27 Jan 1974	@Min	2	3	5
Wayne Connelly	27 Jan 1974	@Min	2	3	5
Rejean Houle	5 Apr 1975	@Que	2	3	5
Robbie Ftorek	17 Nov 1978	Cin	2	3	5
Don Blackburn	7 Nov 1973	@NE	2	3	5
Mike Rogers	23 Jan 1975	@Edm	2	3	5
Ron Ward	3 Nov 1972	NY	2	3	5
Robbie Ftorek	28 Nov 1976	Phx	2	3	5
Marc Tardif	20 Jan 1979	@Que	2	3	5
Rene Leclerc	20 Nov 1976	@Ind	2	3	5
Ken Linseman	28 Jan 1978	@Bir	2	3	5
Ron Climie	23 Jan 1975	@Edm	1	4	5
Serge Bernier	5 Apr 1975	@Que	1	4	5
Bobby Whitlock	24 Mar 1974	@LA	1	4	5

Playoffs

Player	Date	Opp	G	A	Pts
Ron Chipperfield	18 May 1979	@Edm	5	1	6
Larry Lund	13 Apr 1974	@Hou	4	2	6
Larry Pleau	6 May 1973	@NE	3	1	4
Tom Webster	6 May 1973	@NE	2	2	4
Real Cloutier	22 May 1977	@Que	2	2	4
Dennis Sobchuk	18 May 1979	@Edm	2	2	4
Real Cloutier	26 May 1977	@Que	1	3	4
Andre Lacroix	16 Apr 1977	@SD	1	3	4
Serge Bernier	22 May 1977	@Que	1	3	4
Tommy Williams	2 May 1973	NE	1	3	4
Tommy Williams	6 May 1973	@NE	0	4	4

The Top Opponents

No less than 389 different players scored against the Jets in their seven seasons in the WHA and 26 of those players had played with the Jets either before or after scoring against the Jets. Following is a listing of the top all-time scorers against the Jets in both regular season and playoff competition:

Regular Season

Player	G	A	Pts
Real Cloutier	33	39	72
Robbie Ftorek	29	42	71
Marc Tardif	34	36	70
Andre Lacroix	22	47	69
Serge Bernier	19	40	59
Ron Chipperfield	29	29	58
Mark Howe	24	30	54
Danny Lawson	27	24	51
Mike Rogers	18	26	44
Gordie Howe	15	28	43

Playoffs

Player	G	A	Pts
Mark Howe	11	8	19
Real Cloutier	7	9	16
Marc Tardif	8	7	15
Tim Sheehy	6	8	14
Larry Lund	5	9	14
Serge Bernier	5	8	13
Ron Chipperfield	9	3	12
Ted Taylor	5	7	12
John French	5	7	12
Tom Webster	4	7	11
Tommy Williams	2	9	11

In The Nets

The following is a listing of the goaltenders that made the most appearances against the Jets. Don "Smokey" McLeod led the way in both regular season and playoff competition, while original Jet Ernie Wakely makes the top five, including an appearance in the last regular season WHA game at the WinnipegArena while with the Birmingham Bulls.

Regular Season

Goaltender	Appearances
Don McLeod	38
Dave Dryden	34
Richard Brodeur	32
Al Smith	31
Ernie Wakely	29

Playoffs

Goaltender	Appearances
Don McLeod	11
Richard Brodeur	10
Ron Grahame	10
Dave Dryden	9
Al Smith	7

Shutouts

Following is a listing of all the shutouts the Jets were involved in. The Jets shut out their opponents 20 times during regular season play and four times in the playoffs. They were shut out themselves 12 times, all in the regular season, and never failed to register at least one goal in all the post-season games they participated in. Joe Daley, not surprisingly, led all Jets goaltenders with 12 shutouts during the regular season and two more in the playoffs. The Los Angeles Sharks were the team the Jets shut out the most often, followed by the Alberta/Edmonton Oilers and the Cincinnati Stingers. The Minnesota Fighting Saints blanked the Jets most often, with three shutouts, followed by the Quebec Nordiques, Cincinnati Stingers and Houston Aeros, with two each. Mike Curran and Richard Brodeur each shut out the Jets two times and no other goaltender registered more than one shutout against the Jets. Jack McCartan of the Minnesota Fighting Saints, who shut out the Jets on 21 December 1972, registered his only WHA shutout on that night, the second last game played at the Saint Paul Auditorium before the Fighting Saints moved into the new Saint Paul Civic Center.

Jets Shutouts – Regular Season

Date	Opponent	Score	Goaltender
14 Nov 1972	Los Angeles Sharks	8-0	Ernie Wakely
28 Nov 1972	Alberta Oilers	3-0	Ernie Wakely
11 Feb 1973	@Los Angeles Sharks	3-0	Joe Daley
16 Feb 1973	Houston Aeros	7-0	Joe Daley
14 Dec 1973	Los Angeles Sharks	1-0	Ernie Wakely
22 Dec 1973	@New England Whalers	2-0	Ernie Wakely
1 Feb 1974	Los Angeles Sharks	4-0	Ernie Wakely
18 Oct 1974	Edmonton Oilers	4-0	Joe Daley
15 Nov 1974	Indianapolis Racers	5-0	Ernie Wakely
26 Nov 1974	@Indianapolis Racers	4-0	Curt Larsson
12 Oct 1975	@Phoenix Roadrunners	4-0	Joe Daley
21 Oct 1975	Cincinnati Stingers	7-0	Joe Daley
26 Oct 1975	Phoenix Roadrunners	5-0	Joe Daley
30 Oct 1975	Cincinnati Stingers	4-0	Joe Daley
18 Jan 1976	New England Whalers	8-0	Joe Daley
14 Nov 1976	@Calgary Cowboys	2-0	Joe Daley
8 Mar 1977	San Diego Mariners	5-0	Joe Daley
15 Mar 1977	Edmonton Oilers	7-0	Joe Daley
8 Feb 1978	Birmingham Bulls	9-0	Gary Bromley
18 Feb 1978	@Cincinnati Stingers	4-0	Joe Daley

Jets Shutouts - Playoffs

Date	Opponent	Score	Goaltender
22 Apr 1973	Houston Aeros	2-0	Ernie Wakely
26 Apr 1973	@Houston Aeros	3-0	Ernie Wakely
2 May 1976	Calgary Cowboys	4-0	Joe Daley
20 Apr 1977	San Diego Mariners	3-0	Joe Daley

Shutouts by Opponents – Regular Season

Date	Opponent	Score	Goaltender
1 Nov 1972	@Minnesota Fighting Saints	0-3	Mike Curran
21 Dec 1972	@Minnesota Fighting Saints	0-3	Jack McCartan
19 Dec 1973	@Houston Aeros	0-10	Don McLeod
28 Feb 1974	@Toronto Toros	0-3	Gilles Gratton
1 Mar 1974	Minnesota Fighting Saints	0-4	Mike Curran
27 Mar 1975	@Houston Aeros	0-8	Ron Grahame
2 Nov 1975	Quebec Nordiques	0-1	Richard Brodeur
6 Jan 1976	@Calgary Cowboys	0-5	Wayne Wood
27 Jan 1977	@Birmingham Bulls	0-3	John Garrett
11 Feb 1977	@Cincinnati Stingers	0-4	Jacques Caron
9 Feb 1979	@Cincinnati Stingers	0-4	Mike Liut
30 Mar 1979	Quebec Nordiques	0-2	Richard Brodeur

Playmakers From The Crease

The following is a listing of all the points recorded by Jets goaltenders, as well as goaltenders that recorded points while playing against the Jets. Gary "Suitcase" Smith had the most prolific game as a scorer, setting up no fewer than three goals on 10 April 1979 as the Jets defeated the Oilers by a score of 6-4 in Edmonton. Joe Daley had the highest regular-season assist total, recording four points in the 1976-1977 season, and he also added one more in the playoffs that year.

Jets Goaltenders

Regular Season

Goaltender	Date	Opp	Scorer
Joe Daley	8 Feb 1973	@Hou	Bobby Hull
Joe Daley	31 Mar 1974	Van	Bobby Hull
Joe Daley	1 Dec 1974	Que	Anders Hedberg
Curt Larsson	24 Jan 1975	@Van	Anders Hedberg
Curt Larsson	16 Nov 1975	Ind	Peter Sullivan
Joe Daley	23 Nov 1975	@NE	Peter Sullivan
Joe Daley	31 Oct 1976	SD	Ulf Nilsson
Curt Larsson	9 Nov 1976	NE	Dan Labraaten
Joe Daley	16 Nov 1976	Que	Anders Hedberg
Joe Daley	6 Feb 1977	Cal	Peter Sullivan
Joe Daley	27 Feb 1977	NE	Peter Sullivan
Joe Daley	13 Dec 1977	Cze	Anders Hedberg
Joe Daley	11 Jan 1978	Bir	Ted Green
Gary Bromley	28 Mar 1978	@Hou	Bob Guindon
Markus Mattsson	25 Oct 1978	Bir	Lyle Moffat
Gary Smith	10 Apr 1979	@Edm	Rich Preston
Gary Smith	10 Apr 1979	@Edm	Morris Lukowich
Gary Smith	10 Apr 1979	@Edm	Morris Lukowich
Joe Daley	18 Apr 1979	@Edm	Peter Sullivan

Playoffs

Goaltender	Date	Opp	Scorer
Joe Daley	23 Apr 1976	Cal	Willy Lindstrom
Joe Daley	18 May 1977	Que	Anders Hedberg
Joe Daley	14 Apr 1978	Bir	Bob Guindon
Gary Smith	27 Apr 1979	Que	Morris Lukowich

Opposing Goaltenders

Regular Season

Goaltender	Date	Opp	Scorer
Jack Norris	12 Oct 1973	@Edm	B.J. MacDonald
Gary Kurt	03/11/74	@Jer	Gene Peacosh
Don McLeod	2 Apr 1975	Van	Danny Lawson
Gary Kurt	19 Oct 1975	@Phx	Robbie Ftorek
Wayne Wood	29 Feb 1976	@Tor	Gavin Kirk
John Garrett	23 Mar 1976	@Tor	V. Nedomansky
Wayne Rutledge	27 Mar 1977	@Hou	Larry Lund
Ken Broderick	4 Apr 1977	@Edm	Bill Flett
Don McLeod	7 Apr 1977	@Cal	Butch Deadmarsh
Jim Corsi	11 Nov 1977	Que	Marc Tardif
Mike Liut	3 Mar 1978	Cin	Greg Carroll
Richard Brodeur	12 Dec 1978	Que	Real Cloutier
Al Smith	30 Jan 1979	@NE	Andre Lacroix
Al Smith	10 Feb 1979	@NE	Mike Antonovich

Playoffs

Goaltender	Date	Opp	Scorer
Jack McCartan	15 Apr 1973	Min	Ted Hampson
Don McLeod	14 Apr 1974	@Hou	John Schella
Ron Grahame	28 Apr 1977	@Hou	Mark Howe
Louis Levasseur	27 Apr 1979	Que	Real Cloutier

Bad Boys

Following is a listing of the penalty minute leaders among opposing players in games against the Jets.

Regular Season

Player	PIM	Breakdown
Curt Brackenbury	98	19 minors, 4 majors, 3 misconducts, 1 match
Ron Busniuk	94	27 minors, 8 majors
John Hughes	89	27 minors, 1 major, 3 misconducts
Gord Gallant	87	16 minors, 7 majors, 1 misconduct, 1 game misconduct
Paul Baxter	87	21 minors, 5 majors, 2 misconducts
Al Hamilton	87	31 minors, 1 major, 2 misconducts
Frank Beaton	86	13 minors, 4 majors, 2 misconducts, 2 game misconducts
Gilles Bilodeau	83	19 minors, 7 majors, 1 game misconduct
Doug Barrie	83	24 minors, 7 majors
Brad Selwood	82	26 minors, 2 misconducts, 1 game misconduct

Playoffs

Player	PIM	Breakdown
Dave Hanson	48	4 minors, 4 majors, 1 misconduct, 1 game misconduct
Serge Beaudoin	46	8 minors, 3 misconducts
Gilles Bilodeau	42	6 minors, 4 majors, 1 match
Larry Lund	39	12 minors, 1 major, 1 misconduct
Terry Ruskowski	34	12 minors, 2 majors
Curt Brackenbury	30	10 minors, 1 misconduct
Ted Taylor	30	15 minors
John Schella	29	12 minors, 1 major
Gordie Howe	29	7 minors, 1 major, 1 misconduct
Ray Adduono	26	3 minors, 2 majors, 1 game misconduct
Dave Hunter	26	8 minors, 1 game misconduct

For Openers

On 24 occasions over seven seasons, a Jet opened the scoring in two or more consecutive games. Bobby Hull, as expected, did it the most often, with seven such streaks. Hull was also the only Jet to open the scoring in four consecutive games, when he scored the first goal in games between 18-27 March 1977. Following is a listing of all game-opening scoring streaks recorded by a Jet.

Player	Dates
Christian Bordeleau	8 Mar 1973 @Que 10 Mar 1973 @NY
Norm Beaudin	26 Apr 1973 @Hou 29 Apr 1973 @NE 2 May 1973 NE
Bobby Hull	3 May 1973 NE 5 May 1973 @NE
Ron Snell	31 Oct 1973 @Cle 2 Nov 1973 NY
Ulf Nilsson	15 Oct 1974 @Van 18 Oct 1974 Edm
Bobby Hull	19 Jan 1975 Cle 22 Jan 1975 Ind
Anders Hedberg	23 Feb 1975 NE 25 Feb 1975 Min
Howie Young	8 Mar 1975 @SD 9 Mar 1975 @Min 11 Mar 1975 @NE
Bobby Hull	26 Oct 1975 Phx 30 Oct 1975 Cin
Mike Ford	13 Nov 1975 @Cal 14 Nov 1975 Edm
Bobby Hull	23 Nov 1975 @NE 26 Nov 1975 @Cin 27 Nov 1975 @Ind
Bobby Hull	4 Dec 1975 @SD 5 Dec 1975 @Hou
Bobby Hull	23 Dec 1975 @Edm 26 Dec 1975 Cal
Ulf Nilsson	20 Feb 1976 Edm 25 Feb 1976 Cle
Duke Asmundson	2 Apr 1976 @Cal 4 Apr 1976 @Edm

Dan Labraaten	7 Nov 1976 Edm 9 Nov 1976 NE
Anders Hedberg	30 Dec 1976 @SD 2 Jan 1977 Hou
Anders Hedberg	8 Mar 1977 SD 11 Mar 1977 Cal
Bobby Hull	18 Mar 1977 @Ind 20 Mar 1977 @Bir 22 Mar 1977 Edm 27 Mar 1977 @Hou
Anders Hedberg	7 Apr 1977 @Cal 10 Apr 1977 SD
Anders Hedberg	22 Apr 1977 @SD 24 Apr 1977 SD
Bobby Guindon	25 Mar 1978 @Bir 28 Mar 1978 @Hou
Morris Lukowich	17 Dec 1978 Cin 22 Dec 1978 @Edm
Morris Lukowich	4 Feb 1979 Cin 7 Feb 1979 Bir

Ben Hatskin's Investment Paid Off
Goals by Bobby Hull

In addition to all the off-ice benefits that Bobby Hull's signing had for both the Jets and the WHA, Hull was a tremendous success on the ice as well. Following is a listing of all 303 regular season goals and 43 playoff goals Hull scored in a Jets' uniform from the day he was freed by Judge Leon A. Higginbotham to when he left the team early in the 1978-1979 season. His favorite victims during the regular season were the Alberta/Edmonton Oilers followed by the Houston Aeros and the Ottawa Nationals/Toronto Toros/Birmingham Bulls franchise. He scored more against the Aeros than any other franchise in playoff competition, followed by the San Diego Mariners, New England Whalers, and the Birmingham Bulls. Hull lit the red lamp behind 55 different goaltenders, the most popular being Don "Smokey" McLeod (22), Ernie Wakely (15) and Dave Dryden (13) during the regular season, while McLeod (6), Al Smith (6), Ron Grahame (5) and John Garrett (5) were the goaltenders Hull beat most often during the post season.

1972-1973

Regular Season

Date	Pd	Time	Opponent	Date	Pd	Time	Opponent
12 Nov 1972	1	3:18	Los Angeles Sharks	4 Feb 1973	3	1:21	@Alberta Oilers
12 Nov 1972	3	16:56	Los Angeles Sharks	4 Feb 1973	3	7:01	@Alberta Oilers
14 Nov 1972	2	12:53	Los Angeles Sharks	8 Feb 1973	3	12:52	@Houston Aeros
19 Nov 1972	2	0:24	@Los Angeles Sharks	10 Feb 1973	1	1:06	@Los Angeles Sharks
19 Nov 1972	2	8:16	@Los Angeles Sharks	10 Feb 1973	1	8:18	@Los Angeles Sharks
23 Nov 1972	3	16:52	@ Houston Aeros	11 Feb 1973	3	13:06	@Los Angeles Sharks
24 Nov 1972	1	14:01	Quebec Nordiques	15 Feb 1973	1	3:08	@Chicago Cougars
24 Nov 1972	3	10:11	Quebec Nordiques	15 Feb 1973	1	9:07	@Chicago Cougars
26 Nov 1972	2	9:27	Quebec Nordiques	15 Feb 1973	2	18:19	@Chicago Cougars
5 Dec 1972	3	19:51	Quebec Nordiques	15 Feb 1973	3	15:36	@Chicago Cougars
6 Dec 1972	2	9:41	Chicago Cougars	16 Feb 1973	3	2:49	Houston Aeros
8 Dec 1972	3	1:30	Houston Aeros	16 Feb 1973	3	8:27	Houston Aeros
8 Dec 1972	3	6:50	Houston Aeros	25 Feb 1973	1	4:54	Philadelphia Blazers
9 Dec 1972	3	4:34	@Cleveland Crusaders	25 Feb 1973	2	10:11	Philadelphia Blazers
13 Dec 1972	2	18:30	@Philadelphia Blazers	27 Feb 1973	1	19:13	Chicago Cougars
15 Dec 1972	3	8:38	@Philadelphia Blazers	27 Feb 1973	3	7:22	Chicago Cougars
15 Dec 1972	3	19:43	@Philadelphia Blazers	8 Mar 1973	3	1:52	@Quebec Nordiques
17 Dec 1972	3	1:14	@New York Raiders	10 Mar 1973	3	17:40	@New York Raiders
22 Dec 1972	1	10:05	@Chicago Cougars	14 Mar 1973	1	7:01	New England Whalers
1 Jan 1973	3	18:29	@Alberta Oilers	14 Mar 1973	2	11:08	New England Whalers
12 Jan 1973	1	13:10	Cleveland Crusaders	14 Mar 1973	3	0:50	New England Whalers
16 Jan 1973	3	11:02	Minnesota Fighting Saints	18 Mar 1973	2	6:45	Ottawa Nationals
23 Jan 1973	2	2:53	@Cleveland Crusaders	25 Mar 1973	2	10:55	New York Raiders
28 Jan 1973	3	13:31	@Ottawa Nationals	28 Mar 1973	2	10:12	@Chicago Cougars
2 Feb 1973	3	10:41	Alberta Oilers	28 Mar 1973	4	0:55	@Chicago Cougars
4 Feb 1973	2	18:01	@Alberta Oilers				

Playoffs

Date	Pd	Time	Opponent	Date	Pd	Time	Opponent
6 Apr 1973	1	6:37	Minn Fighting Saints	29 Apr 1973	3	11:07	@New England Whalers
6 Apr 1973	3	10:03	Minn Fighting Saints	3 May 1973	1	15:23	New England Whalers
8 Apr 1973	3	19:15	Minn Fighting Saints	3 May 1973	3	18:56	New England Whalers
20 Apr 1973	2	1:42	Houston Aeros	5 May 1973	1	15:50	@New England Whalers
24 Apr 1973	2	17:37	@Houston Aeros				

1973-1974

Regular Season

Date	Pd	Time	Opponent	Date	Pd	Time	Opponent
12 Oct 1973	1	15:13	@Edmonton Oilers	13 Jan 1974	3	15:29	Chicago Cougars
14 Oct 1973	1	1:52	Vancouver Blazers	18 Jan 1974	2	16:08	Cleveland Crusaders
14 Oct 1973	3	9:02	Vancouver Blazers	18 Jan 1974	3	10:49	Cleveland Crusaders
21 Oct 1973	1	2:39	Minnesota Fighting Saints	20 Jan 1974	1	19:26	Jersey Knights
26 Oct 1973	2	11:12	Toronto Toros	20 Jan 1974	2	8:48	Jersey Knights
31 Oct 1973	2	3:35	@Cleveland Crusaders	20 Jan 1974	3	15:37	Jersey Knights
2 Nov 1973	3	19:13	New York Golden Blades	25 Jan 1974	3	9:11	@Edmonton Oilers
4 Nov 1973	1	0:25	Quebec Nordiques	3 Feb 1974	3	18:55	Chicago Cougars
4 Nov 1973	2	11:02	Quebec Nordiques	8 Feb 1974	1	14:15	Minnesota Fighting Saints
4 Nov 1973	2	12:18	Quebec Nordiques	8 Feb 1974	2	18:39	Minnesota Fighting Saints
4 Nov 1973	3	15:47	Quebec Nordiques	8 Feb 1974	3	2:40	Minnesota Fighting Saints
11 Nov 1973	1	1:30	Los Angeles Sharks	17 Feb 1974	3	14:48	New England Whalers
16 Nov 1973	3	17:57	Edmonton Oilers	22 Feb 1974	3	18:00	Toronto Toros
16 Nov 1973	3	19:41	Edmonton Oilers	24 Feb 1974	2	1:29	Chicago Cougars
18 Nov 1973	1	1:10	@Toronto Toros	24 Feb 1974	3	19:31	Chicago Cougars
23 Nov 1973	2	9:34	Vancouver Blazers	3 Mar 1974	1	17:03	Quebec Nordiques
30 Nov 1973	3	16:14	Los Angeles Sharks	3 Mar 1974	2	0:29	Quebec Nordiques
5 Dec 1973	3	6:55	Edmonton Oilers	3 Mar 1974	3	9:44	Quebec Nordiques
14 Dec 1973	2	11:02	Los Angeles Sharks	15 Mar 1974	2	14:00	Vancouver Blazers
26 Dec 1973	3	3:38	Chicago Cougars	15 Mar 1974	2	15:12	Vancouver Blazers
29 Dec 1973	2	8:24	@Quebec Nordiques	17 Mar 1974	2	12:53	New England Whalers
1 Jan 1974	3	1:21	@Edmonton Oilers	22 Mar 1974	1	6:20	Houston Aeros
4 Jan 1974	3	0:30	New England Whalers	29 Mar 1974	3	13:02	Houston Aeros
9 Jan 1974	1	2:43	@Vancouver Blazers	31 Mar 1974	1	11:55	Vancouver Blazers
9 Jan 1974	1	15:07	@Vancouver Blazers	31 Mar 1974	2	19:13	Vancouver Blazers
11 Jan 1974	1	1:31	Edmonton Oilers	3 Apr 1974	1	2:40	Edmonton Oilers
11 Jan 1974	2	9:33	Edmonton Oilers				

Playoffs

Date	Pd	Time	Opponent
14 Apr 1974	3	13:52	@Houston Aeros

1974-1975

Regular Season

Date	Pd	Time	Opponent	Date	Pd	Time	Opponent
25 Oct 1974	1	4:09	@Toronto Toros	23 Jan 1975	2	2:46	@Edmonton Oilers
27 Oct 1974	3	8:55	Michigan Stags	23 Jan 1975	3	17:43	@Edmonton Oilers
30 Oct 1974	1	7:40	Phoenix Roadrunners	28 Jan 1975	1	19:41	@San Diego Mariners
30 Oct 1974	2	6:49	Phoenix Roadrunners	28 Jan 1975	3	3:24	@San Diego Mariners
30 Oct 1974	4	9:19	Phoenix Roadrunners	30 Jan 1975	3	19:15	@Phoenix Roadrunners
1 Nov 1974	1	7:20	Toronto Toros	2 Feb 1975	1	17:13	@Minnesota Fighting Saints
1 Nov 1974	2	6:43	Toronto Toros	7 Feb 1975	2	0:32	New England Whalers
1 Nov 1974	3	11:37	Toronto Toros	8 Feb 1975	1	6:21	@Chicago Cougars
3 Nov 1974	1	8:05	Michigan Stags	14 Feb 1975	1	1:42	Houston Aeros
3 Nov 1974	2	18:24	Michigan Stags	14 Feb 1975	2	16:47	Houston Aeros
5 Nov 1974	3	9:34	Minnesota Fighting Saints	14 Feb 1975	3	18:22	Houston Aeros
9 Nov 1974	2	13:54	@Vancouver Blazers	18 Feb 1975	2	1:46	@Baltimore Blades
13 Nov 1974	2	6:18	@Edmonton Oilers	18 Feb 1975	2	6:29	@Baltimore Blades
18 Nov 1974	1	19:07	@Edmonton Oilers	25 Feb 1975	3	6:25	Minnesota Fighting Saints
18 Nov 1974	2	5:39	@Edmonton Oilers	28 Feb 1975	1	13:37	San Diego Mariners
20 Nov 1974	1	18:53	Minnesota Fighting Saints	28 Feb 1975	3	17:17	San Diego Mariners
20 Nov 1974	3	12:59	Minnesota Fighting Saints	2 Mar 1975	2	8:13	San Diego Mariners
26 Nov 1974	1	5:56	@Indianapolis Racers	5 Mar 1975	3	19:30	Cleveland Crusaders
27 Nov 1974	1	15:55	@Cleveland Crusaders	7 Mar 1975	1	2:15	@Phoenix Roadrunners
29 Nov 1974	1	4:13	Michigan Stags	7 Mar 1975	1	12:27	@Phoenix Roadrunners
29 Nov 1974	2	14:40	Michigan Stags	9 Mar 1975	2	18:07	@Minnesota Fighting Saints
29 Nov 1974	2	18:58	Michigan Stags	12 Mar 1975	1	15:55	@Quebec Nordiques
29 Nov 1974	3	5:05	Michigan Stags	12 Mar 1975	2	1:56	@Quebec Nordiques
10 Dec 1974	1	18:47	@Indianapolis Racers	14 Mar 1975	3	11:36	Quebec Nordiques
12 Dec 1974	3	8:46	@Michigan Stags	16 Mar 1975	2	6:04	Edmonton Oilers
14 Dec 1974	1	7:58	@Houston Aeros	16 Mar 1975	3	2:42	Edmonton Oilers
15 Dec 1974	1	8:24	New England Whalers	16 Mar 1975	3	18:48	Edmonton Oilers
17 Dec 1974	1	9:00	@Toronto Toros	19 Mar 1975	3	11:12	Vancouver Blazers
17 Dec 1974	1	16:16	@Toronto Toros	19 Mar 1975	3	15:54	Vancouver Blazers
22 Dec 1974	2	2:14	Phoenix Roadrunners	21 Mar 1975	3	11:30	@New England Whalers
28 Dec 1974	1	1:02	@San Diego Mariners	22 Mar 1975	2	10:37	@Chicago Cougars
28 Dec 1974	2	5:05	@San Diego Mariners	25 Mar 1975	1	6:00	@Indianapolis Racers
29 Dec 1974	1	6:21	@Houston Aeros	25 Mar 1975	1	13:16	@Indianapolis Racers
29 Dec 1974	2	6:01	@Houston Aeros	29 Mar 1975	2	10:38	@New England Whalers
7 Jan 1975	1	16:29	@Cleveland Crusaders	29 Mar 1975	2	19:55	@New England Whalers
9 Jan 1975	1	4:59	@Michigan Stags	29 Mar 1975	3	12:30	@New England Whalers
19 Jan 1975	1	8:30	Cleveland Crusaders	5 Apr 1975	3	19:40	@Quebec Nordiques
19 Jan 1975	3	5:54	Cleveland Crusaders	6 Apr 1975	2	19:26	San Diego Mariners
22 Jan 1975	1	15:25	Indianapolis Racers				

1975-1976

Regular Season

Date	Pd	Time	Opponent	Date	Pd	Time	Opponent
12 Oct 1975	2	19:45	@Phoenix Roadrunners	18 Jan 1976	1	9:22	New England Whalers
12 Oct 1975	3	10:53	@Phoenix Roadrunners	18 Jan 1976	2	4:12	New England Whalers
26 Oct 1975	1	5:36	Phoenix Roadrunners	18 Jan 1976	3	6:17	New England Whalers
30 Oct 1975	2	18:47	Cincinnati Stingers	23 Jan 1976	2	0:47	Edmonton Oilers
4 Nov 1975	2	10:08	New England Whalers	30 Jan 1976	3	0:46	@New England Whalers
14 Nov 1975	1	13:34	Edmonton Oilers	30 Jan 1976	3	4:40	@New England Whalers
14 Nov 1975	3	1:31	Edmonton Oilers	6 Feb 1976	3	0:54	@Toronto Toros
18 Nov 1975	3	14:30	Houston Aeros	7 Feb 1976	2	15:36	@Cleveland Crusaders
23 Nov 1975	1	17:31	@New England Whalers	8 Feb 1976	1	10:02	Calgary Cowboys
26 Nov 1975	1	0:54	@Cincinnati Stingers	20 Feb 1976	3	16:52	Edmonton Oilers
27 Nov 1975	1	6:42	@Indianapolis Racers	27 Feb 1976	1	11:23	Edmonton Oilers
30 Nov 1975	1	2:13	Minnesota Fighting Saints	29 Feb 1976	2	10:38	@Toronto Toros
2 Dec 1975	4	4:00	@Denver Spurs	7 Mar 1976	1	4:39	Calgary Cowboys
4 Dec 1975	2	1:31	@San Diego Mariners	9 Mar 1976	2	13:32	@Toronto Toros
4 Dec 1975	3	11:03	@San Diego Mariners	10 Mar 1976	3	6:53	Quebec Nordiques
5 Dec 1975	1	0:59	@Houston Aeros	14 Mar 1976	1	4:55	Edmonton Oilers
5 Dec 1975	3	9:31	@Houston Aeros	21 Mar 1976	2	7:23	@Toronto Toros
10 Dec 1975	4	0:44	Toronto Toros	28 Mar 1976	1	2:16	San Diego Mariners
14 Dec 1975	1	18:59	@Edmonton Oilers	28 Mar 1976	1	18:58	San Diego Mariners
21 Dec 1975	1	12:49	Minnesota Fighting Saints	31 Mar 1976	1	17:42	Toronto Toros
23 Dec 1975	1	9:10	@Edmonton Oilers	31 Mar 1976	3	12:50	Toronto Toros
23 Dec 1975	2	1:36	@Edmonton Oilers	31 Mar 1976	3	14:05	Toronto Toros
26 Dec 1975	1	18:17	Calgary Cowboys	4 Apr 1976	2	0:34	@Edmonton Oilers
26 Dec 1975	2	17:49	Calgary Cowboys	6 Apr 1976	2	8:22	@Calgary Cowboys
30 Dec 1975	2	13:01	@Houston Aeros	6 Apr 1976	3	7:29	@Calgary Cowboys
3 Jan 1976	3	12:21	@Calgary Cowboys	6 Apr 1976	3	8:44	@Calgary Cowboys
11 Jan 1976	3	14:28	Ottawa Civics				

Playoffs

Date	Pd	Time	Opponent	Date	Pd	Time	Opponent
9 Apr 1976	1	3:32	Edmonton Oilers	25 Apr 1976	1	9:53	Calgary Cowboys
11 Apr 1976	2	17:10	Edmonton Oilers	25 Apr 1976	1	13:35	Calgary Cowboys
14 Apr 1976	3	10:22	@Edmonton Oilers	28 Apr 1976	1	19:26	@Calgary Cowboys
16 Apr 1976	1	4:25	@Edmonton Oilers	20 May 1976	3	16:43	@Houston Aeros
16 Apr 1976	2	15:27	@Edmonton Oilers	23 May 1976	3	18:06	@Houston Aeros
23 Apr 1976	2	2:42	Calgary Cowboys	27 May 1976	1	5:37	Houston Aeros

1976-1977

Regular Season

Date	Pd	Time	Opponent	Date	Pd	Time	Opponent
30 Nov 1976	2	1:07	San Diego Mariners	27 Mar 1977	1	19:17	@Houston Aeros
8 Dec 1976	3	13:32	@Calgary Cowboys	27 Mar 1977	2	9:03	@Houston Aeros
28 Dec 1976	1	12:13	@Houston Aeros	27 Mar 1977	3	8:04	@Houston Aeros
2 Jan 1977	3	4:43	Houston Aeros	31 Mar 1977	2	2:44	@San Diego Mariners
11 Jan 1977	2	1:41	Phoenix Roadrunners	31 Mar 1977	3	17:27	@San Diego Mariners
8 Mar 1977	1	16:34	San Diego Mariners	2 Apr 1977	1	16:25	@Birmingham Bulls
13 Mar 1977	1	9:26	Edmonton Oilers	2 Apr 1977	1	19:13	@Birmingham Bulls
18 Mar 1977	1	0:38	@Indianapolis Racers	3 Apr 1977	1	7:42	Calgary Cowboys
18 Mar 1977	2	17:54	@Indianapolis Racers	4 Apr 1977	2	8:52	@Edmonton Oilers
20 Mar 1977	1	7:51	@Birmingham Bulls	7 Apr 1977	1	7:11	@Calgary Cowboys
22 Mar 1977	1	1:50	Edmonton Oilers				

Playoffs

Date	Pd	Time	Opponent	Date	Pd	Time	Opponent
10 Apr 1977	1	17:50	San Diego Mariners	30 Apr 1977	1	8:40	Houston Aeros
10 Apr 1977	2	13:02	San Diego Mariners	5 May 1977	2	8:05	Houston Aeros
12 Apr 1977	1	11:01	San Diego Mariners	22 May 1977	2	13:53	@Quebec Nordiques
12 Apr 1977	3	16:55	San Diego Mariners	24 May 1977	1	1:26	Quebec Nordiques
17 Apr 1977	2	12:28	@San Diego Mariners	24 May 1977	2	6:28	Quebec Nordiques
24 Apr 1977	3	0:32	San Diego Mariners	24 May 1977	3	12:36	Quebec Nordiques
24 Apr 1977	3	1:03	San Diego Mariners				

1977-1978

Regular Season

Date	Pd	Time	Opponent	Date	Pd	Time	Opponent
12 Oct 1977	1	16:35	@Edmonton Oilers	20 Dec 1977	1	15:11	Soviet All-Stars
12 Oct 1977	2	8:30	@Edmonton Oilers	21 Dec 1977	2	15:56	@Houston Aeros
12 Oct 1977	3	13:26	@Edmonton Oilers	6 Jan 1978	3	12:52	@Edmonton Oilers
13 Oct 1977	1	13:24	Quebec Nordiques	8 Jan 1978	2	4:32	Indianapolis Racers
16 Oct 1977	1	12:40	Indianapolis Racers	11 Jan 1978	2	7:35	Birmingham Bulls
16 Oct 1977	1	17:27	Indianapolis Racers	11 Jan 1978	2	11:18	Birmingham Bulls
23 Oct 1977	1	8:15	Birmingham Bulls	15 Jan 1978	1	12:26	Edmonton Oilers
23 Oct 1977	1	12:02	Birmingham Bulls	18 Jan 1978	2	6:48	Quebec Nordiques
23 Oct 1977	2	2:54	Birmingham Bulls	20 Jan 1978	1	5:12	New England Whalers
28 Oct 1977	1	4:59	Cincinnati Stingers	26 Jan 1978	3	5:12	@Houston Aeros
30 Oct 1977	3	13:22	Edmonton Oilers	4 Feb 1978	1	0:56	@Cincinnati Stingers
30 Oct 1977	3	17:01	Edmonton Oilers	8 Feb 1978	3	9:41	Birmingham Bulls
2 Nov 1977	3	12:51	@Edmonton Oilers	12 Feb 1978	3	1:58	@Houston Aeros
9 Nov 1977	3	8:01	Houston Aeros	15 Feb 1978	3	0:46	Edmonton Oilers
13 Nov 1977	1	6:37	Cincinnati Stingers	19 Feb 1978	3	18:18	Quebec Nordiques
15 Nov 1977	3	15:13	@Quebec Nordiques	22 Feb 1978	1	1:06	New England Whalers
3 Dec 1977	3	1:53	@Quebec Nordiques	26 Feb 1978	1	5:49	Houston Aeros
7 Dec 1977	1	9:46	Houston Aeros	26 Feb 1978	2	16:14	Houston Aeros
7 Dec 1977	3	1:27	Houston Aeros	1 Mar 1978	3	12:46	@Birmingham Bulls
11 Dec 1977	3	1:51	Indianapolis Racers	3 Mar 1978	1	10:35	Cincinnati Stingers
13 Dec 1977	2	12:26	Czechoslovakia	11 Mar 1978	2	17:27	@Quebec Nordiques
17 Dec 1977	2	0:58	@New England Whalers	22 Mar 1978	1	0:49	@New England Whalers
18 Dec 1977	2	12:39	New England Whalers	22 Mar 1978	1	7:12	@New England Whalers

Playoffs

Date	Pd	Time	Opponent	Date	Pd	Time	Opponent
14 Apr 1978	1	10:18	Birmingham Bulls	19 Apr 1978	2	5:24	@Birmingham Bulls
14 Apr 1978	3	13:19	Birmingham Bulls	21 Apr 1978	3	15:06	@Birmingham Bulls
16 Apr 1978	1	13:41	Birmingham Bulls	19 May 1978	1	6:32	New England Whalers
16 Apr 1978	2	11:31	Birmingham Bulls	22 May 1978	3	3:26	New England Whalers

1978-1979

Regular Season

Date	Pd	Time	Opponent	Date	Pd	Time	Opponent
13 Oct 1978	2	0:53	@Birmingham Bulls	14 Oct 1978	1	19:21	@Indianapolis Racers

Hull's Victims

In scoring his 346 regular season and playoff goals with the WHA Jets, Bobby Hull lit the red lamp behind 55 different goaltenders. Following is a listing of all the netminders who fell victim to the Golden Jet at least once.

Christer Abrahamsson	Michel Dion	Miroslav Kapoun	Jacques Plante
Serge Aubry	Peter Donnelly	Gary Kurt	Pat Riggin
Bill Berglund	Dave Dryden	Bruce Landon	Wayne Rutledge
Les Binkley	George Gardner	Norm Lapointe	Jim Shaw
Ken Broderick	John Garrett	Jacques Lemelin	Al Smith
Richard Brodeur	Andre Gill	Louis Levasseur	Dave Tataryn
Andy Brown	Russ Gillow	Mike Liut	Mikhail Vaselinok
Ken Brown	Ron Grahame	Ken Lockett	Ernie Wakely
Gerry Cheevers	Gilles Gratton	Jack McCartan	Ian Wilkie
Jim Corsi	Paul Hoganson	Don McLeod	Wayne Wood
Rich Coutu	Leif Holmquist	Jim McLeod	Chris Worthy
Mike Curran	Gary Inness	Cam Newton	Bob Whidden
Michel DeGuise	Bob Johnson	Jack Norris	Lynn Zimmerman
Gerry Desjardins	Joe Junkin	Bernie Parent	

Note: Miroslav Kapoun was a member of a touring Czechoslovakian team and Mikhail Vaselinok was a member of a touring Soviet team. Neither goaltender played for a WHA team, but because those games counted in the WHA standings, the goals Hull scored in those games counted as well.

No Ordinary Joe

Joe Daley was the only player on the Jets roster to last throughout all seven seasons the team played in the WHA, appearing in 308 regular season games and 49 playoff games for the Jets. His first appearance came on 13 October 1972 at the Saint Paul Auditorium, and he finished his career with a mop-up relief effort in Edmonton in Game 5 of the 1979 AVCO World Trophy final on 18 May 1979. While 318 different shooters beat him, Marc Tardif beat him most often in regular season competition, and Mark Howe scored against him more often than any other player in the playoffs.
Following is a listing of all the games he played in as a Jet.

1972-1973

Regular Season

Date	Opp		Date	Opp		Date	Opp	
13 Oct 1972	@Min	W	7 Jan 1973	@Min	W	25 Feb 1973	Phi	W
17 Oct 1972	@Alb	L	12 Jan 1973	Cle	W	2 Mar 1973	LA	W
20 Oct 1972	Min	T	16 Jan 1973	Min	W	6 Mar 1973	@Ott	L
24 Oct 1972	Phi	W	21 Jan 1973	NE	L	10 Mar 1973	@NY	L
29 Oct 1972	Hou	W	24 Jan 1973	@NE	L	14 Mar 1973	NE	L
1 Nov 1972	@Min	L	28 Jan 1973	@Ott	W	18 Mar 1973	Ott	L
5 Nov 1972	NY	W	4 Feb 1973	@Alb	W	25 Mar 1973	NY	W
22 Dec 1972	@Chi	L	8 Feb 1973	@Hou	W	28 Mar 1973	@Chi	W
26 Dec 1972	Chi	W	11 Feb 1973	@LA	W	30 Mar 1973	@Cle	L
1 Jan 1973	@Alb	-	16 Feb 1973	Hou	W			

Playoffs

Date	Opp		Date	Opp	
8 Apr 1973	Min	W	29 Apr 1973	@NE	L
11 Apr 1973	@Min	W	3 May 1973	NE	W
20 Apr 1973	Hou	W	6 May 1973	@NE	L
24 Apr 1973	@Hou	W			

1973-1974

Regular Season

Date	Opp		Date	Opp		Date	Opp	
12 Oct 1973	@Edm	L	12 Dec 1973	Hou	L	15 Feb 1974	@Min	L
17 Oct 1973	@NE	W	16 Dec 1973	Min	L	20 Feb 1974	@Edm	L
21 Oct 1973	Min	W	19 Dec 1973	@Hou	L	24 Feb 1974	Chi	W
27 Oct 1973	@Min	L	23 Dec 1973	@Jer	L	28 Feb 1974	@Tor	L
31 Oct 1973	@Cle	L	29 Dec 1973	@Que	W	3 Mar 1974	Que	W
4 Nov 1973	Que	W	1 Jan 1974	@Edm	W	9 Mar 1974	@Chi	L
7 Nov 1973	@NE	L	6 Jan 1974	@Hou	L	13 Mar 1974	@Cle	L
11 Nov 1973	LA	W	9 Jan 1974	@Van	W	17 Mar 1974	NE	W
16 Nov 1973	Edm	W	13 Jan 1974	Chi	W	22 Mar 1974	Hou	L
21 Nov 1973	Cle	W	20 Jan 1974	Jer	W	24 Mar 1974	@LA	L
25 Nov 1973	@Min	L	27 Jan 1974	@Min	L	29 Mar 1974	Hou	W
28 Nov 1973	@Hou	T	3 Feb 1974	Chi	W	31 Mar 1974	Van	W
2 Dec 1973	Que	W	8 Feb 1974	Min	L	3 Apr 1974	Edm	L
7 Dec 1973	Tor	-	12 Feb 1974	@LA	W			

Playoffs

Date	Opp		Date	Opp	
8 Apr 1974	Hou	L	10 Apr 1974	Hou	L

1974-1975

Regular Season

Date	Opp		Date	Opp		Date	Opp	
15 Oct 1974	@Van	W	17 Dec 1974	@Tor	W	19 Feb 1975	Edm	W
18 Oct 1974	Edm	W	22 Dec 1974	Phx	L	23 Feb 1975	NE	L
25 Oct 1974	@Tor	L	7 Jan 1975	@Cle	T	25 Feb 1975	Min	T
27 Oct 1974	Mic	W	9 Jan 1975	@Mic	L	28 Feb 1975	SD	W
1 Nov 1974	Tor	W	10 Jan 1975	Que	L	2 Mar 1975	SD	T
5 Nov 1974	Min	W	19 Jan 1975	Cle	W	5 Mar 1975	Cle	W
9 Nov 1974	@Van	T	22 Jan 1975	Ind	-	7 Mar 1975	@Phx	L
13 Nov 1974	@Edm	L	23 Jan 1975	@Edm	L	9 Mar 1975	@Min	W
17 Nov 1974	Tor	L	26 Jan 1975	Hou	L	11 Mar 1975	@NE	L
18 Nov 1974	@Edm	-	28 Jan 1975	@SD	-	14 Mar 1975	Que	W
1 Dec 1974	Que	W	30 Jan 1975	@Phx	W	21 Mar 1975	@NE	W
4 Dec 1974	Hou	L	5 Feb 1975	@Cle	L	22 Mar 1975	@Chi	W
6 Dec 1974	@Min	L	8 Feb 1975	@Chi	L	23 Mar 1975	Chi	W
8 Dec 1974	Chi	W	12 Feb 1975	Tor	L	29 Mar 1975	@NE	W
12 Dec 1974	@Mic	L	15 Feb 1975	Cle	W	31 Mar 1975	Ind	W
14 Dec 1974	@Hou	L	16 Feb 1975	@Chi	W	2 Apr 1975	Van	L
15 Dec 1974	NE	L	18 Feb 1975	@Bal	W	5 Apr 1975	@Que	L

1975-1976

Regular Season

Date	Opp		Date	Opp		Date	Opp	
9 Oct 1975	@Que	W	10 Dec 1975	Tor	W	8 Feb 1976	Cal	W
12 Oct 1975	@Phx	W	12 Dec 1975	Cal	W	11 Feb 1976	Que	L
18 Oct 1975	@SD	L	14 Dec 1975	@Edm	W	15 Feb 1976	Tor	W
19 Oct 1975	@Phx	L	18 Dec 1975	@Que	L	18 Feb 1976	Phx	W
21 Oct 1975	Cin	W	20 Dec 1975	@Min	L	20 Feb 1976	Edm	W
24 Oct 1975	Den	W	21 Dec 1975	Min	L	25 Feb 1976	Cle	W
26 Oct 1975	Phx	W	26 Dec 1975	Cal	L	27 Feb 1976	Edm	W
30 Oct 1975	Cin	W	3 Jan 1976	@Cal	W	28 Feb 1976	@Que	W
2 Nov 1975	Que	L	4 Jan 1976	@Edm	W	29 Feb 1976	@Tor	-
9 Nov 1975	Tor	W	7 Jan 1976	Tor	W	7 Mar 1976	Cal	W
11 Nov 1975	Cle	L	9 Jan 1976	Ind	L	10 Mar 1976	Que	W
13 Nov 1975	@Cal	W	11 Jan 1976	Ott	W	12 Mar 1976	Que	-
14 Nov 1975	Edm	W	18 Jan 1976	NE	W	14 Mar 1976	Edm	W
18 Nov 1975	Hou	L	21 Jan 1976	Cal	W	17 Mar 1976	Cal	W
20 Nov 1975	@Que	W	23 Jan 1976	Edm	W	19 Mar 1976	@Edm	L
23 Nov 1975	@NE	W	28 Jan 1976	@Min	L	21 Mar 1976	@Tor	L
26 Nov 1975	@Cin	W	30 Jan 1976	@NE	W	24 Mar 1976	Edm	L
27 Nov 1975	@Ind	-	31 Jan 1976	@Cin	W	28 Mar 1976	SD	W
28 Nov 1975	@Tor	W	3 Feb 1976	@Que	L	31 Mar 1976	Tor	W
4 Dec 1975	@SD	W	6 Feb 1976	@Tor	W	6 Apr 1976	@Cal	W
7 Dec 1975	Que	L	7 Feb 1976	@Cle	T			

Playoffs

Date	Opp		Date	Opp		Date	Opp	
9 Apr 1976	Edm	W	25 Apr 1976	Cal	W	20 May 1976	@Hou	W
11 Apr 1976	Edm	-	28 Apr 1976	@Cal	W	23 May 1976	@Hou	W
16 Apr 1976	@Edm	W	30 Apr 1976	@Cal	L	25 May 1976	Hou	W
23 Apr 1976	Cal	W	2 May 1976	Cal	W	27 May 1976	Hou	W

1976-1977

Regular Season

Date	Opp		Date	Opp		Date	Opp	
8 Oct 1976	Cal	W	4 Dec 1976	@NE	W	13 Feb 1977	@Ind	W
10 Oct 1976	NE	W	7 Dec 1976	Phx	W	15 Feb 1977	Cal	T
15 Oct 1976	@Edm	W	8 Dec 1976	@Cal	W	18 Feb 1977	@Edm	L
16 Oct 1976	@Phx	L	26 Dec 1976	Que	L	20 Feb 1977	Edm	W
17 Oct 1976	@SD	L	28 Dec 1976	@Hou	L	22 Feb 1977	Hou	W
19 Oct 1976	Ind	W	30 Dec 1976	@SD	L	26 Feb 1977	@Cin	W
22 Oct 1976	Phx	L	2 Jan 1977	Hou	W	27 Feb 1977	NE	L
24 Oct 1976	Bir	W	4 Jan 1977	Ind	W	1 Mar 1977	@Cal	-
29 Oct 1976	Edm	W	9 Jan 1977	Bir	W	2 Mar 1977	Que	W
31 Oct 1976	SD	W	11 Jan 1977	Phx	W	5 Mar 1977	@Phx	L
2 Nov 1976	Hou	L	14 Jan 1977	@Cal	W	8 Mar 1977	SD	W
6 Nov 1976	@Cin	L	16 Jan 1977	Cin	L	11 Mar 1977	Cal	W
7 Nov 1976	Edm	W	21 Jan 1977	Cin	W	13 Mar 1977	Edm	W
14 Nov 1976	@Cal	W	23 Jan 1977	Cal	W	15 Mar 1977	Edm	W
16 Nov 1976	Que	W	25 Jan 1977	@Hou	L	17 Mar 1977	@Edm	L
19 Nov 1976	@NE	W	27 Jan 1977	@Bir	L	20 Mar 1977	@Bir	W
21 Nov 1976	Cin	L	29 Jan 1977	@SD	L	22 Mar 1977	Edm	W
23 Nov 1976	@Que	L	30 Jan 1977	@Phx	L	27 Mar 1977	@Hou	W
26 Nov 1976	@Hou	T	1 Feb 1977	@Edm	W	29 Mar 1977	Hou	L
28 Nov 1976	Phx	L	4 Feb 1977	SD	W	31 Mar 1977	@SD	L
30 Nov 1976	SD	W	6 Feb 1977	Cal	W	3 Apr 1977	Cal	W
3 Dec 1976	@Min	W	11 Feb 1977	@Cin	L			

Playoffs

Date	Opp		Date	Opp		Date	Opp	
10 Apr 1977	SD	W	26 Apr 1977	@Hou	W	15 May 1977	@Que	L
12 Apr 1977	SD	W	28 Apr 1977	@Hou	L	18 May 1977	Que	W
16 Apr 1977	@SD	L	30 Apr 1977	Hou	W	20 May 1977	Que	L
17 Apr 1977	@SD	L	1 May 1977	Hou	W	22 May 1977	@Que	L
20 Apr 1977	SD	W	3 May 1977	@Hou	L	24 May 1977	Que	W
22 Apr 1977	@SD	L	5 May 1977	Hou	W	26 May 1977	@Que	L
24 Apr 1977	SD	W	11 May 1977	@Que	W			

1977-1978

Regular Season

Date	Opp		Date	Opp		Date	Opp	
13 Oct 1977	Que	W	13 Dec 1977	CSSR	W	28 Jan 1978	@Bir	L
16 Oct 1977	Ind	W	18 Dec 1977	NE	W	31 Jan 1978	@Que	W
21 Oct 1977	NE	L	20 Dec 1977	USSR	W	5 Feb 1978	Edm	W
30 Oct 1977	Edm	W	23 Dec 1977	@Cin	W	12 Feb 1978	@Hou	W
4 Nov 1977	@Bir	W	26 Dec 1977	Que	W	15 Feb 1978	Edm	W
11 Nov 1977	Que	L	8 Jan 1978	Ind	W	18 Feb 1978	@Cin	W
15 Nov 1977	@Que	-	11 Jan 1978	Bir	W	22 Feb 1978	NE	W
18 Nov 1977	@NE	L	14 Jan 1978	@Ind	W	26 Feb 1978	Hou	W
22 Nov 1977	@Edm	L	15 Jan 1978	Edm	-	4 Apr 1978	@Hou	L
27 Nov 1977	Bir	L	18 Jan 1978	Que	W	7 Apr 1978	@Edm	L
2 Dec 1977	@NE	L	20 Jan 1978	NE	T	9 Apr 1978	Hou	-
4 Dec 1977	Edm	L	22 Jan 1978	Ind	-			
7 Dec 1977	Hou	W	25 Jan 1978	@Bir	L			

Playoffs

Date	Opp		Date	Opp		Date	Opp	
14 Apr 1978	Bir	W	23 Apr 1978	Bir	W	22 May 1978	NE	W
19 Apr 1978	@Bir	L	14 May 1978	@NE	W			

1978-1979

Regular Season

Date	Opp		Date	Opp		Date	Opp	
13 Oct 1978	@Bir	W	1 Jan 1979	CSSR	T	20 Feb 1979	@Cin	L
15 Oct 1978	Cin	L	9 Jan 1979	Edm	W	21 Feb 1979	NE	W
22 Oct 1978	Edm	L	17 Jan 1979	Edm	L	23 Feb 1979	@Bir	L
27 Oct 1978	@NE	W	20 Jan 1979	@Que	-	25 Feb 1979	@NE	W
29 Oct 1978	Ind	T	27 Jan 1979	@Que	W	2 Mar 1979	NE	L
9 Nov 1978	@Bir	L	30 Jan 1979	@NE	L	4 Apr 1979	NE	-
1 Dec 1978	Cin	L	4 Feb 1979	Cin	W	18 Apr 1979	@Edm	L
10 Dec 1978	Que	T	9 Feb 1979	@Cin	L			

Playoffs

Date	Opp		Date	Opp		Date	Opp	
25 Apr 1979	@Que	-	15 May 1979	Edm	-	18 May 1979	@Edm	-

The following charts show how goaltender Joe Daley fared against each franchise.

Regular Season

Franchise	W	L	T	Pct.
Denver Spurs/Ottawa Civics	2	0	0	1.000
Soviet All-Stars	1	0	0	1.000
Philadelphia Blazers/Vancouver Blazers/Calgary Cowboys	21	2	2	0.880
Indianapolis Racers	7	1	1	0.833
Chicago Cougars	9	3	0	0.750
Czechoslovakia	1	0	1	0.750
Los Angeles Sharks/Michigan Stags/Baltimore Blades	6	3	0	0.667
Quebec Nordiques	17	10	1	0.625
Alberta/Edmonton Oilers	24	16	0	0.600
New York Raiders/Jersey Knights/San Diego Mariners	10	7	1	0.583
Cleveland Crusaders/Minnesota Fighting Saints	7	5	2	0.571
Ottawa Nationals/Toronto Toros/Birmingham Bulls	16	13	0	0.552
New England Whalers	15	13	1	0.534
Cincinnati Stingers	9	8	0	0.529
Houston Aeros	10	13	2	0.440
Phoenix Roadrunners	6	8	0	0.429
Minnesota Fighting Saints	6	11	2	0.368
Totals	**167**	**113**	**13**	**0.592**

Playoffs

Franchise	W	L	Pct.
Minnesota Fighting Saints	2	0	1.000
Edmonton Oilers	2	0	1.000
Calgary Cowboys	4	1	0.800
Houston Aeros	10	4	0.714
Birmingham Bulls	2	1	0.667
New England Whalers	3	2	0.600
San Diego Mariners	4	3	0.571
Quebec Nordiques	3	4	0.429
Totals	**30**	**15**	**0.667**

Overtime

The WHA used a 10-minute sudden death overtime period to attempt to decide regular-season games tied after regulation time and a game was declared a tie only if neither team scored in overtime. A more traditional 20-minute overtime period was used to decide playoff games, which were played until a goal was scored. Following is a listing of all overtime goals scored both by and against the Jets in this extra period.

Regular Season

For

Scorer	Date	Time	Opponent	Goaltender
Milt Black	9 Dec 1972	3:15	@Cleveland Crusaders	Gerry Cheevers
Norm Beaudin	10 Feb 1973	6:07	@Los Angeles Sharks	George Gardner
Bobby Hull	28 Mar 1973	0:55	@Chicago Cougars	Andre Gill
Christian Bordeleau	21 Oct 1973	7:17	Minnesota Fighting Saints	Mike Curran
Fran Huck	1 Jan 1974	0:46	@Edmonton Oilers	Jack Norris
Fran Huck	31 Mar 1974	2:00	Vancouver Blazers	Peter Donnelly
Bobby Hull	30 Oct 1974	9:19	Phoenix Roadrunners	Gary Kurt
Veli-Pekka Ketola	9 Mar 1975	3:02	@Minnesota Fighting Saints	Mike Curran
Norm Beaudin	25 Mar 1975	1:32	@Indianapolis Racers	Andy Brown
Mike Ford	4 Nov 1975	4:06	New England Whalers	Christer Abrahamsson
Ulf Nilsson	20 Nov 1975	1:13	@Quebec Nordiques	Richard Brodeur
Bobby Hull	2 Dec 1975	4:00	@Denver Spurs	Bob Johnson
Bobby Hull	10 Dec 1975	0:44	Toronto Toros	Dave Tataryn
Anders Hedberg	11 Jan 1976	8:01	Ottawa Civics	Lynn Zimmerman
Lyle Moffat	28 Feb 1976	1:51	@Quebec Nordiques	Richard Brodeur
Ulf Nilsson	9 Nov 1976	8:53	New England Whalers	Christer Abrahamsson
Anders Hedberg	21 Jan 1977	3:57	Cincinnati Stingers	Norm Lapointe
Anders Hedberg	2 Mar 1977	9:19	Quebec Nordiques	Bill Humphreys
Ulf Nilsson	20 Mar 1977	1:35	@Birmingham Bulls	John Garrett
Willy Lindstrom	16 Feb 1978	3:15	@New England Whalers	Al Smith
Bill Lesuk	13 Oct 1978	3:24	@Birmingham Bulls	Pat Riggin
Kent Nilsson	9 Jan 1979	6:22	Edmonton Oilers	Ed Walsh
Peter Sullivan	15 Apr 1979	9:00	Birmingham Bulls	Ernie Wakely

Against

Scorer	Date	Time	Opponent	Goaltender
Ron Walters	17 Oct 1972	4:53	@Alberta Oilers	Joe Daley
Keke Mortson	23 Nov 1972	4:03	@Houston Aeros	Ernie Wakely
Ray Clearwater	23 Jan 1973	0:29	@Cleveland Crusaders	Ernie Wakely
Brian Bradley	10 Mar 1973	7:41	@New York Raiders	Joe Daley
Jim Adair	10 Oct 1973	3:50	@Vancouver Blazers	Ernie Wakely
Bryan Campbell	23 Nov 1973	5:28	Vancouver Blazers	Ernie Wakely
Brian McDonald	27 Nov 1973	1:59	@Los Angeles Sharks	Ernie Wakely
Mike Walton	8 Feb 1974	7:05	Minnesota Fighting Saints	Joe Daley
John Cunniff	17 Feb 1974	5:52	New England Whalers	Ernie Wakely
Larry Mavety	9 Mar 1974	7:46	@Chicago Cougars	Joe Daley
Tom Gilmore	3 Apr 1974	3:13	Edmonton Oilers	Joe Daley
Jim Harrison	27 Nov 1974	9:54	@Cleveland Crusaders	Ernie Wakely
Steve West	9 Jan 1975	4:40	@Michigan Stags	Joe Daley
Butch Deadmarsh	24 Jan 1975	4:22	@Vancouver Blazers	Curt Larsson
George Morrison	2 Feb 1975	2:16	@Minnesota Fighting Saints	Curt Larsson
Paul Hurley	7 Feb 1975	8:02	New England Whalers	Curt Larsson
Tom Webster	23 Feb 1975	5:21	New England Whalers	Joe Daley
Al Karlander	9 Jan 1976	5:44	Indianapolis Racers	Joe Daley
Marc Tardif	11 Nov 1977	6:32	Quebec Nordiques	Joe Daley
Pierre Guite	15 Nov 1977	1:11	@Quebec Nordiques	Markus Mattsson
Bob Stephenson	27 Nov 1977	2:57	Birmingham Bulls	Joe Daley
Robbie Ftorek	9 Dec 1977	3:25	Cincinnati Stingers	Gary Bromley
Ron Chipperfield	15 Jan 1978	6:04	Edmonton Oilers	Gary Bromley
John Tonelli	26 Jan 1978	0:19	@Houston Aeros	Gary Bromley
Peter Driscoll	3 Nov 1978	6:02	@Edmonton Oilers	Markus Mattsson

Playoffs

For

Scorer	Date	Time	Opponent	Goaltender
Norm Beaudin	11 Apr 1973	3:12	@Minnesota Fighting Saints	Mike Curran
Ulf Nilsson	11 Apr 1976	0:54	Edmonton Oilers	Dave Dryden
Peter Sullivan	26 Apr 1977	8:05	@Houston Aeros	Ron Grahame

Against
The Jets were never scored against in WHA playoff overtime competition.

Top 10 Dramatic Goals

Following is a listing of what are arguably the 10 most dramatic goals the Jets scored through their seven seasons of WHA competition.

	Date	Description of Goal
1.	6 February 1977	Anders Hedberg returned to the ice after suffering a knee injury in the second period to take a pass from Bill Lesuk and fire a shot past Calgary Cowboys' goaltender Gary Bromley at 11:21 of the third period for his 50th goal in his 47th game. With the goal, he became only the third player in major pro hockey to score 50 goals in 50 games or less. Hedberg went on to score his 51st goal into an empty net with just one second remaining to cap the historic accomplishment. Unfortunately, Hedberg's knee later had to be fitted with a cast and he missed the next 10 games.
2.	11 April 1976	Ulf Nilsson's slap shot 54 seconds into overtime beat goaltender Dave Dryden and gave the Jets a 5-4 victory over the Edmonton Oilers in Game 2 of the Canadian Division semi-final. Nilsson's blast was the Jets' 62nd shot of the game and enabled the Jets to take a 2-0 lead in the series.
3.	15 April 1979	Peter Sullivan's goal with one minute remaining in overtime gave the Jets a 5-4 victory over the Birmingham Bulls to secure third place for the Jets and eliminate the Bulls from playoff contention in their last season of existence. Sullivan's shot found its way through Bulls' goaltender, and original Jet, Ernie Wakely in the last WHA regular-season game at the Winnipeg Arena. The third-place finish enabled the Jets to avoid a preliminary round best-of-three series with the Cincinnati Stingers.
4.	11 April 1973	Substituting for an injured Christian Bordeleau on the Luxury Line, Bill Sutherland scored off a rebound from Cal Swenson with 45 seconds left in the third period to tie the score at 2-2 in Game 4 of the Western Division semi-final. The Jets went on to win when Norm Beaudin took a pass from Swenson and fired a shot past goaltender Mike Curran at 3:12 of overtime.
5.	14 February 1975	Bobby Hull scored his third of the game at 18:22 of the third period against the Houston Aeros for his 50th goal in his 50th game, becoming only the second player in major pro hockey to score 50 goals in 50 games. The goal capped a four-goal comeback as the Jets rallied from a 3-1 deficit to win by a score of 5-3.
6.	22 March 1973	Needing to capture one more point to clinch first place in the Western Division, the Jets trailed the Alberta Oilers by a score of 1-0 going into the final minute of the third period. With goaltender Ernie Wakely on the bench in favor of the extra attacker, Norm Beaudin took a pass from Dunc Rousseau and beat Jack Norris to tie the game with just 16 seconds showing on the clock. The tie score held through overtime and the Jets secured their first division title.
7.	26 April 1977	With his wife Dorothy at home overdue in expecting the couple's first child, Peter Sullivan scored eight minutes into overtime to lift the Jets to a 4-3 victory over the Houston Aeros in Game 1 of the Western Division final. The game came just two days after the Jets had eliminated the Mariners in a hard-fought seven-game series.

8.	3 May 1973	37 seconds after Tim Sheehy scored to tie the game, Bobby Hull scored with 64 seconds left in the third period to give the Jets a 4-3 lead in Game 3 of the AVCO World Trophy final. The Jets hung on to win and took their first game of the series after the Whalers won the first two.
9.	30 October 1974	Bobby Hull's goal in the final minute of overtime gave the Jets a come-from-behind 6-5 victory over the Phoenix Roadrunners. The goal was Hull's third of the game as the Jets stormed back from a 5-3 third period deficit.
10.	22 April 1973	Dunc Rousseau scored off a rebound from a shot from Larry Hornung at the point to break a scoreless tie at 15:29 of the third period against the Houston Aeros in Game 2 of the Western Division final. The Jets went on to win by a score of 2-0 and grabbed an identical lead in the series.

In Memoriam

The following is a listing of some of the men who made meaningful contributions to the Jets during their seven seasons in the WHA who have since passed on (as of this wiriting in 2013).

Benjamin Hatskin, Jets' founder, passed away peacefully at the age of 73 when his heart failed on the night of 18 October 1990 at the Health Sciences Center in Winnipeg. He was confined to a wheelchair for the last seven years of his life after suffering a stroke in 1983 that cost him the use of his left side. He was inducted into the Manitoba Sports Hall of Fame in 1985 and was posthumously inducted into the Winnipeg Citizens Hall of Fame in 1992. His bust remains on public display in Assiniboine Park.

Despite considerable losses during the Jets' first two seasons that prompted Hatskin to put the team up for sale, he gave the community ownership group a substantial discount on the price so that the team could remain in Winnipeg. Even after selling the Jets in 1974, he remained involved with the WHA and served as the league's CEO and Chairman of the Board through the WHA's last season in 1978-1979.

Terrance John Hind, the Jets' first Business Manager, passed away on 9 January 2007 at the age of 86. Hind was named to the Order of Manitoba in July 2005 for his service to many charitable and sporting organizations. He is also a member of the Manitoba Baseball Hall of Fame, Manitoba Hockey Hall of Fame, and the Manitoba Sports Hall of Fame.

William Byrn's Robinson, former Jets' Director of Player Personnel and Chief Scout, passed away on 25 June 2008 at the age of 86 at Seven Oaks Hospital in Winnipeg after a battle with cancer.

Ken "Friar" Nicolson, the voice of the Jets, passed away on the morning of 31 December 1992 as the result of a heart attack.

Dave Simkin, former Jets' Vice-President for Finance and Ben Hatskin's good friend and business partner, suddenly passed away on 4 December 1972 at the age of 59. He was born on 21 April 1913 and received his Bachelor of Arts from the University of Manitoba in 1931. He joined the family business, Universal Printing Limited, and served as the President and General Manager of the company for more than 20 years, in addition to being active in many community activities and charities.

Ted Hargreaves, former Jets' player, passed away in Nelson, British Columbia in November, 2005 after an eleven-month battle with cancer.

Nicholas Mickoski, former Jets' coach, passed away at Grace Hospital in Winnipeg on 13 March 2002 at the age of 74. Mickoski was born in Winnipeg on 7 December 1927, and had a playing career in the NHL that encompassed 705 regular season and 18 playoff games. His last NHL season came in 1959-1960, when he played 18 games for the Boston Bruins. Mickoski was later inducted into the Manitoba Hockey Hall of Fame.

Daniel Douglas Johnson, former Jets' player and captain, passed away in 1993 as a result of amyotrophic lateral sclerosis (Lou Gehrig's Disease).

Howard John Edward Young, former Jets' player, passed away on 24 November 1999 in Thoreau, New Mexico at the age of 62 as a result of pancreatic cancer.

John Bowie Ferguson, former Jets' Vice President and General Manager, passed away on 14 July 2007 after a lengthy battle with cancer. He helped lure both Anders Hedberg and Ulf Nilsson to New York in 1978, then after he was fired by the Rangers, he accepted the job as Vice President and General Manager of the Jets on 22 November 1978. After the Jets were admitted to the NHL, Ferguson held his post through nine full seasons until his dismissal on 30 October 1988.

Annis Stukus, the Jets' first General Manager, passed away at his home in Canmore, Alberta, at the age of 91 in May, 2006. He had a 12-year playing career in the CFL with the Toronto Argonauts and went on to work in various off-field capacities for the Edmonton Eskimos and B.C. Lions before joining the Jets. He was a member of the Canadian Sports Hall of Fame and the Canadian Football Hall of Fame.

Lars-Erik Sjoberg, former Jets' player and captain, passed away in his native Sweden in October 1987 at the age of 43 as a result of cancer. After his playing career ended following the 1979-1980 season, he became the chief European scout for the New York Rangers.

Bob Woytowich, **Larry Hornung**, **Danny Lawson**, former Jets' players, and **Rudy Pilous**, former Jets' coach and general manager, have each passed on.

Bibliography

Winnipeg Free Press,
- April, 1972 through May, 1979

Winnipeg Tribune,
- May, 1976
- October, 1977
- May, 1978
- October ,1978
- May, 1979

JetStream, the Official Newspaper of the Winnipeg Jets Booster Club
- Volume 1, Number 1
- Volume 1, Number 3
- Volume 1, Number 4
- Volume 1, Number 5
- Volume 3, Number 1
- Volume 4, Number 3
- Volume 4, Number 5
- Volume 4, Number 6
- Volume 4, Number 7
- Volume 5, Number 1
- Volume 5, Number 2
- Volume 5, Number 4
- Volume 5, Number 5
- Volume 5, Number 6
- Volume 6, Number 1
- Volume 6, Number 3
- Volume 6, Number 6

Winnipeg Jets Hockey Club 1972-73 Official Year Book

Winnipeg Jets 1975-76 Media Guide

Winnipeg Jets 1976-77 Media Guide

Winnipeg Jets 1977-78 Media Guide

Winnipeg Jets 1978-79 Media Guide

Winnipeg Jets Magazine
- January, 1973, Volume 1, Number 20
- 16 December 1973
- 25 February 1973
- 18 October 1974
- 7 February 1975
- 14 March 1975
- 27 February 1976
- 2 November 1976
- 3 April 1977
- 21 October 1977
- 7 December 1977
- 26 December 1977
- 11 December 1977
- 4 February 1977
- 11 March 1977
- 22 March 1977
- 26 February 1978
- 9 January 1979
- 7 February 1979

The Official Web Site of the St. Louis Blues, **http://www.stlouisblues.com/**

The Ubyssey, 26 January 1971

The Internet Hockey Database, **http://www.hockeydb.com/**

The Manitoba Historical Society, **http://www.mhs.mb.ca/**

Souvenir Yearbook of the Winnipeg Jets 1972-1976, Winnipeg Jets Booster Club

Hockey Hall of Fame, **http://www.hhof.com/**

Winnipeg Free Press Obituary Listings, **http://www.passagesmb.com/**

Manitoba Hockey Hall of Fame, **http://www.mbhockeyhalloffame.ca/**

Toronto Star, 7 November 1979

The Globe and Mail, 25 November 2008

Canadian Broadcasting Corporation Archives, **http://www.cbc.ca/**

Environment Canada Historical Weather, **http://www.weatheroffice.gc.ca/**

Official Home of the Toronto Argonauts Football Club, **http://www.argonauts.ca**/

The Birmingham News, 31 August 2008

European Hockey.Net – Ice Hockey News and Stats for Europe, **http://www.eurohockey.net/**

Trail Historical Society, **http://www.trailhistory.com/**

Edmonton Oilers Heritage Website, **http://www.oilersheritage.com/**

Alberta Oilers Magazine, 5 January 1973

Interview with Anders Hedberg, 1 June 2009

Conversation with Joe Daley, 22 September 2007

The Complete Historical and Statistical Reference to the World Hockey Association 1972-1979, Scott Adam Surgent, Xaler Press, ISBN 0-9644774-0-8

Red, White & Blues: a personal history of Indianapolis Racers Hockey 1974-1979, Timothy Gassen, PCMP Press, ISBN 978-0-9797337-0-3

International Hockey: Izvestia Cups 1970-1980,
http://www.chidlovski.com/personal/1974/world/izvestia.htm

www.ingramcontent.com/pod-product-compliance
Lightning Source LLC
Chambersburg PA
CBHW080459110426
42742CB00017B/2942